Global Indigenous Communities

Lavonna L. Lovern

# Global Indigenous Communities

## Historical and Contemporary Issues in Indigeneity

Lavonna L. Lovern
Valdosta State University
Valdosta, GA, USA

*With Contrib. by*
Carol Locust
Department of Medicine
University of Arizona
Tucson, AZ, USA

ISBN 978-3-030-69936-9    ISBN 978-3-030-69937-6  (eBook)
https://doi.org/10.1007/978-3-030-69937-6

© The Editor(s) (if applicable) and The Author(s), under exclusive license to Springer Nature Switzerland AG 2021

This work is subject to copyright. All rights are solely and exclusively licensed by the Publisher, whether the whole or part of the material is concerned, specifically the rights of translation, reprinting, reuse of illustrations, recitation, broadcasting, reproduction on microfilms or in any other physical way, and transmission or information storage and retrieval, electronic adaptation, computer software, or by similar or dissimilar methodology now known or hereafter developed.

The use of general descriptive names, registered names, trademarks, service marks, etc. in this publication does not imply, even in the absence of a specific statement, that such names are exempt from the relevant protective laws and regulations and therefore free for general use.

The publisher, the authors and the editors are safe to assume that the advice and information in this book are believed to be true and accurate at the date of publication. Neither the publisher nor the authors or the editors give a warranty, expressed or implied, with respect to the material contained herein or for any errors or omissions that may have been made. The publisher remains neutral with regard to jurisdictional claims in published maps and institutional affiliations.

Cover credit: Alexpunker/shutterstock.com

This Palgrave Macmillan imprint is published by the registered company Springer Nature Switzerland AG
The registered company address is: Gewerbestrasse 11, 6330 Cham, Switzerland

# Acknowledgements

This book is the culmination of some thirty years of research and conversation with Carol. She is my aunt, my mentor, and my close friend and we have enjoyed many adventures, some of which we can speak and others best left undiscussed. Learning from her and working with her has been an incredible journey. I can't express how grateful I am to Carol for all that she has taught me and the hours we have spent together over the years. Our adventures and travels have brought humor, knowledge, and purpose to my life. While the issues we have faced often entail tragedy, human suffering, and discrimination, Carol has always remained a Hope Warrior and an inspiration for so many people, and I am lucky to have been one. Thank you, Carol, for all you have given to so many. I hope this work does justice to your legacy and I look forward to many more years of conversation.

Carol and I would also like to thank our families for the support they have given us throughout our work together and on this project. They have sacrificed time for what we all believed to be important projects. We want to recognize the gift they have given us and include them as part of the foundation for this work. I also want to thank Sydney Beckman for the time she spent editing this manuscript and for the many late-night conversations regarding content, organization, and writing suggestions. Her contributions to this work have been invaluable. Thank you to F. E. Knowles, Jr. for his help with legal questions and confirmation regarding the law.

Thank you to Palgrave Macmillan for believing in this project and for making it a reality. In contacting my past editor Milana Vernikova, I was put in contact with Mary Al-Sayed. The encouragement, professionalism, and guidance from these individuals have made the process easy and enjoyable. Mary offered suggestions and obtained reviews that helped to improve the manuscript and I am grateful for her efforts. Thank you to the reviewers for your suggestions and the time you spend contributing to this manuscript. I want to especially thank Liam McLean for the help and support in completing this work. Liam has gone above and beyond the role of editor to support me and this project. We have shared several challenges, an incredible number of emails, and humor bringing this project to completion and I am grateful for Liam's comments and kindness. All of this took place in the middle of the global pandemic of 2020 and all was done with kindness, a lovely sense of humor and understanding, as well as a sense of community that helped me stay inspired and encouraged me to complete the project. Indeed, the entire Palgrave staff has made this project easy and enjoyable in the middle of chaos. Thank you.

# Helpful Colonization Dates[1]

Caribbean

    Christopher Columbus lands 1492
    Slave Trade in Caribbean by 1502
    Bartolomé de Las Casas in Caribbean 1502

American Indian

    Treaty Era 1774–1828
    Removal began 1830
    Boarding Schools began 1860
    Allotment 1887
    Reorganization 1934
    Termination (House Concurrent Resolution 108) 1953
    Self-Determination Act 1975

---

[1] The dates involving colonization are neither exact, nor free of debate. The list here is offered merely as a guideline for context and orientation. The selection of dates does not represent a complete list or a list of all significant dates.

## Helpful Colonization Dates

Canada

   John Cabot discovers North American coast 1497
   Colony of New France founded 1534
   New France ceded to the United Kingdom 1763
   Dominion of Canada established 1867
   Custodial Schools established by 1880

Central and South America

   The Treaty of Tordesillas divides globe into Castilian and Portuguese 1494
   Vespucci in South America 1499–1502
   Colonization fully underway by 1499
   Cortes invaded Mexico 1519
   Spanish invasion of Aztec by 1519
   Spanish explorer Francisco Pizarro invaded Inca 1532
   Spanish invade Maya by 1550
   Bolivia and Ecuador declare independence from Spain 1809
   Mexico declares independence 1810
   Most of South America independent by 1830

Sami

   Silver discovered in Sweden's Sami land 1634
   Lappmark Proclamation 1673
   First National Congress held 1917a

Africa

   Slave Trade began by 1480
   British Joined Slave Trade 1564
   European division of Africa fully involved by 1880
   Decolonization of Africa began 1954

Pacific

   Magellan reaches the Philippines 1521
   Europeans in Australia 1720
   Captain Cook in Tahiti 1769
   Captain Cook in Australia 1770
   Captain Cook in Hawaii 1778
   Abel Tasman in New Zealand/Aotearoa 1642
   Britain annexed New Zealand/Aotearoa 1840

Britain transfer of prisoners to Australia by 1788
Australian Stolen Generation began in late 1800s
Australian official removal of half-castes 1905

India

Britain trading presence on coast by 1750
British rule declared 1858
Indian gained independence 1947

# Contents

| | | |
|---|---|---|
| **1** | **Introduction** | 1 |
| | Overview of Purpose | 1 |
| | Organization | 4 |
| | International Law | 5 |
| | UNDRIP | 7 |
| | Intergenerational Trauma | 10 |
| | Terms | 12 |
| | Methodology | 16 |
| | Works Cited | 19 |
| **2** | **Earth** | 21 |
| | Ties to the Earth | 21 |
| | Environmental Issues | 23 |
| | Colonization | 25 |
| | The Impact of Origin Narrative Differences | 30 |
| | Sovereignty | 34 |
| | Environmental Issues in Indigenous Cultures | 37 |
| | Traditional Environmental Knowledge | 41 |
| | Additional Readings | 44 |
| **3** | **Sacred** | 49 |
| | Ties to the Sacred | 49 |
| | Colonization of the Sacred | 53 |
| | Loss of the Land | 54 |

| | | |
|---|---|---|
| | Loss of the Sacred | 58 |
| | Global Indigenous Issues Involving Freedom of Religion | 65 |
| | Repatriation | 70 |
| | Indigenous Ways Regarding Sacred | 77 |
| | Additional Readings | 81 |
| 4 | **Social Organization** | 85 |
| | Reciprocal Relations | 85 |
| | Colonization: Relations Disrupted | 90 |
| | The Underdeveloped | 92 |
| | Colonized/Colonizer Differences | 93 |
| | Loss of Sovereignty | 97 |
| | Gendered Violence | 104 |
| | Indigenous Responses to Violence | 113 |
| | Additional Readings | 116 |
| 5 | **Language** | 123 |
| | Good Words | 123 |
| | Endangered and Dying Languages | 127 |
| | Oral Vs. Written Language | 134 |
| | Language and Natural Geometry | 139 |
| | Indigenous Language | 142 |
| | Additional Readings | 149 |
| 6 | **Education** | 153 |
| | Civiliza"tion" | 153 |
| | Indian 101 | 155 |
| | Educa"tion" | 159 |
| | A Brief History of Laws | 160 |
| | Children, Boarding Schools, and Being Stolen | 167 |
| | Resistance and Trauma | 174 |
| | Decolonizing and Indigenizing Education | 178 |
| | Additional Reading | 183 |
| 7 | **Economics** | 189 |
| | Aprons and Cradleboards | 189 |
| | Indigenous Economics | 191 |
| | Economic Conflict and Sacred Sites | 204 |
| | Economic Sovereignty and Data Control | 207 |
| | Additional Readings | 212 |

| | | |
|---|---|---|
| **8** | **Health** | 217 |
| | Five Hundred Years and Three Seconds | 217 |
| | Post-colonization Stress Disorder | 219 |
| | Healthcare | 220 |
| | Indigenous Health Data | 221 |
| | Specific Statistics | 225 |
| | Eugenics | 230 |
| | Indigenous Peoples on Wellness | 238 |
| | Body and Mind Differences | 243 |
| | Additional Readings | 247 |
| **9** | **We Are More Than Our Trauma** | 253 |
| | Time and Healing | 253 |
| | Beyond Trauma | 256 |
| | Academic Transparency | 259 |
| | Equity and Inclusion | 262 |
| | Decolonizing | 264 |
| | Indigenizing | 268 |
| | Concluding Thoughts | 275 |
| | Works Cited | 278 |
| **Index** | | 279 |

# 1

# Introduction

## Overview of Purpose

This project stems from Dr. Locust's life-work and reflects her dedication to advancing global Indigenous knowledge. Born in 1937, Carol grew up Eastern Cherokee and after following her father during his stint in the military, she followed the sun to the west to serve in several American Indian communities. She obtained a degree to teach and later, after experiencing a serious family event, turned to disability and health work. Her journey took her to live and work in several American Indian communities in Arizona focusing on education, healthcare, and disability issues. Personal experiences and her work among the people led her to the realization that she needed to gain her doctorate in education so that she could further work for improvement in American Indian communities. Her work helped to improve educational programs and extended into the Native American Cardiology program at the University of Arizona where she worked as a translator, facilitator, and spokesperson for American Indian patients and their families. Over the years, Carol traveled internationally to assist in Indigenous programs striving to advance traditional knowledge and to build bridges between Indigenous and non-Indigenous people. Her work in education, healthcare, and disability allowed her to focus on the intergenerational trauma associated with colonization and assimilation.

Carol and I began to work together after I had completed my Ph.D. and my children were older. My degree is in philosophy, but I taught philosophy and religious studies with an emphasis on alternative epistemologies and global Indigenous religions. Having been born in 1962 to a family in trauma, I went to live with a white foster family as an early teen, the dark-haired child in the midst of blond and red hair. While considered odd in behavior and attitudes, I was fortunate in gaining their support. As with all children in crisis, interpretation of information and experiences from those chaotic times become a kaleidoscope of events. Reflecting on those events as an adult provides much perspective, but often important data remains closed off and unremembered. However, there were several conversations from those early times that remain clear including advice and instruction given by a great-grandmother, a grandmother, and an aunt.

Each of these women gave me information that was important. While still quite young, my grandmother gave me two things to keep and told me to show no one, not even family members. She said she was told I would know what to do with the items when I was older. I am still unclear as to what to do with these, but investigating them helped me find Carol, and I continue to think about these items as she and I work together. My great-grandmother and aunt gave me stories, but all of these conversations were quietly given and not to be shared broadly. They were also given to me when I was quite young, so I imagine I have not fully remembered the details. I give this information only as a means of introduction to my place in this work, not as a claim to any community positioning. As with many foster and adopted people, I occupy the space between families, communities, and cultures which, for good or for bad, allows a unique perspective. So, I come to this work making no cultural claims, but only to use what talents I may have to bring together many perspectives that may advance an understanding involving global Indigenous issues.

With the introductions concluded, as this work is not about us, it is important to turn to the existing global Indigenous crisis. Indigenous issues continue to be largely ignored, both politically and academically, unless they are seen as beneficial to the State or academic institution. In both politics and academics, Indigeneity often serves as nothing more than window dressing for discussions of diversity and inclusion. The imagery is spectacular, but institutions shy away from giving teeth to the recognition of Indigenous peoples. Even with the United Nations Declaration on Indigenous Rights (UNDRIP), limited work has been done to fully engage the impacted communities, and meaningful dialogue with Indigenous communities remains largely perfunctory. Many governments fail to recognize, or only recognize in a limited way, the continued impact of colonization on Indigenous peoples. Governments that have put in place Reconciliation efforts again lack the legal statutes necessary to fully address or heal the competing assimilation practices.

Recognizing the expansive nature of colonization, the examples used in this book represent a fraction of the information available. Each Indigenous community deserves an in-depth voice. However, because the pages of this book are limited, we are unable to provide the details of each global Indigenous community, the impact of colonization on those communities, and the current situations regarding the legacy of colonization. This book is a single voice in a larger discussion using information found primarily in Indigenous communities and in Indigenous and decolonization scholarship. It is designed as a beginning for students interested in further research and for those outside of academia who wish to advance their knowledge of Indigeneity and global issues. To that end, we will attempt to use examples from as many Indigenous communities as possible in order to build our case that intergenerational trauma, resulting from colonization and assimilation practices, is not an isolated phenomenon.

The complexity of these topics and the uniqueness of each Indigenous community require that essentialist treatments and universalist claims be avoided. No single, or in this case no two, people can speak for any single community, let alone for all Indigenous communities. Instead, we intend to use as many voices as possible so as to create a collective body of knowledge.

For this reason, we will establish what many of my students have come to call the important disclaimer. This disclaimer is important because one must recognize that each Indigenous community is unique with its own history, knowledge, traditions, language, and community institutions. There is no single element that all share and no universal element with which one can describe them. Additionally, these communities are made up of individuals with differing histories, experiences, and beliefs. Colonization and assimilation differences also work to define experiences as do issues such as in-community and out-of-community populations. Essentializing members of a community leads to stereotyping, which has been all too common politically and scholastically and continues as a standard colonizing strategy. We recognize in our project, as is recognized in the studies of colonization and decolonization, that no such essentialism or universalization should be used.

This text will use the concept of Indigeneity only to distinguish from the colonizing populations, histories, and politics noting that colonization techniques also fail the essentialist/universalist test. There is, however, a pattern of dominance that can be studied between oppressors/oppressed, dominant/non-dominant, and colonizer/colonized. These are the patterns that will be explored throughout this book. In investigating global Indigenous populations, it becomes clear that these patterns are not anomalies, but rather the norm. Indigenous populations have become enclosed in colonial States that have subsequently denied sovereignty, self-determination, and often violate human rights standards established in international law. These States continue to dominate, oppress, and destroy large populations of Indigenous people in what has been called cultural and physical acts of genocide.

This book does not claim to make any profound or "earth-shattering" claims that have not been explored by numerous scholars in the area of Indigenizing or decolonization studies. While we will often offer original perspectives on material, much of our work involves bringing together the voices of activists, scholars, leaders, and medicine people in a way that allows them a platform. The text is an interdisciplinary work designed to combine as many voices as possible on the issues so that those unfamiliar with this area of study can seek out additional information in a way that continues to expand the conversation. Additionally, having spent decades in these areas of study, we know that finding material is challenging and finding Indigenous written or supported material is even more of a challenge. This book is therefore dedicated to Indigenous and accomplice voices.

Finally, this book is dedicated to the many students we have had and their questions regarding Indigenous communities. It could even be said that the structure, discussions, and information flow from past student questions. In large part, it is their questions, concerns, and discussions that have framed what is contained here, and it is their concerns that work in our minds as we present the material.

## Organization

The organization of this text allows us to focus on Dr. Locust's work with Indigenous people throughout her life. She carries the heritage, experience, and traditions of a lifetime of activism and scholarship. Dr. Locust's dedication to Indigenous rights, health, and education continues to provide both inspiration and a traditional knowledge foundation to the book. Her voice will be used throughout this text to represent traditional ways and experiences and to keep the text grounded in a non-Western epistemology that takes seriously Indigenous knowledge. Her inspiration and knowledge are the heart of this project and, in my opinion, the thread that unifies the text. I am indebted to her teachings and thankful for the decades we have spent together along with the projects and adventures we have had on this journey that have allowed me to be part of her work.

My contribution to this manuscript involves compiling the voices and offering some original perspective from having worked to build this collaboration. I have attempted to collect scholarship from a broad array of disciplines and activists/scholars to give a comprehensive understanding of the issues along with a variety of perspectives. I have been unable to include all voices, but I hope the ones I have included will begin to expand the dialogue beyond what is offered here.

As a final caveat involving organization, it is important to recognize that not all colonization is Western colonization, which itself should not be treated in an essentialist manner, and that not all non-Indigenous academics should be considered Western. However, the focus of this manuscript will be limited to Western colonization and assimilation practices involving Indigenous communities.

## International Law

Our reason for the use of international law in the discussion of Indigenous rights is threefold. First, practically speaking, there is no possibility of discussing the specific Indigenous/State legalities of all populations. Second, International law/organizations represent much of the current impetus for Indigenous human and sovereignty/self-determination rights. Finally, it seems appropriate to begin where colonization began, in the colonial mindset that justified the imperializing and subjugation of one culture over another.

So, we begin with a brief history lesson to create context starting with Pommersheim, who supports the use of international law as a way of understanding historic treatments of "state sovereignty" and "domestic affairs, relating to Indigenous populations". Additionally, this examination serves to explain current international perspectives that address the differences involving "individual human rights and [the] collective rights of indigenous people within nation-states" (2009, p. 259). Pommersheim explains that discussions involving international law and the treatment of Indigenous people can be observed in early European discussions of Indigenous people. Accordingly,

> …both de las Casas and Vitoria argued that in accordance with most natural law thinking of the day, indigenous people were indeed rational human beings with rights largely equivalent to those of non-Indian people…[with] special conditions attached…[with] responsibilities [that] included the European right

to travel to indigenous lands, to trade with indigenous people, and to proselytize in favor of Christianity. Refusal to permit any of these three activities was grounds for a just war. (p. 260)

Pommersheim, however, notes that the majority of "scholars at the time" defined Indigenous communities as non-nation states according to "international law because they lacked the defining characteristics of exclusivity of 'territorial domain and hierarchical, centralized authority'" (p. 260). Indigenous people were then treated according to individual rights, but as they were defined as being without government, denied collective or governmental rights. These interpretations of international law and definitions of nation-state justified domestic laws and decisions such as the Marshall Trilogy, which was based on the Doctrine of Discovery. What this allowed, according to Pommersheim, was the instigation of domestic "tyranny over Indigenous people" by the U.S. government which, ironically, had itself recently fought a war against the implementation of international tyranny (pp. 261–263).

Pommersheim chronicles the rise of Indigenous rights beginning in the 1960s and the creation of internationally focused events such as the 1977 International Non-Governmental Organization Conference on Discrimination against Indigenous Populations in the Americas and the 1989 International Labor Convention, which led to the ILO Convention 169 (2017, pp. 271–274). Specifically, the ILO establishes a foundational system for Indigenous rights. For many, the culmination of these efforts came in the form of the United Nations Declaration on the Rights of Indigenous Peoples (UNDRIP). UNDRIP has, indeed, become the standard bearer for global Indigenous rights focusing on self-determination and what Pommersheim designates as the "five components" of self-determination "nondiscrimination, cultural integrity, land and natural resources, social welfare and development, and self-government" (p. 274). Acknowledging the ambiguous nature of these terms, he claims that the components themselves come into conflict creating "unresolved paradoxes".

Pommersheim further asserts that

> Because colonialization was primarily concerned with obtaining the riches of indigenous land and natural resources, it is the area most fraught with opposition and resistance by nation-states. Land and natural resources have both a spiritual and an economic nexus within indigenous cultures. In this view, land and natural resources constitute both an essential human right and a property right. (p. 276)

Understanding the conflict between Indigenous interpretations of human and property rights and those of nation-states' wishing to maintain land and economic control, one begins to understand why documents such as UNDRIP are unable to eliminate either paradoxical language or nation-state dominance.

Pommersheim gives the example of one such paradox in the language involving, on the one hand participation, what "is understood as the opportunity for indigenous people to participate as full citizens in the dominant society" and, on the other hand, that which references Indigenous rights to self-governance and autonomy regarding land and resources (pp. 278–279). It is unclear how both positions can be held at the same time by the same people. Documents, such as UNDRIP, that participate in this type of language ambiguity fail to resolve land dispute conflicts and, according to some, simply foster hidden colonial advantage.

Pommersheim continues to illustrate such conflicts in his discussion of consent, as implied in international documents, regarding the use of Indigenous land and resources. He describes the

> …catch-22 element at play. If indigenous people possess recognized rights in their land and natural resources, 'consultation' would inhere in the nature of the recognized right itself. It is only when such a right is missing, usually as a result of the process of colonialization, that the shadow or penumbral right of consultation becomes necessary. (p. 279)

When documents call for consent, it appears to be supportive of Indigenous rights, and that may be the intention. However, the language itself belies the colonizer/colonized hierarchy and represents an ongoing language struggle addressed in later chapters.

## UNDRIP

UNDRIP was adopted by the United Nations General Assembly in 2007 and was heralded as a document establishing the rights of global Indigenous peoples. While it is neither a document that applies to all nations, nor a document with consequences regarding its non-adoption, it represents an attempt to bring to light issues involving Indigenous peoples. With 144 votes in favor, 4 against and 11 abstentions originally, the document became a baseline for United Nations (UN) discussions on Indigenous rights. New Zealand, Canada, Australia, and the United States were the original four dissenting countries. All four have since acknowledged support for UNDRIP[1], but vary in the degree to which that stated support is implemented.

From the perspective of logic, language is important as it can both express and hide information. For example, "support of" or "endorsement of" does not entail adoption.[2] So, a nation-state may support the spirit of UNDRIP without implementing a single concept of the document into law. What remains in question for these four reluctant supporters is the level of commitment to the "letter of the law" expressed in the articles of UNDRIP, especially regarding self-determination and land.

Much continues to be written regarding UNDRIP and the possible implications of its articles, but the document does represent a call for the global recognition of Indigenous rights and the responsibilities of nation-states to recognize those rights.[3] Some of the concerns regarding language ambiguity and the colonial framework of UNDRIP can be found in White Face's, Wobaga, critique of the Indigenous created and the published versions of the document (White Face, Wobaga 2013).

According to this argument, UNDRIP represents a second draft formatted and worded by non-Indigenous UN authors. White Face, Wobaga, claims that the original draft, which was created by Indigenous people, was rewritten to favor colonial language and ideals. In this text, we recognize the drawbacks and the potential for documents such as UNDRIP to provide a hidden colonial agenda along with less than hidden assimilationist orientations given the "required structure" of such documents. Such documents are indeed an attempt to dismantle the colonizers' house using colonizer language and run the risk of failing its objective. Furthermore, we recognize both the limitations and irony of such attempts but will use these international documents to help contextualize current situations in Indigenous populations.

Our strategy is to allow those who are primarily familiar with Western constructs and language games to understand within their own structures the impact of ongoing colonial practices and to provide the possibility of

---

[1] It is interesting to note the dates of support in or near 2010, 2016, 2009, 2010, respectively. The reference to "in or near" refers to various governmental discussions of support. Issues involving actual adoption remain.

[2] Readers should also look at the Truth and Reconciliation Acts involving Indigenous people and various countries. One can start with Canada (The Truth and Reconciliation Commission of Canada 2015), but additional acts exist in various countries, not all of which are focused so specifically on Indigenous people. A good source for general information, as well as resources on Indigenous issues regarding these acts, is the *International Justice Research Center* (Truth Commission Digital Collection 2020).

[3] We recommend *Realizing the UN Declaration on the Rights of Indigenous People* and *In the Light of Justice* (Hartley et al. 2010; Echo-Hawk 2013).

a conversational bridge to be constructed. Additionally, the use of such language and structures remains the currency of the realm in Western political and scholarly arenas. If nothing else, UNDRIP, and similar Western documents, represent nation-state and international organizational recognition of and responsibility for the current conditions experienced by Indigenous people around the world.

Finally, it should be noted that UNDRIP is not a claim of "special" rights regarding Indigenous people, but a recognition of the same rights experienced by non-Indigenous people. The document establishes that there are rights attached to all individuals simply by virtue of being human and such rights are not subject to colonizer/colonized status. Accordingly, Indigenous people do not hold a "lesser portion" or a "lower level" regarding human rights. Furthermore, UNDRIP, along with the Permanent Forum on Indigenous Issues (PFII), is a Western acknowledgment of human rights violations in Indigenous communities. Subsequent documents and agencies further legitimize the impact of colonization on Indigenous communities and the continued implications for these communities in what is commonly referred to as the post-colonization era.

Finally, the UN has become a clearinghouse for Indigenous information (United Nations, UNDESA 2018). While neither a complete catalog, nor above critique, the information represents a global picture of Indigenous communities and includes documents by Indigenous peoples. Indeed, the resource pages offer a starting place for those wishing to gain either a general world picture, or investigate a specific region, community, or issue (United Nations, UNDESA 2018).

Additionally, baseline information has been compiled in documents such as the State of the World's Indigenous People report (United Nations, SOWIP 2013). Recognizing that the statistical data for Indigenous populations are often neither collected according to Indigenous requirements, and so incomplete, nor is collected data decimated to the communities from which the information is collected, and so is not a collaboration according to Indigenous standards. Nonetheless, what is available is still quite grim.[4]

---

[4]It should be noted that the UN statisticians, along with many scholars, acknowledge non-collected or disaggregated data involving Indigenous communities and individuals. Many governments and scholars fail to recognize or collect data regarding Indigenous people causing an invisibility. Reasons for non-collection or disaggregation vary but indicate that the concerns represented in the collected data are underrepresented. In other words, the situation in many communities is far more desperate than current statistics represent.

- Indigenous people constitute approximately 317 m or 5% of the global population, yet they make up 15% of the world's poorest, and categorized as most vulnerable and marginalized.
- Historic and continuing marginalization, as well as, institutionalized racism and discrimination have made Indigenous people vulnerable and marginalized in mainstream development processes in both developed and developing countries.
- Most indicators of well-being demonstrate that Indigenous Peoples are disadvantaged on the grounds of discrimination compared to other populations in all countries where they live (Balawag 2016).

In this book, UN documents and information will often be used to open discussions but should be understood as only one way of gaining entrance into specific populations and issues, not as the only way to gain information or as the ultimate authority. The final authority concerning all Indigenous populations and their issues must remain within those populations, especially since with one hand the UN continues to advance Indigenous rights, while with the other hand it has been criticized for contributing to Indigenous invisibility in the wording of its own Sustainability Development Goals (Borrero 2015).

## Intergenerational Trauma

Indigenous scholars, practitioners, and activists face similar issues involving colonial wording and structure when discussing and treating the impact of colonization. Scholars and activists have been forced to use Western constructs to bring awareness to the continued violation of Indigenous rights, collective and individual, resulting from colonization and continued assimilation efforts in "post-colonization" periods.

This text represents just such an initiative involving the recognition of post-colonization stress disorders experienced by Indigenous individuals and communities. Post-colonization disorders begin with an understanding of intergenerational trauma. As will be explored more completely throughout this text, colonization was not a single event in history, nor did it impact a single generation. Colonization has been continual and so continues to create trauma. Initial contact trauma and subsequent generational trauma have become "blood memory" and as such is part of the physical, mental, and communal/individual lived experiences of Indigenous populations. Additionally, it must be understood that the interdependent nature of Indigenous communities establishes that individual trauma has a communal component, and communal trauma has an individual component.[5] Relational patterns involving interdependent communities, such as those represented in Indigenous populations, are markedly different than those found in independently oriented communities such as those represented by Western populations.[6] Trauma experience and recovery in Indigenous communities therefore involves multiple dimensions.

> The psychological effects of colonization, discriminatory policies, inhumane treatment, racism, and forcible removal of children from families cannot be ignored in an analysis of individual and community psyche and capacity. Contemporary social and economic disadvantage…continue to impact… the well-being and capability of Indigenous Australians to effect change. (Rees et al. 2004)

Brave Heart's research involving intergenerational trauma is considered by many to be foundational in this area of study. Her experience in social work, along with her research on the intergenerational trauma experienced in Jewish communities after the Holocaust, exposed similar patterns of trauma and disorder in American Indian populations. Brave Heart's research revealed that the manifestations of "cumulative wounding across generations" existed in the high rates of depression, self-destruction, psychic numbness, physical disorders, and mortality issues in American Indian populations (2000).[7] According to Brave Heart, these findings involve kinship and spiritual understandings, which are significant components in both grief expressions and in healing both individually and communally.

While information about post-colonization stress disorders will be discussed later in this book, it is worth mentioning two works here for those wishing to begin research in these areas. For those wishing a psychological examination, *Postcolonial Disorders* offers a set of essays that link subjectivity and politics to the understanding of intergenerational trauma and subsequent disorders (Good 2008). For anyone wanting to explore intergenerational trauma from the perspective of Indigenous treatment, *Decolonizing*

---

[5] It could certainly be claimed that this statement is true for all communities, but the emphasis on "individuality" in non-Indigenous culture is not stressed in Indigenous communities, creating a relational difference that will be more fully explored in later chapters.

[6] More research needs to be done on the impact of trauma and the transference of trauma in independent and neo-liberally oriented cultures. We are not claiming that intergenerational trauma is non-existent in such cultures, only that differences between interdependent and independent cultures tend to represent and present differently regarding such trauma.

[7] Recommended literature on intergenerational trauma include *Social Suffering* (Kleinman et al. 1997) and *Genocide and Mass Violence: Memory, Symptom, and Recovery* (Hinton and Hinton 2015).

*Trauma Work: Indigenous Stories and Strategies* represents, not only an excellent discussion of Indigenous lived experiences and healing strategies, but also is a remarkable source for additional references (Linklater 2014).

## Terms

With a background in Western philosophy and logic, I find definitions to be both fascinating and profound. When dealing with colonization issues, a great deal of information can be gained by understanding how individuals or groups define their terms and craft their arguments. Words are neither benign nor are they neutral, and arguments can be crafted to manipulate and hide implications and meaning. In general, communication reveals cultural dynamics, institutions, and values. This is not the place for a long discussion of linguistics or a history of language and paradigms, but paradigm context is a necessary component for understanding this text.

The text is, of scholastic necessity, embedded in Western academic constructs. This allows it to be understood by students and readers educated in Western paradigms. However, the text is also designed to give non-Indigenous readers a glimpse into a different set of Indigenous paradigms. Attempting such a glimpse, however, is perilous in its own right as it teeters on the edge of a knife. By using the outsider constructs involved in Western academics, one risks interpreting Indigenous paradigms based on non-Indigenous structures. Using entirely Indigenous constructs is a more authentic treatment of Indigenous paradigms but is unfamiliar to non-Indigenous populations, allowing for misinterpretation and mistranslation which has been a primary problem in Western treatments of Indigenous knowledge both politically and academically. This text will attempt to blend the paradigms in a way that puts them in a dialogue that establishes partnership equity.

The term "Indigenous" is a broad term and often not used by people designated as fitting within that category. Indeed, many who would be considered Indigenous would prefer to identify according to their nation, community, clan, or kinship designators. The difficulty is that non-Indigenous, or Indigenous from differing areas, may not be familiar with those designators. For many, "Indigenous" is considered to be synonymous with terms such as "First Nations", "Indian", or "Aboriginal". For others, the term is an umbrella term that encompasses all such terms. According to the UN Forum on Indigenous Issues,

[A]n official definition of "indigenous" has not been adopted by any UN-system body. Instead the system has developed a modern understanding of this term based on the following:

- Self-identification as indigenous peoples at the individual level and accepted by the community as their member.
- Historical continuity with pre-colonial and/or pre-settler societies
- Strong link to territories and surrounding natural resources
- Distinct social, economic, or political systems
- Distinct language, culture, and beliefs
- Form non-dominant groups of society
- Resolve to maintain and reproduce their ancestral environments and systems as distinctive peoples and communities (United Nations Forum on Indigenous Issues).[8]

This broad definition is designed to allow people and communities to self-identify as a means of promoting self-determination. This definition also allows for the distinction between "Indigenous" and "Aboriginal", with the latter specifically designating communities that are descended from first occupants to a geographic region or who inhabited the region prior to colonization. These determinations are important if one is examining Indigenous issues in Africa for example as populations may have inhabited a geographic region prior to colonization but Aboriginal status may be difficult to establish because of the imposition of colonial borders or because of nomadic lived experiences (Anderson et al. 2016).

In this text, the term "Indigenous" will be used in accordance with the UN and the ILO Convention 169 definition of tribal and Indigenous peoples so as to allow for communities to self-identify and focus on the culture, economic, and social aspects of a culture that make it distinct from the dominant culture. Additionally, this text will capitalize "Indigenous" in alignment with terms such as "European".

We recognize the debates surrounding the term "Indigenous" and acknowledge the importance of these discussions. For example, some require individual's claiming Indigeneity to be accepted by a community and to possess one or all of the following; language, traditions, ceremonial knowledge, and tribal history. For many, however colonization impedes or has destroyed the

---

[8]The International Labor Organization (ILO) set some similar criteria to establish Indigeneity and Tribal designations in Convention No. 169 using both objective and subjective standards to determine "indigenous and tribal" people (International Labor Organization).

possibility of possessing these, which is part of the focus of this book. Especially hindered in the possession of these requirements are the children who were stolen, adopted, or fostered out of their communities. These children and the generations that followed have been denied the very requirements that some say must be possessed to claim Indigeneity.

Enforcing such requirements then can be understood as nothing more than continuing what colonization began, the denial of identity that leads to erasure. We are conscious of and respect the need to stop all forms of cultural misappropriation. However, it is not the function of this book to determine specifically who is or is not Indigenous. Instead we will use what Locust describes as the teachings from her childhood and welcome all who approach the fire while watching their actions to determine whether they come with a good heart, or in an Indigenous way of being. According to Locust, it is actions, not labels that reveal the person.

Recognizing similar definitional issues, Yellow Bird examines the terms "American Indian" and "Native American" giving the issues with each term and the preferences among Indigenous people (1999). The discussion of terms was published in 1999, so preferences for some may have changed. However, the reasoning behind usage concerns has remained constant. These terms carry with them negative colonial contexts and imagery that must be recognized. Furthermore, both terms are recognized as being related to stereotypes, discrimination, and intergenerational trauma issues. We will use both terms primarily to avoid repetition, but with a recognition of the concerns regarding each.

The terms "colonization" and "post-colonization" involve temporal issues as well as issues regarding continued assimilation. In general, colonization is understood to indicate time frames involving initial invasion, destruction of pre-existing communities, and primary acts of assimilation. What is difficult to determine is exactly when these conditions and acts ceased. Initial contact and invasion may be relatively easy to date, but many Indigenous communities consider colonization to be an ongoing experience. In other words, if complete independence and withdrawal of the colonizing force has not occurred, colonization can be defined as continuous. The question is then one of establishing "post-colonization" periods. For example, many U.S. textbooks state or imply that colonization ended long ago with the establishment of the U.S. government, implying that the country is in a post-colonization period. However, for the Indigenous people of America, acts of assimilation as well as the colonization of mind and community have never ceased. The lack of recognized sovereignty means that these populations continue to exist in a colonial relationship with the American government.

Sovereignty and self-determination will be reoccurring terms throughout this text. These concepts are considered essential for Indigenous human rights to be considered in equal portion to non-Indigenous and colonizing populations. The definitions of such terms will be explored within the text but should be understood as needing to come from Indigenous paradigms, rather than non-Indigenous paradigms. What it means to have sovereignty or to be self-determined must be understood according to Indigenous cultural standards, and as such may change from community to community. For example, determining "poverty" should not be based solely on Western materialistic constructs. For Indigenous populations, "poverty" may be defined wholly or in part according to spiritual standards. Indigenous definitions of "wealth" and "poverty" must be the "gold standard" to pardon the pun. Needs and wants must be established from an insider, rather than an outsider, perspective. Understanding this insider perspective helps to avoid embarrassing instances in which Western communities send winter coats to Indigenous people in the Caribbean or send laptops to children in areas without electricity.

Terms such as "primitive", "savage", and "uncivilized" will not be used in this text and have largely fallen out of vogue when discussing Indigenous people. Additionally, while Huston Smith used the term "primal" intending great respect for Indigenous people, the term will not be used as many confuse it with "primitive". This is not to say that these terms are not still employed by non-Indigenous populations, only that such terms have largely been eliminated from academic discussions involving Indigenous people. One can certainly find them used in older history, sociology, and anthropology texts, but the disciplines have largely ceased such practices.

Again, this is not to claim that the sentiment involved in these terms has ceased to exist, but only that other terms have taken their place, terms such as "developing", "underdeveloped", and "third or fourth world". While these terms may sound better to Western academics and politicians, they are no more than synonyms for "primitive", "savage", and "uncivilized". The implication is that those who are developing or are underdeveloped have yet to reach the level of the developed, more civilized, West. It is, therefore, the obligation of Western cultures to assist underdeveloped populations in becoming more "developed". This language belies the underlying colonization and assimilation practices. For many Indigenous people, such language is a mere continuation of that used to justify boarding schools and stolen generation practices that wanted to "kill the savage but save the man". Unfortunately, even organizations such as the UN, as illustrated above, fall prey to this "developing" terminology.

Ironically, if one changes the definitional referent of "developing" and "developed" to indicate ecological responsibility, sustainability, or the ability to live in harmony with nature, Indigenous communities become designated as developed and Western communities as developing. Beyond the definitional issue, claiming to be "developed" also indicates that there is no need for further development. This is not a concept one generally finds in Indigenous knowledge. By and large, Indigenous languages are verb oriented. In other words, these languages, and by connection these paradigms, are founded on "coming to be" or "becoming", not on "are" or "is". The differences in perspective are significant when one is attempting to "come to understanding", rather than "understanding" what counts as developing and developed societies.

The list here represents some of the significant terms used in this text which required highlighting. Additional definitions and cultural constructs will be discussed throughout this text allowing the reader to consider the impact of imagery and perspective along with definition and argumentation.

## Methodology

The methodology in this text involves an interdisciplinary approach. I represent, by academic training, the humanities. Carol represents traditional knowledge in both health and education. We do not claim that our perspectives are superior to areas such as ethnography, sociology, or anthropology. Instead, we offer simply another voice, another perspective, in order to broaden the discussion. This interdisciplinary and integrational approach allows for equal legitimacy to be given to qualitative and quantitative data. Additionally, using Indigenous methodology allows for evidence and structures often not legitimized in Western academics. Attempting to build a bridge between the Western academic and Indigenous traditional knowledge is not unique to this text, but the use of the humanities background in combination with the Indigenous traditional knowledge does allow for a unique exploration of the lived experience. Again, we recognize that any adoption of Western academic standards represents a continuing element of colonization and assimilation. However, such standards are required in the universities and for publication. Peer review requires the adoption of Western standards and Indigenous and accomplice scholars continue to struggle with these issues.

Where possible, this text will use Indigenous scholarship, with the recognition that Indigenous scholars have often been discriminated against in academia and publication. Some advancement has been made to remediate this discrimination and Indigenous scholars are continuing their attempts to decolonize and to indigenize academia.[9] These advancements, however, still occupy the position of academic and political *Other* and tend to be relegated to specialty courses or to Native American and Indigenous Studies programs.

Given these issues, this text will also employ the terms allies and accomplices, to borrow Marinucci's designations (2016). According to Marinucci, allies are those who are positively disposed to the cause, people, or issue, but who retain their position in the dominant group. Allies have the comfort of being able to withdraw back into the dominant paradigm when faced with conflict. There is no judgment of positioning here, as academic politics require even those in the dominant group to be cautious when supporting non-dominant issues, especially in pre-tenure positions. Accomplices, according to Marinucci, represent those who have opted out of the dominant position or those from other non-dominant groups who work in conjunction with the demographic at issue. Indigenous accomplices may come in the form of scholars or activists, but in the academy, accomplices may be more likely to be those who have already attained tenure or are from universities with strong Indigenous programs and organizations.

A final methodological statement must be made regarding issues of language and syntax. This text intends to enter into a dialogue between Western and Indigenous communities and individuals. As such, syntax will change. Indigenous languages tend to be verb oriented while Western language tend to be more noun oriented. Additionally, Indigenous traditions tend to employ passive voice whereas Western scholarship employs active voice. The recognition of these differences is necessary to create a communicative arena where all participants are recognized as equal partners. To establish equity of positioning, all manners of communication must be given legitimacy, with none claiming the dominant position. Shifting syntax allows for the legitimacy and authenticity of Indigenous voices and allows non-Indigenous readers to experience some of the struggles Indigenous populations experience when participating in Western language syntax. This book, then, intends to complicate Western scholarship by calling for the addition of Indigenous voices and by allowing these alternative voices equal legitimacy in obtaining and establishing knowledge.

The structure of the chapters in this text was designated by Carol based on her teachings and what was communicated to her. The chapters should

---

[9]Some of the scholars used in this text, involving the decolonization of methodology, include *Decolonizing Methodologies* (Smith 2012), *Indigenous Knowledge Inquires* (Sillitoe et al. 2010), *Indigenous Research Methodologies* (Chilisa 2012), and *A Handbook of Critical and Indigenous Methodologies* (Denzin et al. 2008).

be understood as situated within a web of understanding. While marked numerically and positioned linearly, the chapters are neither separate nor compartmentalized. No topic can be completely separated from the others, so the discussion of education and wellness, for example, should not be taken as independent from that of the environment or community. They are all parts of an integrated lived experience. The separation here is merely an abstraction for discussion purposes. For this reason, Western readers may be perplexed by some overlap and repetition. However, this too is a product of Indigenous knowledge and is used to help with understanding integrative cultures as well as to assist with memory.

At this point, we will forgo the common chapter descriptions as the titles are self-explanatory. Instead, let it be noted that each chapter will begin with a discussion flowing from Carol and represents an Indigenous preparatory statement to the more academic discussion that follows. These preparatory statements should not be taken as being either universal or essential positions, nor are they representative of any other Indigenous person's understandings or experiences. They are the statements of a single Indigenous person based on what she was taught and has come to understand. It should also be recognized that the first chapters introduce many foundational concepts and Indigenous issues and so are longer than subsequent chapters. We believe that a great deal of contextualizing must be done to allow the reader to more fully understand the issues and to promote dialogue. In many cases, topics will be introduced in an abbreviated manner to give context and to allow the reader to more fully investigate the topic at a later date. To this end, additional readings have been placed at the end of each chapter.

It should also be noted that, as with this entire book, this chapter will be written, to the best of our ability, from a position of peace and harmony. However, the reader should understand the passion felt by many individuals regarding the issues discussed in this book. Many of the writings and discussions involved in these issues come from a place of intense individual and communal pain, which is often exhibited through anger. Readers should be prepared for some of the raw emotions presented by some of the activists and scholars in this text. Historical and current experiences of Indigenous people are often brutal. Discussions of those events and the trauma that follows can be equally brutal. Many times, there is no other way to express these experiences, and sorrow often gives way to anger for Indigenous individuals and communities.

Equally, Indigenous readers may experience new or exacerbated pain in these pages. It is not our wish to open old wounds and we apologize for any upset that may come from this text. It is not possible to write about these issues without embracing the devastating impact on both individuals and communities. If we could bring to light these issues without visiting or revisiting the pain, we would. So, for those experiencing intergenerational colonial trauma, we ask that you tread carefully for both yourself and your community and that you honor your position and reactions. Seeking community and Elder assistance may be important in healing. According to Carol, "anger is all too often the lid on pain. Remove the lid and the pain springs out like a beast and lays bare the true impact of the trauma". This book attempts to recognize the pain, to acknowledge the anger, and to write for healing.

## Works Cited

Anderson, I. et al., (2016, July 9). Indigenous and Tribal Peoples' Health (The Lancet-Lowitja Institute Global Collection): A Population Study. *The Lancet, 388*, 131–157.

Balawag, G. (2016). *Current Work Undertaken by Indigenous Peoples Related to SDGs and Data Disaggregation.* UNICEF, Tebtebba-Indigenous Peoples' International Center for Policy, Research and Education. New York: United Nations.

Borrero, R. (2015). *Indigenous People Cannot Be Left Behind in the Post-2015 Development Agenda.* International Indian Treaty Council. United Nations Non-Governmental Liaison Service. Retrieved from https://unngls.org/index.php/80-home/1794-indigenous-peoples-cannot-be-left-behind-in-the-post-2015-development-agenda-roberto-borrero,-international-indian-treaty-council-2#edn1.

Brave Heart, M. Y. H. (2000). Wakiksuyapi: Carrying the Historical Trauma of the Lakota. *Tulane University of Social Work,* 245–266. Retrieved from http://discoveringourstory.wisdomoftheelders.org/ht_and_grief/Wakiksuyapi-HT.pdf.

Chilisa, B. (2012). *Indigenous Research Methodologies.* Los Angeles: Sage.

Denzin, N. K., Lincoln, Y. S., & Smith, L. T. (Eds.). (2008). *Handbook of Critical and Indigenous Methodologies.* Los Angeles: Sage.

Echo-Hawk, W. R. (2013). *In the Light of Justice: The Rise of Human Rights in Native America and the UN Declaration on the Rights of Indigenous People.* Golden, CO: Fulcrum.

Hartley, J., Joffe, P., & Preston, J. (Eds.). (2010). *Realizing The UN Declaration on the Rights of Indigenous People: Triumph, Hope, and Action.* Saskatoon, SK: Purich Publishing Limited.

Hinton, D. E., & Hinton, A. L. (Eds.). (2015). *Genocide and Mass Violence: Memory, Symptom, and Recovery.* New York: Cambridge University Press.

International Labor Organization. (2017). *Employment Policy Recommendation No. 169.* https://www.ilo.org/dyn/normlex/en/f?p=NORMLEXPUB:12100:0::NO::P12100_ILO_CODE:R169.

Kleinman, A., Das, V., & Lock, M. (Eds.). (1997). *Social Suffering.* Berkeley, CA: University of California Press.

Linklater, R. (2014). *Decolonizing Trauma Work: Indigenous Stories and Strategies*. Halifax: Fernwood Publishing.

Marinucci, M. (2016). *Feminism Is Queer: The Intimate Connection Between Queer and Feminist Theory* (2nd ed.). London: Zed Books.

Good, M. D., Hyde, S. T., Pinto, S., & Good, B. J. (Eds.). (2008). *Postcolonial Disorders*. Berkeley: University of California Press.

Pommersheim, F. (2009). *Broken Landscape: Indians, Indian Tribes, and the Constitution*. New York: Oxford University Press.

Rees, S., Tsey, K., Every, A., Williams, E., Cadet-James, Y., & Whiteside, M. (2004). Empowerment and Human Rights in Addressing Violence and Improving Health in Australian Indigenous Communities. *Health and Human Rights, 8*(1), 94–113. Retrieved from http://www.jstor.org/stable/4065377.

Sillitoe, P., Dixon, P., & Barr, J. (2010). *Indigenous Knowledge Inquiries: A Methodologies Manual for Development*. Warwickshire: Practical Action Publishing.

Smith, L. T. (2012). *Decolonizing Methodologies: Research and Indigenous Peoples* (2nd ed.). London: Zed Books.

The Truth Commission Digital Collection. (2020). *United States Institute of Peace*. https://www.usip.org/publications/2011/03/truth-commission-digital-collection (2008). *United Nations Declaration on the Rights of Indigenous Peoples*. New York: United Nations Publisher. Retrieved from http://www.un.org/esa/socdev/unpfii/documents/DRIPS_en.pdf.

The Truth and Reconciliation Commission of Canada. (2015). *Honoring the Truth, Reconciling for the Future: Summary of the Final Report of the Truth and Reconciliation Commission of Canada*. Canada: Library and Archives Canada Cataloguing in Publication. Retrieved July 2018, from http://www.myrobust.com/websites/trcinstitution/File/Reports/Executive_Summary_English_Web.pdf.

United Nations. (2013). *State of the World's Indigenous Peoples: Indigenous Peoples' Access to Health Services*. New York: United Nations. Retrieved from https://www.un.org/development/desa/indigenouspeoples/wp-content/uploads/sites/19/2018/03/The-State-of-The-Worlds-Indigenous-Peoples-WEB.pdf.

United Nations. (2018). *UNDESA Division for Inclusive Social Development Indigenous People*. Retrieved from https://www.un.org/development/desa/indigenouspeoples/.

United Nations Forum on Indigenous Issues. (n.d.). *Who Are Indigenous People? Fact Sheet*. New York: United Nations. Retrieved from http://www.un.org/esa/socdev/unpfii/documents/5session_factsheet1.pdf.

White Face, C. (Zumila Wobaga). (2013). *Indigenous Nations' Rights in the Balance: An Analysis of the Declaration on the Rights of Indigenous People*. St. Paul: Living Justice Press.

Yellow Bird, M. (1999). What We Want to Be Called: Indigenous Peoples' Perspectives on Racial and Ethnic Identity Labels. *American Indian Quarterly, 23*(2), 1–21.

# 2
# Earth

## Ties to the Earth

*We rise in the morning to sing up the sun. It is important to begin the day by setting one's self in place. A place of respect for all things and a respect for the balance of all that is. In the evening, we sing down the sun and again look at our place in the world and honor that place. That place is not above or below the rest of existence, but a part of all that was, is, and will be. Framing the day reminds us to focus on what is important, rather than what is not. Minor frustrations such as a mess on the floor or a lost bit of work should not overwhelm. What should overwhelm is the beauty of the sun rise and sun set and all that exists in the world. When one sings the rise and setting of the sun, one is reminded of the beauty that exists all around us. It reminds us to focus on the beauty and the calm that comes at those moments that separate the light and the dark. The harmony of the two experiences requires that we should honor both in all aspects of life. Both light and dark teach us the lessons we came to learn, and we need to take the time to honor those lessons.*

*Place is who we are. It is that from which we were created. We call the Earth "Mother" both to honor and to remind. We honor that which is the living being that created and houses all life. We remember that we are created from the Earth. We grow in our biological Mother. It is our Earth Mother that forms us. What our birth Mother eats and drinks forms the cells of our body, and so we have two Mothers, each owed love, honor, and respect. Spirit completes the trinity of creation when it joins with the two Mothers. Taking the time to sing the sun helps to* remind us where we came from and what our place is in the world. It keeps us focused beyond ourselves to the web of relationships to which we belong. It reminds us that we are the result of all the ancestors, human, plant, animal, and earth, that came before us and that we will be the ancestors of those who come after us. This establishes the responsibilities we have past, present, and future. The dirt on which we walk, which grows our food and holds the water that created our ancestors, is our ancestors. It created us and will be us for later generations. It is important to respect that and know one's place.

It was taught to me that Mother Earth can heal all things as all things first came from her. I was taught to take sorrow and upset and dig a hole. By placing these in the ground and covering them, they can be healed. But, I was taught to be careful of placing the negative too much in one place or too close to certain plants or places. Too much sorrow in one place can cause an imbalance. It can do harm to that which is around it. Offerings of thanks and respect for what one is asking of our Mother is essential to the healing. As humans, we have asked our Mother to heal too much with the pollution and toxic waste we are putting back into our Mother. We have dug too deeply and stripped out things that should have been left buried deep. I was taught that there were things that humans should leave, there was never any talk of "having rights" to what lay below the Mother's skin. We do not define ourselves by rights, but by responsibilities and we have a responsibility to live with what is given as enough. To live in harmony with all beings and not to take what is not meant for us. But the world has shifted to place humans above all else and so the balance is lost. Some say that the quakes, floods, fires, and storms have gotten worse because we have shifted the balance. I have heard some say that it is the anger of a Mother mistreated. Others have told me it is Mother shaking her skirt to rid herself of the toxins and to balance once again.

There are prophecies, some shared openly, and others kept close by those who tend such things, that warn of what may result from the misuse of the Mother and what she houses here on Earth. There are stories of water that went away because people disrespected it and stories of animals that sent the illnesses because humans disrespected them and refused to live in balance with all things. In these stories, the plants endeavored to help the humans by giving healing. But the sympathy of the plants has been returned with destruction and so many healers are gone. One Elder told me that for all illnesses in the world there is a cure, unless humans destroy it. It is important for us that we fulfill our responsibilities and act in reciprocity with all things. This is fundamental to us and our place in the world.

We do not rank beings as the West does in a hierarchy with humans at the "top of the food chain". All things are created equally from Mother Earth and with equal Spirit. Spirit is whole and not given in degrees but shared equally. This equality puts humans no higher than rocks, plants, or animals. We do not rank beings higher if they can move, leaving plants below animals and rocks below plants. Some things move by self and some things do not. It is the way of things, not *a judgement of importance. Some things have talents for moving and some things do not. All things, however, do have talents as given by the Creator. Because we as humans do not know, or fail to recognize, a talent given by the Creator, does not mean it doesn't exist.*

*Knowing our place means being able to learn from all that is around us and not being so arrogant as to think we can't learn from animals, plants, or rocks. It means listening to what they have to teach us and learning the lessons we need to know. I was told that the prophecies that call for the consequences of our actions are not inevitable. None of the prophecies speak of a punishment from Mother Earth or from the Creator, rather they are prophecies regarding the consequences of our actions. Disrespect and destruction come at a cost, a cost we must pay if we do not change our behavior. The choice is ours, to learn the lessons or to experience the results of our actions. I have been told that it is not possible to always reverse our course. There is a point at which we cannot avoid the consequences and for many they believe that time is at hand. But even if we have reached that point, there is hope and there is beauty in the world. In the darkest of times there are lessons to be learned and knowledge to be honored. To continue to sing up the sun and to sing down the sun reminds us of these things. Beauty will exist and even in difficult times, we can balance with the difficulty and find harmony with Mother Earth and all of the beings she birthed. —Carol Locust*

## Environmental Issues

As the opening chapter in this book, environmentalism will be used to establish context for most of the discussion involving sovereignty, self-determination, and colonization. The chapter will briefly discuss these concepts as they work within Western and Indigenous paradigms in order to understand different perspectives involving evidence and argumentation. The use of differing narratives will allow the reader to better understand why perspectives, or paradigm differences, matter and how they result in differing cultures, sciences, and interpretations regarding the environment. Throughout the chapter, the concepts of interdependence and reciprocity will also be used to further explain Indigenous perspectives and paradigms regarding nature.

According to many, intense interest in the environment did not begin to grab the American public until the 1960s as environmental concerns such as pollution began to gain more attention. Environmental groups brought attention to threatened land, animals, and water making conservation rhetoric part of the conversation as groups worked to save what they believed to be threatened resources. Interestingly, Western conservation arguments tended to focus on securing the threatened resource for future generations of humans. Ironically, conservation efforts often focused on the inability of future human use of the resource while ignoring the fact that human usage created the environmental issue in the first place. Many of these conservation attempts employed strategies that usurped Indigenous imagery to promote environmental movements, with little investigation done regarding accuracy or the impact of these practices on Indigenous communities.

In fact, respect for Indigenous traditional environmental knowledge was, and continues to be, dismissed and replaced with trivial platitudes. Even now, conservation groups often invite the Indigenous voice to their events but prefer Western conservation messages rather than Traditional Environmental Knowledge (TEK). Such events often focus on the elimination of fossil fuels for the introduction of "clean" energy. When Indigenous people note that "clean" energy also comes with negative environmental impact and call for significant human cut-backs in usage that would give preference to plants or animals, they are often ignored or not invited a second time to the event. In general, TEK requires significant reduction in the use of environmental resources, which would, in turn, require a significant reduction in materialism and extreme changes to Western lifestyles.

In 1990, groups such as the *Indigenous Environmental Network (IEN)*[1] began to collect data and to focus on the relationship between Indigenous cultures and environmental issues. As scholars and activists such as Winona LaDuke[2] worked to gain recognition of and support for Indigenous TEK, the grassroots efforts continued to be largely unrecognized in Western environmental movements. LaDuke, along with other Indigenous activists and scholars, gained more recognition around the turn of the century but often still found their voices largely ignored especially in the political arenas.

Supporting Indigenous efforts, the United Nations published the *State of the World's Indigenous People* (SOWIP) report in 2009 highlighting the impact of environmental trauma on Indigenous cultures. In the report, Indigenous communities were identified as some of the "world's most vulnerable" populations. The document states that there are "approximately 370 million indigenous peoples occupying 20 per cent of the earth's territory". It is also estimated that they represent as many as "5,000 different indigenous cultures" and that these cultures "often coincide with areas of high biological diversity"

---

[1] The IEN offers expansive source information for global environmental and Indigenous issues.
[2] LaDuke has written and presented widely on environmental issues, her works *All Our Relations* (1999) and *The Winona LaDuke Reader* (2002) continue to inspire both Indigenous and non-Indigenous activism.

(p. 84). The SOWIP also acknowledges that the spiritual and physical relationship between Indigenous peoples and the land is unique and should be respected both culturally and politically (pp. 53–54).

In support of this position, SOWIP referenced article 26 of the 2008 *United Nations Declaration on the Rights of Indigenous People* (UNDRIP), which states that Indigenous peoples have a "right to maintain spiritual relationships with the land, the right not to be forcibly removed or dispossessed, the right for indigenous peoples to have their own land tenure systems, the right to redress for land that has been taken or damaged and the right to conservation and protection of the environment" (p. 55). While not focused specifically on environmental issues, SOWIP created both a foundation and a global platform for Indigenous scholars and activists in their discussions of TEK.[3]

## Colonization

One of the major aspects of trauma resulting from colonization continues to be Indigenous loss of land and the denial of access to traditional resources. Referencing both SOWIP and UNDRIP, this loss and denial of access continues to hinder individual and collective human rights in Indigenous communities. This book cannot give full representation to the damage caused by colonization, nor can it do justice to a discussion of global colonization of Indigenous populations. However, the basis of Indigenous trauma and the resulting designation of being "among the most vulnerable populations" on the planet is a direct result of colonization and continued colonial practices, which were primarily motivated by the desire to possess Indigenous land and resources. Colonial desire for Indigenous land created a history of Indigenous removal and dispossession that profited the colonizing forces. The continuation of early colonial institutions and practices that deny Indigenous access to resources continue to advance financial profits for the colonizing States. To more fully understand the continued impact of colonization practices, this section will give a brief history of colonization in the Americas with the understanding that these events are not unique but have been perpetrated on a global scale in Indigenous territories.

Beginning with the "Doctrine of Discovery" established largely by the Papal Bull "*Inter Caetera*" of 1493, Western ideology created international

---

[3]UNDRIP establishes a more complete history of the United Nations involvement in Indigenous rights.

legal precedent for claiming all "discovered" land in the name of the discovering country. Pope Alexander VI put forth this proclamation to ensure that all "discovered" lands would fall under Christian control by claiming that any land "discovered" and found to be inhabited by non-Christians could be claimed by Christian rulers. The inhabitants were then to be either converted to Christianity or eliminated. This Doctrine was the foundation for the Doctrine of Discovery justification in the Marshall Trilogy that established the standard treatment of Indigenous populations by the US government.

In the 1823 case *Johnson v. McIntosh*, Chief Justice Marshall stated that the Doctrine of Discovery gave legal justification for Europeans to claim lands in the Americas. Manifest Destiny and racial superiority, which later became associated with Social Darwinism, worked as powerful allies to the doctrine justifying a multitude of atrocities associated with the conquering and dispossession of Indigenous land. While it is debated as to whether or not Manifest Destiny was an official State position, the doctrine claimed that the Christian god gave the right to certain European populations to rule over all the "dusky nations". Embedded in the concept was the idea that the "savage" and "uncivilized" populations failed to properly use the lands that they inhabited justifying the more "civilized" Western population, who better understood resource usage, to claim rightful ownership. This ideology implied that Indigenous populations failed to have the knowledge or industry to properly use the resources given to humans by the divine. For this reason, Indigenous inhabitants were often viewed as "childlike" or given titles such as "noble and ignoble savages".[4]

Social Darwinism, largely attributed to Spencer in 1898, provided "scientific" justification for conquering and dispossessing Indigenous populations of their land by establishing a system of cultural hierarchy which placed European cultures at the pentacle and Indigenous cultures further down the evolutionary hierarchy. Indigenous or "savage" cultures were described either as vastly inferior to their European counterparts or as being in decline and so on their way to what was considered a natural extinction. The choice was then either raise these inferior cultures to the civilized level of Europeans or to allow them to pass into inevitable extinction. It should be noted that "being allowed to pass" into extinction often justified colonial actions that worked to hasten that extinction. Removal, dispossession, and even genocide became scientifically justified as the lamentable, but the inevitable end for these "savage" and "uncivilized" populations.

---

[4] These terms will be more fully discussed in the culture chapter of this text.

Reports of the destruction of life and land under colonization vary and have been debated often being minimized by using the same apologist strategies applied to discount the conditions of slavery and the Jewish Holocaust. It has been argued that little destruction occurred within the Indigenous populations or that the majority peaceably chose conversion and assimilation to European and Christian ways of being. However, there is ample evidence that much of the "peaceful" conversion took place within the ravages of colonization and should more correctly be considered conversion under duress.

Significant evidence, however, reveals no conversion or acquiesce in many Indigenous communities but rather attempted, and partially completed, cultural and physical genocide. Early documentation describing the violence associated with colonization can be found in Bartoleme de Las Casas' 1542 account which gave descriptions of the destruction in the Indies including what he claimed to be both the depopulation and the land devastation by European citizens. In his account, he chronicled the wanton killing and torturing of Indigenous populations including descriptions of dismemberments, games involving the dismembering and beheading of men, women, and children, and the tossing of infants into crags or rivers along with the accompanying merriment and laughter inspired by these events (de Las Casas 1992). Some scholars have discounted these claims stating that they are the over-exaggeration of a man attempting to gain the favor of the Spanish rulers and to control Spanish behaviors in the islands. Other scholars insist that any exaggeration along with the appeal to cease the killing of Indigenous people and the dispossession of land indicate that to some extent the events described contained at least some level of truth.

Additional accounts of colonial destruction are cited as involving the "plantation masters' hunger for slaves and the padres' desire for souls" (Voeks 1997, p. 34). According to these reports, while the practice of enslavement was generally disallowed in Brazil, the taking of Indigenous slaves was possible if acquired during a "just war". The need for plantation workers was then used to justify many small "just wars". Enslavement of Indigenous people was further justified as a way to save the workers from uncivilized practices such as being eaten by other "cannibalistic captors". While no such captors have been documented, the propaganda justified the conscription of Indigenous workers to European authorities local and abroad. While enslaved, conscripted, or forced to work (terminology differs according to perspective differences) Indigenous people suffered high mortality rates because of poor working conditions, lack of traditional food, and the introduction of European diseases.

In parallel colonial efforts, the Jesuits worked to convert and baptize the Indigenous people, and, to that end, thousands were herded into small villages with little food and poor sanitation. While held in this captivity, the introduction of European diseases such as smallpox killed as many as thirty thousand in the 1562–1563 pandemic alone. Subsequent pandemics devastated the Indigenous populations until it is estimated that ninety-five percent of the Indigenous people of the region disappeared. The understanding was that it was better for these people to be baptized and dead than alive and "pagan" (pp. 34–35). In general, the justification and tactics of European colonizers in the Americas often mimicked the elimination of undesirables in the Inquisition and Witch trials.

Two Western origin narratives can be seen in early, and indeed in many continuing, colonial attitudes involving the environment. The first narrative involves religious concepts associated with the Hebrew Bible, designated by Christianity as the Old Testament, with connections to Indo-European and Zoroastrian knowledge. The second narrative involves scientific theories of Pangaea, plate tectonics, and migrations. The result of these narratives places humans in a different relationship to the environment than that found in Indigenous communities.

Indigenous origin stories vary between communities but tend to be significantly different from Western traditions. Because Indigenous origin stories are markedly different from Western versions, they continue to be largely discredited by Western belief systems and scholars. The plethora of Indigenous origin traditions prohibit recounting them in this text, but recurring themes include reciprocity and constructions of interconnectedness especially related to the Earth. For Indigenous people, origin stories place and define people according to the geographical region. The land and the people are thus linked and often considered to be integral parts of each other, each being necessary to complete the other. The justification for these origin traditions is based on empirical evidence, oral testimony, and rational theory. These traditions take seriously spiritual evidence and use that evidence as foundational for understanding human existence.

In contrast, Western scientific origin stories deny spiritual evidence and focus primarily on empirical evidence, written testimony, and rational theory. While Western religious traditions do often allow for spiritual, or faith, evidence in justifying beliefs, they do not focus on earth-human constructs of interrelation or reciprocity as evidence for either the divine or for human ways of being. According to logicians and Western post-modern philosophers, the type of evidence allowed or disallowed in any argument shapes the conclusion. As Indigenous and Western origin narratives allow differing types of evidence, it is not surprising that the conclusions, or theories, are significantly different.

The strength of each argument, or theory, is therefore a matter of perspective based on what one understands to be justifiable as evidence as well as what standards are set in place to claim an argument, or theory is strongly inductive.[5] While it is reasonable to be able to judge arguments as stronger or weaker within a given paradigm, as discussed in Western post-modern philosophy, attempting to make similar judgments across paradigms is problematic and understood to be inauthentic. The standards of justifiability and argument strength are not objective, but are themselves imbedded within paradigms, making the judgment of other paradigms subjective and often both self-serving and circular.

Western dismissals of Indigenous origin stories based on a dismissal of oral or spiritual evidence fail to effectively counter Indigenous knowledge, but instead indicate the types of information and phenomena labeled as legitimate within Western paradigms. Indeed, most dismissals of Indigenous evidence and knowledge are done without reason other than the information simply does not fit within the Western constructs, or narrative. Ironically, this violates Western logical rules that require the dismissal of evidence or theories using reasoned arguments, rather than unsupported dismissals.

Given that individuals are assimilated into their cultures with all the traditions, "truths", and ideas inherent to their specific paradigm, it is not surprising that phenomenal experiences will also differ. Human experience of the world and what is considered legitimate, and justifiable evidence for theories stemming from that experience, is therefore paradigm dependent. As no "objective", or non-paradigm human positioning exists, no claim of "objective", "absolute", or "truth" positioning can be asserted. Judgments of "objectivity", "absolute", and "truth" remain subjective and paradigm dependent. Claims of knowledge superiority therefore also remain subjective and paradigm specific.[6] The history of Western religions belies a complicated relationship with Western science but shares a dismissal of Indigenous origin

---

[5]A strong inductive argument entails that the conclusion that follows from the premises is strongly probable. The degree to which a conclusion is strongly probable is largely based on individual or community beliefs involving the truth of the premises in the argument. As inductive arguments tend to contain assumptions, which cannot be determined to be true or false, and background information based on linguistic and cultural constructs, determinations of the strength with which the conclusion follows from the premises are variable.

[6]While Western philosophy still debates post-modern argumentation involving paradigm and cultural differences and what "truth" is, it is significant to note that these arguments represent a significant body of scholarship especially in the areas of critical theory, feminist theory, critical race theory, and decolonization/Indigenizing studies. The concept of an essentialist "Truth" or an absolute "Truth", however, was fortified in the Enlightenment and has since found a place in neoliberal and conservative theories.

narratives and spirituality associated with nature. Indeed, the distinction of what is classified as "spiritual" and the types of experiences housed within this classification is significantly different in Indigenous and Christian paradigms.

## The Impact of Origin Narrative Differences

Examining origin narratives for both Indigenous and Western cultures highlights the treatment and use of environment as resource within the different paradigms. Western constructs involve concepts such as dominion and stewardship, along with scientific and technological concepts of industrialization. Indigenous constructs focus on reciprocity and a science of interrelation. The differences are not a simple matter of focus or "saying the same thing in different ways". Instead, the paradigm differences establish different phenomenal experiences leading to vastly different understandings of what counts as evidence and what it takes to establish a strong argument, or theory.

What this means is that culturally different people living within the same geographical region likely experience vastly different realities, which cannot be ranked on a hierarchical scale of superiority as they do not share the same standards regarding what makes something "superior". Additionally, the idea of separate but equal paradigms is understood to be more problematic for Western paradigms than Indigenous ones because of the Western need to establish epistemic and cultural hierarchies. However, Western philosophy and science both allow for the justification involving equity claims using post-modern and quantum theories.

To better understand just how differing paradigms can establish conflicting environmental knowledge we will briefly examine Western and Indigenous narratives involving the Bering Strait. According to Western tradition, which uses an interweaving of religion and science, humans came into existence in what is now considered the Middle East, or North Africa, and through a process of migration, came to inhabit the rest of the world. This narrative also relies on a theory of plate tectonics and additional scientific evidence along with archeological and anthropological evidence. While science, anthropology, and archeology have often run afoul of religious ideologies, there is a rather belabored agreement involving the origin/migration narrative. Western religions agree that origins began in the Middle East and that humans spread beyond that. There is, however, a marked difference on the how and why for these ideals, but the broad outline of the narratives can be woven together.

Given these narratives, the Bering Strait narratives[7] have become largely accepted as sacrosanct even though scientific archeological evidence is questionable and, according to some, completely absent. The debate hinges largely on the definition of "mass-migration". Establishing the possibility of small numbers of people passing back and forth in the region presents as reasonable. Establishing a "mass-migration" is more problematic, but what constitutes a "mass"? Setting aside the definitional problem, establishing the origins of the theory of a "mass-migration" from Asia itself is problematic. In reality, much of the early Bering Strait work focused on theories of plant migration (Hopkins 1967). In the forward to *Across Atlantic Ice*, Collins describes the continued debate within Western circles as different sectors attempt to use various methods, including DNA analysis, to support the various narratives, many of which use an ice-thaw/ice-free corridor. The theories offer various time frames and methods for possible human migration. He notes that there continues to be debate and "spirited objections" to newer theories. Indeed, Collins claims that the older versions of the Bering Strait narratives are so ingrained that scholars have been known to make comments such as "I hate to see him…throw away his career" aimed at those espousing the newer theories that dispute the Bering Strait narratives. Nonetheless, Collins does admit that there is a growing willingness to "at least give a listen" to new interpretations. He himself denounces the newer DNA-based claims as he claims they lack physical evidence from an ancient era (Collins 2011, pp. xiii–xv).

Cremo and Thompson add to the controversy with human archaeological evidence that predates the accepted 12,000–20,000-thousand-year Clovis time frame. Indeed, their book is more about exposing the "anomalies" and evidence that has been dismissed by archaeology, rather than directly countering the Bering Strait narratives specifically (1999). They point to evidence such as the artifacts discovered under the Tuolumne Table Mountain site which were found in gravel dating "from 9 to 55 million years" ago (1999, pp. 94–95). In many cases, the evidence they put forth has been dismissed as anomalous, poor archaeology, or simply as mistaken. However, the plethora of such anomalies listed in the text at least brings into question the Bering Strait narratives. As Collins states, "good science requires critical examination of evidence and ideas, but it is not served by the unsupported dismissal of either. Thoughtful, well-argued, and evidence-based challenges" are important (p. xv). Even with detractors such as Cremo and Thompson, the narrative

---

[7] It should be noted that there are several Bering Strait narratives. Here we are referring to the collection as a whole and not specific versions, although the details in the different versions should be addressed in other works.

of the Bering Strait migration remains strong and continues to hold a place of sacred narrative in Western populations and scholarship.

Indeed, the intensity with which Western scholars and laity hold to the Bering Strait narratives is often baffling to Indigenous scholars and scientists as it seems more reminiscent of religious fervor, than to Western claims of rational, objective science. When scholars such as Deloria call for evidence and justification regarding such narratives, the response is often one of disbelief and even indignation that such a question could be raised. In the West, while the time frame and specifics of any mass migration may be debated, the narrative itself remains largely unquestioned. The importance of this theory appears to be as much a matter of tradition based on oral testimony as on actual physical evidence, which is ironically one of the primary reasons for dismissing Indigenous origin narratives.

Indigenous communities in North America largely deny the Bering Strait narratives based on evidence provided in oral histories, historical rock depictions, and cultural knowledge involving plants and animals all of which have been gathered before, during, and after the "freezing times". Often these communities allow for the possibility of small migration from one area to the other, but they deny "mass-migration". Additionally, many origin stories evidence that, migrating communities, did not do so from Asia, but had always done so in association with Turtle Island. For Deloria, along with other Indigenous scholars, the Bering Strait mass-migration narratives are additionally problematic given evidence related to general migration patterns in Asia, geological issues involving glacial and non-glacial passages over multiple mountain ranges, global weather patterns necessary to create the ice or non-ice conditions for the bridge, and the lack of empirical evidence to substantiate a claim of "mass-migration" (Deloria 1997).

Additionally, civilizations such as the Inca, which was the fourth civilization associated with that era according to Incan evidence, are also problematic to Western narratives. Given that civilizations take hundreds and sometimes thousands of years to rise and fall, the speed with which these migrations would have had to occur belies a determination of human spirit. Finally, even if one admits to a mass-migration, that does not logically entail that there were not already people in the areas into which these people migrated.[8] Supporting Indigenous evidentiary concerns, Waters points out that the Bering Strait theories contain logical fallacies including begging the question and false cause which undermine the strength of the arguments (Waters, Bering Stait 2004). She argues that the narratives themselves fail

---

[8]It is interesting to note that similar discussions of land bridges have been associated with the Caribbean and the Pacific Islands to explain population origins.

to meet Western standards required for strong inductive arguments. Given Indigenous arguments, Western narratives claiming a vacant continent and mass-migration are largely a product of tradition, rather than empirical evidence or logical argumentation.

Like Collins, many Indigenous scholars question recent DNA-based arguments as the focus of these arguments is a matter of how one interprets the DNA evidence. For example, one interpretation found a DNA marker that shows up in many American Indian populations as well as within one small Asian population. The study used this shared marker as evidence supporting Bering Strait migrations. However, the explanation for how and when such a marker might have been shared is indeterminate. More importantly, the stronger logical argument would be that migration occurred from Turtle Island to Asia, not the other way around. Granted this is a rather specific DNA claim and others are not so obviously logically flawed, but it indicates the depth of tradition involved in Western interpretations of evidence. The assumption that the migration flowed East to West is just that, an assumption, and indicates a paradigm bias. Logically speaking, arguments could be made for groups of humans traveling in either direction, but such arguments fail to give sufficient evidence to support any mass-migration of humans. Regardless of the direction of any migration, it does not undermine the argument that humans existed in Turtle Island prior to any migration.

What is important for this discussion is to see how differing origin narratives influence human relationships with the environment. As stated by Deloria and other Indigenous scholars, the polarizing nature of Bering Strait discussions is less about science and evidence than about politics. Deloria claims that hidden in the sacrosanct nature of these Western narratives is the need to separate the Indigenous of Turtle Island from their places of origin. The Bering Strait tradition eliminates the possibility that Indigenous people were created from the lands later known as North, Central, and South America. The argument then is that these people migrated to this empty land "shortly" before the Europeans.

Migration then works to negate reciprocal and interrelated Indigenous claims based on direct creation from or with their lands of origin. In this way, Indigenous spiritual and physical land connections are considered later developments rather than a part of original creation. Colonization is then nothing more than two non-aboriginal groups struggling over what was originally vacant territory (Deloria 1997, pp. 67–70). When joined with Western religious understandings of dominion over the earth and literary images of heroic exploration, narratives like the Bering Strait, alongside Manifest

Destiny and Social Darwinism, worked to justify arguments for colonization and Indigenous removal and assimilation.

In contrast to Western origin narratives, Indigenous narratives vary considerably. There are claims that certain communities originated above and traveled to Turtle Island and others that evidence that people came from below and tunneled or were brought to their place. Others indicate migrations, but do not include stories of coming over the Bering Strait area. Instead, the migration stories tend to be within the areas now called North, Central, and South America. What these stories do have in common is the reciprocal relationship between the Earth and the people based on a science of interconnection. These stories focus on the reciprocity between the geographical areas and the animals, including humans, that originated in these areas. The connection between humans and nature can then be described as child to mother or part to whole. Regardless of the descriptor, the physical and spiritual connection is understood to be both necessary and intimate. Indigenous scholars have then pointed to the fact that, as opposed to Western concepts of being separate, superior to, or dominate over nature, Indigenous people identify as part of, in harmony with, and familial with nature.

## Sovereignty

Indigenous sovereignty issues are a continuing theme within this text as they underlie Indigenous continuity and continue to be observed in intergenerational trauma. Some readers may wonder at the placement of this discussion in a chapter devoted to environmental issues. However, understanding the relationship between nature and sovereignty is essential to understanding Indigenous ontology. Ontology is the study of being and posits questions about what it means to "be" human. As explained above for Indigenous people, to be human is to be part of nature, it is a relationship of mother and child or part to whole. There is an interconnectedness and reciprocal relationship that bonds individual to nature in a way that does not accept division easily.

Dividing Indigenous from the geographical region of origin is a division of self. The two are not separate entities; each requires the other for completion of the self. Many Western students struggle to understand why Indigenous transplantation or removal was, and remains, problematic. "Why can't they just go to another region and put down new roots?" To ask questions such as this belies a Western mentality. It is not that Indigenous individuals have not survived removal or dysphoria, it is that survival comes with the loss of the self, the part that was physically and spiritually connected to the individual's origin. That place is the connection to the larger self, that will be discussed in later chapters. For this chapter, it is the natural part of the self that creates the intersection between sovereignty and environmental issues.

Using the U.S. as an example in exploring sovereignty issues, one must consider federal Indian law. A comprehensive treatment of sovereignty can be found in *Cohen's Handbook of Federal Indian Law*, which, since his death, has been amended but continues to be referred to as *Cohen's*. Deloria and DeMallie also offer a detailed two-volume text entitled *Documents of American Indian Diplomacy: Treaties, Agreements, and Conventions, 1775–1979* that deals extensively with sovereignty. While informative reads, these works present a challenge for those not trained in legal semantics.

For the purposes of this text, sovereignty discussions will focus on some rudimentary information with an understanding that more in-depth scholarship both exists and is important to the advanced study of sovereignty. Providing a foundation for discussions of sovereignty and land, Echo-Hawk identifies *Worcester v. Georgia* as elemental in the establishment of four components.

1. The Indian tribes enjoy a sovereign right of self-government that is not divested by their inclusion in the United States and is free from interference by the states,
2. Indian treaties must be honored as the supreme law of the land,
3. The doctrine of discovery and edicts of Europe do not divest Indian land or sovereignty, and
4. Reservation borders are protective barriers against hostile states and land-hungry settlers (Echo-Hawk 2013, p. 120).

*Worcester* established "the legal status of Indian tribes as 'domestic dependent nations' with inherent sovereignty that exist as separate political communities within the United States" (p. 120). However, the wording of *Worcester*, along with its implications, and its relevance to treaty rights became a legal quagmire.[9]

Tsosie explains that within the United States, there are "three classifications: Indian tribes, Alaska Native people, and Native Hawaiians" (Tsosie 2013, p. 241). The different classifications designate different statuses regarding rights. Indian tribes and Alaska Natives have rights as "federally

---

[9]As further evidence of the legal quagmire, Echo-Hawk gives a comprehensive discussion of the implications and lessons involving plenary power involving *Lone Wolf v. Hitchcock* in his work *In the Courts of the Conqueror* (2010).

recognized Indian tribes", although specific rights may differ based on the specifics of each treaty. Further, territorial rights are tied to the designation of "Indian Country", which limited Alaskan rights to a "single reservation (Metlakatla) and allotments still held in Native title". In this case, sovereignty was tied to a community's ability to tax and to form regulatory jurisdiction (p. 241).

While Tsosie explains the mistaken, but common, conflation of the different classifications and the rights allotted to these communities, the reality is that "only federally recognized tribes have jurisdiction to govern their lands and resources" (p. 242). Furthermore, non-federally recognized people do not "have the ability to receive statutory delegations of federal authority, which would allow them to exercise meaningful control over air, water, or land resources" (p. 242). This in turn leaves only federally recognized tribes with the right to "generate environmental laws of their own choosing and apply them to their lands and resources" (p. 242).

According to Tsosie, the designations distinguish the political rights of sovereignty from cultural rights of sovereignty. The former being possessed by only some Indigenous communities, while the latter is possessed by all. Tsosie's discussion states that moving beyond domestic law to the use of international law, including UNDRIP, can assist Indigenous communities in developing strategies to argue for self-determination as International documents tend to focus on the connection between cultural rights and human rights. Indeed, moving beyond domestic law and using international documents represents a viable strategy for communities attempting to protect TEK. Tsosie chronicles U.S. governmental strategies involved in discussions of environmental damage and the negation of Indigenous rights in which the government stipulates that "environmental claims and religious claims are completely separate under U.S. domestic law" making Indigenous environmental claims legally ambiguous. This definitional loophole, and others like it, allow the government to override Indigenous claims to sacred sites and allow for government-supported mining or pipeline operations because tribal claims are not seen as falling either under the "First Amendment Free Exercise Clause or the Religious Freedom Restoration Act" (pp. 248–249).

While employing Tsosie's strategy regarding the use of both domestic and international documents to argue for sovereignty can be seen in global Indigenous efforts, the results are varied. International documents, including those from the UN, face challenges regarding definition and interpretation. For example, UNDRIP, considered by many to be the preeminent model for Indigenous discussion of rights, fails to use the term "sovereignty" to describe Indigenous rights to land, preferring the term "self-determination". While related, the terms are not synonymous. The only time the document references "sovereignty" is in Article 46 and, from a logician's perspective, this reference has some potentially concerning ramifications.

> Nothing in this Declaration may be interpreted as implying for any State, people, group or person any right to engage in any activity or to perform any act contrary to the Charter of the United Nations or construed as authorizing or encouraging any action which would dismember or impair, totally or in part, the territorial integrity or political unity of sovereign and independent States. (UNDRIP 2008, p. 14)

Since it is embedded in the UNDRIP document, the assumption may be that this reference is in support of Indigenous populations regarding the dismemberment or impairment of "sovereign and independent States". However, the article can be read to support the non-disruption of colonizing Nation-States such as the U.S. or Australia. This second interpretation appears to deny Indigenous populations the right to impair the running of sovereign colonizing Nation-States in any quest to regain the use and self-determination over current or past Indigenous lands and resources. Finally, the terms sovereignty and self-determination continue to be used ambiguously. The terms refer to collective rights, as indicated by Tsosie, however many people slide usage of the terms between individuals and groups. As Tsosie points out, it is strategic to tie sovereignty and self-determination to human rights, but it must be understood that human rights tend to be individually defined. This is again part of the difficulty regarding legal actions in Nation-States that recognize individual human rights of religion but fail to recognize group rights. This will be discussed more fully in the next chapter.

## Environmental Issues in Indigenous Cultures

To illustrate the environmental issues resulting from Western and Indigenous paradigm differences and to further explain the ties between colonization, sovereignty, and intergenerational trauma, we will examine issues found in Indigenous communities. It does not take intensive research to uncover why the UN designates Indigenous people as some of the most "at risk" people on the planet as Indigenous communities are facing a multitude of environmental disasters. Additionally, continued colonization and assimilation efforts deny Indigenous populations access to traditional geographic regions necessary for continued spiritual and physical well-being resulting in increased poverty, health issues, and cultural destruction. The separation from geographical origins, or traditional migratory patterns, is more than a matter of cultural self-determination, it involves both individual human rights issues and community sovereignty, a topic that will be more fully explored in this chapter.

For examples of Indigenous cultures under threat, one need only to search topics such as "pollution in Indigenous territories" or "Indigenous water rights issues" to find a plethora of global environmental crises impacting Indigenous populations. Caution must, of course, be used as the Internet can be said to have both helped and hindered Indigenous rights. However, Internet reporting has increased global environmental and Indigenous awareness.[10] In Canada, for example, there remains a drinking water crisis among First Nations populations, which is often not covered in mainstream media accounts or, at least not, from Indigenous perspectives.

The crisis involves drinking water that is polluted with harmful agents including bacteria, heavy metals, and persistent organic pollutants (POPs).[11] POPs are defined as including pesticides and industrial chemicals, most of which people outside the industry can neither pronounce nor spell. These are defined as persistent because they do not breakdown readily, but instead stay in the water, soil, or air and can travel great distances. Among the chemical compounds still found in First Nations water supplies is arsenic used in gold mining. In Great Slave Lake, the adjacent gold mine used a particularly virulent form of arsenic. While the government passed the Safe Drinking Water in First Nations Act in 2013, little has been done to resolve the issues keeping some communities under a more than seventeen-year boil order.

Similar drinking water issues associated with mining can be found in the U.S. and other industrialized countries with a large proportion impacting primarily Indigenous communities. Little coverage of these crises occur as the mining is seen to be essential for Nation-States to maintain quality of life or, as in the U.S., much of the mining was stopped years ago and so is considered a thing of the past regardless of the toxic waste that remains in reservoirs around the defunct mines.

Dioxins, chemicals associated largely with pesticides, herbicides, bleaching of pulp and paper, and burning, have gained some media attention in the U.S. in the recent past; however, little of this press has focused on the impact of dioxins in Indigenous communities. Dioxins are found in the fats of

---

[10]The information in this section is gleaned from news outlets, personal conversations, and conference dialogues over the years to give an Indigenous perspective on environmental concerns.

[11]In recent medical literature, POPs have been named as potential triggers for health issues such as type II diabetes, cancers, kidney and liver ailments, as well as spontaneous abortions and birth defects.

animals such as beef, poultry, and fish as well as in dairy products and eggs. The negative health impacts of large dose exposure are generally agreed to, but what continues to be debated is what constitutes "acceptable" levels.

The concern for Indigenous populations, particularly in the far North, includes the rise of dioxin levels in human breast milk. Several industrialized countries along with the UN have conducted studies, not widely disseminated, indicating higher dioxin intake for infants and toddlers largely because of the use of breast milk and dairy supplements. Indigenous infants in the Arctic appear to be at higher risk as evidence indicates that global dioxins tend to concentrate in the Northern, cooler climates. Sources indicate that the Arctic region has become dense with dioxins to the point that Inuit women have begun to consider alternatives to breast feeding their children. What is clear is that the sovereignty and self-determination of the Indigenous people living in the Arctic are threatened by the industrial pollutants of industrialized countries to their South. The Inuit people are faced with abandoning traditional diets or preserving them at the expense of their children.

Another example of an environmental crisis involves petroleum production. While oil and gas production, including fracking and the use of pipelines, has gained a great deal of press in the U.S. and Canada, many are unaware of the devastation of pipelines in the Amazon. Western Amazon oil is being heavily produced with much of it flowing through species-rich areas of the Amazon and areas either titled to or used by Indigenous people. Production of the oil requires deforestation, toxic drilling chemicals, increased human/industrial waste, and oil spills from persistent leaks. The combination of these pollutants threatens the human, animal, and plant biodiversity in the region.

Experiencing no benefit from the oil production, Indigenous populations suffer the brunt of the consequences. As issues have arisen, Amazonian Indigenous people have been faced with the destruction of culture, the impairment of lifestyle, and even removal. In some cases, military tactics have been used to preserve the oil production. While the Achuar tribe in Peru and the Indigenous in Ecuador have had some recent success in the courts, the legal battles represent years of work and financial commitments beyond the resources of most tribes. Various lawsuits have claimed that the deaths, birth defects, and environmental destruction, including polluted water supplies, were the responsibility of government-supported oil companies. While the Indigenous in Peru won an undisclosed amount of money, tribal representatives state that no amount of money will reverse the damage suffered by the Amazon or reinstate traditional ways of being. The money gained will neither reestablish the lost cultural or political sovereignty, the species of plants and animals eliminated from the region, nor will it replenish the lost drinking water. Furthermore, the win does not ensure that oil production will not occur in the future.

Islands throughout the world are facing their own threats with the loss of resources, specifically drinking water. These threats come, not only from climate change, but also from increased industrial production and tourism.[12] Many islands in Oceania are experiencing rising waters and high tides that threaten to make areas on the islands uninhabitable or in some cases to sink the island entirely. In part, the lack of media coverage stems from a history of island exploitation by industrialized countries. Beginning with Captain Cook, Oceania has been billed as an exotic playground for tourists and as important military sites.

Between 1946 and 1996, the U.S., France, and Britain conducted nuclear testing throughout the region with little or no concern for Indigenous populations. Among the areas impacted were Rongelap, Bikini, and Enewetak, with Bikini experiencing the March 1, 1954 Bravo test involving a 5-megatonne bomb. The people of Bikini were removed from their island for the tests and remain displaced with the exception of a brief time from 1970 to 1978 when the United States deemed the island safe. The second removal came after high levels of radioactivity were detected in the food being consumed by the Indigenous people.

The people of Rongelap also returned to their islands in 1957 only to leave again in 1985 as fears of radioactive contamination were confirmed. To date, only one of the islands of Rongelap is considered "cleaned up" by the U.S., but uncertainty remains. In an unprecedented occurrence, the people of the Marshall Islands won compensation for the devastation to their lands, but the funds were insufficient, and many people remain uncompensated.

To this day, many Oceania Indigenous fear returning to their traditional homes because of the nuclear testing, especially as much of the environmental impact remains under investigation. The health impacts from exposure to the initial tests and to the residual radioactivity continue to be the subject of investigation making these islands and populations some of the most studied scientific subjects involving radioactive contamination. As noted earlier in this chapter, removal negatively impacts Indigenous ways of being and eliminates sovereignty regarding tradition and origin lands. It is a misunderstanding to think that the removal of island people to a different island does not seriously impact or destroy culture. As with other cultures, island

---

[12]The authors recognize that not all people accept global warming or the human component of global warming. However, both Indigenous and Western science have established evidence for a strong inductive argument regarding the reality of human participation in global warming.

cultures are not interchangeable, they are unique in language, tradition, spirituality, and history. The loss of a single island entails the loss of culture and Indigenous knowledge.

As with other Northern Indigenous people, dioxins have negatively impacted the Sami, and like island Indigenous peoples, the Sami are struggling with the impacts of global warming. The Sami inhabit Northern areas of Sweden, Finland, Norway, and Russia and face the extinction of their culture with the warming of the land and the melting of the permafrost. Traditionally, the Sami have hundreds of words to describe snow, but climate change has eliminated the need for many of these. Instead of traditional snows, the region is experiencing more ice which inhibits traditional foods, medicine, and reindeer herding. Add to these issues governmental regulations involving land usage and the rising dioxin levels and the Sami populations are facing potential cultural extermination. With reports of the loss of valuable resources within their traditional territories, Arctic populations such as the Sami are not only being denied sovereignty, but potentially face the denial of existence. Already, the increase in mining has become more prevalent, shrinking the diminishing availability of land for reindeer herds. The threats to traditional ways of life are reflected in reports that document the increased suicide rates in these communities much of which is being attributed to the burden felt by the young Sami as they face being the last of their people.

## Traditional Environmental Knowledge

In bringing this chapter to conclusion it is important to highlight specific elements of Indigenous traditional knowledge as it impacts environmental awareness and involvement. We have already discussed reciprocity and interconnection and the role of origin stories in understanding TEK, but some explanation needs to be given as to why many Indigenous individuals and communities separate themselves from Western conservation movements. Western conservation movements, and in many cases Western preservation movements, continue to focus on humans as the primary reason to conserve or protect resources. For Indigenous populations, the interrelationship requires that preservation be done for the sake of nature itself. There is an understanding that nature has agency and must be protected and assisted in its own sovereignty. For this reason, phrases such as "for seven generations" are common in Indigenous communities. The idea being that a reciprocal debt is owed to all of nature for at least seven generations beyond one's life or beyond a community's existence.

Employing Western strategies to ensure the seventh-generation moral requirement has become necessary, but also risks the loss of traditional knowledge as success in Western legal systems continues to require the use of Western evidence, terminology, and strategy. To speak of land, water, plants, and animals as resources in Western terms commodifies them in a way that is in direct opposition to Indigenous paradigms. Such discussions risk turning the lands into ownership battles between groups of humans and dismissing the equity of agency built into the Indigenous-nature ontology.

O'Neill claims that commodification language focuses on limiting the risk of environmental pollution or minimizing the damage rather than on efforts to reduce environmental risks all together including significantly limiting human consumption and use of resources to give preference to the agency of nature (O'Neill 2003). Not only does Western language fail to incorporate Indigenous calls to minimize usage, but O'Neill argues that Western views regarding human-nature relations also support Indigenous removal and inhibits Indigenous sovereignty by claiming that it is "more efficient" to move impacted Indigenous populations than to stop using or to stop polluting the "resource". Her argument calls for policymakers to embrace Indigenous knowledge, tradition, and spirituality in making decisions regarding geographic regions and their inhabitants. She also argues that TEK be included to advance environmental justice and to avoid continued patterns of cultural and racial discrimination.

To help Western policymakers understand Indigenous science, Cajete explains that rather than humans attempting to control or dominate nature, Indigenous ontology places humans alongside all other beings in a mode of creativity (2000). Reality is understood to be in flux with no single point or way of being having preferential standing. Existence is then continuously changing as the beings participate in creativity driven by Spirit, which may also be referenced as energy as will be explained in Chapter 2. The understanding is that all things are animate and so share in creative participation. Indigenous cosmology, therefore, embodies a "natural democracy" focused on balance and harmony (p. 52). He explains that the dynamic balance of the transformative creativity is understood by Indigenous people by engaging, not just the rational mind, but also the metaphorical mind. The metaphorical mind "decodes layers of meaning" and is the catalyst for creativity as it understands beyond reason to other areas of truth much of which involves symbolism and metaphorical knowledge tied to deeper levels of universal knowledge. As a result, the foundation of Indigenous knowledge requires not only the rational experience of phenomena and mind, but also the engagement of the metaphoric mind to enlist deeper levels of understanding regarding things both seen and unseen.

Creating a more practical list for policymakers, Cajete's science of interrelation establishes a list of guiding thoughts for human-nature interrelationship.

- Native Science integrates a spiritual orientation.
- Dynamic multidimensional harmony is a perpetual state in the universe.
- All human knowledge is related to the creation of the world and the emergence of human; therefore, human knowledge is based on human cosmology.
- Humanity has an important role in the perpetuation of the natural processes of the world.
- Every "thing" is animate and has spirit.
- There is significance to each natural place because each place reflects the whole order of nature.
- The history of relationship must be respected with regard to places, plants, animals, and natural phenomena.
- Technology should be appropriate and reflect balanced relationships to the natural world.
- There are basic relationships, patterns, and cycles in the world that need to be understood; this is the proper role of mathematics.
- There are stages of initiation to knowledge.
- Elders are relied upon as the keepers of essential knowledge.
- Actin in the world must be sanctioned through ritual and ceremony.
- Properly fashioned artifacts contain the energy of the thoughts, materials, and contexts in which they are fashioned and therefore become symbols of those thoughts, entities, or processes.
- Dreams are considered gateways to creative possibilities if used wisely and practically (pp. 64–65).

Support for Cajete's list is evidenced in a variety of origin narratives including that found in the Havasupai, which reference the Grand Canyon as Grandmother and Grandfather. They are whole when they are there and can join with the land in ceremony, thus allowing them to balance with the whole of creation (Hirst 2006). Similar evidence is revealed in collections of Elder wisdom such as *Every Day Is a Good Day* (Mankiller 2004), *Elders* (Yunupingu and O'Donoghue 2003), and *Voices of Wisdom* (Harden 1999). These collections share voices that focus on the natural democracy embedded in Indigenous knowledge. The role of humans is to live harmoniously within nature in a mode of reciprocity with all other inhabitants.[13] The chapter on education will again reference these ontological understandings.

We will conclude this chapter with three voices that help to solidify what has been evidenced above. According to Henare, the ethic of reciprocity is "a 'generative relation' that exists between individual human hearts and minds, as well as between human beings and [all] matter" (Henare 2001, p. 205). For Gonzales and Nelson "land is everything". It is the foundation of spiritual practices, history, and oral traditions. It is the bodies of our ancestors that we ingest in food, and it is that from which we get medicines (Gonzales and Nelson 2001). Finally, Namunu's description of Indigenous "life, before the Europeans came, was [one] surrounded with creative energies flowing through trees, grasses, streams and rivers, mountains, sea, sky and all the galaxies" all intertwined to create an understanding of harmonious existence (2001).[14]

## Additional Readings

Birns, N. (2015). *Contemporary Australian Literature: A World Not Yet Dead*. Sydney University Press.
Craven, M. (2007). *The Decolonization of International Law: State Succession and the Law of Treaties*. Oxford: Oxford University Press.
Deloria, V., Jr. (2006). *The World We Used to Live In: Remembering the Powers of the Medicine Men*. Golden: Fulcrum Publishing.
Deloria, V., Jr., & Lytle, C. M. (1983). *American Indians, American Justice*. Austin: University of Texas Press.
Feng, P. (2002). Ritual Rememory: Afro-Caribbean Religions in 'Myal' and 'It Begins with Tears.' *Melus, 27*(1), 149–175.
Goldtooth, T. B. K. (2004). Stolen Resources: Continuing Threats to Indigenous People's Sovereignty and Survival. *Race, Poverty & the Environment, 11*(1), 9–12.
Grande, S. M. A. (1999). Beyond the Ecologically Noble Savage: Deconstructing the White Man's Indian. *Environmental Ethics, 21*(3), 307–320.

---

[13]It should be noted that there is a similarity between deep ecology constructs and Indigenous ecology, but they should not be considered the same as deep ecology does not employ spirit in the same manner. Additionally, one can look at the list provided by Cajete and see where deep ecology differs. Ecofeminism also shares some similarities in the relationship between women and nature, but it too differs from Indigenous understandings, primarily in its gender construction. In fact, both deep ecology and ecofeminism continue to argue from Western paradigms using human-centered constructs.

[14]*Indigenous Traditions in Ecology* edited by John A. Grim is an excellent source for this discussion and if we could include every entry, we would as they reflect the interrelationship expressed in Indigenous science.

Grim, J. A. (Ed.). (2001). *Indigenous Traditions and Ecology: The Interbeing of Cosmology and Community*. Cambridge: Harvard University Press.

Jackson, S. (2011). Indigenous Water Management: Priorities for the Next Five Years. In D. Connell & Q. Grafton (Eds.), *Basin Futures: Water Reform in the Murray-Darling Basin* (pp. 163–177). ANU Press.

Johansen, B. E. (2002). The Inuit's Struggle with Dioxins and Other Organic Pollutants. *American Indian Quarterly, 26*(3), 479–490.

Kryzanowski, J. A., & McIntyre, L. (2011). A Holistic Model for the Selection of Environmental Assessment Indicators to Assess the Impact of Industrialization on Indigenous Health. *Canadian Journal of Public Health, 102*(2), 112–117.

MacKenzie, M. K., Serrano, S. K., & Kaulukukui, K. L. (2007). Environmental Justice for Indigenous Hawaiians: Reclaiming Land and Resources. *Natural Resources & Environment, 21*(3), 37–42.

Mankiller, W., & Wallis, M. (1993). *Mankiller: A Chief and Her People*. New York: St. Martin's Press.

McGaurr, B. T., & Lester, L. (2016). Environmental Leaders and Indigenous Engagement in Australia: Cosmopolitan Endeavor? *Conservation and Society, 14*(3), 254–266.

Reed, T. V. (2009). Toxic Colonialism, Environmental Justice, and Native Resistance in Silko's 'Almanac of the Dead'. *MELUS, 34*(2), 25–42.

Stevenson, M. G. (1996). Indigenous Knowledge in Environmental Assessment. *Arctic, 49*(3), 278–291.

Tang, R., & Gavin, M. C. (2016). A Classification of Threats to Traditional Ecological Knowledge and Conservation Responses. *Conservation and Society, 14*(1), 57–70.

Thorson, J. E., Britton, S., & Colby, B. G. (Eds.). (2006). *Tribal Water Rights: Essays in Contemporary Law, Policy, and Economics*. Tucson: The University of Arizona Press.

## Works Cited

Cajete, G. (2000). *Native Science: Natural Laws of Interdependence*. Santa Fe: Clear Light Publishers.

Collins, M. B. (2011). Forward. In D.J. Stanford & B.A. Bradley (Eds.), *Across Atlantic Ice: The Origin of America's Clovis Culture*. Berkeley: University of California Press.

Cremo, M. A., & Thompson, R. (1999). *The Hidden History of the Human Race*. Los Angeles: Bhaktivedanta Book Publishing.

de Las Casas, B. D. (1992). *The Devastation of the Indies: A Brief Account*. Baltimore: John Hopkins University Press.

Deloria, V., Jr. (1997). *Read Earth, White Lies*. Golden: Fulcrum Publishing.

Deloria, V., Jr. (1999). *Documents of American Indian Diplomacy: Treaties, Agreements, and Conventions, 1775–1979* (Two Volume Set). Oklahoma: University of Oklahoma Press.

Echo-Hawk, W. (2010). *In the Courts of the Conquerors: The Ten Worst Indian Law Cases Ever Decided.* Golden: Fulcrum.

Echo-Hawk, W. R. (2013). *In the Light of Justice: The Rise of Human Rights in Native America and the UN Declaration on the Rights of Indigenous People.* Golden, CO: Fulcrum.

Gonzales, T. A., & Nelson, M. K. (2001). Contemporary Native American Responses to Enviornmental Threats in Indian Country. In J. A. Grim (Ed.), *Indigenous Traditions and Ecology: The Interbeing of Cosmology and Community* (pp. 495–583). Cambridge: Harvard University Press.

Harden, M. J. (1999). *Voices of Wisdom: Hawaiian Elders Speak.* Kula: Aka Press.

Henare, M. (2001). Tapu, Mana, Mauri, Hau, Wairua: A Maori Philosophy of Virtalism and Cosmos. In J. A. Grim (Ed.), *Indigenous Traditions and Ecology: The Interbeing of Cosmology and Community.* Cambridge: Harvard University Press.

Hirst, S. (2006). *I Am the Grand Canyon.* Grand Canyon: Grand Canyon Association.

Hopkins, D. M. (Ed.). (1967). *The Bering Land Bridge.* Stanford: Sanford University Press.

*Indigenous Environmental Network.* (n.d.). Retrieved from IENEarth.org: https://www.ienearth.org/home/.

*Johnson v. McIntosh.* https://www.lexisnexis.com/community/casebrief/p/casebrief-johnson-v-m-intosh.

LaDuke, W. (1999). *All Our Relations: Native Struggles for Land and Life.* Cambridge: South End Press.

LaDuke, W. (2002). *The Winona LaDuke Reader: A Collection of Essential Writings.* Stillwater: Voyageur Press.

Mankiller, W. (2004). *Every Day Is a Good Day: Reflections by Contemporary Indigenous Women.* Golden: Fulcrum Publishing.

Namunu, S. B. (2001). Melasian Religion, Ecology, and Modernizatin in Papau New Guinea. In J. A. Grim (Ed.), *Indigenous Traditions and Ecology: the interbeing of cosmology and community.* Cambridge: Harvard University Press.

Newton, N. J., Anderson, R., et al. (2012). *Cohen's Handbook of Federal Indian Law* (2012 ed.). LexisNexis.

O'Neill, C. A. (2003). Risk Avoidance, Cultural Discrimination, and Environmental Justice for Indigenous People. *Ecology Law Quarterly, 30*(1), 1–57.

Tsosie, R. (2013). Climate Change and Indigenous Peoples; Comparative Models of Sovereignty. *Tulane Environmental Law Journal., 26*, 239–257.

UNDRIP. (2008). *United Nations Declaration on the Rights of Indigenous Peoples.* New York: United Nations Publisher. Retrieved from https://www.un.org/esa/socdev/unpfii/documents/DRIPS_en.pdf.

United Nations. (2013). *State of the World's Indigenous Peoples: Indigenous Peoples' Access to Health Services.* New York: United Nations. Retrieved from https://www.un.org/development/desa/indigenouspeoples/wp-content/uploads/sites/19/2018/03/The-State-of-The-Worlds-Indigenous-Peoples-WEB.pdf.

Voeks, R. (1997). *Sacred Leaves of Candomblé: African Magic, Medicine, and Religions of Brazil*. Austin: University of Texas Press.

Waters, A. (2004). *That Alchemical Bering Strait Theory; America's Indigenous Nations and Informal Logic Courses* (A. Waters, Ed.). Malden: Blackwell Publishing.

*Worcester v. Georgia*. https://www.lexisnexis.com/community/casebrief/p/casebrief-worcester-v-georgia.

Yunupingu, M., & O'Donoghue, L. (Eds.). (2003). *Elders: Wisdom from Australia's Indigenous Leaders*. Cambridge: Cambridge University Press.

# 3

# Sacred

## Ties to the Sacred

*1997-I was very tired, very stressed, and I was not pleased to be awakened in the middle of the night by someone calling my name, "CAROL!". Jolted awake, I said "What?" in a voice more grumpy than responsive. No answer. I sighed, thinking that a member of my large family had awakened me and then, because of my tone of voice, was now reluctant to tell me what they wanted, such as money for gas, fix a flat tire, or can they sleep on the couch for the remainder of the night.*

*"CAROL!" This time I raised up on my elbows, looked over at my three little grandchildren that shared the big bed with me. Fast asleep; the voice had not disturbed them. I looked out the open bedroom door, down the hall; no lights. What is this, I thought, and said aloud "What do you want?", thinking that whoever it was might still be at the front door. A long silence; no response.*

*Disgruntled, I was in the process of turning over when I heard "YOU WILL WRITE THE BOOK."*

*Of all the… in the middle of the night you tell me that? Write a book? With three grand–babies to care for? Working full time? Trying to pay bills and keep food on the table? Do you know what you are asking?*

*I was too tired to even think of writing a book. If I had time to write, I thought, I'd clean out my refrigerator. Clean the stove. But write a book?*

*"YOU WILL WRITE THE BOOK!". This time I half sat up, coming wide awake and realizing that something was going on that I didn't really understand, wished desperately would go away. This is crazy, I thought. I was mentally arguing with a voice out of nowhere, with a presence I couldn't even see, wasn't sure there*

*was anything there to see. Who – or what – is talking to me? And why me? Is this something from the Light, or from the Darkness? I felt no evil, no crawling skin, no hair raising, no cold chills. This was good, then, whatever was happening.*

"What book?" I said out loud, a bit uneasily, a whole lot cautious, all grumpiness gone. Being raised in a household where such unusual things occurred frequently, I was not really frightened by what was going on, but I was a whole lot uncertain. The little winky–blinky lights that flashed on and off like tiny fireflies were familiar to me; they often were present when two realms of existence intermingled. But a very audible voice, quite loud and authoritative, telling me to do something that had not even entered my mind, was a new experience. Write a book? What book?

Suddenly in front of my face, close to my nose, was a book. There was a jacket on it, printed in blue, gray, and white, and the lettering was in big, bold letters: **INDIGENOUS CIVILIZATIONS AND POST COLONIZATION STRESS.**

No, no, no, I thought, I don't have time to write any kind of book, and I certainly don't want to start on one like that. Besides, I usually say "Indigenous populations", not "Indigenous civilizations". And the book looked awfully big and thick…

"Look," I argued, "I have way too much to do as it is. I just don't have time to write a book, especially not one like that."

"YOU ALREADY HAVE THE CHAPTERS OUTLINED."

"I have? What are you talking about?"

The book vanished, and in front of my nose was a typed page, a paper I had used frequently for over ten years in my lecturing and writing. Ten concepts of American Indian beliefs… behaviors associated to those beliefs… the fundamental cause of post-colonization stress. I had never thought about it that way, but suddenly I could see the connection. Well, I thought, this might not be so hard, and it will be good for American Indians.

"NO!"

"No? No what?"

"INDIGENOUS CIVILIZATIONS ARE ALL OVER THE WORLD."

"Now wait just a minute! You expect me to write a book and include Indigenous cultures from around the world? I can't do that!"

"YOU WILL HAVE HELP.

How does he or she—or what—that's talking to me know what kind of help I might need? Only a few people in the Center where I work knew anything about that sheet of paper listing the nineteen items. And even fewer from international events knew about it…. yes, I remember now, that meeting that we had in British Columbia in 1991. Many people with disabilities from Indigenous cultures all over the world were at the meeting. They spoke about not only having a disability but having a disability and also being members of minority cultures in their countries. Cultures that had been conquered by colonizers… Which ones from among those individuals would help me? Or would they assist me to meet others who would help?

*"How do you know..."* I was asking the unseen speaker a question when I realized the presence had vanished. Whoever it was that conversed with me had departed. I lay back on my pillow slowly, trying to decide what had just happened. Although I had answered in English and rather loudly at that, the voice had not really been in any specific language. The volume had been great, the loud sound bouncing about in the room so intensely that it seemed I had been surrounded by it, yet it had no specific point of origin except from inside my bedroom, or maybe inside my head. Strange, too, that it had not awakened my grandchildren. And it was almost as if there had been thought–forms rather than words spoken, like whole concepts and meaning occurring in the communication rather than one word at a time. Needless to say, I was wide awake by then, my mind racing as I thought about what I had been instructed to do. Daylight was near when I finally fell asleep.

That is how this project began. First, I began asking for verification of what had happened from traditional people I knew. Was this for real or was it a dream? Was it good or was it not good? What should I do about it?

The answer was always the same—it was not evil; therefore, it is good. And you should write the book. Next, I asked a larger circle of friends and associates; the same answers. Most of these people had great stores of knowledge about colonization stress. I was reluctant to speak about the happening with white–race friends but realized I must get their input. I shared the experience with many non–Native friends and found them excited and positive about the book. They offered help, something I was not expecting from that corner of my environment. Some wanted to help by proof reading what I wrote. One kind and generous friend offered to supply a new computer for the project, knowing my 1984 IBM was sadly outdated. Indigenous friends agreed to read topic areas and tell me if I was on target or needed to modify something. I was promised help and I was getting it even before the actual writing began. We began referring to the person or entity that provided instructions as *"THE SPEAKER"* for lack of a better term or identity.

Then, about three weeks into the initial work on the book, I was awakened in the middle of the night again. This time THE SPEAKER jarred me awake with a single word:

*"INTRODUCTION."*

Before I had time to fully awaken the voice started to dictate, word by word, the introduction of the book!

*"Wait!"* I said loudly. *"That's not how I planned to start the introduction. I wanted to – ."*

I was totally ignored. THE SPEAKER kept dictating slowly and clearly. Well, I thought, if the whole book is going to be dictated, I won't have much to do. This will be easier than I thought. At that point I really began to listen, to try to distinguish a style or a theme of some kind:

*"... AND DOMINATION OF THE CULTURES BEING INVADED. AND JUST AS USUAL, THE TALE OF SUCH WARS, SURRENDERS, AND DOMINATION WERE RECORDED IN ..."*

Not much new in that, I thought to myself, a bit disappointed. History books are full of accounts of wars, surrenders, and domination.

"THIS BOOK CONTAINS STORIES OF THE SURVIVORS OF THE DOMINATION AND COLONIZATION PROCESS AS TOLD BY SURVIVORS OR DESCENDANTS OF SURVIVORS…"

"What? But you said I already had chapters outlined. How do personal stories fit into this?"

At that point the voice ceased to dictate and began to read a text to me that I guessed had not been written yet. It was as if I was being given a verbal pattern of how to organize the information, what categories to use, and methods of presenting critical issues in a non–threatening manner. I can't say how long the voice continued, but the message was clear in my mind of what the voice wanted and how I was to go about doing it.

The book has been organized according to the outline provided by "THE SPEAKER". Because we are including indigenous cultures from the world, we need to define terms used so the readers would know how certain words are being used. Also, we must write so that Indigenous people can understand what we are saying and perhaps gain peace from our words.

more as time goes on…

The situation occurred when the text I was putting on the computer disk at 2:23 a.m. each morning was not being accepted, morning after morning, and I didn't understand why. One morning, after yet another feeling of being abandoned, of sensing the emptiness of the room that meant THE SPEAKER had departed and thus my text was unacceptable, I shut off the computer and grabbed a handful of the hard copy, headed for the coffee pot and then my place of quiet, my garden. First light had come but not full daylight; I sat down on the old tree stump and tried to read the papers in my hand, but it was too dark yet. So I sat there, frustrated and upset, not knowing what I needed to change to meet the requirements for the material I was writing. I thought about what was printed in that hard copy in my hands; hadn't THE SPEAKER given most of the words? Wasn't I trying very hard to follow the pattern set out for me? In my mind I reviewed what I had been told; the purpose of the book was to educate both the Indigenous people and the other races of people. It was to be a guide book to tell future generations how not to proceed in the quest for cultural expansion, mining of minerals, harvesting other natural materials, and the quest for land itself. And it was to be written in a non–threatening manner so that it would not further increase the chasm between races.

I thought about what I had written that morning. My writing had not been non–threatening. There was truth in my words, but it was sharp–edged truth, stated in phrases that were not healing. The sentences were harsh and condemning, pouring out anger, listing one by one the unjust acts of the past that still caused pain today. I was writing from PCSD (Post-Colonization Stress), the "D" being disharmony. And that was why I was getting nowhere.

*Non–threatening. Threat: a menace; portending something undesirable (Webster 1987). Abusive, intimidation (Roget's Thesaurus 1987). Non–threatening, then, would be a what? Roget's Thesaurus: benevolence; loving kindness; brotherly love; having one's heart in the right place. A place of peace? A place of harmony?*

*July and August were two very difficult months for me. By coincidence or not, I was experiencing pain and frustration from discrimination and domination in my work place, and it was most difficult to deal with. Add to that the immediate family problems involving my beloved grandchildren, and I was not only physically exhausted but financially in a bind. And then my job was threatened.*

*Those things were just the surface of the problem, though. There was an undercurrent of stress constantly, day and night, interrupting my sleep, destroying my appetite, producing massive headaches. I knew I had to deal with the cause of the stress, but I couldn't.*

*"Why do I have to write from a place of peace and harmony?" I demanded. "Look what has happened in the past, what is happening today, right now! How can I – ". I could never finish the sentence. Over and over again my mind played the same tape, I asked the same question, running, running like a mouse in a cage trying to find a way out, an answer other than "from a place of peace and harmony."*

*Years would pass as life got in the way of the book and eventually help came in the form of a friend and niece. We worked on many projects together and spend much time talking. Although we lived far apart, it was as if what happened to one happened to the other. Although she was much younger, we were bonded in a way that she always knew what was happening to me and when I needed to talk. She called at moments when I was distraught and at moments when I was happy. We shared a reality that included spirit, knowledge, experiences, and adventures. Our lives and spirits were bound in a journey.*

*Together we now write, as I am 83 from harmony and peace. While the content of this book may have threatening sources, we offer it in a non-threatening spirit. The facts are what they are, threatening, and the feelings of colonized people will always hold pain and suffering and so this book must contain these. The events cannot be changed, nor the experiences deleted from reality. However, the words and writing are offered in love and balance.—Carol Locust*

## Colonization of the Sacred

Native American religious traditions are rich in aesthetics and symbolism. Each tribal group has its own cultural pattern, language, and way of life, which generate the cosmological core of its unique belief system…Most non-Indians have as yet failed to comprehend the full impact of conquest on Native Americans whose lives were forcibly transformed by systematic efforts to replace their cultures and religious beliefs with various forms of Christianity and Euro-American political structures. (Talamantez 1985, p. 33)

Colonizing forces and dominant demographics have yet to comprehend the impact of historic and continued colonization efforts involving the physical, cultural, and spiritual erasures of Indigenous peoples. This chapter is designed to continue Talamantez's call for dialogue to make visible what has often been hidden in scholastic and dominant discussions of Indigenous people. The chapter will examine some of the misrepresentations, misunderstandings, and general dismissals of Indigenous spirituality and the sacred and will discuss how colonizing interpretations continue to impact the treatment of and disrespect for Indigenous knowledge. To this end, the chapter will document continued colonial dismissal and disrespect involving Indigenous attempts to repatriate remains and sacred objects as a means of healing intergenerational trauma.

We will begin this chapter with a focus on Indigenous communities in the Americas, not because they are more important, but as a way of opening the larger global dialogue. This case study approach should also not be taken as an indication that the Indigenous of this geographical area suffer greater historical and cultural destruction or that they are under greater threat to their sacred beliefs. The choice to begin with America's Indigenous communities is merely a way to begin the conversation. Global Indigenous issues will be evidenced later in order to dismiss any argument that the situation in the Americas is an anomaly. Again, we caution the reader to remember that this chapter is only a beginning discussion and that Indigenous beliefs should be neither essentialized nor universalized.

## Loss of the Land

As has been noted in Chapter 1, conflict between the inhabitants of the Americas and European colonizers[1] occurred, if not from the beginning, from quite early on after encroachment on Turtle Island. This chapter is

---

[1] It is difficult to know which term to use for European settlers/colonizers as there is no single way in which they came to the land, nor was there a single attitude. French trappers appeared to be more inclined to work with or assimilate to Indigenous cultures while other groups such as Puritans were more inclined to "civilize" what they considered the heathens. There is also a difference between those who came to settle and find a new place, those seeking military goals, and those seeking economic advancement. There are also issues of time that differ from the earliest contact to later periods of settlement, or in the case of Georgia, imprisonment. Finally, there is the matter of perspective depending on whether one is in the colonizer or colonized position. For this reason, we will use "European colonizers" to encompass the variety of European individuals, groups, and attitudes.

not intended to chronicle first conflicts nor is it attempting to identify all conflicts. Instead, it will focus on colonial attempts to limit or destroy Indigenous spirituality and concepts of the sacred as a strategy to deny Indigenous sovereignty. These colonization practices, including attempts to assimilate Indigenous peoples to Western ways of being, continue to be manifested in intergenerational trauma. Recognizing that the timelines involving conflict and Indigenous reactions to the attempted elimination of spiritual beliefs is as unique as each community, we will only be able to focus on the patterns and a few specific examples. The reality is that conflict began immediately in some areas and later in others, and attitudes involving both colonizers and colonized differed, creating unique situations that shared the common aim involving Indigenous desires for physical and cultural survival. However, the patterns and strategies of colonization can be recognized and must not be dismissed, or remain unexamined, simply because specific implementation differed.

Encroachment on Indigenous spirituality can be traced to early attempts by religious organizations to convert or "save" the savages, some of which were referenced in Chapter 1. Indeed, the rather unholy marriage in Western history of Christianity and concepts such as Manifest Destiny and Social Darwinism supported and encouraged a continuum of conversion tactics ranging from friendly encouragement to genocide. Throughout much of the interaction between colonizers and Indigenous populations, missionaries were used as the sharp tip of the spear, working to penetrate Indigenous communities and establish entry points for the larger political and military colonizing troops.

For many colonizing forces, Christianity was, and continues to be, not only the justification for the assimilationist practices, but the driving force involved in the implementation of those practices. Among many Indigenous peoples, forced conversion was, and remains, a symbol of death and the destruction of their ways of life. For many Indigenous communities, being rounded up and imprisoned in small unclean areas was considered a death sentence and baptismal waters were often referred to as "waters of death". For the ones that survived, many faced forced labor or removal. Negative Indigenous reactions were largely ignored by colonizers or attributed to "evil and savage ways", "simple mindedness", or "childlike misunderstandings". From a European perspective, being saved but dead or saved and forced into European ways of being was preferable to being free and a "savage".

What was, and often continues to be, unrecognized in colonial paradigms was the complex and sophisticated cosmologies exhibited in Indigenous ontologies. For many initial missionary and colonizing groups, there was not only an inability to understand these ontologies because of language barriers, but also an unwillingness to acknowledge Indigenous spirituality as organized or sophisticated. In many cases, there was simply no desire to dialogue with or explore Indigenous spiritual knowledge as it did not appear in any way similar to Christianity in structure or belief. Indigenous spirituality of reciprocity, interrelation, and connections to spiritual dimensions were neither part of European cultures nor were they acceptable according to Abrahamic religions. Indigenous religions, therefore, represented a threat to Christianity as a negative or "evil" Other. The Indigenous community of believers and individuals were then viewed and dealt with in the same manner as the unholy and heretical of the Inquisition and Witch Trials.

Cajete gives an example of how these early misunderstandings continue to infiltrate modern colonial thought and education in the Western narratives surrounding the arrival of Cortes (2000). According to many colonizer interpretations, Indigenous inhabitants of the land did not know what ships were and thought the sails were clouds and so thought Cortes to be the return of Quetzalcoatl. This myth goes on to claim that these inhabitants worshipped Cortes as their god Quetzalcoatl and welcomed his troops. The authors of this text continue to hear this myth in college classrooms couched in the condescending language that implies that the Indigenous peoples of the region were "childlike" and "unsophisticated".

Cajete and other Indigenous scholars describe a quite different account of the events from the Indigenous perspective. To begin, many of the Indigenous peoples were involved in sailing as a means of trade and exploration and so certainly understood that the vehicles were boats, even if they were large boats. Additionally, while one could say that the sail material was unfamiliar to the Indigenous people, it is a rather prejudicial assumption, and somewhat ridiculous, to claim that Indigenous people could not tell the difference between the material of a sail and a cloud. Nevertheless, this myth continues to invade the classroom even at the collegiate level.

Turning to the colonial belief that the Aztecs worshipped Cortes as the "second coming" of Quetzalcoatl, not only does the wording embrace the Christian colonizer interpretation, but it also misrepresents Aztec linguistic and paradigm constructions. The colonial interpretation ignores the complex Aztec "*calmecac* in which the *tlamatinimine* (astronomer-philosopher poets) taught the calendar, medicine, astronomy, religion, mathematics, and architecture using poetic chants" (Cajete 2000, pp. 260–261).

> According to the Aztec great calendar, 1,144 years comprised an epoch of time. The epoch consisted of twenty-two cycles of fifty-two years each. Thirteen of

the cycles were described as 'heavens of decreasing choice,' and the remaining nine as 'hells of increasing doom'.

Quetzalcoatl died when he was fifty-two years old. One short cycle of the sacred calendar, one of the Lord of Life's thirteen heavens was all he was given. The date of his birth by the Christian calendar was 947 A.D., and his departure, 999 A.D. His death marked the beginning of the fourth cycle, or heaven. Before his death, Quetzalcoatl promised to return to close the thirteen heavens and open the nine hells. Hernan Cortes reached the shores of Mexico on April 21, 1519, on the day one reed, the year one reed, which was the birth date of Quetzalcoatl and the first year of the first fifty-two-year cycle of the nine hells. (pp. 261–263)

Given the Indigenous description of their experience, there are at least two ideas that should be gleaned from Aztec understandings of the situation. First, the descriptions involved in the encounter with Cortes were not celebratory or filled with excitement and joy given that the event represented the opening of the nine levels of descending hell. Second, there is no reason to understand the complex and sophisticated Aztec spiritual constructs to contain the simplistic language that would have interpreted Cortes as a "second coming" or "incarnation" of Quetzalcoatl. Indeed, as pointed out by Cajete, Indigenous language, and particularly spiritual language involves a metaphoric mind and would most likely not involve such a direct or concrete translation.[2]

On one level, it might be that Cortes' coming on one reed, one year was perceived as Quetzalcoatl's return. However, this does not entail that they were understood to be one and the same being. What is significant for this book is the recognition that the Indigenous communities of this era employed complex ontologies involving empirical evidence including astronomy and natural geometry in the foretelling and interpretation of these events. Indeed, Leon-Portilla's research supports depictions that the Indigenous of the region documented negative omens foretelling the events to come and that attitudes involving the impending encounters were filled with trepidation (2006).

While employing different justifications and tactics, Christianity and military forces proved an effective two-pronged strategy in the physical and cultural conquering of people and subsequent attempts to annihilate Indigenous spirituality. The two-pronged strategy can certainly be witnessed in early contact but become undeniable with the onset of the boarding school era. These institutions involved the intertwining of Christianity and military organization to conquer the minds and bodies of children as a means of indoctrination into the general "settler" narrative. These narratives promoted

---

[2] Details of the language use will be discussed in the later chapter on language.

the heroic explorations such as those of Columbus in 1492 as sanctioned by God. Other narratives were then used as evidence of God's continued approval such as the first Thanksgiving 1637, which in the European version celebrates an almost utopian harmony between Settlers and Indigenous peoples. Current American k-12 education continues these myths, ignoring alternative Indigenous perspectives and dismissing the chronicled events that surrounded this "first Thanksgiving".

Indigenous narratives and scholarship recount a different sequence of events including the fact that Winthrop established the "Thanksgiving" event in celebration of the returning militia who killed 700 Pequot men, women, and children. Similar narratives explain that the King Phillip's War of 1675 was a reaction against Indian "uprisings and threats".[3] However, Talbot argues that Indigenous responses of the time were primarily in response to the continued dispossession of land, trespassing by non-Indigenous people, and colonist laws, which made "blasphemy" and non-sanctioned Christian ideals punishable by death. Additionally, colonists required the ceasing of Indian activity on the Puritan sabbath and outlawed medicine people.[4] Civilizing or annihilating the savages became the mission of both the religious and the military prongs of colonization, and phrases such as those calling for the death of American savages were their rallying cries (Leon-Portilla 2006, p. 10).

Indigenous resistance to conversion, loss of land, or violence continues to be framed within Western narratives as savage uprisings or unprovoked attacks, and massacres, of innocent settlers. As will be discussed in the later chapter focusing on language, such narratives are neither innocent, nor are they accidental. Indeed, they not only continue colonization strategies but significantly contribute to intergenerational trauma in Indigenous cultures as Indigenous students are forced to learn and be tested on uncontested Western narratives.

## Loss of the Sacred

By 1819, the U.S. had established the Indian Civilization Fund which called on "benevolent societies" to civilize the savage, establishing government funds

---

[3] It should be noted that there has been a historic division of tribes in terms of support in events such as the King Phillip's War, the Revolutionary War, and the Civil War. One can find tribes on different sides of these conflicts, expressing differing reasons for supporting each side. Indigenous social and political responses have always been varied.

[4] It is interesting to note that throughout American colonizer history, medicine is the exclusive domain of the male. This fails to recognize complex Indigenous understandings of medicine and gender, both of which will be discussed later in this text.

to assist in these efforts. The motivation for this, and similar administrative policies, was to continue the "kill the Indian, save the man" campaign. While the Treaty of Hopewell in 1785 is often considered the progenitor to the official removal and reservation era, official displacement intensified with multiple efforts in the 1800s. What is often unrecognized is that these strategies of dispossession involved both official removal policies as well as individual and community "land grabs". In these unofficial dispossessions, Indigenous people and communities had no legal recourse. There were no legal ramifications for settlers illegally occupying Indigenous lands or eliminating Indigenous populations. Indeed, such efforts were often praised as civilizing efforts regarding both land and Indian.

Among the governmental strategies for removal was the use of incentives for Indigenous people and communities willing to relocate "of their own accord" in advance of what promised to be a forced removal. Groups such as the Old Settlers[5] agreed to these incentives in the hope of avoiding what they saw as the dire consequences of forced removal and in hope of salvaging their way of life. While exact dates are disputed, the time between 1778–1871 has been called the treaty era because it produced treaty agreements establishing the government's recognition of and responsibility to Indigenous communities regarding issues such as protection, economic advancement, education, and health care, primarily in exchange for land and loyalty. During this time, more than 500 treaties were negotiated, each unique in its construction. However, many of these treaties were never ratified and arguably all of them, ratified and unratified, have been broken as the Plenary Powers allow Congress to unilaterally abrogate treaties. Interestingly, while the government has failed to uphold its part of these treaty agreements, Indigenous populations continue to be held accountable to their part, especially in cases regarding governmental dispossession of land. These contractual disputes continue to be a significant part of Indian Law litigation.

The Indian Removal Act of 1830 began the forced removal of Indigenous people from their geographical and origin lands, creating the loss of sacred sites, medicines, ancestors, and non-human relations along with a loss of self. Removals took place throughout the U.S. In fact, focusing only on Cherokee removal in the Trail of Tears appears to be part of a larger strategy to define all American Indians as one people, thus eliminating the memory of other Tribes and Nations who experienced similar destruction of self and communities.

---

[5] "Old Settlers" is a title given to Cherokee who relocated to Indian Territory before the Trail of Tears. It should be noted that other American Indians also moved West, including to Indian Territory, prior to the Trail of Tears. There were also removals from other parts of the Americas that are rarely discussed in academia. However, focusing on the Cherokee Trail of Tears has the effect of erasing all of the other removals.

For example, on the Trail of Tears, multiple Indigenous communities were forced on separate marches resulting in thousands of deaths. In many cases, the deaths would result in the mingling of different communities as the remaining individuals attempted to care for those who were still living. This intermingling often created a great loss of familial relationships and knowledge as people from differing Tribes and communities banded together for survival. Remarkably, what is often lost in Western accounts is the heroic attempts by Indigenous people on the march as well as those from communities along the way who would sneak in at night attempting to rescue as many of the vulnerable as they could. Colonizing narratives recount an estimated 4,000 Cherokee who died on the Trail but fail to document the numbers lost from the other Southeastern Tribes, nor do they account for those who died in the initial fight against removal. With the establishment of the 1851 Indian Appropriations Act, the government solidified the reservation system further asserting control over Indigenous economics, movement, education, health, and spirituality.[6]

In 1868, President Grant established the Peace Policy designed to eliminate corrupt Indian supervisors on reservations and replace them with, what he claimed to be, more trustworthy missionaries. This was followed by the 1883 Indian Religious Crimes Code developed by Secretary of the Interior Henry Teller. Irwin's examination of the Code reveals the government's active participation in the elimination of American Indian spiritual traditions and sacred places by threatening those caught with imprisonment. Irwin's research claims that Morgan, acting as the Commissioner of Indian Affairs, established the "Rules for Indian Courts" which codified the outlawing of dances, ceremonies, and medicine people. Irwin argues that the codification of these official restrictions ensured governmental suppression of Indigenous ways of being and made essential the "establishment of the office in 1832 through the appointment in 1934 of John Collier" (1997, pp. 35–36). With the codification of the Dawes Act in 1887, Indigenous ways of being were threatened with extinction.

While some of the above information is shared in both colonizer and Indigenous narratives, the treatment and interpretation of events are often significantly different. To provide perspective, Irwin recounts Indigenous reactions to removal missing from Western narratives. He describes Indigenous resistance and commemorates many of the leaders and strategies undocumented in Western accounts of "settler" history. Beginning with the Papounhan religious leader Mansee in 1752 and the Delaware prophet

---

[6]Conditions on which were marked by increasing poverty, starvation, disease, violence, and death culminating in the devastating Indigenous lived experiences chronicled in the 1928 Meriam Report.

Neolin in the 1760s, Irwin chronicles prophets and leaders in Indigenous communities that espoused traditional knowledge, the "old ways". Many of these leaders reestablished traditional knowledge and created new ways of incorporating older knowledge into the Indigenous diaspora, which at times involved the inclusion of Christian elements.[7] Irwin argues that both the Ghost Dance and Sun Dance became integral in the retention and renewal of traditional knowledge. His research traces a continuation of resistance leadership from this earlier period to the more modern that includes the American Indian Movement (AIM) (pp. 38–46).[8]

The exclusion of Indigenous information, such as resistance efforts, in part accounts for why students continue to ask questions such as "why did Indigenous people not fight back or resist colonization". American history and education deny the reality of Indigenous history and resistance to colonization in a way that exacerbates intergenerational trauma. By ignoring complete accounts of Tribes impacted by forced removal as well as Indigenous strategies of resistance, non-Indigenous students are given a skewed account of events, and Indigenous students are denied accurate depictions of their ancestors that include heroic endeavors and honorable sacrifices for the preservation of the sacred and the honoring of the Creator.

This heroic imagery is readily available to students descended from European populations but greatly lacking for other races. For example, in one Missouri school district, fourth graders were given an assignment to write a report on a famous historical person from Missouri. The list consisted of approximately twenty names. Of those twenty, only two African Americans were listed and one female American Indian, Sacagawea who was not from Missouri but did travel through it. The message in this assignment was that no other people of color or women of note had ever existed in that state.

A large part of intergenerational trauma is the dismissal of those people of color and women who contributed ideas, inventions, literature, art, and other valuable knowledge, not the least of which includes those who gave their lives in historic battles to protect their communities and ways of life. As Irwin points out, Indigenous people did resist cultural extinction with sacred ceremonies often with a significant loss of life such as that at Wounded Knee in 1890. Because of religious and governmental supported prejudice,

---

[7] The use of Christianity in Indigenous ceremonies is attributed to many factors. According to some, Christian elements represent different levels of assimilation. Others claim the use of Christian elements was similar to the use in many Caribbean practices, to hide the continuation of traditional ways from Western government and religious powers.

[8] Heroic figures such as Dragging Canoe and resisting communities such as the Chickamauga are dropped from k-12 and academic accounts greatly biasing the narratives received by both Indigenous and non-Indigenous populations.

approximately three hundred men, women, and children were killed. The catalyst for this massacre was a fear that the Ghost Dance, a peace-oriented spiritual ceremony, would spread and threaten Christian settler communities.

Suppression of American Indian spirituality has not been confined to the past but remains a virulent mind-set that continues to actively influence American religion and governmental policy. Most readily apparent is the continued failure to recognize Indigenous freedom of religion. Using the two-pronged strategy, Christianity and political/military forces continue to work together to limit Indigenous access to sacred places and deny the freedom to peruse spiritual practices. One example of these struggles can be observed in the Native American Church's use of the peyote sacrament.[9] Founded in the late 1800s in Oklahoma, this movement has been linked to older sacred practices in the American Southwest and Central America where the use, in several forms, was understood to have been given by the Creator to promote spiritual balance and health. Some have attributed the spread of peyote to revitalize old ways of being as well as to the resistance movement.

In 1978, Indigenous communities experienced progress toward religious freedom with the establishment of the American Indian Religious Freedom Act (AIRFA), which was enacted to protect American Indigenous peoples' rights under the Free Exercise Clause. However, AIRFA is a policy statement and includes no legally binding consequences if it is not implemented or observed. Additionally, the wording of the act leaves it vulnerable as terms such as "beliefs" and "actions" are definitionally ambiguous. Effectively, AIRFA allows Indigenous individuals the right to believe as they will, but it fails to provide adequate protection for actions and ceremonies stemming from those beliefs. AIRFA does not protect Indigenous access to sacred sites necessary for many ceremonies, nor does it ensure access to or possession of sacred objects such as peyote or ceremonial feathers. Additionally, the wording can be interpreted as supporting individual beliefs, similar to human rights policies discussed in chapter one, but offering little or no legal avenue of support for collective, or communal, rights.

Echo-Hawk et al. argues that the deficiency of AIRFA lies in its failure to embrace Indigenous ontologies.

> The law squarely addressed itself to the long-standing classic cultural conflict between the Indigenous people of this hemisphere and the newcomers from the old world recorded in Columbus's diaries, in which he stated on his very

---

[9] This movement has been referred to by other names including the American Indian Church and Peyotism.

first day in the hemisphere that the Indians 'will easily be made Christians because it seems to me they have no religion'. (2004, p. 154)[10]

The argument against AIRFA, according to Echo-Hawk, is that it calls for "special rights", not basic or human rights. These arguments against AIRFA claim that if sites are claimed to be sacred by Indigenous groups and usage is restricted to those Indigenous groups that it denies the rights of others who wish to use the area for sacred purposes regardless of whether these individuals or groups can produce evidence involving traditional use of the site (Echo-Hawk 2013).

New Age religions and Individuals wanting to use sites, objects, and medicines such as peyote have therefore claimed that AIRFA affords Indigenous people a right not allowed to others. Echo-Hawk argues for congressional laws to clarify the reasons why AIRFA is not a creation of "special rights", but the assurance of Indigenous rights as colonized people that have been denied access to sacred sites and objects. Echo-Hawk argues that recognizing the religious and governmental policies that dissociated Indigenous people from their lands and objects of worship is essential to understanding AIRFA and to ensuring that Indigenous people are guaranteed the same religious freedom experienced by other Americans under the Free Exercise Clause. Other Indigenous activists have argued that the claim of special rights is another example of Western bias as Indigenous people would not be allowed free access to Churches or Temples in the way that those arguing against AIRFA claim access to Indigenous sacred sites. This conflict will be revisited in later chapters discussing economic designs on Indigenous sacred sites (pp. 157–181).

Returning to the discussion of peyote, the limitations of AIRFA are apparent. In 1981, in a move that continues to undermine the veracity of AIRFA, the FDA restricted the harvesting, transportation, and use of peyote based on the Western classification of peyote as a hallucinogen, a classification that legally restricts the invocation of the Free Exercise Clause (FDA 1981). It should be noted that Western classification of peyote as a hallucinogen is based on both religious and government biases. From a Christian perspective, peyote does not hold the qualities necessary to be classified as sacrament. From a governmental perspective, academic and medical research claims it can be used to induce hallucinations, that is experiences classified by Western definitions as hallucinations.

---

[10] In this same article, Echo-Hawk and Foster talk about the limitations of religious freedom in the correctional facilities in the U.S. They note the struggle to allow Indigenous ceremonies, objects, and personal expression to be a part of the healings process in prisons.

In contrast to Western evidence, Indigenous evidence cites the use of peyote as medicinal based on generations of research and practice. Among other uses, Indigenous medical experts emphasize the use of peyote for joint pain, snakebites, fevers, and women's health. These same experts note that proper use of this medicine, as with all medicines, is important. Improper use, as with other medicines, can indeed produce negative or hazardous results. Indigenous medical experts note that, as with all Indigenous medicine, spiritual guidance and the respect for the spiritual nature of the healing must be respected. For this reason, it is not recommended that Indigenous medicines or forms of healing be attempted without the requisite Indigenous expertise.

Indigenous proponents also note that visions may occur with medicines such as peyote, but these are not the same as hallucinations, and the experience of a vision may be unsettling or misinterpreted by Westerners who deny the existence of such phenomena. Peyotists argue that any ill effects are the result of mis-use by non-Peyotists and that there is no evidence of harm, "bad trips", or overdosing within the history of its traditional sacred usage.

Legal escalation of the peyote issue came in *Smith* which involved the ceremonial use of peyote and on-the-job drug testing (*Employment Division v. Smith* 1990). The case involved the denial of unemployment benefits to an individual after he participated in sacred ceremony that included the use of peyote, which was classified as a prohibited substance. The *Smith* case was heard twice by the U.S. Supreme Court. In the first hearing, it was remanded. The second hearing upheld the violation of state law and the denial of benefits but noted that there was a conflict with the Free Exercise Clause.[11] Huston Smith and Reuben Snake recount the Native American Church's fight for religious freedom, the use of peyote, and the sacred understandings of the ancient traditions through the voices of the Indigenous people impacted by this decision (1996). Their efforts and the continued Indigenous resistance culminated in the 1993 Religious Freedom Restoration Act which states that the government must give "compelling reasons" to inhibit the Free Exercise Claus.[12] However, the wording of the Act allows "compelling reasons" to be defined according to Western legal and evidentiary standards.

Supportive and reformative views regarding Indigenous knowledge of spirituality and the sacred have appeared throughout the above timeline but have largely gone without political or scholarly support. In other cases, Indigenous knowledge and tradition have been associated with or appropriated by various New Age movements, which is regarded negatively by Indigenous

---

[11] Paulik gives an account of the rational for the Supreme Court decision beginning with *Sherbert v. Verner* 1963 through *Peyote Way Church of God v. Thornburgh* (1992, pp. 30–39).

[12] This Act was amended in 1997.

communities. The association with New Age religious practices denies the impact of colonization on Indigenous spirituality while the appropriation of Indigenous ceremonies, objects, and traditions by these groups simply continues the colonial destruction of Indigenous ways of being.[13] Western religious politics and scholarship are not devoid of support for Indigenous rights including aspects of liberation theology and Catholic feminism, but such support remains marginalized and specialized.

## Global Indigenous Issues Involving Freedom of Religion

At this juncture, it is important to digress in order to clarify some theological discussions used to justify colonization. These will not be complete, nor will they be in depth, but the discussion will offer insight into many colonizer/colonized religious conflicts around the world. There exists a component of Christian tradition that emphasizes the need for conversion, or at least the need to tell the story of the Christ to all people, as a precursor for the second coming. This tradition has motivated many evangelicals and fundamentalists and is largely responsible for missionary practices in Indigenous communities. In many cases, missionaries have not been educated in Indigenous traditions or have chosen to ignore Indigenous knowledge. They are then often surprised when they are not welcomed into the Indigenous community or when their religion is not taken as "the one, true, and only" religion.

As part of the missionary tradition, Christianity has historically worked to "renew" or "rebrand" the sacred sites, traditions, and objects of other religions in the hope of making assimilation easier. Examples of rebranding, from older religions, can be observed in many Christmas and Easter celebrations as well as titles such as "Our Lady of the Lake" church. Much of this re-purposing of other cultures' sacred sites, concepts, and objects can be traced to early arguments for Supersessionism. The doctrine of Supersessionism began in the first century C.E. and claimed that Christianity fulfilled Judaism, making Christians the new chosen people of God.

When connected to the theological move from Jesus as regional spiritual leader, or the historical Jesus, to Jesus as the Christ, Christianity began

---

[13] Acts of appropriation misrepresent Indigenous knowledge, ceremony, and sacred traditions by taking them out of context and denying the intrinsic value of these elements in Indigenous cosmology. Acts of misappropriation are not limited to religious groups, but also include media and advertising, organizations such as the boy scouts and Indian scouts, and mascots.

to see itself as the final or superior religion and Jesus as the fulfillment of all existing prophecies in every tradition, thus subordinating all other spiritual and religious beliefs. Supersessionism may have originally developed in response specifically to Judaism, but it quickly expanded to include all religions and became a primary pillar supporting colonization. According to Joseph, Supersessionism justified early missionary strategy that worked to subsume non-Christian traditions into Christian doctrine and imagery such as equating the Lakota ceremonial pipe with Christ, which was not set aside until after Vatican II.

> It would not be until the post-Vatican II's more inclusive approach to non-Christian religions that the theological supersessionism of the Pipe *as* Christ could be replaced by the recognition that the Pipe *and* Christ represented two complementary religious approaches present in contemporary Lakota society. (Joseph 2018, p. 369)

Ballantyne reports a similar strategy when missionaries attempted to "reshape" the Maori *Te Ao Hurihuri* as a Christian way of being (2018). Ballantyne argues that the justification for reshaping was largely the result of colonizer's interpretations of Indigenous religions, not actual beliefs present in Indigenous ontology. Such interpretations originated strictly in Western attempts to infuse Maori traditions with Christian doctrines, which misrepresented Maori cultural practices. Additionally, Ballantyne notes that Western interpretations of Indigenous cultures and spiritualities envision them as stagnant and passive in opposition to what they see as the dynamic and active cultures and religion of the West (2018, pp. 118–122).

According to Ballantyne, these interpretations ignored the dynamic and active elements involved in Indigenous cross-cultural trade patterns. The failure, or intentional ignoring, of dynamic Indigenous cultural patterns provided justification for the missionaries to introduce written texts designed to permanently alter Indigenous trade interactions, which, in turn, impacted culture and spiritual traditions. These texts were to provide the dynamic/active knowledge that was missing in Maori understanding.

Straight provides similar evidence of missionary attempts to undermine spiritual traditions in Kenya. According to Straight, missionaries interpreted the offerings given to the god Nkai in Kenya as superstitious and inappropriate (Straight 2008). In order to disprove the Samburu belief, one missionary named Scudder fired a gun into the cave that was understood to be spiritually inhabited. While narratives differ, with some claiming hyenas ran from the cave, Straight argues that the hyper-masculinity of such narratives and the use of violence and pseudo-heroic acts to support Christian superiority were common.

According to the missionaries, these acts served as evidence in the "unmasking" of false or superstitious Indigenous claims. Straight argued that it was the masculine power dynamic that allowed Scudder to interpret his actions as the superior or as the Christian God defeating the inferior Indigenous God. Straight claims that Scudder's interpretation reflects a common Western interpretation that fails to account for two things. First, that his actions may have simply desecrated that particular sacred site causing Nkai to remove to another location. Second, given the complex understanding of Samburu cosmology involving the manifestation of spirit, shooting a gun would neither kill, nor would it touch Nkai regardless of his presence in the cave. The fleeing hyenas, then, do not represent a "win" by the Western God or the unmasking of a false belief, but rather the desecration of a sacred site making interaction with the sacred at that place no longer possible (pp. 839–843). Straight further argues "that acts of metaphysical violence quintessentially exemplify such exceptional moments and that the shared imaginaries that tended to follow such acts prove that point by *forgetting difference*" (843). Straight's point being that gods of differing people are often quite ontologically different.[14]

Recently in Kenya, another religious conflict involving a sacred place found its way into court. The court found in favor of the Indigenous people and ruled that Kenya had violated "the Ogiek peoples' right to land, religion, culture, development, and non-discrimination" (2017). However, the people continue to fight for the right to the land even after this ruling (Omuka 2021). The African Court on Human and Peoples Rights (AfCHPR) stated that the forcible removal of the Ogiek peoples by the Kenyan government violated Ogiek rights to their sacred land. While cases such as that filed by the Ogiek have been favorably resolved for the Indigenous communities, the majority of cases continue to be resolved in favor on non-Indigenous interests, such as in the case of *Ktunaxa Nation v. British Columbia*.

This case involved building a ski resort on the sacred site of the Grizzly Bear Spirit, thus "irrevocably impairing their religion, and significantly impacting the vitality and well-being of the community" (Shrubsole 2017, p. 1). Shrubsole articulates two particularly disturbing elements in the ruling.

---

[14] Further argumentation, by Straight, involves Western use of the Cartesian spirit/matter dichotomy that is not used by the Samburu ontological construction of spirit. Additionally, the Western concept of God being only in heaven is different from the Samburu concept that "Nkai is in both places" (p. 849).

First, religion continues to be defined using Western/Christian standards. Second, despite the recognition of the Ktunaxa as Aboriginal people, their position was considered to be no different than other non-Indigenous litigants. Again, the issue of individual rights to believe as one wished was recognized, but the collective, community, right to place was denied. As Shrubsole argues, although Canada endorses UNDRIP, the court ignored the components of UNDRIP regarding sacred land and self-determination. Too often, it is the Western interpretations of religion including the identification of religion as the ability to believe without necessarily requiring access to sacred sites, the focus on individual rights, and economic advancement that undermine UNDRIP in the courts.

Using the American Convention on Human Rights (ACHR), which makes no specific provision for sacred sites, and the findings of the Inter-American Court of Human Rights (IACtHR), which claims that Indigenous rights to ancestral lands should be "full title", Newman, Ruozzi, and Kirchner examine the use of international human rights documents in cases such as the Moiwana community in Surinam and the Awas Tingni of Nicaragua in an attempt to expose Western biases regarding issues of land and sacred sites (2017, pp. 448–460).

Similar issues have been exposed regarding the limitations of the European Convention on Human Rights (ECHR), which fails to include Indigenous peoples. For example, the Sami peoples inhabit Norway, Sweden, Finland, and areas of Russia. While the Sami within these first three countries have legal and political standing because of the National Sami Parliaments, they do not possess the ability to "overrule" in cases of sacred land disputes, which leaves the majority of Sami land, including sacred land, under the control of "state and public interests". This means that the Sami peoples may have limited or controlled access to sacred sites. Compounding this issue is the Sami understanding that sacred sites may be specific to an individual, a group, or may be shared by multiple villages, but are not obviously designated. Indeed, the "essence of [a] Sami sacred site is that its location not be known to outsiders" (p. 428).

The obvious problem involves the Western emphasis on physically identifiable religious structures and the dismissal of spiritual practices that do not readily fit into Western religious constructs. The ECHR's failure to specifically recognize Indigenous peoples and the dogmatic adherence to Western religious definitions continues to create a bias that denies the Sami the right to attend and protect sacred sites. Finally, Newman, Ruozzi, and Kirchner argue that the emphasis on Western constructs allows for the interpretation that all peoples have the right to believe as they will. However, that right does not translate into a right to act on or practice those beliefs. For Indigenous peoples, beliefs and practices are not separable. In this way, belief requires and involves practice, or ceremony which in turn requires access to sacred sites.

Within the complex study of global religions, Creolized traditions provide an interesting study of the intertwining of differing cultures and spiritualities as well as a unique strategy for resistance to colonization attempts.[15] In many ways, Caribbean Creolized religions resisted supersessionism and sublimation by interweaving African, Indigenous, and Christian traditions. Discussions of why and how creolization occurred must be left for another time, but the occurrence reflects the ability for multiple belief systems to unite in such a way as to create new coherent belief systems. This is not to claim that these traditions have gained equality in colonized States, only that within themselves they represent unique and coherent cosmologies.[16]

Caribbean creolization incorporates African spiritual beliefs from areas such as Yoruba, Kongo, Guinea, Benin, Nigeria, and Ghana. Knowledge including the spirit's ability to separate, time, specific deities, and rituals can be traced back to these specific African populations. Additionally, Indigenous island traditions including those from the Ciboney, Arawak, and Taino can also be observed. Indeed, many of the medicines and ceremonies in Vodou, Santeria, and Candomblé can be traced directly to both Indigenous Island cultures and Indigenous African cultures.

Christian, specifically Catholic, elements are also present in these Creolized religions including the saints, religious calendar, and liturgical elements; however, many Christians fail to recognize, or flatly deny, Caribbean religions as Christian denominations or Christian affiliates. Additionally, as many "adepts affirm that the beliefs and practices of their religion are rooted in African culture and that, although the popular *Santeria* associates the religion with Catholic sainthood, the African orishas are its dominant references, not the saints" (Murrell 2010, p. 97).[17] As these Creolized religions are

---

[15]The term Afro-Caribbean religions is also used but focuses primarily on the African-European aspects of Caribbean religions. Some scholars claim that Indigenous island elements are either no longer existent or that they are not easily identifiable given the African-European counterparts. However, within the islands, many communities claim knowledge of and connection to their Indigenous island ancestors and we wish to recognize that knowledge.

[16]It is understood that the African populations enslaved and brought to the Caribbean are considered Indigenous people. The designation of African in opposition to Indigenous here simply designates that Africans were not Indigenous to this region. Additionally, "aboriginal" is not used to designate island populations because of the cultural and economic movement between islands prior to colonization.

[17]It should be acknowledged that the different Creolized religions have different Catholic influences depending on the country from which the Catholic colonizers originated. There was, for example, a difference between French and Spanish Catholicism.

oriented more towards individuals and communities, the primary emphasis or affiliation varies.

Representing a rather unique creolization, the Obeah movement in Jamaica intertwined not with Catholic but with Baptist elements. From these roots grew the Garvey movement and Rastafarianism, which interpreted Biblical references in favor of Ethiopia and black empowerment.

> [T]he declaration of Haile Selassie's divinity… involved gaining adherents to the notion of a black living God whose divinity was shared by other blacks, both in Africa and in the Diaspora. Chromolithographs of Haile Selassie as a full-bearded Black Christ were distributed widely at meetings and street corners. (Olmos and Paravisini-Gebert 2011, p. 186)

The Rasta movement embraced Christian elements such as the trinity and the messiah gleaned from the King James Bible, but interpreted these using *The Glory of the Kings* of Ethiopia. The adoption of the *Holy Piby* helped establish the construct of "reasoning", a process by which oral and written tradition were brought together (pp. 192–193). For many in the Rasta movement, the culmination of these religious ideals embodied African Zionism, a physical or spiritual reunion in Ethiopia. As with other religions, there is no single interpretation or practice of Rastafarianism or the other creolized movements. The generalizations here are meant only to further evidence of active and dynamic Indigenous cultures and cosmologies.

The active and dynamic nature of these religions is evidenced in their historical resistance to colonialism which inspired revolution as Caribbean creolized religions have been and continue to be powerful social and political forces.

## Repatriation

There are many reasons for this text to include an examination of the colonization and collection of human remains, not the least of which is the issue of sovereignty. Beyond the issue of sovereignty are issues of humanity, dignity, and the respect for the spiritual beliefs of other beings. For most communities, including Indigenous peoples, it is important to have the bodies of loved ones respected and handled with dignity. It is understood that the dead are involved in that which is considered sacred or that which involves the sacred. Unfortunately, for Indigenous communities around the world, colonization has ensured the denial of this basic respect and dignity regarding thousands of human remains. One of the greatest failures of colonizing forces has been the inability to understand the devastation to Indigenous communities and the level of rage experienced by Indigenous people who have had ancestors and loved ones collected and placed in labs, stored in boxes, or placed on display in museums.

For most Indigenous peoples, the placement of the dead, the ceremony associated with that placement, and the continuation of that placement being undisturbed is of great importance. For many Indigenous cultures, once an individual is placed, the details of which vary from community to community, the idea of disturbing the individual is not just distasteful, it is unimaginable. According to one Indigenous woman, disturbing the dead is done only by evil persons for unholy purposes. Her understanding was that nothing good can come from disturbing those who were returning to Mother Earth. In this section, we will forego any discussion involving the obvious concerns of dignity and humanity (as we believe these issues should be self-evident) in order to focus on the violation of sovereignty and the role that repatriation plays in healing intergenerational trauma.

Western collection of bodies has been largely attributed to scientific studies along with anthropological and archaeological scholarship. However, there continues to be interest in the collection of Indigenous remains for individual and voyeuristic purposes. While academic areas have changed practices, as they no longer openly employ grave robbers, they continue to excavate Indigenous graves in the name of scholarship and for personal advancement in their fields. Bendremer and Richman argue that neither the Code of Ethics for the American Anthropology Association nor the Principles of Archaeological Ethics ensure Indigenous informed consent or sufficient guidelines for dealing with human subjects living or dead (2006, pp. 103–110).

Instead, he claims the codes are biased in favor of body collection and provide the minimum of ethical consideration for Indigenous paradigms or the people who inhabit those paradigms. His contention is that the collection, study, and displaying of Indigenous remains fail to recognize the humanity of what is being collected and, instead, treats the bodies and the parts as specimens. In this way, specimens can be scraped, written on with permanent markers, piled in cardboard boxes or plastic bins, and displayed as trophies on desks or in glass cabinets.

The nature of Western science along with archeology includes the collection, examination, and storage of specimens. Even with the best of intentions and the use of what is considered by Western standards to be ethical practices, academics are confronted with the need to remain employed and that means producing results for tenure, raises, attending conferences and publishing. These are not inherently bad practices, but they are concerning when the need to produce scholarship evolves into the collection of Indigenous bodies, artifacts, and data.[18]

It must then be understood that "American anthropology [was] developed in large to preserve Native American culture for posterity—not to help Native Americans" (Powell et al. 1993, p. 10). While Powell's article refers primarily to early anthropological attempts at Native American study, the statement can be applied to many academic practices involving Indigenous populations. The purpose of collection and examination is not to help those being studied, but to increase the knowledge or to advance the careers of those doing the studying. According to Powell,

> Most archaeologists would not characterize themselves as racists who exclude and dehumanize contemporary (and past) American Indians. But most also view themselves as operating in a context narrowly constrained by disciplinary boundaries—for the most part archaeology has been by and for archaeologists. (p. 13)

Powell further argues that the 1984 Society for American Archeology (SAA) resolution recommends "close and effective communication with appropriate groups", but it does not define any of these terms leaving them ambiguous and open to broad interpretation, nor does the resolution do more than encourage "close and effective" communication (p. 14).

In an attempt to fully chronicle the history of Indigenous remains collection, Platt notes that

> Between the 1780s, when Thomas Jefferson excavated a thousand human remains near his home in Virginia, and the 1960s, when the Red Power movement successfully challenged the right of archaeologists and scientists to treat their dead as specimens, between 600,000 and 1 million Native grave sites were excavated. (pp. 18–19)

During this time, the expansion of collections in museums, private collections, and universities created a market for Indigenous remains and artifacts worldwide. According to Platt, scientists and museums "joined the hunt in the hope that Native bodies would shed light on the origins of the species or on racial typologies of human difference" (p. 19).

The market encouraged grave robbing and the trading of remains in the name of scholarship and science. Platt notes that these practices were based on "scientific racism", such as Social Darwinism, and "American eugenics". This

---

[18] A discussion of data collection will be held for consideration in later chapters.

scholarship included studies that measured skulls as a means of advancing the claim of White superiority and were carried out by scholars such as "Morton, Hrdlicka, and Gifford [who] 'encouraged armature archaeologists to dig up graves and send them any remains they discovered'" (p. 20). According to Platt, the procurement of vast numbers of remains made the study of each set virtually impossible, meaning that the collection was unnecessary for the actual scholarship being done. Moreover, the remains were often poorly cataloged and mixed together hindering proper scientific study as well as later identification.

> In the 1920' and 1930s, Ralph Glidden, a self-styled archaeologist, filled and decorated the Catalina Museum of Island Indians with hundreds of crania and bones taken from Tongva and other graves. By 1948, Berkeley was boasting…'more than 10,000 Indian skeletons, many of them complete'. (p. 21)

Indigenous groups gained some success in the repatriation of "corpses and artifacts" with the 1990 passage of the Native American Graves Protection and Repatriation Act (NAGPRA). NAGPRA established a process for the return of artifacts and human remains, but Platt states that "after twenty-three years…less than 5% of human remains [had] been repatriated". In fact, "as of June 2013, Berkeley had repatriated only 315 of its 10,000 remains" (p. 21).

He identifies four reasons why the process of repatriation has been slow: the difficulty in identifying tribal origin because of the mishandling and cataloging issues, scholars not wanting to lose their specimens "that might reveal new findings in the future", federally unrecognized tribes having no rights to legally claim remains, and the burden of proof needed by the tribes to recover the remains (p. 22).

Platt also explains that for some Indigenous communities the process of repatriation presents challenges such as how to deal with spiritually and physically contaminated remains as those that are buried, or placed by other means, are intended to remain where they are so as to allow the spirit to journey to its destination, the process of exhumation disturbs, or denies the possibility of, this journey (p. 22). Additionally, in many Indigenous communities, only specific individuals handle the dead and specific ceremonies are required in the handling and in the aftermath. There are no traditional ceremonies or medicines for the repatriation of bodies, especially when the bones have been marked with permeant marker or mixed with the remains of others. How does one go about "unmixing" body parts so that each can be dealt with according to the proper tribal ceremonies? What if the parts cannot be properly identified, how does one respect the proper ceremonies if the tribal origin is not identifiable? These questions have required tribal and intertribal spiritual investigation and the redesigning of ceremonial practices to accommodate these violated and displaced individuals.

In one article, Riding In et al. addresses a loophole in NAGPRA that allows institutions and scholars to claim that specific tribal designations are not possible for some remains, meaning that they do not have to adhere to NAGPRA repatriation guidelines. Riding In argues that, even when specific tribal designations cannot be established remains identified as Indigenous should be understood to fall within Indigenous sovereignty rights (2004, pp. 171–175). He argues that the issue of identification along with how and where to place Indigenous remains is not a question for scholars, these questions are for Elders with spiritual knowledge. "A reburial is a very spiritual undertaking…we have removed the spirits of our ancestors from those places where they've been incarcerated, and… we are putting them back into the womb of Mother Earth where they belong" (pp. 172–173).

In the case of the Ancient One, Echo-Hawk, in the Riding In et al. article, the Indigenous/Western debate regarding the proper application of NAGPRA (2004).[19] "The Yakama Nation, the Nez Perce Tribe, the confederated Tribes of the Colville Reservation, Confederated Tribes of the Umitilla Nation, and the Wanapum Band" claimed the remains as evidenced by oral traditions (pp. 182–183). Scientists contested the reburial claiming it was important to study the remains. According to Western academics, because of the ancient nature of the remains, empirical evidence required for tribal identification could not be acquired and "the location where the remains were discovered is outside of aboriginal tribal areas as determined by the Indian Claims Commission in NAGPRA.

Therefore, "there is a geographic loophole that puts the Ancient One in an area that is not clearly covered by the statute" (p. 183). In 2002, the Appeals Court found for the scientists, who stated that the remains showed no markers related to Native Americans. However, the remains were kept in storage pending the tribes' appeal.[20] In 2004, the U.S. Court of Appeals for the 9th circuit claimed that no direct link could be made to the tribes and allowed for the study of the remains. Ironically, although denied by some

---

[19] The Ancient One, has largely been referred to, by Western academics, as Kennewick Man.

[20] Western claims of skeletal markers are influenced by Western conceptions involving global migration including the Bering Strait narrative. Logically speaking, this calls into question the argument involving marker application and identification.

scientists, the study of the remains gave evidence supporting tribal connections. In 2016, the U.S. Congress ordered the repatriation of the remains to the five tribes, and in 2017 the Ancient One was reburied.

While the above discussion has focused on the U.S., it is important to note that repatriation of artifacts and remains is a global Indigenous concern. Lambert-Pennington, describes the issues of culture and identity involved in the repatriation of remains to La Perouse in Australia (2007). Western colonization supported the collecting of bodies from all parts of the world and the exploration period is marked with the collecting of human remains and artifacts along with animal and botanical specimens for placement in museums, private archives, and for scholarly study. Indigenous bodies continue to be studied and placed on display continents away from where they lived and were placed after death, with little thought given to their repatriation. School children are brought to look at these specimens, instilling in new generations the idea of privilege regarding ownership rights and knowledge collection along with the inculcation of the idea that Indigenous people are specimens, not humans.

Because Western scholars tend to view themselves as the keepers of truth and knowledge, often identifying themselves as the stewards of the past or as experts regarding the cultures they are studying, the trauma experienced in Indigenous communities subjected to these practices can be deemed to be collateral damage or an unfortunate but necessary consequence. Within Western knowledge constructs is the belief that people, particularly scholars, have the right to explore and learn about anything and everything they choose. Indigenous paradigms tend to believe that certain knowledge is for certain people. There is not an understanding that everyone, or even one specific person, has a right to know all things or whatever she wishes.

Generally, in Indigenous cultures, knowledge comes with responsibilities including protection, especially when it could be used for harm. An example of Western and Indigenous paradigm difference can be seen in the recent media frenzy involving a "never discovered tribe" in the Amazon. The tribe indicated its desire to be left alone by threatening outsiders attempting to photograph and document their way of life. This did not detour investigating scholars and paparazzi who used aircraft to gain access. Actions such as these and the misuse and misrepresentation of information gained from Indigenous cultures have created a distrust of Western academics. These misappropriations include but are not limited to Indigenous end-of-life rituals and ceremonies.

Academics have spent a great deal of time in body collection attempting to gain knowledge regarding cultural practices. In many cases, this same knowledge could be gained through dialogue, but, as will be discussed later in this text, Indigenous dialogue is considered academically suspect because it is primarily oral. For this same reason, many scholars ignore or dismiss Indigenous corrections regarding "scientific" discoveries and theories. For example, scholars continue to perpetuate the idea that Indigenous communities regularly committed infanticide or the killing of disabled or elderly individuals. While we will not claim that these acts never occurred in Indigenous cultures, there appears to be no evidence that they occurred on a regular basis or with any more frequency than is observed in Western cultural practices. Moreover, given Indigenous spiritual views regarding children, differences, and Elders, such acts are not likely to occur with any frequency or regularity.

Dismantling these false narratives requires not only the elimination of Western constructs involving "savage", "infidel", and "uncivilized", but also the decolonization of academic narratives. For example, in many Indigenous communities, the time prior to body death is considered sacred as the spirit of the individual is moving closer to what comes next, be it a reunion with ancestors, advancing toward the Creator, or other destinations. Regardless of the journey specifics, the individual is preparing for the journey and will often be surrounded by one or only a few individuals who assist through ritual and prayer. For this same reason, many communities remove individuals from dwellings to allow the spirit to leave the body and begin the journey unencumbered by enclosures.

Spirits confined to a dwelling may become trapped or have difficulty moving beyond the confinement. Interpretations by Western scholars may claim that this is "throwing away the ill, dying, and disabled", but Indigenous paradigms view this as allowing a respectful and dignified crossing from this life to the next place. Indeed, the "knowledge" gained from misinterpretations and body collection tends to say more about Western cultures and their understanding of end-of-life and their religious cosmologies than about the Indigenous cultures they are "studying".

Deloria gives a more in-depth explanation of the Western scholarly treatment of Indigenous remains and communities in his works titled *Ethnoscience and Indian Realities; Indians, Archaeologists, and the Future* and *A Flock of Athros* (1999). Deloria recounts the failed scholarship associated with Western academic disciplines and their misuse of Indigenous people and artifacts that supported that scholarship. LaDuke's book *Recovering the Sacred: the power of naming and claiming* also confronts the history of collection, control, and display along with how these practices impacted the Indigenous communities (2005). Finally, we would be remiss if we did not mention *Indians & Anthropologists: Vine Deloria, Jr. and the critique of anthropologists* (Biolsi and Zimmerman 1997). This work explores Deloria's critique of anthropology along with the ensuing debate caused by that critique.

## Indigenous Ways Regarding Sacred

Although Indigenous constructs and paradigms have been discussed throughout this chapter, this section will examine specific Indigenous constructs involving the sacred. Admittedly, discussing what is meant by the sacred requires one to define that which cannot be defined. Attempting to describe that which Indigenous people claim to be beyond human understanding feels disingenuous and, as each Indigenous community has its own unique understanding of spirit, spirituality, and relationship, the task becomes almost ludicrous. Finally, dropping any such project into the absurd, to discuss Indigenous sacred concepts using Western language requires the translation of Indigenous ideas and paradigms into Western constructs that are not designed for the very topics being discussed.

However, as one of the goals of this text is to bridge the gap between Indigenous and non-Indigenous paradigms in order to correct some of the Western media and scholarly misinterpretations, we ask for the indulgence of Indigenous readers in the following attempt. Additionally, we will rely on Indigenous scholars and Elder testimony to do justice to the complex Indigenous cosmologies. From the beginning, one must understand that

> The Americas are an ensouled and enchanted geography, and the relationship of Indian people to this geography embodies a 'theology of place'…The land has become an extension of Indian thought and being because, in the words of a Pueblo elder, 'It is this place that holds our memories and the bones of our people…This is the place that made us.' (Cajete 1999, p. 3)

According to Cajete, place is not just a physical place, but "a spiritual place, a place of being and understanding" that is tied to "the lives and relationships of all participants" (p. 4). Beck et al. describe Native American concepts of the sacred as containing the personal, which is individually experienced and felt, along with the communal, which "is shared and defined year after year through oral histories, ritual, and other ceremonies and customs" (1992, p. 6). According to these authors, the experience of the sacred is not separate from the "ordinary" but comes when one "experiences a hidden meaning—*sacred* moments".

The person's life is then twofold requiring the individual to balance the components of "wisdom and divinity" (pp. 6–7). The authors also state that Native Americans tend to hold the following six beliefs.

1. A belief in or knowledge of unseen powers, or what some people call The Great Mystery.
2. Knowledge that all things in the universe are dependent on each other.
3. Personal worship reinforces the bond between the individual, the community, and the great powers. Worship is a personal commitment to the sources of life.
4. Sacred traditions and persons knowledgeable in sacred traditions are responsible for teaching *morals* and *ethics*.
5. Most communities and tribes have trained practitioners who have been given names such as medicine men, priests, shamans, caciques, and other names. These individuals also have titles given them by *The People* which differ from tribe to tribe. These individuals are responsible for specialized, perhaps secret knowledge. They help pass knowledge and sacred practices from generation to generation, storing what they know in their memories.
6. A belief that humor is a necessary part of the sacred. And a belief that human beings are often weak—we are not gods—and our weakness leads us to do foolish things; therefore clowns and similar figures are needed to show us how we act and why (pp. 8–9).

Accordingly, the Creator, or the Great Mystery, is understood in conjunction with the Great Mysteries, which are reflected in the changing seasons and other cycles present in nature. The mysteries reflected in the cycles and seasons are understood to have their own "personality", each of which is to be respected for its knowledge. Ceremonies and rituals done in coordination with the cycles of life, both the positive and negative aspects of life, along with the cycles of the universe are understood to bring the person, community, and universe into balance and to show respect for the knowledge each brings (p. 10).

Cajete explains that, in general, cosmologies are used to organize existence; they explain, create guidelines, and give answers. "It is a culture's guiding story" (2008, p. 495). Cosmologies disclose values, truths, organization, and relationships. They also represent the community's answers to questions such as how life began, what is the function of life, and how things are related within the universe and tend to come with origin stories that place beings within existence.[21]

Indigenous cosmologies tend to understand Spirit as a primary "life force connected to all other life forces" (Meyer 2008, p. 218). For those uncomfortable with the use of the term "Spirit" because of Western religious connotations or the implications from Western science, some Indigenous traditions will translate constructs using the term "energy."[22] The understanding is that this energy/spirit flows through, or constitutes, all matter and non-matter, connecting all things and allowing for a primary spiritual level communication. According to Deloria, spirit/energy is that which stands beyond the limits of science. He states that, using the Western reductionist model, what is beyond the smallest "stuff" of the universe is this spirit/energy (2006, pp. 193–214). It is then the "spiritual nature [that] enhances the physical" aspects of the universe (201). Because energy/spirit stands in a position of primacy and enhances the physical, Indigenous paradigms tend to consider spirit positioning first when interacting with other beings. As described by Cajete, "The spirit and the spiritual were at the center of each human being and all that made up the universe" (2008, p. 490). For this reason, Indigenous knowledge transmission tends to focus on the spirit/energy metaphorical level in narratives, or what are often called "stories". This level of communication itself makes up one of the Great Mysteries of the universe.

The interconnectivity of all things at the level of spirit creates a natural democracy in which all beings must be considered equally. For this reason, many Indigenous cultures will often refer to non-human people such as geese people and tree people when considering any action (Fienup-Riordan 2001, p. 551). Additionally, oral literature often refers to "brother wolf" or "cousin crane" as indicators that nature is not for the use of humans but has its own spiritual value and purpose, its own autonomy. This interconnectivity requires one to consider all relations before making a decision, and, as mentioned in the chapter on environmentalism, the actions and interactions of any given being has consequences for all other beings. When one considers the Indigenous interdimensional nature that includes spirits, one begins to understand the ethical complexities of choice and action.

In contrast to many Indigenous ontologies, Mbiti claims that much of the Indigenous "African ontology is firmly anthropocentric; and this makes man

---

[21] Western cosmologies can be understood as twofold, the scientific and the religious. The scientific relates to theories such as the big bang and string theory and the religious are centered on the Religions of Abraham. Both sets of cosmologies, and their origin stories, require faith, a faith in God or a faith in scientific theory.

[22] We will not be discussing the translational issues with these terms or the difference between energy and energies, but such topics certainly warrant more in-depth discussions.

look at God and nature from the point of view of his relationship with them" (2006, p. 48). Using an Ashanti proverb stating that, "everybody knows of God's existence almost by instinct, and even children know him", Mbiti illustrates the concept that all aspects of being involve the spiritual (p. 29). While God is predominantly discussed in proverb and multiple designators are used such as "He who sees and knows all" and "the Wise One", many of the African constructs hold God to be omniscient, omnipresent, and omnipotent.

An important aspect of this theology is that God is understood as transcendent, and so distant from humans, yet immanent, so ever present with the world. Mbiti states that this is not pantheism, but a more complex understanding of God being both beyond time and place, yet ever present in it, which allows humans to communicate with God in times of need (pp. 30–33). Mbiti also notes that there are few images of God in Africa, and while God may be discussed using anthropomorphic terms, in general, God is thought of as Spirit. He notes that "the Ga, Langi and Shilluk compare Him with the wind or air" and "it is particularly as Spirit that God is incomprehensible" (pp. 34–35). In addition to God, Mbiti states that African cosmologies contain spiritual beings, spirits, and the living dead all of which may be, but are not necessarily encountered by humans. Spiritual beings may then be those who have experienced bodily death or may have never been human.[23]

While differing on specific concepts and orientations, the primacy of Spirit is a staple in Indigenous cosmologies. Additionally, Indigenous cosmologies tend to inspire a focus on spirituality over religion. In fact, Indigenous languages often have no traditional words for religion. Their experience of the world is therefore understood as predominantly spiritual, in a way that denies dichotomous constructions of sacred and secular as it is often through the secular that the sacred is revealed or experienced. We do not claim that similar concepts cannot be found in Western construction, the claim is that, within Indigenous cultures, these conceptions of sacred hold a primary position that function to allow individuals and communities to experience life first and foremost as spiritual. It is essential to the healing of intergenerational trauma to consider Indigenous perspectives regarding the treatment of their ancestors, both historically and physical, and the role of community in the spiritual understanding of reciprocity and harmony as these are required constructs for healing intergenerational trauma.

---

[23] For a more complete understanding of the spiritual and the concepts of time and death, one should read his earlier chapters dealing with potential and actual time along with the African constructions of past, present, and future.

# Additional Readings

Brown, B. E. (1999). *Religion, Law, and the Land: Native American Sand the Judicial Interpretation of Sacred Land*. Westport: Greenwood Press.
Caplan, P. (Ed.). (2003). *The Ethics of Anthropology: Debates and Dilemmas*. London: Routledge.
Christen, K. (2011). Opening Archives: Respectful Repatriation. *The American Archivist, 74*(1) (Spring/Summer), 185–210.
Deloria, V., Jr. (1994). *God Is Red: A Native View of Religion*. Golden: Fulcrum Publishing.
Deloria, Jr., V. (1999). *Singing for a Spirit: A Portrait of the Dakota Sioux*. Santa Fe: Clear Light Publishers.
DeLucia, C. (2018, January). Fugitive Collations in New England Indian Country: Indigenous Material Culture and Early American History Making at Ezra Stiles's Yale Museum. *The William and Mary Quarterly, 75*(1), 109–150.
Hanna, M. G. (2005). The Changing Legal and Ethical Context of Archaeological Practice in Canada, with Special Reference to the Repatriation of Human Remains. *Journal of Museum Ethnography*, No. 17, Pacific Ethnography, Politics, and Museums. Museum Ethnographers Group, 141–151.
Helander, E., & Kailo, K. (Ed.) (1998). *No Beginning No End: The Sami Speak up* (Circumpolar Research Series No. 5.). Finland: Nordic Sami Institute.
Hernández-Ávila, I. (1996). Meditations of the Spirit: Native American Religious Tradition and the Ethics of Representation [Special Issue: To Hear the Eagles Cry: Contemporary Themes in Native American Spirituality]. *American Indian Quarterly, 20*(¾), 329–352.
Hooker, A. M. (1994). American Indian Sacred Sites on Federal Public Lands: Resolving Conflicts Between Religious Use and Multiple Use at El Malpais National Monument. *American Indian Law Review, 19*(1), 133–158.
Kelsey, P., & Carpenter, C. M. (2011). In the End, Our Message Weighs': Blood Run, NAGPRA, and American Indian Identity. *American Indian Quarterly, 35*(1) (Winter), 56–74.
Koehler, E. M. (2007). Repatriation of Cultural Objects to Indigenous People: A Comparative Analysis of U.S. and Canada Law. *The International Lawyer: A Quarterly Publication of eh ABA/Section of International Law, 41*(1) (Spring), 103–126.
Lyver, P. O., Davies, J., & Allen, R. B. (2014). Settling Indigenous Claims to Protected Areas Weighing Maori Aspirations Against Australian Experiences. *Conservation and Society, 12*(1), 89–106.
Macpherson, C., & Macpherson, L. (2011). Churches and the Economy in Samosa. *The Contemporary Pacific: A Journal of Island Affairs, 23*(2), 304–337.
Marcos, S. (2009). Mesoamerican Women's Indigenous Spirituality: Decolonizing Religious Beliefs. *Journal of Feminist Studies in Religion, 25*(2) (Fall), 25–45.
Mihesuah, D. A. (Ed.). (2000). *Repatriation Reader: Who Owns American Indian Remains?* Lincoln: University of Nebraska press.

Miller, B. G. (1998). Culture as Cultural Defense: An American Indian Sacred Site in Court. *American Indian Quarterly, 22*(½) (Winter-Spring), 83–97.

Pavlik, S. (1992). The U.S. Supreme Court Decision on Peyote on Employment v. Smith: A Case Study in the Suppression of Native American Religious Freedom. *Wicazo Sa Review, 8*(2), 30–39.

Pickering, M. (2010). Where Are the Stories? *The Public Historian, 32*(1) (Winter), 79–95.

Poirier, C. (2011). Drawing Lines in the Museum: Plains Cree Ontology as Political Practice. *Anthropologica, 53*(2), 291–303.

Pui-lan, K. (Ed.). (2010). *Hope Abundant: Third World and Indigenous Women's Theology*. Maryknoll: Orbis Books.

Salomon, F., & Urioste, G. (Trans.). (1991). *The Huarochiri Manuscript: A Testament of Ancient and Colonial Andean Religion*. Austin: University of Texas Press.

Tedlock, D. (Trans.). (1996). *Popol Vuh: The Mayan Book of the Dawn of Life* (Revised Ed.). New York: Simon & Schuster.

Waldron, D., & Newton, J. (2012, November). Rethinking Appropriation of the Indigenous: A Critique of the Romanticist Approach. *Nova Religio: The Journal of Alternative and Emergent Religions, 16*(2), 64–85.

Wilcox, M. (2010, April). Saving Indigenous People from Ourselves: Separate But Equal Archaeology Is Not Scientific Archaeology. *American Antiquity, 75*(2), 221–227.

Wooten, H. (2006). Resolving Disputes over Aboriginal Sacred Sites: Some Experiences in the 1990s. In E. B. Coleman & K. White (Eds.), *Negotiating the Sacred: Blasphemy and Sacrilege in a Multicultural Society* (pp. 193–204). Canberra: ANU Press.

## Works Cited

African Court on Human and People's Rights. (2020). https://www.african-court.org/wpafc/.

American Convention on Human Rights. (1969). www.un.org›esa›socdev›enable›comp302.

Ballantyne, T. (2018). Entangled Mobilities: Missions, Maori and the Reshaping of the Te Ao Hurihuri. In R. Standfield (Ed.), *Indigenous Mobilities: Across and Beyond the Antipodes* (pp. 115–144). Canberra: ANU Press.

Beck, P. V., Walters, A. L., & Francisco, N. (1992). *The Sacred: Ways of Knowledge, Sources of Life* (Redesigned Ed.). Tsaile: Navajo Community College Press.

Bendremer, J. C., & Richman, K. A. (2006). Human Subjects Review and Archaeology: A View from Indian Country. In C. Scarre & G. Scarre (Eds.), *The Ethics of Archaeology: Philosophical Perspectives on Archaeological Practice* (pp. 97–114). Cambridge: Cambridge University Press.

Biolsi, T., & Zimmerman, L. J. (Eds.). (1997). *Indians and Anthropologists: Vine Deloria, Jr. and the Critique of Anthroplogy*. Tucson: The University of Arizona Press.

Cajete, G. (Ed.) (1999). *A People's Ecollogy: Explorations in Sustainable Living*. Santa Fe, New Mexico: Clear Light Publishers.

Cajete, G. (2000). *Native Science: Natural Laws of Interdependence*. Santa Fe: Clear Light Publishers.

Cajete, G. (2008). Seven Orientations for the Development of Indigenous Science Education. In N. K. Denzin, Y. S. Lincoln, & L. T. Smith (Eds.), *Handbook of Critical and Indigenous Methodologies* (pp. 487–489). Los Angeles: Sage.

Deloria, V., Jr. (1999). Indians, Archaeologists and the Future. In B. Deloria, K. Foehner, & S. Scinta (Eds.), *Spirit & Reason: The Vine Deloria, Jr. Reader*. Golden: Fulcrum Publishing.

Deloria, V., Jr. (2006). *The World We Used to Live in: Remembering the Powers of the Medicine Men*. Golden: Fulcrum Publishing.

Echo-Hawk, W., Foster, L., & Parker, A. (2004). Issues with the Implementation of the American Indian Religious Freedom Act: Panel Discussion. *Wicazo Sa Review, 19*(2), 153–167.

Echo-Hawk, W. R. (2013). *In the Light of Justice: The Rise of Human Rights in Native Americ and the UN Declaration on the Rights of Indigneous Peoples*. Golden, CO: Fulcrum.

*Employment Division v. Smith*. (1990). 494 US 872. Retrieved from: https://www.oyez.org/cases/1989/88-1213.

European Convention on Human Rights. (2020). https://www.echr.coe.int/Pages/home.aspx?p=basictexts&c=.

FDA. (1981). *Peyote Exemptions for Native American Church*. Retrieved from: https://www.justice.gov/file/22846/download.

Fienup-Riordan, A. (2001). A Guest on the Table: Ecology from the Yup'ik Eskimo Point of View. In J. A. Grim (Ed.), *Indigenous Traditions and Ecology: The Interbeing of Cosmology and Community* (pp. 541–558). Cambridge: Harvard University Press.

Inter-American Court of Human Rights. (2021). https://www.corteidh.or.cr/index.cfm?lang=en.

Irwin, L. (1997, Winter). Freedom, Law, and Prophecy: A Brief History of Native American Religious Resistence. *American Indian Quarterly, 21*(1), 35–55.

Joseph, S. J. (2018, June). Yuwipi: A Postcolonial Approach to Lakota Ritual Specialization and Religious Revitalization. *Journal of the American Academy of Religion, 86*(2), 365–393.

LaDuke, W. (2005). *Recovering the Sacred: The Power of Naming and Claiming*. Chicago: Haymarket Books.

Lambert-Pennington, K. (2007). What Remains? Reconciling Repatriation, Aboriginal Culture, and the Past. *Oceania, 77*(3), 313–336.

Leon-Portilla, M. (2006). *The Broken Spears: The Aztec Account of the Conquest of Mexico* (expanded and updated ed.). Boston: Beacon Press.

Mbiti, J. S. (2006). *African Religions & Philosophy* (Second revised and enlarged ed.) Blantyre: Heinemann.

Meriam Report. (1928). *National Indian Law Library*. https://narf.org/nill/resources/meriam.html.

Meyer, M. A. (2008). Indigenous and Authentic: Hawaiian Epistemology and the Triangulation of Meaning. In N. K. Denzin, Y. S. Lincoln, & L. T. Smith (Eds.), *Handbook of Critical and Indigenous Methodologies* (pp. 217–232). Los Angeles: Sage.

Migiro and Thomson Reuters Foundation. (2017). *African Court rules Kenya violates forest people's land rights*. Reuters. https://www.reuters.com/article/us-kenya-rights-ogiek/african-court-ruleskenya-violates-forest-peoples-land-rights-idUSKBN18M1ZC.

Murrell, N. S. (2010). *Afro-Caribbean Religons*. Philadelphia: Temple University Press.

National Sami Parliaments.

Newman, D., Ruozzi, E., & Kirchner, S. (2017). Legal Protection of Sacred Natural Sites Within Human Rights Jurisprudence: Sápmi and Beyond. In L. Heinämäki & T. M. Herrmann (Eds.), *Experiencing and Protecting Sacred Natural Sites of Sámi and other Indigenous Peoples: The Sacred Arctic* (pp. 11–26). New York: Springer.

Olmos, M. F., & Paravisini-Gebert, L. (2011). *Creole Religions of the Caribbean* (2nd ed.). New York: NYU Press.

Omuka, S. (2021). *Despite a landmark ruling, Kenya's Ogiek community are still fighting to return to their ancestral land*. Equal Times. https://www.equaltimes.org/despite-a-landmark-ruling-kenya-s?lang=en#.YHtuzD8pCUk.

*Peyote Way Church of God v. Thornburgh*. (1991). https://www.leagle.com/decision/19912132922f2d121011958.

Paulik, S. (1992, Autumn). The U.S. Supreme Court Decision on Peyote in Employment Division v. Smith: A Case Study in the Suppression of Native American Religious Freedom. *Wicazo Sa Review, 8*(2), 30–39.

Powell, S., Garcia, C. E., & Hendricks, A. (1993). Ethics and Ownership of the Past: The Reburial and Repatriation Controversy. *Archaeological Method and Theory, 5,* 1–42.

Riding In, J. Seciwa, C., Shown, S., & Echo-Hawk, W. (2004, Autumn). Protecting Native American Human Remains, Burial Ground, and Sacred Places: Panel Discussion. *Wicazo Sa Review, 19*(2), 169–183.

*Sherbert v. Verner*. (1963). https://www.lexisnexis.com/community/casebrief/p/casebrief-sherbert-v-verner.

Shrubsole, N. (2017, November 13). A Recent Ruling on Religious Freedom Shows the Supreme Court Is Unable to Recognize Its Own Colonial and Culturally Located Position Under the Charter. *Policy Options Politiques*. Montreal.

Straight, B. (2008, October). Killing God: Exceptional Moments in the Colonial Missionary Encounter. *Current Anthropology, 49*(5), 837–860.

Talamantez, I. N. (1985). Use of Dialogue in the Reinterpretation of American Indian Religious Traditions: A Case Study. *American Indian Culture and Research Journal, 9*(2), 33–48.

UN. (2008). *United Nations Declaration on the Rights of Indigenous Peoples*. New York: United Nations Publisher. Retrieved from http://www.un.org/esa/socdev/unpfii/documents/DRIPS_en.pdf.

# 4

# Social Organization

## Reciprocal Relations

*My family has made talking sticks for many years and they have been used for as long as I can remember in sacred ceremony. I will share some of what I know about the meaning. I will share what is appropriate. Other knowledge will remain with those for whom it is intended.*

*Native people did not have Robert's Rules of Order. Centuries before the Rules were developed on other continents, we had a method of accomplishing essentially the same thing as the Rules. However, our method included elements not found in the Rules. Talking sticks have items attached to them. Each item is a symbol of something. People sitting in a talking circle for a talking stick ceremony must abide by the meaning of the symbols. The meaning of each symbol is explained, and if someone desecrates the Stick, that person must leave the circle.*

*Examples: There is a gifted feather from a specific flying relative tied to my personal talking stick. When I use the stick, I explain that the feather represents the Creator, and because the feather is present in the circle, we must speak the truth because the Creator is in the circle with us. The gifted fur from a four legged relative on the end of the stick reminds people to speak soft words, never hard or hurtful words. Sometimes a person will need strength to speak what is in his or her heart. They grasp the hair from our buffalo relative hanging from the stick, grasping the strength of the powerful animal to strengthen themselves so they can speak.*

*Talking circles using a talking stick are not focus groups or open forums. These should not be misappropriated by non-Indigenous people or those who have not been educated in the ceremonies and the spirit of the ceremony. To do so treats talking circles as secular and promotes the possibility of harm. It is never good to misappropriate a sacred ceremony of a community or adopt it for outsider use. Those leading the circle will have spent years learning the knowledge and often weeks to prepare for the specific circle. While non-Indigenous people may be invited in, it is not appropriate for them to claim or attempt leadership of a talking circle or the use of a talking stick.*

*These ceremonies have spiritual elements that cannot be denied. Every time I have used the stick, I start the ceremony with a prayer, and the stick takes over from there. The buffalo hair was the first item that needed to be replaced; it had been worn off by many fingers reaching for inner strength. The feather from the flyer became tattered and was replaced. The blue stone (turquoise) representing the sky fell off when the string broke. The fur from the four-legged one became thin and the hair fell out, so it was replaced. Replacement takes cleansing, ritual, and sacrifice and must be done in ceremony. Replacement is never casual or without spirit.*

*Only once was someone asked to leave the circle that I can recall, and that was during arbitration before a court hearing on domestic violence. Hard, angry words were spoken by a man; he was asked to leave the circle. He did; then he left the room but returned a few minutes later to apologize and ask to rejoin the circle. He sat again in the circle, was handed the talking stick, and that time his tears spoke for him.*

*Talking circles and talking sticks should never be used lightly or without Elders and Medicine People as there are always consequences when dealing with the spirits of all the relations. These consequences must be managed responsibly and with care. These are sacred places and sacred places involve trust, love, and reciprocity.*

*I have known of academics, businesses, and money makers who have misappropriated talking circles and talking sticks. They have changed terms or used different items but the events lack authenticity and understanding. These are hollow and often do nothing more than allow people the time they wish to speak. These lack the deeper experiences that bring the primacy of spiritual understanding and the interconnectedness that develops into unification and healing consequences.—Carol Locust*

## SPLIT FEATHER SYNDROME

*We used the talking stick and its lessons in my research on Split Feathers. We used this term for those children taken from our families and communities because of the American social services were prejudiced against the Indian way of being. The children were taken and fostered or adopted to White families as a way to continue boarding school assimilation. We continue to see these practices in*

Canada, America, and Australia as social services deny the legitimacy of Indigenous ways of being and insist that all families look like Western family structures. These children are often called lost or stolen generations. Even the American Indian Child Welfare Act, that tried to stop the stealing of these children has failed to protect our children as the social workers and the government ignore or find loopholes in ICWA. The stealing of these children and placing them with White families is simply a continuation of boarding school cultural and physical genocide. The result has been that these children suffer from loss, some for their whole life, of identity and community. We talked with some of these children now that they have grown, below is what they reported to us and what we share now with their approval.

The loss of Indigenous identity appears to be one of the most important factors in the development of the Split Feather Syndrome. The data indicates that the loss of the Indian identity is not the same as the loss of personal identity, although it is included in the personal aspect. Additionally, however, it is the loss of belonging to one's real culture.

The loss of culture, heritage and language seemed to encompass the total lifestyle that the respondents had missed. One said, "I was supposed to have a naming ceremony when I was two years old, and I didn't get it. I don't have a name. How can I go back to my tribe if I don't have a name?" Another wrote, "Somebody said that we could learn all we needed to learn about our culture and heritage from books and videos from our school. What a laugh! What we got was a watered down, Indian-style-Sesame-Street version of what some White person thought all Indians were like."

All of the Split Feathers said they read books, watched TV shows and saw movies about Indians when they were children. No matter what the plot of the story, they championed the Indians, even when John Wayne was on the winning side, even when the majority said the Indians were portrayed as brutal savages, drunks or dirty thieves. Their feeling toward real life Indians was not any different.

They told me my parents were alcoholics and that I was lucky to be out of the home," one respondent said. "But I don't feel that way. Poor Mom, poor Dad, maybe I could have helped some way. I'll never know. I never had the chance to find out. Nobody ever asked me if I wanted to stay or not. They just drove up one day and took me. My mother had this horrible, disbelieving look on her face. I never saw her again.

Despite the negative portrayal of Indian people in the media and in most of the non-Indian adopted parents, the respondents were proud to be Indian.

Many of them had been told horror stories about their birth families, which always ended with "aren't you glad you came to live with us?" The fact was that most of the stories expounded on the negative aspects – rather than the positive aspects – of the biological families and were twisted versions of the truth or were outright lies. None of the respondents said they were "glad" about their adoptive placement.

*Tribal spirituality seemed to transcend the adoptive experience. All of the respondents regarded themselves as being spiritual, either in an organized church, a personal religious way or in their tribal belief system. Many of the respondents claimed to have spiritual experiences, beyond Christian norms, from childhood, ranging from knowing about things before they happened, having dreams that came true, knowing what someone else was thinking and being able to communicate with animals. Some of the respondents said they had actively sought more information about their tribal traditional beliefs, hoping to find explanations for the mystical experiences in their lives or learn more about their own tribal beliefs.*

*Most of the respondents viewed tribal ceremonial experiences as an integral part of spirituality. While some had been able to experience at least one tribal ceremony, others had not had the opportunity. Several had attended at least one Indian pow-wow or celebration, while others had been denied the privilege but expressed optimism about attending one in the future. A few of them had taken part in sweats. One said he was allowed to attend Indian celebrations as a child.*

*Re-entry into the culture took place after the Split Feathers had reclaimed their Indian identity. Many of the respondents said they were ignorant or knew very little about traditional ceremonies that they would miss over the years, although a few of them knew about several of their tribal customs and traditions associated with ceremonies. All of them felt they had been robbed of the ceremonies that other tribal children were given but that they had never experienced. All of them said they had several pieces of Indian art, such as jewelry, pottery, basketry or such that held a ceremonial meaning for them.*

*One individual had been given a ceremonial eagle feather. Tribal affiliation – being enrolled in a tribe – was a serious subject for all of the Split Feathers. Some had had their enrollment cancelled when they were adopted into non-Indian homes. The names of very few had remained on tribal rolls. At the time of this study, several of them had two sets of birth records, one of Indian ancestry bearing their birth names and family names, and another set bearing their adoptive names. The one respondent who had not yet found his Indian identity had been searching archival records for years trying to locate some clue to his tribal affiliation.*

*"Those pieces of paper – the adoption papers – took away my Indian rights," another respondent wrote.*

*Although fear of not being accepted was a major personal issue, and threats of being disowned came from adoptive parents, all of them said they were glad they had pursued their quests to find out who they were.*

*Descriptors used for the experience were: "I felt whole for the first time in my life."*

*Thank God I finally know who I am!" "I finally found what I am, what is part of me, what I am part of." "I found the missing part of me and put it back in place. Now I can really be alive.*

*I found where I really belonged, my place, my home, my true identity.*

When asked how they felt about rejoining a cultural group that was frequently described in degrading terms (drunk Indians, lazy, dirty, stupid) and against which there were many racist, bigoted and prejudiced people, not one of the Split Feathers said they would change their minds. From their responses, it appeared that social, economic and cultural labels had no impact whatever on their repatriation decisions. Most of them said they began helping their birth families and relatives as soon as they found out who they were.

They received tribal teachings in return, a reciprocal process that satisfied the needs of the whole family.

*They gave me everything a child could ever ask for, except my Native American identity. All my years growing up in school I was cut down and made fun of because I was Indian. I was darker, had dark hair, and I was 'different.' I grew up resenting who I was, what I was; of course, I kept all the shame to myself, therefore building resentment. I am waiting now for enrollment in my tribe and waiting to establish contact with my biological family. I wish I had grown up being proud – like I am proud today.*

*My foster mother was very abusive. She always said we were dirty because we were dark. She beat us often, made our noses bleed. But the worst thing she did was denying us our Indian heritage. Courts should never let anything like this happen. Indian children need to be with Indian families, not White families that are so different from Indian.*

*Adoption causes such intense inner pain that you do anything just to get away from it. No one understands you, you are different, and there's no one to talk to. You withdraw into yourself, keep it all inside. That's how I got into trouble with alcohol: it was pain medicine.*

*I was adopted at age four, started school just before five, grew up in a middle-class family that was okay. But I started having dreams about age five about being taken away (from the adoptive home), taken back to my family, by Indians. My family didn't pay much attention to the Indian spirit within me, or to me, either. I communicated more with animals than I did people. In the sixth grade I started having problems with the other kids. Whites, Mexicans and others didn't like me because of being Indian. I got into lots of fights and became a loner.*

*I am 72 years old. I was adopted into a White family at age one-and-a-half when my mother died. I realized I was different before I ever went to school. When I asked, my foster parents told me I was Indian, and from that day I identified with Indians because that was what I was. I didn't know who I was, and that heartache and anguish has been with me for nearly 70 years. I hope your study can help me find out who I am before I die. I don't want to die not knowing my true identity. They (the government) sealed my birth certificate so I could never find my identity and never see my blood relatives. The pain of this is never ending.*—Carol Locust

## Colonization: Relations Disrupted

As mentioned in the introduction, the terms colonization and post-colonization are problematic as there is the implication that colonization was a historical event rather than a continuing set of circumstances. By relegating colonization to history, it is more easily dismissed making current social and political situations related to, or resulting from, colonization invisible. Admittedly, the invisibility tends to be found more by the colonizer than the colonized and often represents a desire by settler descendants to ignore or dismiss the action of their ancestors. Indeed, it is the case that descendants are neither responsible for, nor are they able to undo the acts of their ancestors. However, as recipients of the privilege that stems from ancestral acts, descendants do participate in continuing acts of colonization and assimilation, whether such participation is realized or unrealized.

The actions of all of our ancestors, collectively and individually, have created the communities that currently exist, and impact individual and group lived experience. The foundation of intergenerational trauma takes seriously the understanding that those currently living are not disconnected from generations past, and, in fact, acknowledges the fact that current generations are the legacy of what came before them.

Colonized people wish to acknowledge the past and to actively work to decolonize detrimental aspects of society that have been, consciously or unconsciously, brought forward into descendant generations. This decolonization may then be followed by a process of re-indigenizing community institutions. From this perspective, the colonized understand colonization to be perpetual as it has, and continues, to enforce colonizer social and political constructs, which replace traditional ways of being. For Indigenous people, the continued enforcement of Western social constructs and institutions disrupts identity not only because of the historical loss of community, but also because much of the historical loss was the product of force and efforts to reestablish traditional ways continue to be met with discrimination and violence.[1]

---

[1] Issues of Indigenous identity globally are a complex mix of tribal and State dynamics. Imposed identity standards such as blood quantum practiced in the U.S. deny traditional identity structures. Additionally, issues involving reservation, or reserve, identities are a factor in individual and community identity. Whether an individual can or should identify as Indigenous in general or with a specific tribe or nation involves a complex layering of Indigenous and Colonizer traditions and politics. As

Assimilation into colonizer ways of being often brings forth concerns as to who should identify as Indigenous and who is too removed from tradition to identify as Indigenous. Can a person, removed because of intergenerational trauma and forced assimilation, claim Indigeneity in general or an affiliation with a specific tribe or nation? As one young Indigenous academic explained, issues of identity are individually significant in that they help us define ourselves, but continued colonization has created situations where claiming one's heritage can be problematic not only in the colonizing society but in the colonized as well. Lost and stolen social organization, traditions, and teachings impact not only the original generation but subsequent generations, creating patterns of intergenerational trauma.

The original destruction of Indigenous communities did not die with first contact generations or even with the removal generation. The impact of dispossession, re-education practices, and violence involved in the destruction of ceremonies and spiritual ways of being continues to impact generations of Indigenous people as they experience colonization consequences in the form of poverty, poor education, inadequate health care, and discrimination. Beyond these social and political experiences, subsequent generations struggle with the loss of cultural and spiritual identity in a colonized system that is alienated from nature and traditional ways of being. This chapter will briefly examine colonization as a continuing factor in Indigenous lives by examining issues related to the destruction of communal ties and traditional social organization.

Additionally, this chapter uses Sarah Deer's construction of political and individual sovereignty as a means of understanding communal and individual self-determination (Deer, p. xv). The interrelation of the two illustrates reciprocity relations readily identified in Indigenous communities. As stated by Deer, "[a]ll other challenges faced by tribal nations are linked to the history and trauma of rape" (p. xv). The colonization of Indigenous women's bodies represents not only a microcosm of the larger community colonization, but as Indigenous tribes tend to value the spiritual and leadership roles of women, such acts represent the rape of the entire community making the violence against women a destruction of both the individual and communal spirit (p. 13).

Current trends involving the assault on and the trafficking of Indigenous women around the world represent the continued colonization and genocidal efforts against Indigenous people as evidenced by the lack of media concern and the failure of dominant communities to prosecute what they themselves

---

one Indigenous scholar noted, while self-identification is the standard in the U.S., recognition by the American government or by individual tribes remains a matter of dispute.

have designated to be illegal acts. While it is easy to get lost in the devastation of Indigenous cultures and Indigenous women, it is important to note, as Deer states, that the Indigenous story is not simply one of destitution, but, in the face of hundreds of years of colonization efforts by the West, it is a story of resistance, resiliency, and strength. Finally, this chapter will focus on Indigenous efforts to maintain their traditional lifeways in the face of continued colonial violence and the significance of decolonization/indigenizing efforts in establishing a sustainable future for all relations.

## The Underdeveloped

In many cases, Western denial of continued colonization and assimilation efforts has become propagandized as "assistance" efforts. Historically, such efforts were claimed under the "domestic dependent" categorization and used to justify removal of reservations and boarding schools, or workhouses in the case of Australia. The violence perpetuated in these events represented a malignant paternalism designed to eliminate savage ways of being. Both education and media continue to present colonization as occurring "long ago" and being specific to eras, which are unrelated to current notions of equality and justice.[2] Examples of malignant paternalism can be observed in assertions of assistance for "developing" or "underdeveloped" communities.

Inevitably, this call to assist is a call to eliminate traditional ways of being in favor of the more "advanced", "civilized", and "technologically superior" lived experiences. As with past assimilation efforts, little or no consent or deference is given to the communities being aided in their "development". There is often no discussion of the historical factors that have influenced a community's need for assistance. Indeed, there is largely no effort to historically contextualize the situations of communities deemed "underdeveloped" or "developing". Instead, discussions are couched in the paternalistic language of colonization that claims these communities have failed to evolve or failed to embrace modern advancements, which have led to the consequences of "being on the edge of extinction", to reference Social Darwinism. It is then the task of the more advanced dominant culture to educate and bring the Indigenous communities into the developed ways of civilization. The terms themselves, developing and underdeveloped, disguise colonizer prejudice.

---

[2]The text does not allow for a complete discussion of terms such as "domestic dependent" and "ward" (and other such social and legal terms applied to Indigenous communities). Two sources recommended for those who are interested in a more complete discussion are *The Legal Universe* (Deloria 2011) and "A Civic-Republican Vision of 'Domestic Dependent Nations" in the twenty-first century (Babcock 2005).

These terms claim that cultures failing to embrace what colonizer cultures deem important must be inferior and in need of education.

When confronted with the popular Western propaganda involving paternalistic assistance and the idea that Indigenous cultures were considered less developed than dominant cultures, one Indigenous Elder responded by asking the colonizer skeptic to name a single Indigenous community that claims to be "better off" as a result of colonization or admits to being inferior to its more "developed" counterpart. As a follow-up when no response was given, the Elder asked the skeptic to name a single Indigenous community that is considered by Westerns social and political organizations, or even within educational realms, to be equal to or superior to Western cultures. The point the Elder was trying to make was that it is assumed in the standard Western rhetoric that Indigenous cultures and communities are inferior. This rhetoric is part of the continued intergenerational colonization that exacerbates the trauma that exists in Indigenous communities.

The global reality of Indigenous cultures is that they continue to be placed in the "uncivilized" (underdeveloped) position in need of "civilizing" (development). The wording may have changed from "uncivilized", "unsophisticated", and "savage", but the sentiment remains. As long as the sentiment remains part of education and media representations, Indigenous attempts to regain recognition of their sovereignty rights, which were not ceded in colonization, and efforts to heal intergenerational trauma will be denied legitimacy.

## Colonized/Colonizer Differences

Both Western and Indigenous epistemologies and ontologies are complex and deny singular treatment. However, Western theories are, to a greater extent, more formalized involving academic uses of logic, theory, and science. While allowing for some subjective knowledge, Western epistemology elevates the notion of "objective" knowledge. Indigenous systems tend to promote subjective epistemologies alongside objective social epistemologies in a way that creates an interactive system of individual and communal knowledge, which fosters an individuality within a broader interrelated dynamic. This section will examine some of the differences between Western and Indigenous paradigms while acknowledging the existence of the plurality of theories and variations within both paradigm sets. The use of generalities is to create a foundational understanding of conflicting worldviews and how such conflicts impact existing colonized/colonizer social and political relationships. While other examples exist and could have been chosen, the ones used in this section were chosen to illustrate the conversation at hand.

While not necessitated by Western paradigms, Western epistemic and ontological claims tend to embed dualistic constructs more commonly expressed in orientations such as good/bad (evil), right/wrong, and normal/abnormal. This is not to claim that Western knowledge is simplistic or fails to have non-dualistic components. Rather, the claim is that Western descriptions of phenomenological experiences, language, and the discussions of self tend to involve the use of foundational binaries. Moreover, these binaries are structured in a hierarchy with good, right, and normal in the preferential position and bad, wrong, and abnormal in the inferior position.

From this perspective, dualities involving civilized/uncivilized, developed/developing, and colonizer/colonized inherently place the civilized/developed/colonizer in a preferential/positive position relegating the uncivilized/developing/colonized to the inferior/negative position. Within this binary hierarchy, Indigenous communities and individuals inhabit the negative/inferior position with little or no real possibility of advancing to the preferential/positive position unless they complete assimilation into that preferential position.

Indigenous communities then remain the Other and as such support the justification for continued colonization and assimilation efforts. The ideology and subsequent propaganda include the unexamined belief that everyone does, or should, want to be in the hierarchically preferential position. The potential for equity of social and political position between the superior and the inferior remains elusive, if not impossible. Using this model, hierarchical duality theories such as Social Darwinism and Manifest Destiny were formed, and colonization and assimilation efforts became not only justified but mandated, prompting historical and current acts of cultural and physicalgenocide[3].

As acknowledged by Cajete, Indigenous-lived experiences tend to be predicated on the interrelatedness of all beings (2000). Deloria supports this claim by explaining that the primal element in most Indigenous ontologies is Spirit, which unites all things. He notes that while Spirit exists in Western ontologies, it is not generally discussed in Western science. Additionally, Indigenous understandings of Spirit do not resemble theologically oriented religious and academic studies (2001, p. 23). It is not that Indigenous people possess less

---

[3] Western perceptions involving science, technology, and religion also reflect the dichotomous hierarchy in relation to what the Western perspective identifies as the unscientific, un-technological, and the incorrect spiritual orientation of Indigenous populations. As noted throughout this text, Indigenous communities possess complex systems of science, technology, and spirituality that tend to go unrecognized in Western paradigms.

scientific understanding or curiosity, but rather that some things are understood to be beyond human characterization and knowledge or are simply not the focus of Indigenous epistemic discussions.

In phenomenological terms then, Spirit is among those things experienced, but not subject to definition, analysis, or explanation. This Indigenous orientation to Spirit leads to what Deloria calls the "predisposition [of Indigenous people] to live in the world as opposed to living on, above, or in control of the world" (p. 53). Indigenous people tend to live with the phenomenological mystery rather than being driven to solve it.

Indigenous constructs may also involve negative and positive orientations of Spirit, but they do not inherently define these designators as dichotomous. Instead, the relationship between "good" and "bad" is ambiguous and fluid as the designation is largely determined by the individual or group experiencing the phenomena. For this reason, too much "positive" Spirit can be experienced as "negative" by individuals or communities as such an experience can overwhelm and unbalance. In the same way, "negative" spiritual phenomena can produce "positive" learning experiences if it assists in harmonizing relations. The determination depends on the relationship of the beings involved in the event. For example, unexpected money for an individual in need may still be considered a negative experience if it results in the harm of others or comes from practices that damage the environment. Similarly, a loss of relation can lead an individual to a deeper understanding of self or others, thus creating a valuable understanding that can promote communal balance and harmony.

Thompson furthers this analysis by examining the difference between interdependent and independent cultures. Specifically, Thompson's work describes the importance of interdependent and independent orientations involving the self within these differing cultures (1997). According to Thompson, interdependent societies emphasize the success and advancement of the entire society with the individual being an integral part of the success, but not the focus. Independent societies emphasize the success and advancement of the individual with the society functioning as the support to that success. Given the different emphasis, the definition of self in the interdependent society involves a relation to others and the responsibilities entailed by those relations, while the definition of the self in independent societies focuses on individual rights and individual accomplishments.

As argued by Thompson, the difference in orientation further determines which emotions a society promotes as socially preferable. For interdependent societies, the emotions advanced tend to be associated with cooperation and empathy. For independent societies, the promoted emotions tend to be associated with competition and aggression (Markus, pp. 226–239). The emotions, promoted by each paradigm, then establish behavior patterns or cultural norms. For interdependent cultures, behaviors involving the imposition of one's own feelings on others tend to be discouraged so as not to violate the other's immediate and unique experience. Independent cultures, however, often encourage the expression of one's emotions in public as not only appropriate, but a desired endeavor (pp. 229–230). It is not that interdependent and independent communities do not exhibit elements of the other, but rather that these communities differ according to the emphasis placed on interdependence or independence and how that emphasis works to define the experience of self.[4] For example, reciprocity in Indigenous communities is the mutual responsibility of beings and is a direct result of the understanding of interdependence (Kovach 2009, p. 63).

Western philosophical treatments involving the self tend to focus on whether humans have spirit/mind/souls and bodies or just bodies. The materialistic theories that claim humans have only physical bodies are relatively straightforward, claiming that humans possess no elements beyond the physical. Admittedly, the physical is exceedingly complex in order to allow for the entirety of human experience. However, there remains only the physical. In contrast, dualistic, or multiple elements, theories while diverse tend to claim that humans are composed of both the physical and the spirit/mind/soul. We will not attempt a discussion of the various theories as the specifics are only tangential to this discussion. It is sufficient to recognize that the use of "spirit", "mind", or "soul" in these theories adds an additional element to the physical element in defining humans. Regardless of what the second component is or how it is defined, a dualistic, or multielement, model of humans is common in Western traditions, especially when considering Western religious ideology.

Within Indigenous communities, the discussion tends to involve a three- or four-part division with the understanding that all beings are not just physical beings but possess additional elements such as mind, spirit, and emotions that are uniquely different from the physical, not unlike Western models. However, Indigenous populations tend to accept a body-mind-spirit scenario with some communities adding emotions as a fourth element, while others connect the element of emotion to an aspect of one of the other elements. The fluidity of these elements defies any strict division and mimics the

---

[4]It is often the case that readers infer from this discussion that interdependent cultures deny or discourage individuality. That is not the case. It is often a matter of noting that individuality is essential for the success of any given community, but independent behaviors undermine the interrelationships involved in interdependent communities.

external relationships to others, making the self a microcosm of the external universal macrocosm.

While not related hierarchically, Indigenous ideologies do tend to understand Spirit as the primary mode of being insofar as it is that which was, is, and continues as well as that which functions as the primary interrelational aspect of existence for all beings (Lovern et al. 2013, p. 80). There are distinctions among Indigenous communities involving the Spirit's ability to leave the body or to wander at given times indicating the ability of Spirit to separate entirely or partially from the other elements of self. Unlike Western conceptions of spirit/mind/soul, separation of soul and body does not necessitate a crisis or death orientation unless reunification is inhibited.

Taken individually, the above differences may appear to be only minimal or simply a matter of refining definitions or translations. However, they represent significantly diverse interpretations of human reality and phenomenological experience. For example, Western constructions of binary hierarchies locate Indigenous cultures in the deficient and inferior position precluding the possibility of them being considered equal. In fact, it is this inferior positioning that continues to impose colonial determinations of "developing" and "underdeveloped".

Brown illustrates the significance of cultural ontological and epistemic differences in his discussion involving legal and evidentiary definitions, in discussions of Indigenous claims to sacred land (Brown 1999). He explains that the legal conflicts are not just about the sacred sites themselves, but about the difference in paradigms. He states that Indigenous claims are argued in terms of the land's sacred aspects and the interrelationship between the people, the land, and the plants and animals inhabiting that land using oral and spiritual evidence. Indigenous claims speak of ancestral tradition, ceremonies, and the need to connect with the spiritual elements of a given place. These claims are not recognized as acceptable legal evidence in Western procedures. According to Brown, Western arguments involving land cases focus on legal precedents related to human occupancy, written documentation, and resource development. Given the difference in orientation to land and as to what counts as evidence, the divide between Indigenous and Western paradigms is both real and, in some cases, insurmountable.

## Loss of Sovereignty

The loss of sovereignty recognition represents one of these insurmountable issues as it is entangled in the epistemic and ontological divide that is controlled by colonial legal and political power structures. Adding to the difficulty are the continued changes in both politics and law regarding designations such as "domestic dependent", "freedom of religion", and "self-determination". Politically, Indigenous issues and rights are subject to the whim and political maneuvering of whichever party is in control of the government and whether that party is "pro- Indian". Over the years, this "pro" status has often had less to do with the welfare of the Indigenous communities and more to do with how these communities can be used to advance the given party's agenda. Examples can readily be seen in the history of U.S. policy from the treaty era, to the termination era, and on into the sovereignty era. Internationally, similar State maneuvering is observed in claims made by States to support UNDRIP compared to actual policy changes.

It is important to digress and note that in many discussions of Indigenous sovereignty, the term "self-determination" has been employed as a synonym with "sovereignty". In other cases, self-determination indicates a policy of limited control under the "sovereign" power of the State. This book is limited in its ability to fully examine the legal and political evolution of these terms. Nonetheless, it is important to mark the definitional ambiguity of these terms as lawyers and politicians often manipulate that ambiguity to best suit the colonizing State. Examples of this type of manipulation can be seen in the creation of contractual loopholes. As mentioned before, UNDRIP itself offers just such a loophole related to the word "sovereignty" which appears only once in article 46 and states:

> Nothing in this Declaration may be interpreted as implying for any State, people, group or person any right to engage in any activity or to perform any act contrary to the Charter of the United Nations or construed as authorizing or encouraging any action which would dismember or impair, totally or in part, the territorial integrity or political unity of sovereign and independent States.

For a logician, the phrasing potentially dismantles any previous discussion of Indigenous rights and State responsibilities by allowing any State, as sovereign, to claim that the implementation of Indigenous rights will "dismember or impair, totally or in part, the territorial integrity or political unity of sovereign and independent States". Indeed, returning lands, advancing Indigenous economic progress, or eliminating violence and political discrimination against Indigenous individuals and communities could readily be defined as impairing the State as these practices would require the introduction of funding, changes in political and social institutions, and the reorganization of authority within the State. By showing that there exists a substantial burden for the State if it advances Indigenous equality and self-determination, any State can justify partial or total non-compliance with UNDRIP. Policies and loopholes such as this continue to be the norm in Western practices that justify continued colonization and assimilation.

Dunbar-Ortiz's work *An Indigenous Peoples' History of the United States* (2014) chronicles some of these attempts by Western colonizing States to dismiss Indigenous sovereignty recognition advancements. Using Grenier as a basis for her work, Dunbar-Ortiz explains settler subjugation and elimination strategies beginning with the historic formation of

> irregular units to brutally attack and destroy unarmed Indigenous women, children, and old people using unlimited violence in unrelenting attacks… By attacking civilians and their support systems, such as food supply… [the irregular units] sought to disrupt every aspect of resistance as well as to obtain intelligence through scouting and taking prisoners. (p. 58)

In addition to the destruction of Indigenous food supplies, Dunbar-Ortiz notes that the use of mercenaries gave officials and the government plausible deniability in the killing of Indigenous non-combatants.

For example, Puritans hired John Mason to eliminate the Pequot. There was a choice of two targets, one containing Pequot fighters and the other containing unarmed women, children, and the elderly. Mason chose the latter. After killing most of the Pequot, his forces set fire to the structures, burning the rest alive (p. 62). It could be argued by the State that it did not order the slaughter of civilians, or that Mason acted on his own in the choice of targets except for the fact that violence against non-combatants has been a known Western tactic for demoralizing enemy forces.

Additionally, no formal legal action was taken in response to the attack. Dunbar-Ortiz states that during the Grant administration, Buffalo Soldiers were used to continue the extermination originated with the irregular settler units resulting in events such as that which occurred between 1850 and 1886 when the U.S. government launched its "longest military insurgency" against the Apache Nation (pp. 146–150). Dunbar-Ortiz further argues that the most insidious strategy for Indigenous extinction culminated in the boarding school era, which was designed to, in the words of Pratt, "Kill the Indian and save the man" (p. 151). As will be discussed more completely in the chapter on education, the forcible and coercive removal of children devastated families, destroyed kinship lines, and undermined the foundation of Indigenous spirituality and lived experience, permanently impacting Indigenous communities.

The impact of the specific policies involving boarding schools and stolen generations continues to be a source of intergenerational trauma in the United States, Canada, and Australia. According to Dunbar-Ortiz, one of the most devastating, and effective, strategies used in these countries was to unite State policies with religion, especially the Vatican Doctrine of Discovery. The use of religious institutions in the boarding schools and workhouses further dismantled the recognition of pre-contact Indigenous sovereignty. Dunbar-Ortiz chronicles the continued use of these strategies in the twentieth century highlighting the use of references to Indian policies as justification not only for the denial of Indigenous access to sacred land, but, rather surprisingly, in the establishment of the Guantanamo detention center.

According to Dunbar-Ortiz, the State used the "1873 *Modoc Indian Prisons* opinion", which claimed that if one was defined as an Indian, he could be legally killed without reprisal. She also notes that "John Yoo cited this precedent in the 1865 *Military Commissions* to justify torture in 2003" (p. 224; Indianz 2014). Dunbar-Ortiz outlines the continuous and deliberate strategy to eliminate Indigenous sovereignty, both in recognition and in reality, and to deny Indigenous self-determination and notes that such strategies are not limited to the United States, Canada, and Australia, but have been used throughout the world.

A second strategy used to disrupt sovereignty and self-determination in the U.S. appears in the form of political actions beginning prior to, but culminating in, the treaty era itself. The strategy involved the divestment of Indigenous populations from their lands, food supplies, spirituality, and dignity. Efforts of removal and extinction were in place before Jackson, but the *Indian Removal Act* of 1830 established an official genocidal policy. While most people associate the removal era with the Cherokee and the Trail of Tears, this too represents a colonial reimaging of the events.

As noted in earlier discussions, while most people know the *Trail of Tears* and the Cherokee, other Tribes were forced on that and other *Trails*. Removal and relocation were national policies that impacted Indigenous communities throughout America. The era is marked by the forcible removal of men, women, children, and the elderly using military enforced marches through inhospitable territories. In many cases, these marches were undertaken in winter with few supplies and little shelter. Often, those refusing to leave their homes faced the forced renunciation of their Indigenous identity or death. Military hunting parties were sent after those attempting to avoid removal often with orders to force compliance or to kill all as they were a threat to peace. It is unclear how many thousands of people died during this era.

What is clear is that some Indigenous communities were in fact exterminated, and others suffered the stripping away of identity, self-determination, and sovereignty both individually and communally.

The *Major Crimes Act* of 1885 and the *Dawes Act* of 1887 further eliminated Indigenous rights to organize their lived experiences according to traditional knowledge and communal structures. The use of the earlier discussed two-pronged attack of Christianity and political/military force, as discussed by Dunbar-Ortiz, was an insidious and effective strategy. Media and government reports of potential Indian uprisings and Christian biases against American Indian spiritual beliefs targeted ceremonies such as the Ghost Dance and justified military interventions resulting in events such as the Wounded Knee Massacre in 1890, which killed an estimated 300 men, women, children, and elderly Lakota.

While colonial strategies could be considered historical and as such should be relegated to eras of long ago, it must be recognized that these colonial strategies have persisted into the modern era. In 1928, the *Meriam Report* chronicled the abysmal conditions in Indian communities and boarding schools which prompted the 1934 *Indian Reorganization Act (IRA)*. In the guise of improving reservation and community conditions, offering potential economic gain, and the elimination of allotments, Indigenous populations would be required to create and adopt constitutions and by-laws approved by the U.S. government. According to Deloria and Lytle, the IRA "did not provide them [Indigenous communities] with powers they had not previously possessed, it did recognize these powers as inherent in their status and resurrected them in a form in which they could be used at the discretion of the tribe" (1983, p. 14).

However, tribal use of authority continued to be under the supervision and with the approval of the U.S. government. Following reorganization, the U.S. government began a period of Indigenous termination designed to eliminate the relationship between Indigenous tribes and the federal government. In a move that Deloria and Lytle refer to as "economic and religious Darwinism", tribes were triaged according to those that could survive without federal money, those that needed some federal money, and those that were dependent on federal money (pp. 16–17). Tribes deemed to have too few Indigenous of correct blood quantum were subject to governmental erasure.

According to Deloria and Lytle, the termination era lasted from 1945 to 1961. During this time, strategies were created to entice Indigenous people to leave reservation lands, which could then be classified as abandoned and seized by the government. For many who were enticed by the promise of jobs in the city, they were sorely disappointed to find that no such jobs existed or that competition, from others in the city, limited the potential of being hired. Urban Indigenous populations, therefore, grew, but were subject to poverty conditions and the associated issues experienced by other urban demographics.

In 1953, sovereignty recognition was further eroded with the adoption of PL 280. PL 280 compounded jurisdictional issues, already complicated by the *Major Crimes Act*, by eliminating "federal criminal jurisdiction on reservations" (Agtuca 2014, p. 45). PL 280 turned over jurisdiction in the case of six states to those states but failed to provide adequate funding to ensure proper law enforcement within the Indian lands. As a result, crimes such as sexual assault against Indigenous women went unaddressed in these states (p. 45) The *Economic Opportunity Act* of 1964 and the *Indian Civil Rights Act* of 1968 both stressed American Indian self-determination and economic advancement; however, the *Indian Civil Rights Act* limited the "penalty and punishment" that a tribal court could exact to one year, five-thousand dollars, or both.

The limitations denied appropriate sentencing for major crimes and encouraged the "myth that offenders of such crimes will not incur significant legal consequences or criminal penalties" (Agtuca 2014, p. 44). Agtuca and Sahneyah argue *Oliphant v. Suquamish* was equally damaging to Indigenous sovereignty recognition. In 1978, the U.S. Supreme Court concluded that "Indian nations lacked authority to prosecute crimes committed by non-Indians", denying Indigenous nations the ability to prosecute non-Indian offenders. "This U.S. Supreme Court-created loophole allowed non-Indians to commit heinous acts of physical and sexual abuse without fear of any legal consequences from tribal governments" (pp. 44–45).

Many legal and academic scholars, as well as activists, have claimed that these legal strategies created, or at least encouraged, "open-season" on Indian women as PL 280 states and federal agencies lacked the funding or the desire to investigate and prosecute crimes reported on Indian lands. In 2010, the U.S. passed the *Tribal Law and Order Act*, which did increase tribal authority in sentencing and fines, but only to three years and/or fifteen-thousand dollars (Agtuca 2014, p. 44). Additionally, Indian law within the U.S. continues to be plagued by what Echo-Hawk calls the thirteen legal fictions, which inhibit justice for Indigenous populations (2010). For these reasons, many Indigenous people consider the self-determination era to be an extension and re-branding of the termination era.[5]

---

[5] U.S. Canons of Construction authorized the use of Indigenous definitions and perspectives within the legal system because the laws were designed and implemented by non-Indigenous structures. However, the full implementation of the Canons has yet to be enacted.

Since the establishment of the UN Permanent Forum on Indigenous Issues, it could be claimed that history has moved into an international Indigenous era, or a United Nations Declaration era (Knowles et al. 2015, pp. 79–85). This era appears to be marked by the use of international Indigenous unity and the recognition of international policies along with bodies such as the UN dedicated to the advancement of Indigenous rights. Within this era, Indigenous organizations have found a more global voice and a strength in global identity. However, much of this has yet to be translated into State recognition of Indigenous sovereignty or the actualization of rights. While the UN era has advanced international exposure to Indigenous issues, it remains to be seen if this recognition will culminate in the return of sovereignty recognition.

One example involving the recognition of Indigenous rights can be observed in the creation of the African Commission on Human and Peoples' Rights (ACHPR). Using UNDRIP and the ILO, ACHPR was able to address Indigenous sovereignty issues specific to Africa. In Africa, it is important to note the problems associated with linking the terms Indigenous and Aboriginal, which, in other areas of the world, have been used synonymously. According to the ACHPR, recognizing the African distinction between Aboriginal and Indigenous is necessary to the understanding and advancement of Indigenous rights.[6]

The ACHPR definition, therefore, focused on guidelines including Indigenous claims, uniqueness of culture, and the threat or actual loss of human rights because of the dominant society (International Work Group 2006). Efforts such as the ACHPR represent advancements in eliminating the invisibility of Indigenous people and a recognition of issues but have yet to fully restore sovereignty recognition and self-determination. Even with these types of documents and acknowledgments, global Indigenous rights fail to be actualized. Colonization continues to permeate Indigenous existence, and colonizer populations continue to ignore these documents and the responsibilities described in them.

The issue of place-names in Queensland is another example of States failing to implement "adopted" documents as well as the political power of colonizing populations benefiting from State and political bias. In Queensland, many of the place-names continue to reference colonial or "frontier times" such as "Murdering Creeks" or "Skulls Holes". The use of these place-names represents pro-colonial ideals and State sanctioned violence against

---

[6]For example, African Indigenous people may not be understood to be "Aboriginal" to the area they may now inhabit because of traditional migration patterns, being forced to remove from traditional lands, or seeking asylum in areas as the result of conflict.

Aboriginal peoples (Richards 2014). Richards argues that the continued use of offensive place-names including the controversial "Mount Wheeler" violates any acknowledgment of Indigenous reconciliation.

The "Mount Wheeler" name, while debated, is largely associated with a "cruel" and "sadistic" police officer by the name Fredrick Wheeler (p. 151). According to many, archival information and enhanced legend have created a legacy that not only acknowledges violence against Aboriginal people but celebrates it. The ability of non-Indigenous to "dismiss" the past as unimportant or irrelevant is a luxury associated with colonizing populations. For colonized populations, the trauma is continuously inflicted with the use of these names as "frontier violence is…reiterated by the continuing use of 'racial' placenames" (p. 159). In fact, failing to eliminate these place-names can be understood as a violation of both UNDRIP and reconciliation policies.

## Gendered Violence

The focus on gendered violence, alluded to already in this chapter, works as a lens through which to observe the continued colonization of Indigenous communities. Additionally, this examination, as stated by Deer, illustrates both the devastation colonization brought on Indigenous communities and the remarkable resilience of those same communities and peoples. Examination of gendered violence also allows the reader to observe how the atrocities of the past continue and, in many ways, have become normalized in Indigenous communities.

Western enforcement of binary gender roles along with continued religious and political subordination of women has been used to justify both the subjugation and violence toward Indigenous women globally. Sexual assaults and forced sterilization policies have been a part of these strategies as a way to "breed out the savage", thus eliminating future Indigenous generations. This discussion will begin with a brief overview of engenderment to establish the Indigenous/Western paradigm differences and to highlight Western strategies of violence aimed at cultural and physical genocide.

Recently, a great deal of research has been devoted to Indigenous understandings of gender. Current scholarship argues that while there often existed a division of labor in Indigenous communities, it was part of an egalitarian or complementarity social structure that acknowledged a shared power. Women, and women's work, was neither inferior, nor subordinate in a large portion of Indigenous societies. Indeed, many Indigenous cultures were matrilineal and those using a patrilineal process of inheritance often possessed a balance of power that valued and respected the social positioning of women.[7]

For example, pre-contact Zuni, according to Howell, experienced gender equity, with women in leadership positions (1995). Gilley also attributes changes in traditional Native American gender roles to colonization practices that imposed the Western gender binary supported by Manifest Destiny to empower European heterosexism (Gilley 2011). Western strategies to reorient Indigenous gender roles embedded the hierarchical binary that placed men in the preferential/superior position and women in the negative/inferior position. The inability to recognize or accept alternative engenderment continues to be part of religious and political assimilation strategies of the West.

Scholarship indicates that Indigenous gender constructs tend to be complex and difficult to translate into Western language and constructs as Indigenous roles allow for flexibility and fluidity that does not align with a binary structure. Moreover, this flexibility and fluidity encouraged individuals to choose gender roles regardless of sex organs and, in some cases, allowed the choosing of different roles within different situations and throughout a given individual's life.

American Indian history is then marked with multiple examples of female chiefs and multiple gender constructs including what has recently been affiliated with the political movement called two-spirit. While the term two-spirit is not a traditional term, it has been used by many within the Native American populations to designate traditional non-binary community positioning within various tribes. As tribal languages are unique and complex, the use of one tribe's gender designators to refer to all tribes was deemed inappropriate, which led many to support the use of the term two-spirit.

The two-spirit movement then appears to be more of a political identifier to support and revitalize traditional ways of being undermined by Western colonization. Morgensen argues that non-Indigenous communities could learn a great deal from two-spirit organizing beginning with the understanding that, within many Native American traditions, being two-spirited

---

[7] One does not want to take from this a claim of utopia, but rather a construction of society that promoted the value and the social and political positioning of women as partners. Much of this can be seen in Indigenous origin stories that place women as primordial creators independently or alongside male counterparts. It also does not claim that no violence was experienced by women in these cultures, only that the violence does not appear to have been a product of subordination of women or dominance on the part of men, especially on the level of European acts of violence during the Inquisition and Witch trials. Additionally, traditional justice regarding violence against Indigenous women was often adjudicated by women.

people was not associated with minority positioning.[8] While Morgensen admits to the necessity of modern connections with minority status given Western colonized and governmentally supported discrimination, he explains that no such status was required in traditional Indigenous cultures as being two-spirited did not represent a negative social positioning. Morgensen notes that being a minority in Western cultures tends to be based on either being fewer in number or having less political power. He notes that neither was the case in traditional Indigenous communities, so the designation of "minority" is a Western-imposed construct (Morgensen 2011). Indeed, in some cultures, being two-spirited was understood as a medicine position, and such people were sought for counseling, healing, and the care of orphaned children.

Gender fluidity and flexibility do not seem to be limited to Native American traditions but are also discussed among other global Indigenous communities such as Maori, Andean, and African. According to Aspin, Maori communities not only accepted sexual diversity, but celebrated it. He referenced the adopted term "Takatapui", "an intimate companion of the same sex" (Aspin 2011, p. 118). Aspin offers evidence of archival, pictorial, and oral depictions of sexual diversity within Maori tradition (p. 115). While not directly referencing gender fluidity, Powers recounts the organization of Andean pre-contact communities. She reports a structure involving parallel hierarchies, one female and one male. Each structure had its own organization, rituals, officials, and deities. She argues that at the highest level there was a patriarchal line, but that early cases of women holding the ruling position and of women temporarily holding that position while a husband/brother was at war existed. Additionally, male power at the imperial level was gained through the female (Powers 2000, pp. 511–513). The complementarity parallel structure allowed for a broader understanding of gender and sexual freedom and a flexibility that was disrupted by Spanish colonization. Powers references the cult of Mary, or Marianismo, as one of the strategies used by the Spanish to "indoctrinate" women into the "psychological and spiritual burden of Christian moral precepts" (pp. 527–528).

Similar strategies can be observed in continued attempts to colonize gender and sexuality in Africa. Abidogun gives evidence of missionaries and colonizing binary propaganda strategies in Northern Igbo in Nigeria within the

---

[8]Minority positioning implies a negative power dynamic using the Western normal/abnormal designation. It also tends to imply either fewer or lesser. In other words, there were fewer two-spirits and so they were in need of protection against the larger community; or, lesser implying that there is inferior positioning or a lesser power position and so in need of protection. There is no indication that gender fluidity and flexibility were considered either lesser in power or fewer in number.

twentieth century (Abidogun 2007).[9] Abidogun argues that Western education continues to push gender roles that are not traditionally Northern Igbo and so causes a disruption of family and community relations by dividing students from their elders. The emphasis on Western binary engenderment conflicts with traditional fluidity creating conflict in children as they are forced to accept Western definitions to succeed in school or remain dedicated to traditional beliefs and risk difficulties and discrimination. Abidogun calls for an integration of Igbo traditional knowledge in school representations of communities, genders, and sexuality as a way to decolonize and heal this community divide. The use of both the Western and Igbo gender roles in schools would allow students to remain community oriented and would help to heal continued and intergenerational colonial trauma.

Western constructs of gender binary and the hierarchical positioning of the female gender as lesser or subordinate continue to be the political, social, and religious norm in colonized States. With women clearly in the inferior position, Western treatment of women of color establishes a position of dual discrimination being both female and non-White.[10]

Historically, Indigenous women have been eroticized and sexualized in ways that link them to nature. Both women and nature have been understood by Western patriarchy to be objects in need of, as well as desiring, conquering and domination. It has been argued that the challenge of taming Indigenous women and nature fulfilled the same machismo fantasy of Western colonizers. Indeed, encouraging or forcing the submission of Indigenous women and nature continues to be part of Western language, fantasies, and pornography. Chronicling film history, Marubbio's *Killing the Indian Maiden* recounts the use of the erotic noble and ignoble savage and the Western interpretation of her need to be tamed, which explores the use of the iconic taming of the sexualized savage and the Wild West in film and literature (2006).

According to Marubbio, the sexualized maiden is often aligned with the same unpredictability and potential dangers of nature. She has the potential of being tamed, but also possesses the potential for violence equated with the unpredictability and intensity of natural disasters. Accordingly, it is this unpredictability and the element of danger that intensifies the eroticism toward Indigenous women and continues to justify violence as a strategy

---

[9]We would argue that such practices persist into the twenty-first century, but do not want to ascribe such claims to Abidogun.

[10]In many ways, this dual discrimination is shared with other women of color. However, the manner of discrimination and the strategies used in cultural and physical genocide have often differed. This is not to claim that one set of strategies or discriminatory acts is more important or severe than that of another, as we are not interested in revising a hierarchy, it is simply that we are focusing on Indigenous dual discrimination in this text.

for submission. "Finally, the Sexualized Maiden's combination of racial exoticism, and sexual promiscuity, and physical threat to the hero often emerges in the femme fatale depiction that carries with it certain socially based fears about the sexually aggressive woman" (pp. 7–8).

Marubbio also analyzes the use of the sexualized Queen and the "sexually overused" crone as Western religious and moral designators for evil. This evil was largely a result of these women being aggressive and claiming a power equivalent to the worst of nature. Indeed, the connection between Indigenous women and nature in literature and media is remarkably easy to find, especially in references to sea and land exploration. Terms such as conquering, penetrating, and subduing both unveil Western hierarchical positioning involving the inferiority of women and reveal continued fantasies associated with the domination of women.

It has been argued that the positioning of women in general has contributed to the global violence against Indigenous women as they represent the dual hierarchical inferior positioning of being both female and of-color. Additionally, this inferior positioning has contributed to the lack of media coverage or political concern regarding the violence to this demographic.

As explained by Deer, unlike sexual assaults in Western communities, the experience in Indigenous communities is both individually and communally devastating.

> I listened to women as they realized they represented the fifth generation of women in their family to be victims of sexual assault—a realization that slowly emerged in a woman's eyes, casting a shadow across her face. *This happened to my gramma when she was my age. No one helped her. She was always sad and she never talked about it. Now I know the source of her sadness.* The eyes of these women then looked into the future, emptying out into a hollow vacancy as they considered the next generation, still girls or babies. *My niece, My baby sister. My daughter.* Native women experience the trauma of rape as an enduring violence that spans generations. (Deer 2015, pp. xi)

We chose this quote from Deer because it encapsulates the intergenerational trauma experienced in Indigenous cultures where violence against women has become the norm, to be expected, and to be endured. Deer discusses the often-cited statistic that one in three American Indians and Alaska Native women will be the victim of rape. While she notes that data collection in Indigenous communities is underreported, she states that her research fails to reveal a single study that does not state that Native Americans experience "the highest rates of victimization in the United States" (p. 3).

Deer's research indicates not only a significant level of violence experienced by Native women, but also an increase in the physicality of that violence (p. 4). According to Deer, the high occurrence of rape and the elevated levels of violence during rape have become "normalized" creating an attitude of inevitability.

Citing the Bureau of Justice Statistics from 1999, Deer provides evidence that the rape of Native American women is the only demographic for whom race is a significant factor. With the exception of Native American women, the race of both victim and assailant is primarily the same. While rapes do occur where the assailant is a different race than the victim, the majority of cases involve individuals of the same race. However, in the case of Native American women, the majority of assailants are not Native American. Nine out of ten reported rapes deal with a non-Indigenous perpetrator. Additional research evidences the number of White assailants at over seventy percent. While not wanting to place the frequency of assault entirely at the door of the *Oliphant* decision, Deer explains that rape survivors tend to see this decision as a catalyst stating that *Oliphant* clearly established that "non-Native men who rape Native women on tribal lands completely escape tribal and criminal sanctions" (p. 7).

Deer argues that the experience of rape is a type of "spiritual death that is difficult to describe to those who have not experienced it. It is not only Native women who have been raped but Native nations as a whole" (p. 12). Her discussion further establishes the trauma within Indigenous communities from these attacks as women are traditionally considered the "'backbone' of tribal sovereignty" (p. 13). "The damage being done to sovereignty through sexual violence is so deep and significant that other tribal sovereignty efforts will continue to fail because people are hurting" (p. 97). Throughout her book, Deer recounts the colonial practices that continue to sexualize Native American women, cause the invisibility of their suffering, and encourage the prostitution and human trafficking of these women.

This research is echoed in A. Smith's *Conquest: sexual violence and American Indian genocide* (2005). A. Smith's book outlines the ways in which sexual violence has been used in strategies of control and genocide and even concluding with a chapter entitled "U.S. Empire and the War against Native Sovereignty" (pp. 177–191). According to A. Smith, sexual violence is part of a larger American eugenics program that, while not as blatant as it was in the past, remains in effect. She argues that these practices have been and continue to be government-sanctioned, systemic, and intentional policies aimed at Native American cultural and physical genocide.[11]

Nagy provides additional evidence of violence against Indigenous women in Canada, the United States, and Australia stating that these rates are three, 2.5, and three times higher, respectively, than their non-Indigenous counterparts (Nagy 2015, p. 182). She argues that these rates, in large part, are the legacy of boarding schools and the failure of the judicial systems. Nagy cites the 2013 UNICEF report evidence that states "Mayan women and girls were systemically targeted for gender-based violence, including femicide and rape" claiming that such reports are far from anomalous.

She also cites the Amnesty International report, which states that "370 women were murdered between 1993 and 2003" in Ciudad Juarez with an unknown number of missing as evidence that Indigenous women are being specifically targeted (p. 187). While noting the global pandemic involving violence against Indigenous women, much of Nagy's discussion is devoted to the "1181 missing and murdered indigenous women across Canada" with a specific focus on cases associated with Vancouver's Downtown Eastside.[12]

According to Nagy, "of the approximately 65 missing and murdered women from Downtown Eastside, one-third are indigenous, despite the fact that they represent only 3 percent of the general population" (p. 188). She considered these numbers to be the result of government programs to displace Indigenous people including the *Indian Act* and the "Sixties Scoop", "which saw 11,000 First Nations children, along with many other indigenous children, taken into the child welfare system and adopted out to mainly white homes". The forced removals devastated both families and the removed children as often neither parents nor children knew what happened to the other.

According to Nagy, the experience of removal or being "stolen" increased the probability of these children experiencing violence and sexual assault which, in turn, led to an increased probability of them participating in the sex trade industry (p. 190). Dean's research into the "Disappeared Women" of Vancouver also highlights the impact of colonization and the legacy of

---

[11] Conversations involving the U.S. Violence Against Women Act is significant to the treatment of Indigenous women. Historically, this act has been denied in part because of its support for allowing tribal prosecution of violence against Indigenous women on tribal lands. While the Act was ratified, continued reauthorization remains uncertain.

[12] At a conference in Vancouver in 2017, Lovern was able to sit in on a discussion about Downtown Eastside. The woman giving the presentation offered a publication put out by the *Peers Sex Work Story Collective*. The publication is a collection of stories told by Indigenous women working in the area as sex workers. The stories are not about their work, but about themselves as humans with dreams, values, and love. The project is ongoing and designed to give a voice to the often invisible and voiceless (McKay 2017)

violence experienced by Indigenous women, which has created a pattern of invisibility and a justification for violence (2015). Dean also examines the broader dynamics of gender roles in her examination of "squaw men" and "queered" identity, emphasizing identity fluidity. She argues that this fluidity triggers Western biases and places them in the feminine role. Both Nagy and Dean conclude that the failure of the Canadian government to establish a national inquiry into the violence against Indigenous women, and those identifying as fluid, not only fuels continued violence, but also undermines the possibility of justice within legal systems, reducing many reconciliation claims to pure rhetoric.[13]

According to the United Nations Human Rights Council while the collection of data in Indigenous communities remains problematic, there is "enough to know that indigenous women and girls are three times more likely to suffer violence than other women" (2016). The panel went on to discuss issues including the need for State inclusion, education, and the elimination of poverty as these were contributing factors in the violation of Indigenous women's human rights. The panel stated that Indigenous women represent some of the world's poorest people as a result of colonization, racism, and marginalization, making them highly vulnerable to violence.

UNICEF statistics confirmed the vulnerability of Indigenous women as well as the increased levels of violence (2013). This report linked sexual stereotypes associated with Western society and the inaccurate portrayals of Indigenous women in the media to these increased risks. While the report states a need for more complete data collection in Indigenous communities, it argues that available data indicates a higher rate of violence toward Indigenous women than their non-Indigenous counterparts.[14] The report also acknowledges the increased incidents of child labor, child trafficking, and child domestic servant issues noting that these children, primarily female, face an increased risk of violence and sexual abuse.[15] According to the report, sexual violence is part of the larger economic exploitation of Indigenous women and children that includes child marriage, limited access to health care, and higher health-based childbearing risks, often exacerbated by rural

---

[13] It should be noted that as of the writing of this book, both Canada and the United States have begun to give more media attention turned to missing and murdered Indigenous women. Legislation is being proposed to force both governments to investigate these cases. Activist movements in Indigenous communities have brought significant awareness to these issues largely using social media.

[14] It must be noted that UNICEF found a disturbingly high rate of violence against women in general but noted a higher incidence in Indigenous demographics.

[15] The report notes that both male and female children face increased rates of violence and sexual assault, but that the majority of children in the positions of child labor, trafficking, and domestic servitude are female.

isolation. Overall, the report gives evidence of a disturbing global trend involving the violence and exploitation of Indigenous women and girls.

According to the *Mairin Iwanka Raya*, which is an "Indigenous women's approach to gendered violence" and is the companion report to the UN report on Indigenous women (2006), increased manifestations of violence towards Indigenous people, particularly females, are the result of neoliberal politics and the emphasis on economic models for determining the value and usage of natural and human resources. The report argues that the embracing of neoliberal politics by Western governments has meant the devaluing of Indigenous human rights and sovereignty efforts, which, in turn, devalues Indigenous peoples. This devaluing, then, justifies violence as a means of eliminating that which stands in the way of productivity and economic advancement.

This companion report also examines the role of military conflict in the violence against Indigenous women along with displacement, poverty, economic challenges, education, and health disparities as noted in the UN and UNICEF data. In a unique move, the companion report addresses issues such as compulsory assimilation and forced sterilization practices in government-sanctioned healthcare facilities, topics often unaddressed in research involving Indigenous women (p. 35). Finally, migration and immigration issues, while again not often discussed in reports involving Indigenous communities and violence, are represented in this research and add an essential perspective on the violence and choices faced by Indigenous women attempting to maintain or improve their life and those of their children.

This section has focused on the global violence against Indigenous women as a means of understanding the historical and continuing violence impacting Indigenous communities, but this is not the end of the Indigenous story. Indeed, the impact of both individual and community has produced intergenerational trauma that has gone largely unrecognized by governmental institutions, but the trauma is not the entire Indigenous experience. Acknowledging the devastation of sexual violence to individuals and communities, we again echo Deer's caution that Indigenous women's stories are not oriented only toward suffering but extoll the strength and courage of survivors and the wisdom of Indigenous women to heal both the self and the community.

## Indigenous Responses to Violence

In this new UN and International era, Indigenous activists and communities have advanced efforts to regain sovereignty recognition and to assure self-determination for future generations. Decolonization and indigenizing, in theory and in praxis, have become both a rallying point and a means of organizing. However, it is important to note that while the international efforts have been embraced by some Indigenous populations, others worry that it homogenizes all things Indigenous.

The uniqueness of each community, history, and situation has the potential to be lost in the global struggle. Issues of essentialism and universalization, then, contribute to the invisibility of individual community struggles and needs making the use of the "Indigenous", in terminology and in activism, a double-edged sword. Nonetheless, on community, State, and international stages, Indigenous people have begun to assert their positions and call for a recognition of their human and sovereignty rights.

Willis and Seward credit organizations such as the International Labor Organization (ILO) and the Inter-American Court of Human rights for helping Indigenous communities access global economic arenas and in asserting their rights (2006). As with other researchers, the authors note that these "provisions are often unenforced", which requires the adoption of alternative strategies including the use of traditional knowledge to sway public and political opinion (pp. 18–19).

They reference the success of these strategies as exemplified in cases like *The Mayagna (Sumo)Awas Tingni Community v. Nicaragua* in 2001 and the 2005 *Yakye Axa Indigenous community v. Paraguay* (p. 19). Additionally, they promote strategies that use national and local colonizer statutes to the advantage and protection of Indigenous communities, land, and resources as evidenced by the Otavalo and Quichua communities in Ecuador as well as the Indigenous communities in Peru and Bolivia (pp. 20–21).

Fernández supports these findings, noting that Indigenous communities are entering political arenas in Latin America in spite of the "brutality, daily raids, and the use of firearms against unarmed" populations and threats of "child welfare" checks with the intention of removal, a strategy all too familiar in Western colonization. Regardless of these governmental pressures to submit, Fernández states that there is a "growing level of indigenous activism" as Indigenous communities fail to be "intimidated by the violence or threats of the powerful" (2008, pp. 8–9). Brysk and Bennett chronicle similar struggles within Bolivian Indigenous communities and note some Indigenous success in the face of racialized politics and threats of violence. While these examples are limited, they represent the continuing resistance expressed by global Indigenous communities in the face of ongoing colonization threats of erasure (Brysk and Bennett 2012).

Using Western laws and institutions to re-establish sovereignty recognition and to protect Indigenous communities and traditions does recall Audre Lorde's caution that *The Master's Tools will Never Dismantle the Master's House*. Walking too long in the colonizing world, for many, comes with a great price involving the loss of traditional identity and ways of being. It may in reality be difficult to dismantle colonization while participating in it, but this in no way diminishes the efforts of those attempting to do just that as in many situations there are few alternatives. However, such concerns do reflect the concerns in many Indigenous communities as their members are forced to assimilate, to some extent, in order to protect those same communities and their ways of being.

In reading Deer's work, what is striking is the extent to which Western power structures normalize oppression. Her discussion of rape as a political tool exposes the general subjugation of women and the strategy with which this subjugation has been used, not only against Indigenous women, but against Indigenous communities. Given the interconnectivity of Indigenous culture and reciprocity ethics, the damage or destruction of part destabilizes, and potentially, destroys the whole. Relegating Indigenous women to the subjugated and inferior position of Western women and adding the secondary inferiority positioning of being of-color remains a foundational component of State strategies to disrupt traditional patterns of reciprocity and interdependence.

By destabilizing traditional Indigenous constructs involving complementarity, or redefining it in terms of Western structures, Western hierarchies have attempted to force heterosexism on Indigenous communities. Even in Indigenous societies exhibiting some level of patriarchy, women were understood to have significant value as evidenced in the various origin stories which ascribe both power and equity positions to women. For example, even in societal structures such as the Inca that establish a patriarchy at the highest levels, there was a tradition involving female rulers. These women ruled in place of absent males without a loss or differentiation of powers. In other Indigenous cultures, men may have been considered war chiefs, but often had to have the permission of the Head Woman or the Women's Council before participating in war, especially if the women preferred trading with the contested group. In point of fact, the gender fluidity in many of these cultures established traditions that supported female warriors, male weavers, and an open expression of diversity.

The complementarity institution found in Indigenous cultures continues to confound many Western critics. In defining "complementarity" to include "separate but equal" ways of understanding the reciprocal relationship between gender roles in society is one of equality. While Western theories contain the idea of complementarity, the application of it has not reflected the definition. Western constructions of complementarity often focus on the "valuing" of women, but do not define such value as being equal to men.

As described by a young Indigenous professor, "the Christian and social systems of the West claim that they value women and their role in society and claim that the distribution of labor is a matter of complementarity. However, valuing does not entail equality of power. It is clear that, in many Western religious, social, and political traditions, women are valued, but their labor and position remain inferior; they continue to be subordinate to men". Western women, then, remain positioned as the hierarchical Other placing them in the abnormal or the inferior position. According to this mindset, Indigenous women, along with other women of-color, are placed lower on the hierarchy because of their multiple "deficiencies" or "abnormalities", justifying subordination and violent strategies to subdue this Other.

In the face of this dual Othering, Indigenous women, as chronicled by Deer and other scholars, have begun to reclaim and reassert their unique knowledge involving the healing of themselves and their communities. In this way, these women have embodied Freire's ideal that salvation for both the oppressed and the oppressor can only be achieved at the hands of the oppressed. These initiatives work to move beyond the master's tools so as to reclaim female knowledge and reciprocal relations in an effort to heal self, community, and colonizers and to eliminate the imposed violence and genocidal strategies of Western colonization.

Linklater chronicles these efforts in her recounting of traditional women's practices of healing in her book entitled *Decolonizing Trauma Work* (2014). Her work documents the use of Indigenous healing and wellness as a means of understanding colonization trauma and how to treat the intergenerational impact. Similarly, *Women and Religion in the African Diaspora*, a collection of articles discussing women's traditions and knowledge, promotes the creolization of religions as one possibility to regain balance in colonization-traumatized communities (Griffith and Savage 2006). The articles in this text emphasize the strength and unique ability of Indigenous women to overcome the oppression of colonization and to create a sustainable future. The ability to interweave spiritual constructs in order to produce ceremonial and ideological healing illustrates a potential decolonization and indigenizing that benefit not just the oppressed, but also the oppressor. Given these efforts, re-envisioning the master's tools according to Indigenous paradigms offers a potential avenue to dismantle Western-imposed hierarchical dualism using Western tools.

The legacy involved in women's traditional medicine and what has been called "Grandmother knowledge", while often difficult to find, represents a diversity and plethora of wisdom. Given the uniqueness of each Indigenous community, this combined wisdom encompasses vast amounts of knowledge involving every aspect of human existence. An effective decolonization/indigenizing strategy would be to begin with the reinstatement of Indigenous women's positioning in reciprocity structures and the recognition of their ability to heal their communities.

Our initial intention was to devote the conclusion of this chapter to the recognition of Indigenous female leaders. However, as we began the process, we could not choose from the plethora of historical and current global examples. Female Indigenous activists, scholars, chiefs, and traditional medicine people represent an, all too often ignored, but ever present and essential part of Indigenous communities. Some are outspoken warriors, while others are soft spoken, but their diversity and their knowledge of traditional ways of being represent an indominable spirit that refuses to be silenced and continues to build a place for future generations. According to Locust, these women represent the female line of Hope Warriors beginning in creation and continuing into the generations yet unborn.

## Additional Readings

Akaka, M., Kahaulelio, M., Keko'olani-Raymaond, T., Ritte, L., & Goodyear-Ka'ōpua. (2018). *Nā Wāhine Koa: Hawaiian Women for Sovereignty and Demilitarization*. Honolulu: University of Hawaii Press.

Alderman, P. (1978). *Nancy Ward: Cherokee Chieftainess and Dragging Canoe: Cherokee-Chickamauga War Chief* (2nd ed.). Overmountain Press: Johnson City.

Alfred, T. (2009). *Peace, Power, Righteousness: An Indigenous Manifesto*, 2nd ed. Oxford: Oxford University Press.

Allen, P. G. (1994). *Voice of the Turtle: American Indian Literature 1900–1970*. New York: Ballantine Books.

Allen, P. G. (1991). *Grandmothers of the Light: A Medicine Woman's Sourcebook*. Boston: Beacon Press.

Barker, J. (2006). *Sovereignty Matters: Locations of Contestation and Possibility in Indigenous Struggles for Self-Determination*. Lincoln: University of Nebraska Press.

Canby, W. C., Jr. (2015). *American Indian Law in a Nutshell* (6th ed.). West Academic: St. Paul.

Colloredo, M. (2007). The Power of Ecuador's Indigenous Communities in an Era of Cultural Pluralism. *Social Analysis: The International Journal of Social and Cultural Practice, 51*(2), 86–106. Berghahn Books.

Cotton, A. L., & Acampora, C. D. (2007). *Cultural Sites of Critical Insight: Philosophy, Aesthetics, and African American and Native American Women's Writings.* Albany: State University of New York Press.

Coulter, R. T. (2015). The Situation of the Indigenous People of Rapa Nui and International Law: Reflections on Indigenous Peoples and the Ethics of Remediation. *Santa Clara Journal of Indigenous Law, 13*(1), 293–305.

Coulthard, G. S. (2014). *Red Skin, White Masks: Rejecting the Colonial Politics of Recognition.* Minneapolis: University of Minnesota Press.

De Manuel, D. (2004). Decolonizing Bodies, Reinscribing Souls in the Fiction of Ninotchka Rosca and Linda Ty-Casper. *MELUS, 29*(1), 99–118. Oxford University Press.

Deer, S. (2019). (En)Gendering Indian Law: Indigenous Feminist Legal Theory in the United States. *Yale Journal of Law & Feminism, 31*(1), 2. 2–34.

Deer, S., Clairmont, B., Martell, C. A., & White Eagle, M. L. (Eds.). (2008). *Sharing Our Stories of Survival: Native Women Surviving Violence.* Lanham: Altamira Press.

Elias, M., Hummel, S. S., Bassnett, B. S., & Colfer, C. J. P. (2017). Gender Bias Affects Forests Worldwide. *Ethnobiology Letters, 8*(1), 31–34. Society of Ethnobiology.

Elias, R. (1986). *The Politics of Victimization: Victims, Victimology, and Human Rights.* New York: Oxford University Press.

Fernández, R. V., & Gutiérrez, C. E. (Ed.), and Gelles, P. H., & Escobar, G. M. (Trans.) (1996). *Andean Lives.* Austin: University of Texas Press.

French, L. A. (2016). *Policing American Indians: A Unique Chapter in American Jurisprudence.* Boca Raton: CRC Press.

George, N. (2011). Pacific Women Building Peace: A Regional Perspective. *The Contemporary Pacific: A Journal of Island Affairs, 23*(1), 37–71. University of Hawai'i Press.

Gutiérrez, R. A. (1991). *When Jesus Came the Corn Mothers Went Away: Marriage, Sexuality, and Power in New Mexico, 1500–1846.* Stanford: Stanford University Press.

Hau'ofa, E. (2008). *We Are the Ocean: Selected Works.* Honolulu: University of Hawai'I Press.

Janda, S. E. (2007). *Beloved Women: The Political Lives of LaDonna Harris and Wilma Mankiller.* DeKalb: Northern Illinois University Press.

Kahele, M. (2006). *Clouds of Memories.* Kamehameha Schools: Honolulu.

McGrath, A., & Jebb, M. A. (2015). *Long History, Deep Time: Deepening Histories of Place.* Acton Act: Australian National University Press.

Mankiller, W. (2004). *Every Day Is a Good Day: Reflections by Contemporary Indigenous Women.* Golden: Fulcrum Publishing.

Mann, A. B. (Ed.). (2008). *Make a Beautiful Way: The Wisdom of Native American Women*. University of Nebraska Press: Lincoln.

Maracle, L. (1996). *I Am Woman: A Native Perspective on Sociology and Feminism*. Vancouver: Press Gang Publishers.

Marcos, S. (2009). Mesoamerican Women's Indigenous Spirituality: Decolonizing Religious Beliefs. *Journal of Feminist Studies in Religion, 25*(2), 25–45. Indiana University Press.

Masaharu, M., Stich, S., & McCready, E. (2018). *Epistemology for the Rest of the World*. New York: Oxford University Press.

NCAI Policy Research Center. (2013). *Policy Insights Brief: Statistics on Violence Against Native Women*.

Perrone, B., Stockel, H. H., & Krueger, V. (1991). *Medicine Women, Curanderas, and Women Doctors*. Norman: University of Oklahoma Press.

Pevar, S. L. (2012). *The Rights of Indians and Tribes*. New York: Oxford University Press.

Postero, N. (2017). The Emergence of Indigenous Nationalism in Bolivia: Social Movements and the MAS State". *The Indigenous state: Race, politics, and performance in plurinational Bolivia* (pp. 25–40). Berkeley: University of California Press.

Rosco, W. (1998). *Changing Ones: Third and Fourth Genders in Native North America*. New York: St. Martin's Press.

Rosco, W. (Ed.). (1988). *Living the Spirit: A Gay American Indian Anthology*. New York: St. Martins Press.

Rothenberg, D. (Ed.). (2012). *Memory of Silence: The Guatemalan Truth Commission Report*. New York: Palgrave Macmillan.

Silko, L. M. (1996). *Yellow Woman and a Beauty of the Spirit*. New York: Simon & Shuster.

Simpson, L. B. (2017). *As We Have Always Done: Indigenous Freedom Through Radical Resistance*, 3rd ed. Minneapolis::University of Minnesota Press.

Suzack, C., Huhndorf, S. M., Perreault, J., & Barman, J. (Eds.). (2010). *Indigenous Women and Feminism: Politics, Activism, Culture*. Vancouver: UBC Press.

Tovar-Restrepo, M., & Irazabal, C. (2014). Indigenous Women and Violence in Colombia: Agency, Autonomy, and Territoriality. *Latin American Perspectives, 41*(1), 39–58. Sage.

Trask, H.-K. (1999). *From a Native Daughter: Colonialism and Sovereignty in Hawaii*, 2nd ed. Latitude 20.

United Nations: General Assembly Resolution 48/104 Containing the Declaration on the Elimination of Violence Against Women. (July 1994). *International Legal Materials, 33*(4), 1049–1054. Cambridge University Press.

Villa-Vicencio, C., & Verwoerd, W. (2000). *Looking Back Reaching Forward: Reflections on the Truth and Reconciliation Commission of South Africa*. Cape Town: University of Cape Town Press.

Wall, S. (1993). *Wisdom's Daughters: Conversations with Women Elders of Native America*. New York: Harper Perennial.

Williams, W. L. (1992). *Spirit and Flesh: Sexual Diversity in American Indian Culture.* Boston: Beacon Press.

## Works Cited

Abidogun, J. (2007). Western Education's Impact on Northern Igbo Gender Roles in Nsukka, Nigeria. *Africa Today, 54*(1), 29–51.

African Court on Human and People's Rights. (2020). https://www.african-court.org/wpafc/.

American Convention on Human Rights. (1969). http://www.un.org/esa/socdev/enable/comp.

Agtuca, J. (2014). *Safety for Native Women: VAWA and American Indian Tribes* (Ed., D. Sahneyah). Lame Deer: National Indigenous Women's Resource Center.

Aspin, C. (2011). Exploring Takatapui Identity Within the Maori Community: Implications for Health and Well-Being. In Q.-L. Driskill, C. Finley, B. J. Gilley, & S. L. Morgensen (Eds.), *Queer Indigenous Studies: Critical Interventions in Theory, Politics and Literature.* Tucson: University of Arizona Press.

Babcock, H. (2005). A Civic-Republican Vision of 'Domestic Dependent Nations' in the Twenty-First Century: Tribal Sovereignty Re-envisioned, Reinvigorated, and Re-empowered. *Open Access: Georgetown University Law Center*, 442–471. Retrieved from https://scholarship.law.georgetown.edu/cgi/viewcontent.cgi?referer=https://www.google.com/&httpsredir=1&article=1958&context=facpub.

Brown, E. B. (1999). *Religion, Law, and Land: Native Americans and the Judicial Interpretation of Sacred Land.* Westport: Greenwood Press.

Brysk, A., & Bennett, N. (2012). Voice in the Village: Indigenous Peoples Contest Globalization in Bolivia. *The Brown Journal of World Affairs, 18*(2), 115–127.

Cajete, G. (2000). *Native Science: Natural Laws of Interdependence.* Santa Fe: Clear Light Publishers.

Dean, A. (2015). *Remembering Vancouver's Disappeared Women: Settler Colonialism and the Difficulty of Inheritance.* Toronto: University of Toronto Press.

Deer, S. (2015). *The Beginning and End of Rape: Confronting Sexual Violence in Native America* (3rd ed.). Minneapolis: University of Minnesota.

Deloria, V., Jr. (2011). *The Legal Universe: Observations on the Foundations of American Law.* Golden: Fulcrum.

Deloria, V., Jr., & Lytle, C. M. (1983). *American Indians, American Justice.* Austin: University of Texas Press.

Deloria, V., Jr, & Wildcat, D. (2001). Knowing and Understanding. *Power and Place: Indian Education in America* (pp. 41–46). Golden: Fulcrum.

Dunbar-Ortiz, R. (2014). *An Indigenous Peoples' History of the United States.* Boston: Beacon Press.

Echo-Hawk, W. (2010). *In the Courts of the Conquerors: The Ten Worst Indian Law Cases Ever Decided.* Golden: Fulcrum.

Fernández, S. (2008, February 16–22). Trajectory of Indigenous Politics in Latin America. *Economic and Political Weekly, 43*(7), 8–9.

Gilley, B. J. (2011). Two-Spirit Men's Sexual Survivance Against the Inequality of Desire. In Q.-L. Driskill, C. Finley, B. J. Gilley, & L. Morgensen (Eds.), *Queer Indigenous Studies: Critical Interventions in Theory, Politics, and Literature* (pp. 123–131). Tucson: University of Arizona Press.

Griffith, R. M., & Savage, B. D. (2006). *Women and Religion in the African Diaspora: Knowledge, Power, and Performance.* Baltimore: Johns Hopkins University Press.

Holmes, L. (2008). Heart Knowledge, Blood Memory, and the Voice of the Land: Implication of Research Among Hawai'ian Elders. In G. J. Sefa Dei, B. L. Hall, & D. G. Rosenberg (Eds.), *Indigenous Knowledge in Global Context: Multiple Readings of Our World* (pp. 37–53) Toronto: Toronto University Press.

Howell, T. L. (1995). Tracking Zuni Gender and Leadership Roles Across the Contact Period. *Journal of Anthropological Research, 51*(2), 125–147.

International Labor Organization. (2017). *Employment Policy Recommendation no. 169.* https://www.ilo.org/dyn/normlex/en/f?p=NORMLEXPUB:12100:0::NO::P12100_ILO_CODE:R169.

International Work Group for Indigenous Affairs. (2006). *Indigenous Peoples in Africa: The Forgotten People?* The African Commissions Work on Indigenous People in Africa. Piscataway, NJ: Transaction Publishers. Retrieved from www.iwgia.org.

*Indianz.* (2014, December 14). *Boyd Cothren: Torture Justified by Treatment of Indian Prisoners.* Retrieved from https://www.indianz.com/News/2014/12/17/boyd-cothran-torture-justified.asp.

Knowles, F. E., & Lovern, L. (2015). *A Critical Pedagogy for Native American Indian Policy: Habermas, Freire, and Emancipatory Education.* New York: Palgrave Macmillan.

Kovach, M. (2009). *Indigenous Methodologies: Characteristics, Conversations, and Contexts.* Toronto: Toronto University Press.

Linklater, R. (2014). *Decolonizing Trauma Work: Indigenous Stories and Strategies.* Halifax: Fernwood Publishing.

Lovern, L., & Costello, D. (2013). Native American Issues Involving Diabetes and Balance. In M. Stoltzfus, R. Green, D. Schumm (Eds.), *Chronic Illness, Spirituality, and Healing: Diverse Disciplinary, Religious, and Cultural Perspectives* (pp. 217–237). New York: Palgrave Macmillan.

Mairin Iwanka Raya: Indigenous Women Stand Against Violence. (2006). *Mairin Iwanka Raya: New Beginnings for Women, Miskito.* Retrieved from http://www.fimi-iiwf.org/archivos/7ffd8ee2807b42a0df93d25d70c9cfdb.pdf.

Marubbio, M. E. (2006). *Killing the Indian Maiden.* Lexington: University of Kentucky.

Markus, H. R., & Kitayama, S. (1991). Culture and Self: Implications for Cognition, Emotion, and Motivation. *Psychological Review, 98*(2), 224–253. Retrieved from http://chnm.gmu.edu/courses/honors130/culture.html.

McKay, R. ed. (2017). *Chronicles from Dis'trick to Stroll.* Vancouver: Peers Victoria Resource Society. Retrieved from www.safersexwork.ca.

Meriam Report. (1928). *National Indian Law Library.* https://narf.org/nill/resources/meriam.html.

Morgensen, S. L. (2011). Unsettling Queer Politics: What Can Non-natives Learn from Two-Spirit Organizing? In Q.-L. Driskill, C. Finley, B. J. Gilley, & S. L. Morgensen (Eds.), *Queer Indigenous Studies: Critical Interventions in Theory, Politics, and Literature* (pp. 132–152). Tucson: University of Arizona Press.

Nagy, R. (2015). Combatting Violence Against Indigenous Women. In A. Powell, N. Henery, A. Flynn (Eds.), *Rape Justice* (pp. 182–199). New York: Palgrave Macmillan.

Powers, K. V. (2000). Andeans and Spaniards in the Contact Zone: A Gendered Collision. *American Indian Quarterly, 24*(4), 511–536.

Richards, J. (2014). Many Were Killed from Falling over the Cliffs': The Naming of Mount Wheeler, Central Queensland. In I. D. Clark, L. Hercus, & L. Kostanski (Eds.), *Indigenous and Minority Placenames: Australian and International Perspectives* (pp. 147–161). ANU.

Smith, A. (2005). *Conquest: Sexual Violence and American Indian Genocide.* Cambridge: South End Press.

Thompson, V. C. (1997). Independent and Interdependent Views of Self: Implications for Culturally Sensitive Vocational Rehabilitation Services. *The Journal of Rehabilitation, 63*(4). Retrieved from https://www.thefreelibrary.com/Independent+and+interdependent+views+of+self%3A+implications+for...-a020209740.

UNICEF. (2013). *Breaking the Silence on Violence Against Indigenous Girls, Adolescence, and Young Women.* New York: UNICEF. Retrieved from https://Vilence%20against%20Indigenous%20Girls%25252c%20Adolescents%20and%20Young%20women.pdf.

United Nations. (2008). *United Nations Declaration on the Rights of Indigenous Peoples.* New York: United Nations. Retrieved from http://www.un.org/esa/socdev/unpfii/documents/DRIPS_en.pdf.

*United Nations Human Rights office of the High Commissioner.* (2016, June 16). (United Nations) Human Rights Council Opens Annual Discussion on the Human Rights of Women, Focusing on Violence Against Indigenous Women and Girls. Retrieved from www.ohchr.org/EN/NewsEvents/Pages/DisplayNews.aspx?NewsID=20116&LangID=E.

Willis, F. M., & Seward, T. (2006). Protecting and Preserving Indigenous Communities in the Americas. *Human Rights, 33*(2), 18–21.

# 5

# Language

## Good Words

*As children we were taught early to communicate only in good words, that is how one spoke, it was important, not just what one said. We were told to think long before speaking and to choose our words carefully think about how words would impact all those around us. We were taught to be quiet and listen to the trees, the wind, and the animals, not to speak loudly and startle or disturb them. They had business of their own, and we should not interfere but should watch and learn. Maybe we were never directly told this, but it was understood early. We tried to be so quiet and to see all we could, to learn the lessons taught to us by our human and non-human relations. Each tribe has a language and the language created reality. Words are sacred, not just secular things, and they build the reality in which we live. To speak harshly or in anger, not only damaged the one who heard, but it damaged the spirit of the one who spoke. Once said, the words can't be unheard. The damage is done and even if forgiven, it remains a part of those who spoke and those who heard. Remaking the negative energy created by bad words is a long process and can't always be done. Sometimes the damage is too great. Sometimes ceremonies were needed to change the energy and sometimes the relation was just broken. The sadness of a broken relationship was not just individual but communal.*

*What I have learned in my experience is that languages are particular to each community and should be undertaken with care by outsiders. Often misunderstandings stem from not understanding the wholeness of another's language and the way it shapes reality. For example, humor is not easily translatable. In many tribal settings it is left to those with experience, but often teasing occurs between* those who know each other well. I have tried to explain to non-Indians that teasing should not be done unless close relations exist. In many of my experiences American Indians often tease only when they don't mean it. One would never use teasing language if one truly meant what was being said. Instead, one can learn more from what is unsaid. When many American Indians remain silent, it is not out of agreement, or affirmation, but rather out of disagreement. It is just not, in their opinion, their place to state their disagreement, either because they were not asked or because they were in public. These are the protocols that are so important in American Indian communication, protocols that most non-Indians do not take the time to learn. Protocols such as, never stepping in front of an Elder, not turning one's back to an Elder when a conversation is completed, and in many situations, not directly addressing an Elder, particularly if he or she is in thought.

Understanding Indigenous language is about more than just the words, it is the protocol for how the words are formed and heard. Discussions are often not direct and may not seem to the outsider to even be about the topic of concern. Often stories are used to convey information. There are many reasons for this including the creation of energies and the need for the individual to come to understand. For most, an opinion is not given unless asked for, but if asked one must give as truthful of a statement as possible. And, in all situations, one should control emotions so as not to let the energy, good or bad, impact the other and cause harm. Wisdom was understood to come with age and experience and so as children we watched and listened and learned. We did not argue with our elders when they said something even if they said the noon sky was black as night. We understood that there was something we were to come to understand in that statement and to think on it. Or in cases where someone was wrong, it would be rude to argue, or point out the wrong, especially in front of others. Protocols and ways of being such as this created problems as many children were forced into Western modes of communication where being aggressive and loud were considered the norm; where addressing elders directly and arguing with them was to be expected, even when it was punished. Often Indigenous children were considered shy or unintelligent in school because they kept to the old protocols. Even the teachers often didn't understand the cultural differences. For example, when American Indian children are in trouble, they are not used to being addressed directly or in public over these issues, and they won't look directly at their accuser. Their actions were seen as disrespectful or impertinent to not look directly at the teacher who was speaking harshly. But American Indian people do not generally look into the eyes of others as it is intrusive and rude. Certainly, children do not look into the eyes of elders and to do so to the teacher speaking harshly invites damage or insinuates a potential escalation of the conflict.

And again, we were brought up to understand that conflict was a child's thing. Growing to be an adult meant learning to have controversy and differences of opinion without aggression or conflict. Certainly, such wisdom was not always gained, and it was often a struggle, but it was understood as the goal of the adult to be able to discuss rationally and without aggression. People who were angry were *considered to have a "twisted mind" or were seen as temporarily crazy and to be avoided until they were back in their right mind. They were allowed to calm before addressing the situation and, if needed, Elders and medicine people were called to help. Additionally, if someone was sad, they were watched by family and friends, but not always spoken to. Many times, the people would sit in silence with the sad person until that person spoke so that they could think through what was upsetting them. It doesn't mean they were left without people, more that they were surrounded by a community of kind silence.*

*These protocols came many times with hand signs and body signs as well. There were different signs for the different American Indian communities, but they were as important and often as subtle as the slight change around an elder's eyes or lips that told the children what they should do. A simple crinkle of the eyes or a shift in the lips was enough to address both positive and negative child behaviors. Slight movements of the fingers could signal pleasure or danger. But the hand signs allowed communication when one wasn't talented in hearing or when our languages differed. Some of them came from the times when we ran from the military to avoid reservations or hid from those taking children to boarding schools. Some of those signs are still in use. Other signs came from watching turtles swim or noting the passage of time in storytelling. Pointing, as often done in the Western cultures, was not a sign to be used as it carried energy to another. Instead, the shifting of eyes, pursing of lips, or other signs were used to indicate a direction. These are some of the complexities of Indigenous communication that have been lost in assimilation and even in the attempts by some to archive dying languages. I offer the following as a limited example of protocol within some Indigenous communities.—Carol Locust*

## *DON'T TRY ON IT NO MORE: THE USE OF SILENCE*

"Silence" as the word is used in this paper refers to the use of silence among American Indian tribes. Discussions with San Carlos Apaches about the use of silence brought the response that "When you don't try on it no more, when you just wait" was the best description of silence. Among the Tohono O'odham the reply was "showing respect by not talking all the time." Silence, to the Seminoles in Florida, was an indication of wisdom: "How can you think good if you are always talking?"

"Silence is beautiful," said a Sioux woman. "That is when the spirit world is close."

The use of silence is mandated by tribal behavior codes in some situations. If this code of behavior is not followed, the individual who violates the code is thought to be crude, unlearned, and stupid. The person's behavior also impacts negatively on the social respect of his family and clan; for this reason, few individuals are inclined to violate the code. In other situations, silence is so distinctly a part of a ceremony or event that to trespass could result in an individual's need for schooling using various stories.

*The following is a general overview of the use of silence in social situations.*

I. *In conversation with other persons (one person or several):*
   1. *one does not speak immediately after another person has spoken.*
   2. *one does not speak more often than others.*
   3. *one does not repeat the same statements over and over.*

II. *The reasons are:*
   1. *speaking too soon after another person has spoken does not show respect for her or what she has said. It is like pushing*

   *her words aside too quickly before they can be thought about.*
   *The normal time a non-Indian waits before she speaks after a another person ends a speech is 3 seconds. In Indian communities the wait time is 6–12 seconds.*

   2a. *talking too much does not allow silence in which the person can think about what others have said.*
   2b. *talking too much means a person has not respected silence for others to think before they speak. When a person jumps in and talks when it is not his turn, he is disrespectful. (While no set method of taking turns during speech may be established, it is a behavior code of sharing time equally, much like using the sacred talking stick).*
   3. *saying the same thing over and over indicates that the person speaking really has nothing else to say but is greedy of time. If a person has nothing to say other than what he has already said, it is appropriate to keep silent while others continue to talk.*

III. *Silence before a sentence*
   1. *Silence before speaking a sentence is a continuation of the silence following someone else's speech. Everyone in the conversation will know that the second person is ready to talk, and silence should be given while the second person arranges her thoughts to put into words.*

2. *Silence in a sentence is important so that the speaker choses the right words. The speaker should not rush, or be rushed, as the wrong words can damage or misrepresent what is meant.*

IV. *Words and time are important and should not be rushed.*
   1. *If a conversation is worth having, it should not be rushed. Time should be allowed for those speaking and those hearing. It is important to honor the time and the relation to others.*

2. *Words should be carefully chosen as they create a reality and convey an energy that will impact others. Words should be concrete and not abstract, unless that is the conversation that one is involved in. For many, words should grow from nature and be able to be signed to be good words.—Carol Locust*

## Endangered and Dying Languages

According to the UN, "96 percent of the world's approximately 6,700 languages are spoken only by 3 percent of the world's population. Although indigenous people make up less than 6% of the global populations, they speak more than 4,000 of the world's languages". Additionally, the UN notes that "more than half the world's languages will become extinct by 2100" and that "one indigenous language dies every two weeks" (United Nations, Together). These statistics prompted the UN to declare 2019 the year of Indigenous languages with the intention of bringing awareness to the issue of endangered languages and to assist in language revitalization efforts (International Year of Indigenous Languages 2019).

While the Permanent Forum has called for the use of Indigenous languages in education and in training materials and has linked the usage to issues of human rights and self-determination, it continues to side-step the issue of sovereignty. This chapter will begin with a brief examination of Indigenous/Western linguistic paradigm differences and the impact of these on issues of colonization. Specifically, the chapter will focus on the role and outcomes of oral and written traditions regarding language and the function of language in natural geometry. The chapter will conclude with a brief statement on the significance of Indigenous language for daily activity, ceremonial purposes, the actualization of sovereignty, and the healing of intergenerational trauma.

Indigenous communities understand language endangerment and extinction as a part of colonization strategies promoting assimilation as well as a deterrent to the realization of sovereignty. However, many within the West, including academics, have not been convinced that preservation of Indigenous languages is a significant enough issue to allocate either time or money to the cause. Part of the Western disinterest in dying languages may be because of what Errington called the split in linguists. According to Errington, about thirty years ago linguists split into those who studied cultural anthropology and those that focused on cognitive neuroscience

(2003). The shift in linguistic orientation away from the cultural and political aspects relating to the use and power of languages resulted in an academic disinterest in the impact of colonization on Indigenous languages.

However, "as hundreds of languages become marginalized, endangered, and 'die' around the world", Errington declares that it has become "hard even for the most theoretical and lab-oriented practitioners of this science to ignore" the loss (p. 723). Errington discusses academic strategies that link the demise of languages to the places and people from whence they come but notes that the continued association of language with these abstract studies hinders the experiential connection of languages to human rights. The organic connection made by activists, according to Errington, "has specific practical implications, insofar as it places greater symbolic weight on relatively culturally salient lexicons, over and against phonological and morphosyntactic systems, which are generally more interesting to linguists" (p. 724).

For those who study endangered languages and the impact on culture, Hill cautions against a universalist approach, which focuses on the broader issue of Indigenous loss, opting for a more individuated study. According to Hill, to fully understand linguistic change and endangerment, a detailed examination of the specific language must be made which often involves the specific community usage rather than an esoteric study of the language as a whole, as language usage is unique from one community to the next (1983). Hill uses her studies in Uto-Aztecan to illustrate the need for individualized language study by focusing on the demographics and functional shifts of different communities along with their patterns of decay and loss.

Hill examines one hypothesis involving language loss which claims that often, in an attempt to revitalize an endangered language, original information is no longer being conveyed and that "users" are instead "making a sort of 'phatic' gesture of ethnic identification". This hypothesis understands the language to be used only as a gesture indicating earlier times of language fluency. A second hypothesis claims that the "reduction of frequency of complex sentences in language death is…a manifestation of an antistructural solidarity code" (p. 271). An underlying assumption of both hypotheses is that language decay can be studied separately from cultural decay as the decline of language fits observable patterns. Hill argues that there is no "homogeneity in the process [of decay or death] to justify the current emphasis on universals" (p. 272). Errington also emphasizes the need to focus on individual community language loss rather than an over-simplification or universalizable pattern for language loss. However, her research continues to emphasize theoretical concerns rather than the impact on the communities suffering the loss.

In the study of creolized language, Mufwene engages a type of genetic linguistics, which establishes a system of language birth, death, and creolization (Mufwene 2004). According to Mufwene, the process of creolization and language death is something that can neither be easily traced, nor can it be viewed as a particular historical event, which makes the process complex and easily misinterpreted. According to Mufwene, creolization occurs over time and is "used to describe community-level loss of competence in language, it denotes a process that does not affect all speakers at the same time or to the same extent" (p. 204). While accepting that economic and political globalization is likely to impact language usage, Mufwene argues that there is little "articulation" regarding specifically what is entailed by the term "globalization" and how such a movement specifically impacts language usage (p. 206).

As with Errington, Mufwene claims that the lack of uniformity in loss and endangerment globally and historically implies a need for caution when attempting to establish a universal theory using either political or economic globalization theories (pp. 207–209). Mufwene defines the terms colonization and globalization in terms of "the former [being] interpreted as the political and economic domination of a population by another and the latter [being] interpreted as an economic network in which the more powerful control production and consumption interdependencies. The two seem to go hand in hand but not in the same ways everywhere" (p. 218). Mufwene concludes:

> Linguists concerned with rights of languages must ask themselves whether these rights prevail over the right of speakers to adapt competitively to their new socioeconomic ecologies. Advocates of the revitalization of endangered languages must tell us whether the enterprise is possible without restoring the previous socioeconomic ecologies that had sustained them. Like cultures, languages are dynamic, complex adaptive systems that cannot be considered independent of the adaptive needs of their speakers. (p. 219)

Illustrating creolization theories, Tryon's study states "approximately 6,000 distinct languages spoken in the world today…25 percent, or 1,500, are spoken in the Pacific Islands region" (2009, p. 37). Tryon charts the different Austronesian and Papuan language families noting their pre- and post-contact interactions and explains that with "Polynesian and Micronesian diaspora… there are often more speakers of a given language living outside the homeland than at home…resulting not only in language change in the new country of residence but also serious language endangerment" (p. 52). Tryon does, however, acknowledge the increased threat to languages from globalization and economic requirements in the Pacific. Human migration, forced or voluntary, does create creolized or hybrid languages and in this way those who have moved out of a language region adapt to a new culture and language.

Cook, in turn, examines the phonological variations in dying languages and connects the process to ontogenesis and concludes that "the variations that occur in dying languages are much greater both in quantity and genre than those in healthy languages. Variations resulting from simplifications, including syllable reduction, phonemic mergers, *ad reduction* of allomorphy, are considered to be major characteristics of language death (and pidginization)" (1989, p. 253). The knowledge represented here and in the broader studies certainly advances scholarly work in the field of linguistics. However, for many Indigenous scholars, these articles read like a post-mortem. They have dissected the corpse and attempted to explain the systemic failure; but, instead of identifying the underlying cause of language loss and death, they focus on how the system shut down. Indigenous scholars call for a focus that identifies the *why* rather than the *how* of language decay and death. For these scholars, focusing on the how diminishes and ignores the why associated with colonization. Such discussions also tend to disassociate from the trauma of language endangerment and death experienced in Indigenous cultures.

In examining Western scholarship regarding language endangerment and death, there tends to be an emphasis on language loss as a natural process in which societies choose, or as a matter of course, simply cease to use their traditional languages. Little emphasis has been placed on the role of colonization in these choices or on issues such as the forced assimilation associated with Western practices of boarding schools and stolen generations. The scholarship continues to employ Western assumptions of evolution and the hierarchical designations associated with Western preferential positioning.

These discussions, along with those regarding the legitimacy and wisdom of language revitalization, have been echoed in many neoliberal camps, which place an emphasis on individual choice and adaption in the case of competing language systems. This emphasis embraces theoretical models such as Social Darwinism which claim that languages, like cultures, have a "natural" evolutionary cycle. They are born, they exist so long as they are useful and people choose to use them, and they die when people choose a more "advanced", "civilized", or "economically successful" system.

The emphasis tends to be on "choice" and an individual's decision to trade a less practical or efficient language for a more practical and efficient one. Given the history of colonization and assimilation efforts, Indigenous peoples' "choice" to lose language abilities or to change to dominant languages is highly suspect. Generations of boarding school and stolen children were not given a choice as to which language they would use, and many parents' choices to distance their children from traditional languages continue to be a matter of duress predicated on survival. The determination as to whether this is a natural or an imposed process may depend on whether the reader understands colonization and assimilation itself to be a natural or imposed process.

According to Indigenous scholars, Mufwene is technically correct in stating that Indigenous individuals did creolize or adapt to the dominant languages, but to claim this was a "natural" process or to imply that Indigenous populations freely chose to adapt is at best naive and at worst another colonial strategy that "blames the victim". From an Indigenous perspective, Western academic studies concerning the phenomena of language loss and death continue to be focused on theoretical and abstract constructions that rarely consider Western cultural or linguistic biases in their analysis of the language Other. Few scholars discuss the importance of language diversity as a positive, and others see the rise and fall of languages as a natural part of human evolution. In many cases, the orientation and strategies used in Western research reveal more about Western academic and cultural assumptions than it does the cultures they are analyzing.

Chiswick et al. argue that the economic benefit of linguistic homogeneity is largely a strategy of assumed and "hidden" propaganda (2000). They note that the general lack of research on economics among modern-day descendants of aboriginal people especially in relation to linguistic data fails to offer an inductively strong argument in favor of linguistic homogeneity (p. 350). Their analysis of labor markets and language skills represents significant research in Latin America and certainly points to the need for similar research within global Indigenous populations. While not surprising, the study's results show that earnings increased for monolingual Spanish speakers and decreased for bilingual and monolingual Indigenous speakers, emphasizing Western economic and cultural biases toward linguistically homogeneous populations. Furthermore, the bias is oriented not toward any linguistically homogenous population, but rather toward those favoring Western languages. This scholarship lends academic legitimation to what many Indigenous communities have already known, economic success is a strong incentive to assimilate.

Ironically, many recent approaches to revitalization have come from academic and government sources espousing reconciliation agreements but focused more on political advantage. However, many of these revitalization efforts have less to do with Indigenous peoples and more to do with academic advancement either in the warehousing of dying languages for study or in the form of career advancements for those studying what are considered to be esoteric dead languages. Additionally, government programs to revitalize languages are often led by individuals outside the linguistic culture. This is not necessarily problematic, but often causes a disconnect between the language and the traditional spiritual and cultural connections, especially if language revitalization is approached as an academic exercise. These approaches tend to place the control and methodology of the projects within Western governmental and scholastic traditions rather than within the Indigenous communities.

Rolstad reports the efforts in Central Mexico to revitalize the Nahuatl language and to advance Indigenous education as a means to support economic inclusion but notes that these efforts fail to recognize Indigenous concerns such as suspicion of outsiders in Nahuatl areas and the prejudice faced by Nahuatl speakers in the dominant population (2001–2002). Using Fishman's (1991) "Stages of Reversing Language Shift" in her analysis of data and interviews, Rolstad focuses on literacy acquisition as a joint Indigenous-State endeavor. She acknowledges that literacy acquisition in schools involves community-based Elder involvement but also argues that the control of these programs should remain in the hands of the State. Acknowledging the need for a grassroots effort, Rolstad also recognizes that obstacles such as finding qualified teachers, proper funding, and the need for two-way immersion must be addressed, requiring State management of these efforts. Rolstad does, however, support the unique stance that would require both Native and non-Native students to be taught the Nahuatl language in order to promote cultural understandings and equity (pp. 15–16).

In a similar move to unite Indigenous and dominant communities, Mendoza-Mori argues that acknowledging and supporting Indigenous languages like Quechua at the university level is not only an important part of preserving Latina/o identity, but it also works to decrease the prejudice toward Quechua-speaking individuals (2017). "As scholars, we need institutional and financial backing to accompany and actively support the process of making Indigenous Cultures and languages relevant in a variety of contexts" (2017, p. 54). Mendoza-Mori believes universities should promote Indigenous language curricula as a matter of social justice. The idea being a sort of "trickle-down" model that normalizes Indigenous languages in academia and spreads to the larger dominant culture. There is concern as to whether such an approach could have a positive impact on Western society, or even on a given academic community within the university, as it would require dominant academics, and laity, to acquire the linguistic knowledge. As observed in the Rolstad model, language acquisition remains problematic. Leitner and Malcolm have compiled academic articles discussing the use of and support for similar types of linguistic projects in Australia (2010).

While voices such as Hale, Mithun, and Battiste have chronicled the need to preserve the complexity and value of language diversity because it preserves human wisdom, it may be Harrison that is most familiar within both academic and non-academic circles. Harrison's book *When Languages Die* and the corresponding lecture on YouTube have opened the discussion to the broader population (2007a). Using Indigenous voices and knowledge, Harrison's research gives insight into the Indigenous approaches to language. Allowing the Indigenous people to speak for themselves, he explores the intricacies of languages from their perspective and chronicles the complexities related to community experiences such as those involving reindeer herding and time orientations in specific communities.

He also explores the significance of oral language in cultures that value it above written language for its ability to communicate "tone of voice, loudness, excitement, gestures, facial expression and tempo...all those things that make a story come alive" (p. 145). The significance of storytelling as communication is an intricate and significant part of Indigenous language often neglected or dismissed in Western academics which employ a written model and identify oral communication as less accurate and often as less sophisticated. Harrison's study attempts to provide evidence to dispel these prejudices against oral forms of communication by examining the complexities involved in these forms of dialogue and the sophistication needed to access these complexities.

Western revitalization efforts can be important partners for Indigenous projects as they can provide economic and institutional support, but they can also reinforce colonialism if allowed to overshadow or subjugate the Indigenous needs and voices. As accomplices in the preservation of Indigenous languages, Western scholars can provide valuable resources to assist Indigenous efforts. Examples of such couplings can be found in the Aotearoa/New Zealand university system. Currently, Maori language and knowledge are being incorporated as a way to advance both Maori and non-Maori students. In fact, the university is accepting dissertations written in Maori. This is still primarily a one-way language revitalization, in that it has yet to be the case that non-Maori are required to learn the Maori language, but it represents an advance in inclusion and diversity.

For Indigenous people, maintaining language and establishing language equity is essential to sovereignty and, as such, must begin with traditional ways of knowing and educating. Viatori and Ushigua provide an example of such efforts in Zápara populations (2007). "The Zápara nationality of Ecuador used their language to petition for greater administrative and cultural autonomy from Ecuador's government" (p. 7). Indeed, they argue that "Indigenous Language programs can be important for unifying individuals and communities as a coherent indigenous nation and for gaining recognition from nation-state governments for increased indigenous sovereignty" (p. 8). Viatori and Ushigua chronicle the political advancement of the Zápara using traditional knowledge and language. In a unique discussion, the authors also argue that Indigenous self-determination should not be understood as requiring the use of Indigenous language but can be expressed in both the Indigenous and dominant languages allowing Indigenous people who have lost their language to participate in sovereignty.

Indigenous scholars and activists continue to challenge academic programs to promote Indigenous scholarship, tradition, and voice while acknowledging the difficulty in finding a balance. Romero-Little offers the following caution (2006).

> [T]he models that are created to maintain and revitalize Indigenous languages often fail to meet the needs, goals, and desires of the Indigenous peoples and their communities. Furthermore, these models and approaches fail to include the intellectual traditions of the Indigenous peoples themselves, including their ways of knowing, learning, and teaching. (2006, p. 400)

## Oral Vs. Written Language[1]

Western assumptions of written language superiority have become so normalized that it is now part of the hidden curriculum in education. Among other fallacies, there is a circular argument built into claims of written language superiority, which have manifested in Western designations of "history" and "pre-history". These designations conflate Western development specifically involving written language with advancement and superiority, thus embedding the conclusion in the premises of the argument. When studied in school, it is claimed that "history began" in the Americas when conquering nations

---

[1] It should be noted that oral and written traditions exist in Indigenous and Western cultures, the difference seems to be which is predominantly used and the roles of each in the given traditions.

brought written traditions to the savages. Prior to this, it is assumed that nothing historically noteworthy took place as that time was pre-history.

Indeed, Western scholars occasionally do allow that noteworthy events most likely occurred before contact, but they generally agree that no record of these events exists or survives in Indigenous cultures as Indigenous communities primarily used oral traditions to mark significant events and to transmit significant information. Doubting the veracity of oral histories, Western cultures assign more "legitimacy" to written information, placing it in the preferred hierarchical position. Justification for claims of truth and qualifying information as evidence is given preferentially to written information.

Western bias toward written information then finds orally transferred information suspect and associates it with "primitive" and "unsophisticated" cultures. In contrast, Indigenous communities often value oral tradition over written for reasons that include the ability of oral tradition to transmit spirit, the use of inflection and sound to indicate meaning and context, and the ability of the speaker to gauge the understanding of the receiver. For these, and other, reasons, the oral transmission of sacred or important information was given to those trained in communication often referred to as storytellers. While the title storyteller in Western contexts tends to indicate falsehoods, fantasy, and whimsy, within Indigenous cultures the term storyteller is a revered title referencing wisdom, skilled communication, and a keeper of significant information. This section will discuss some of the misconceptions regarding oral tradition in order to dispel some of the myths perpetuated in media and educational depictions.

While often ignored or denied, many Indigenous cultures had forms of written languages. There are obvious examples such as the Maya, Egyptian, and Indic, but other Indigenous cultures also claim to have had written languages. However, in many cases, the languages did not resemble Western languages and so were dismissed by Western scholars as meaningless pictures or gibberish. However, as indicated in Aboriginal pictorial languages, the symbols convey information, provide meaning, and give evidence to significant events.

The Inca wove similar information into cloth using the cloth as clothing and monuments to important events. In Africa, knowledge was also recorded as evidenced on ancient monuments. American Indians recorded significant information on hides. In other cases, it has been claimed by Indigenous people that certain clans or societies within a community would use written languages for sacred ceremonies, with it being forbidden to reveal or use that language outside of that specific group.

Indeed, around the world, petroglyphs and geoglyphs refute Western claims that Indigenous peoples did not have written languages. These written languages may not have resembled Western languages, but the observation of difference does not logically refute their existence. Again, it belies Western bias to simply state that pictorial or symbolic written languages fail to resemble Western written languages and so are either not a written language or are primitive or unsophisticated attempts.

One need only look at Chaco Canyon to understand the sophistication of Indigenous written languages that used not only petroglyphs to record complex mathematical solar and lunar cycles but also the valley itself as written record. Chaco Canyon is a science written in lines, architecture, and place that gives evidence to solar and lunar movements. This writing is not on paper, parchment, or other materials common in the West. Instead, the information is written using the placement of buildings and roads in the landscape itself many of which are located across vast distances and are separated visually by mesas. In this way, the construction of Chaco reflected the cosmos recorded in the earth itself. Other than to reinforce colonization practices, it is unclear why Western scholarship ignores the preponderance of evidence that written languages existed in Indigenous territories before contact.

While written languages did exist in Indigenous communities, oral narrative was the most common method of information transference, indicating a preference rather than a lack of awareness of other types of communication. To be clear, Indigenous oral narratives are not like the Western children's game of telephone, as often depicted. Rather, Indigenous narratives involve complex and sophisticated systems requiring the memorization of vast amounts of knowledge often "word-for-word and breath-for-breath". Initiations into this knowledge can take years of learning and practice, depending on the information, placing expertise in older generations rather than in younger.

Adding an additional complexity to oral transmissions of information is that such tasks may require multiple days or weeks for the telling. In some cases, information is revealed throughout the year and begun again the next year, or the dissemination of information may require knowledge of cosmological patterns in relation to Earth cycles. The individual responsible for disseminating the information must, therefore, study and prepare for the intensity and responsibility of relating the information through various methods such as stories, songs, and legends (Beck et al. 1992, p. 59). While there is a tendency to reduce all forms of Indigenous communication to a single format, storytelling, Beck et al. explains that "storytelling" is only one form of oral communication used to transmit knowledge. As with any community, there are multiple organizations, uses, and methods involving oral communication (p. 57). Storytelling is, however, the form of Indigenous communication studied most by Western scholars and predominantly perpetuated by Western media.

Within many Indigenous cultures, storytelling is often considered to be one of the most effective systems to communicate complex cosmologies, epistemic knowledge, and ontological information. Ironically, it is the very complexities of this system that can make it the most difficult type of oral tradition to translate or for outsiders to understand. Western interpretations of Indigenous oral narratives tend to miss what Cajete refers to as the metaphoric levels of understanding. Western interpretations tend to represent the narratives in the most simplistic manner possible. One could claim that many of these simplistic interpretations were unintentional results based on a lack of understanding by Western scholars. However, access to Indigenous scholarship and Indigenous denials of these simplistic translations counters any innocence involving their scholastic continuation.

According to McIsaac, unfamiliar audiences find flaws with oral tradition and knowledge because they fail to understand the process (2008, p. 93). For this reason, Couture (2008) suggests the use of "oral literature" to "oral tradition" rather than "storytelling" (2008, p. 162). Non-Indigenous readers tend to be less prejudiced against "literature", or even "narrative" as conveyors of knowledge which may help in advancing understanding. However, it should be recognized that Western listeners/readers and scholars often fail to apply these terms equitably to both non-Western and Western oral information, granting "knowledge" to their own narratives and applying the term "stories" to the narratives of others.

According to many Indigenous traditions, "…knowledge comes first from the family…", but "…may include prayer, prescience, dreams, and messages from the dead" (Holmes 2008, p. 37). For this reason, oral literature often begins young with shorter stories and over time introduces layers of understanding as discussed in Cajete's "metaphoric mind". Accordingly, stories are often used to "…remind us of who we are…" in relation to family, community, and cosmology (Kovach 2009, p. 94). For this reason, LaDuke summarizes the significance of oral literature by stating that "…our language, our teachings, and our cultural practices are one" (2006, p. 24).

Because of its significance in Indigenous communities and its inclusion of spirit, the manner in which oral literature is stated is as important as the information itself. The individuals, surroundings, and events involved are all part of the literature creating a lived experience that binds generations. In some communities, the telling of the events of the past brings those events into the present, creating a lived reality and so must be told carefully and with respect to the ancestors who first gave the words and names involved (Basso 1996). In this way, ancestral knowledge is incorporated into the knowledge of the new generations creating a dynamic and fluid reciprocity. How the ancestors stated information, not just the information itself, remains a significant part of much Indigenous knowledge. Preservation of these aspects of the knowledge is accessible in oral literature but is often not present, misinterpreted, or missed in the written literature. Indeed, the process involved in information transference is often inseparable from the social constructs within Indigenous communities.

Finally, oral literature requires not only great skill in the telling but equal skill in the receiving. Knowledge transference is a dynamic community event. According to LaDuke, the use of oral literature in connecting "teachings and cultural practices" allows for the inclusion of spirit as a significant component of cosmological knowledge (2006, p. 24). Oral literature allows the sacred and secular to connect in a way that brings together past, present, and future in an interconnected experience of reciprocity. According to Meyer, "[k]nowledge that endures is spirit driven" (2008, p. 218). Reciprocity ethics establish that the "truth value" involved in Indigenous knowledge claims is derived from cosmological connections involving spirit (Holmes 2008, p. 42). Finally, for many Indigenous communities, oral language participates in creation because breath itself is an act of spirit that creates reality.

Indigenous and Western understandings of language differ in a variety of ways often inhibiting clear and proper translation and communication. For example, Western constructs tend to view language in the abstract, as a system of sounds or symbols that are connected to meaning. While Western philosophy has debated foundational and coherence theories of language, language is primarily a matter of function and form. Western theories do use the term "organic", but it is largely referencing the languages themselves such as growing, changing, creolizing, and dying. Indigenous peoples tend to use the term "organic" in reference to nature with the understanding that language is directly related to or grows from nature, making languages organic to place and that which carries the Spirit of that place. Language is then a part of all beings derived from that specific place. In this way, beings, place and language, are a whole, meaning that damage to one of the parts harms all. Languages may indeed change, creolize, and die, but this process is not independent of cultures and people. For many Indigenous people, the loss of language is the loss of culture.

While there are many reasons to study Western and Indigenous language differences, one of the most impactful is the study involving legal evidence.

As court battles are being waged over sacred lands and sovereignty, noting and addressing the biases against Indigenous evidence is important. The use of terms such as "evidence" and "objective" continues to deny the legitimacy of Indigenous oral evidence and spirit or traditional knowledge. The lack of Western-accepted documentation and the determination that such oral and ancestral evidence/knowledge is subjective in nature works to disallow Indigenous testimony.

This prejudice against Indigenous evidence continues to make winning legal cases nearly impossible for Indigenous individuals and communities. However, there have been some advancements in Western legal justice systems as Canada has begun to accept oral history and testimony as legitimate in some cases. B. G. Miller chronicles this Canadian shift in his work *Oral History on Trial* (2011). According to Babcock, the reason advancements have been made in Canada and not in States such as the U.S. is because Canada has admitted its past treatment of Indigenous peoples and, under reconciliation, is working to directly address the consequences of colonization. Babcock notes that the U.S. has not officially addressed or attempted reconciliation for past injustices against Indigenous peoples (Babcock 2012–2013).

## Language and Natural Geometry

The above discussion has already introduced many Indigenous views of language, but this section intends to give additional detail in order to promote an understanding of the interrelation of place, beings, and language and to further dispel the myth that Indigenous language fails in complexity and sophistication. As language is understood to be "grown" from place, words tend to mimic the sounds of lived experiences in nature including water, wind, and animals. According to Locust, "a word is good only if it can be connected to nature or if it can be signed, as signing is a visual representation of interactions with nature". She further notes that communication "needs to be tended like a garden, fed and harvested at the correct times".

Locust frequently points out that too often Western languages "over-feed" their words, growing them to "two or three times the required size and so losing the sweetest flavor". The idea here is that language should be accessible to all. For communication to be successful, those involved must be in equitable positions. The use of "12-dollar words" and "specialty jargon" inhibits understanding and asserts a hierarchy of power that diminishes communication and often works to subjugate those unfamiliar with the terms. Similarly, speaking quickly and loudly can intrude on the thoughts of others and, rather than convincing them of a specific position, it beats them into submission. For Indigenous people, language contains both the sacred and secular, and therefore should be approached thoughtfully and cautiously. According to Locust, the proper use of language entails that none be harmed in the process.

One way to better understand Indigenous language construction is to investigate its involvement with natural geometry.[2] Understanding that all things participate in Spirit and that the universe flows from the Creator and that all things continue to participate in the creative process once created, one begins to comprehend the integral relation between the sacred, nature, and language. Each participates in and reveals the other through patterns. As expressed in these cosmologies, there is a direct connection between how things are to be ordered on Earth and the cosmic order established by the Architect (Creator) (Mbiti 2006, p. 39).

For many Indigenous peoples, the reflection of cosmic patterns goes beyond human communal structures and organizations and is found throughout nature, forming what has been called natural geometry which reveals microcosm and macrocosm reciprocity relations.[3] While Indigenous populations recognize various natural mathematical and geometrical patterns, one set of these repeating patterns is of particular interest to Western science, which they refer as fractals.[4]

Indigenous sciences understand these repeating patterns, including fractals, to be the revelation of the sacred. Circles, spirals, triangles, and other shapes are clearly experienced in leaves, sea shells, and other natural phenomena, but, from many Indigenous perspectives, thoughts, emotions, and spirit also participate in these patterns. To illustrate this point, Eglash examines the use of fractal patterns in African societies noting the existence of these patterns in everything from hair braiding, to architecture, to the creation of entire communities (2005). While acknowledging the use of non-fractal repeating patterns in African natural geometry, Eglash argues that the specific use of fractals is prevalent and "quite striking" in African communities. He acknowledges that there are examples in global Indigenous communities involving

---

[2]In the West, it is often called sacred geometry. The term "sacred geometry" has also been used to refer to Indigenous understandings, but it often fails to capture the relation to nature. We prefer the term natural geometry as it places the focus on nature, rather than on theoretical or theological discussions.

[3]Because it too is derived from nature, language also participates in these patterns both organically and through description.

[4]Fractals are generally described as complex patterns that repeat at larger and smaller scales. Western cultures tend to represent these mathematically. Indigenous cultures recognize the mathematics but also relate these patterns to all aspects of existence including language.

fractals, but they are less common with the focus being on other natural geometrical patterns (pp. 20–21).

According to Eglash, while fractals can be linked to some Indigenous cultures, the majority exhibit non-fractal forms of natural geometry (2005). For example, he argues that Ancestral dwellings such as those found in the Chaco Canyon region are "primarily characterized by an enormous circular form created from smaller rectangular components" and, while not fractals, express "the most important design themes in the material culture of many Native American societies, including North and South continents" (p. 40). Additionally, Eglash notes the references to these natural geometries in North and South American Indigenous artifacts as well as in histories and narratives such as Black Elk's dialogue on the power of circles (p. 42).

Two areas in which Eglash did observe fractal patterns, outside of Africa, were in the Pacific Northwest and in the South Pacific. According to Eglash, the Pacific Northwest communities of the Haida, Kwakiutl, and Tlingit evidenced carvings that "have the kind of global, nonlinear self-similarity necessary to qualify as fractals and clearly exhibit recursive scaling of up to three or four iterations" (p. 43). He also describes the fractal patterns exhibited in South Pacific cultures, particularly in the tattoo patterns of the Maori, which he describes as being related directly to the Maori culture as "they emphasize mirror-image symmetries, which are associated with their cultural themes of complementarity" (p. 47).

Eglash provides equally interesting discussions of mathematics, recursives, and infinity, all of which reflect elements of natural geometry known and expressed in Indigenous societies before Western contact. While Eglash notes a general historical and global use of natural geometry including various uses of fractals, he is clear that these occurrences do not claim the existence of a single or universal Indigenous natural geometry.

> Comparing the Mayan snake pattern with the African weaving based on the cobra skin pattern…we can see how geometric modeling of similar natural phenomena in these two cultures results in very different representations. The Native American example emphasizes the Euclidean symmetry *within one* size frame…This Mayan pattern is composed of four shapes in the same size, a fourfold symmetry. But the African example emphasizes fractal symmetry, which is not about similarity between right/left or up/down, but rather similarity *between different* size frames. The African snake pattern shows diamonds within diamonds within diamonds. (p. 43)

Specifically focusing on numbers, Urton gives an account of natural mathematics involving Quechua ontology in *The Social Life of Numbers* (Urton 1997). Urton explains that Quechua arithmetic begins with:

> ...*yapa,* which constitutes what we could call the first principle of Quechua arithmetic and mathematics, is the appropriate logical and cultural point of departure for a study of Quechua mathematical operations because it provides the rationale for the conceptualization of arithmetic and mathematics both as a type of human activity and as a cultural production. It should be clear from this outline how radically Quechua mathematics differs from at least certain traditions of pure mathematics (especially formalism) in the West. (pp. 147–148)

Urton then gives evidence of the difference between Western and Quechua mathematical systems in his discussion of Quechua systems of equilibrium and rectification. His discussions of additions, subtraction, multiplication, and division provide ample evidence of the interrelation of culture, nature, mathematics, and language. The relationship is furthered in his appendix titled "Quechua Number Symbols and Metaphors", which explains this reciprocal relationship in more detail (1997).

The use of these examples is not to confound the reader with mathematical and geometrical theory, but rather to document factors of Indigenous lived experiences defined by the reciprocal and interrelatedness of beings, place, and language. The primacy of Spirit infuses these patterns in all aspects of this lived experience. Two things should be taken from this discussion, if nothing else. First, Indigenous cultures exhibit complex, comprehensive, and sophisticated epistemologies from ancient times that rival anything found in the West. Second, Indigenous ontological systems exhibit a reciprocal and recurring set of patterns that flow through and express reality in all aspects of being. Language is, therefore, simply one part of the larger organic whole that both reflects and participates in Spirit.[5]

## Indigenous Language

This chapter more than any other may seem repetitious to readers, and, in many ways, it is appropriate that such repetition comes toward the center of the book in a discussion of repeating patterns and fractals as this book

---

[5] It may be of interest to some readers that studies coming out of Canada show improvement in Indigenous student scores when mathematics and geometry are related back to community and nature.

wishes to participate in Indigenous epistemology. However, what may appear to be repetitious is, in fact, an attempt to spiral more deeply into Indigenous knowledge claims so as to continuously make connections between different parts of the whole. As can be observed throughout Indigenous communication, repeating patterns are understood to enhance both the transmission and the acceptance of knowledge.

Moreover, the use of breath in language is part of what Cajete called dynamic creation associated with spirit (2000). The energy of the words, then, carries positive and negative connotations which impact all beings to whom one is related. It is understood that words are powerful and oral literature used in its various forms has the power to assist or to harm individuals and communities. For this reason, many Indigenous communities teach children to be careful with language as they have a responsibility to use energy carefully.

While Western cultures understand the idea that words hurt and can shift power, there is not the link to Spirit that exists in Indigenous understandings of language. It is the spirit of language that is unique in Indigenous cultures and the ability to speak things into existence that often means that negative things will not be spoken of in certain cultures or situations. Language energy, therefore, is a significant part of medicine and will be discussed more in the chapter on health.

Language also binds generations and dimensions in many Indigenous traditions. For example, the Maori understands that "individuals had participated in the lives of their ancestors, so that their own lives went backward in time to early events. An orator describing an early event in his people's history might speak as though he himself had been present at the scene" (Orbell 1998, p. 9). The ability of an orator, or storyteller, to bring to life ancestral beings and events, for many Indigenous cultures, is not strictly metaphor. It is a reality and is explained by nonlinear time and connections between, what Westerners might call, different dimensions or realities. The use of song, chant, and words can, for many Indigenous people, create a way to link, spiritually and physically, original creation with continued creation patterns. Understanding the power of voice helps one to understand the power of chants and songs in healing, and in harming other beings. It is also understood that language is used differently in the daily communication of things such as harvesting and cooking than it is in ceremony, but in each Spirit is present.

Silko cautions that "the words most highly valued are those spoken from the heart, unpremeditated and unrehearsed…a written speech or statement is highly suspect because the true feelings of the speaker remain hidden as she reads words that are detached from the occasion and the audience" (1997, p. 48). Silko explains that Pueblo communication is similar to a spider's web in that the lines are not straight but intersect other lines of knowledge. "As with the web, the structure emerges as it is made, and you must simply listen and trust, as the Pueblo people do, that meaning will be made". Silko further explains that language "embraces the whole of creation and the whole of history and time" (p. 49).

Silko continues to explain that storytelling involves both the speaker and the listener and that while language plays its part, it is the meaning that is most important. The speaker must do her best to give the story, but the listener must also do her best to receive the meaning. The stories explain not only creation, but family in a way that allows one to understand her own identity and place (pp. 50–51). She notes that, as the Pueblo were not relocated, their language and geographical area remain intact bringing together the past and the future in a way that removed Indigenous communities may no longer experience. As she states,

> we are still *all* in *this* place, and language—the storytelling—is our way of passing through or being with them, of being together again… 'going over' as a journey, a journey that perhaps we can only begin to understand through an appreciation for the boundless capacity of language that, through storytelling, brings us together, despite great distances between cultures, despite great distances in time. (pp. 58–59)

Basso echoes these statements in his work with Western Apache and the use of place-names. He notes that place-names are essential to the understanding of self and community and "involves multiple acts of remembering and imagining which inform each other in complex ways" (1996, p. 5). He states that "we *are*, in a sense, the place-worlds we imagine" (p. 7). His account of learning and chronicling the place-names for the Apache involves not only obtaining the information, but also learning correctly and taking the time to appreciate just how the ancestors had spoken the place-names (pp. 10–12). Taking the time to correctly pronounce the place-names and to learn the stories to bring the past into the present merges ancestors and times to allow for a complete understanding of reality.

This interconnectivity of place and time is revealed in the languages themselves as they are often "verb based, and the words that describe the world emerge directly from actively perceived experience" (Cajete 2000, p. 27). It is the experience of the active and constantly changing world that disallows a stagnant language, while at the same time establishing a constancy that reveals ancient ways of being. DiNova states that "indigenous theory…is not rooted in a fundamental separation of the name and named. Since the indigenous worldview, like indigenous languages, is process-oriented, such a separation is not conceivable" (2005, p. 52).

DiNova argues that both Western and Indigenous cultures are "steeped" in story that determines "truth and knowledge" making Western interpretations of Indigenous cultures suspect. If, for example, Western discussions of Indigenous ways of being are done using Western "truth and knowledge", great harm is created as Indigenous "truth and knowledge" is denied or destroyed. According to DiNova, "Blood memory, as Momaday presents it, is present in all people, whether acknowledged or not. Blood memory is story in its physical form, which implies a physical basis for the web of relations" (pp. 73–74).

DiNova's indigenist criticism functions to recognize and reassert blood memory in Indigenous narratives that are threatened by Western narratives. Interestingly, in referencing Joy Harjo's statement "ultimately everyone is a relative", DiNova's theory brings forth an aspect of Indigenous understanding that is often overlooked by Western narratives, that if all things are related, so too are all people. She notes that "diversity has always been crucial to survival from an Aboriginal perspective. An indigenist criticism, then, does not abandon non-Native scholars; it simply abandons the intensely isolating and increasingly prevalent dance towards death into which colonialism urges all people of the earth" (p. 180).

It is this understanding of relations that establishes the ethic of reciprocity that often causes Indigenous peoples to refrain from the use of "I" or "me" and instead focus on "we". The use of "we" by Indigenous people has often been misunderstood by non-Indigenous scholars. "We" can be both singular and plural. If one says, "we went to the market", it may, in fact, be the case that only one person went to the market; yet in making the statement, that person may indeed reference "we". After all, in going to the market, one brings all her relations, not only in the way one buys the food, but in the caring for the others and in the traversing through nature to get to the market. Going to the market is not an individual endeavor.

As Locust has explained, the use of "I" and "me" indicates an isolation from all other beings and places, it puts the emphasis on the individual as separate from her involvement with the community. This is not to say that Indigenous communities fail to celebrate individuals, it is to say that celebrations are done within the web of relations. The use of "we" as both singular and plural is a reminder of reciprocity ethics. Cordova explains that "societies based on the principle of the I as the essential bargaining unit see the individual as being 'at war' with each and every other individual" (2004, p. 174). According to Cordova, Indigenous communities have a primary understanding of humans as social animals, making it important to relate choices and actions to the entire community.

Actions and choices, therefore, have consequences, not only for the individual, but also for the community (pp. 178–179). Indigenous children are brought up with the "we" understanding that choices impact one's relations, making it important to consider all potential outcomes before choosing an action. Locust tells of a Cherokee Elder, Standing Wolf, who used to tell the story of the leaf. He would say that before one decides how to act, she must first consider all sides of the leaf.[6] There are, of course, two sides that the children often get quickly, the top and the bottom. However, when running along the edge of the leaf, there are the east, south, west, and north sides of the leaf as well. These sides face each of the four cardinal directions. The children are told to consider the possible consequences for relations in every direction. Only after doing so, is one to put herself in the middle as the "we" that joins the relations. When the joining is complete, the decision can be made. Standing Wolf stated that there are seven directions for seven perspectives before a decision is made or an action is pursued. This does make deliberation a bit lengthy, a factor that many Western individuals find frustrating as they tend to value the quick and decisive decisions. However, quick and decisive does not allow time to consider all positions and all relations. Indigenous ethics require time, and "when one has thought on it long enough", a decision can be made.

The use of "we" can also introduce Indigenous concepts of excellence. Hester explains that in Choctaw, information is given through stories, which indicate that one either has experienced the event or has "known through hearsay" and "the difference between the two is made clear" (2004, p. 183). Hester notes that in Choctaw context is essential as "there are no words for 'he', 'she', 'it', or 'they'… either you know by context of what is being referred to, or you don't" (pp. 183–184). He states that in this way the language itself is efficient, using a few words.

"By speaking few words we allow others their own understanding; we assume others are aware of the context" (p. 184). Hester's discussion focuses on education and the use of respect, without command or correction that allows the individual to come to an understanding. This model allows the individual to experience and consider without being embarrassed or humiliated. It also allows for the importance of the individual's subjective context. Excellence is, then, in the teacher for allowing one to learn as well as in

---

[6]At this point, a leaf is often taken from the ground and placed in a child's hand or a child's hand is held out to resemble a leaf.

the learner who is working through the situation and coming to an understanding. Education is never about enforcing one's opinion or understanding of the other (pp. 186–187). It appears that the excellence is in the context itself.

What becomes understood in reading works such as Hester's is the importance of silence, an often-forgotten aspect of language. Josephs states that her work with the Yolngu in Australia gave her insight into similar concepts of internal and external understanding (2008). She states that, "knowing, for Yolngu, is always being approached as an interior *experience* for the individual" (p. 174). She explains the act of storytelling as being one where "the Ancestors (who are Beings, not necessarily only *human* beings), are the stories—and each is intimately dwelling in Place (in country). The tellers *become* the Ancestors, those who body forth *in* dance *as* Ancestors" (p. 177). Silence is an important process for internal learning, as it is "a necessary part of a sacred epistemology or way of knowing" (p. 180). Josephs points out that respecting the silences is part of the Yolngu protocol in the same way as never making a request twice (pp. 184–186).

Basso also describes the importance of understanding the protocol of silence in Western Apache (Basso 1990). He states that silence is involved with much of Apache communication. For example, when strangers meet, there is no required introduction as in Western practice. Instead, the strangers will often remain in silence for extended periods. Basso states that it is understood that the strangers will eventually speak but that "strangers who are quick to launch into conversation are frequently eyed with undisguised suspicion… [considered to be] intoxicated…[or] 'wants to teach us something'" (p. 85). Basso explains that silence is also protocol in courting, when children arrive home, when people are angry, when people are sad, or in cases of ceremonial healing (pp. 85–94). The importance of knowing silence can allow individuals to adjust to circumstances and energies, which promotes positive communication. Additionally, in the face of anger and sadness, silence can minimize or eliminate the damage already occurring.

In addition to silence protocols, Basso explains protocol cautions in the use of humor. He addresses the fact that humor, in American Indian communities, is frequent and often involves the understanding of things being both sacred and secular. According to Basso, humor plays a vital role in storytelling and educating. However, he also cautions that humor can cause damage. In *Wisdom Sits in Places,* he recounts a situation in which a woman is saddened by her brother's illness (1996). The description of the conversation reveals minimal use of words by her companions to allow her to think and to experience the stories. They primarily speak in place-names, which gives her images. When it is appropriate, one of her companions inserts a place-name associated with humor. The conversation is concluded with similar protocol as the woman speaks to the attending dog (pp. 78–85). The stylized conversation is intentional and meaningful on many levels as described by one of Basso's informants.

> The woman's younger brother acted stupidly. He was stupid and careless. He failed to show respect. No good! We said nothing critical about him to her. We talked around it. Those place-names are strong! After a while, I gave her a funny story. She didn't get mad. She was feeling better. She laughed. Then she had enough, I guess. She spoke to the dog about her younger brother, criticizing him, so we knew we had helped her out. (p. 77)

Indigenous cultures tend to have protocols such as these to navigate the interrelated nature of the community and to honor the emotional place of each relation.[7]

Rather than using place-names, protocols in many African languages use proverbs as a means of information transference. These proverbs, similar to place-names in Western Apache, bring to mind the layers of information associated with specific knowledge. Because of the potential impact, there are specific protocols for when, where, and by whom such language is used. In "A Proverb Never Lies", Masolo explains that proverbs "are…expressions to indicate the people's general impressions, experiences, and thoughts…they are told to acquire deeper understanding of human conduct in life" using variations between simple and complex proverbs (2013, p. 37). Masolo also notes the loss of this knowledge as younger generations no longer know the proverbs. Nevertheless, for now proverbs remain vital to many African languages.

Oduyoye offers a similar discussion of proverbs in her book *Daughters of Anowa* (1995). She explains that "proverbs restate themes that appear in ethical and moral teachings". Her description states that men and women have "parallel" groups of proverbs and these continuously change with the times (p. 55). Her book offers examples of these proverbs and analyzes the reciprocal nature of this male/female parallel, noting challenges as cultural dynamics have changed. She concludes her discussion with an appeal to "weave a new tapestry" involving the relations of men and women.

> With intricate designs of mutual dependence and reciprocity, it has a pattern in which individual strands of thread may be traced, but they cannot be pulled out without destroying the whole. Although we love *adwini asa*, we have

---

[7]This is not to say that Western cultures do not have similar protocols, it is only to point out some Indigenous protocols that often go unacknowledged.

continued to weave new patterns. Remember, no matter how restricted the space is, a hen will find its way to its hatchery. Women have set out on a journey to call society back to its divine origin and back to the dignity of the human person. (pp. 75–76)

In concluding this chapter, it seems appropriate to mention some final tips about language protocol. As expressed in a Lakota text, language is the "bloodline" of the people (White Hat 1999, p. 1). These words should be taken seriously as they encapsulate the significance of Spirit, particularly in the case of oral literature. With that in mind, the narratives and information given by Indigenous people should be understood to be not only carefully stated, but a representation of their ways of being in the world. In some cases, reading Indigenous works aloud can reveal patterns veiled by the written words. For example, it is worth reading *Reinventing the Enemy's Language* edited by Harjo and Bird aloud (1997). In doing so, one can experience the echoes from the women who wrote the various chapters. Reading versus speaking/listening the words are different experiences that create different dynamics. Reading out loud is not the same as being present with the women and participating in the narrative, but, at least in part, it may be possible to be transported to a shared place where the voices still linger.

Finally, we would be remiss if we did not mention that not all literature is meant for all people and must be respected under Indigenous protocols. Additionally, not all literature should be discussed at any given time. As Indigenous scholarship is often ceremony, it is important to note that some literature may be passed over because it is inappropriate for a situation or is "out of season". For example, there is an understanding among some of the Havasupai that certain stories should be told only at certain times of the year. For other Indigenous communities, literature may be restricted to specific places, ceremonies, or times of life. As with all Indigenous protocols, these need to be respected in scholarship not only because of the connection to spirit, but also as part of the sovereignty of the people.

## Additional Readings

Anzaldúa, G. (1999). *Borderlands: La Frontera* (2nd ed.). San Francisco: Ant Lute Books.

Basso, K. H., & Anderson, N. (1973). A Western Apache Writing System: The Symbols of Silas John. *Science, 180*(4090), 1013–1022.

Brysk, A., & Bennett, N. (2012). Voice in the Village: Indigenous Peoples Contest Globalization in Bolivia. *The Brown Journal of World Affairs, 18*(2), 115–127. Providence, RI.

Evans, N. (2009). *Dying Words: Endangered Languages and What They Have to Tell Us*. Maiden: Wiley-Blackwell.
Ezeife, A. N. (2011). A Cultural and Environmental Spin to Mathematics Education: Research Implementation Experience in a Canadian Aboriginal Community. *First Nations Perspective, 4*(1), 2–39. http://mfnerc.org/wp-content/uploads/2012/11/4_Ezeife.pdf.
Floyd, Jr., S. A. (1999). Black Music in the Circum-Caribbean. *American Music, 17*(1), 1–38. University of Illinois Press.
Hinton, L. (2013). *Bringing Our Languages Home: Language Revitalization for Families*. Berkeley: Heyday.
Iseke-Barnes, J. M. (2004). Politics and Power of Languages: Indigenous Resistance to Colonizing Experiences to Language Dominance. *Journal of Thought, 39*(1).
McCarty, T. L. (Ed.). (2005). *Language Literacy and Power in Schooling*. Mahwah: Lawrence Erlbaum Associates, Publishers.
McCarty, T. L., & Nicholas, S. E. (2014). Reclaiming Indigenous Languages: A Reconsideration of the Roles and Responsibilities of Schools. *Review of Research in Education, 38*, 106–136. American Educational Research Association.
Spelek, E., Lee, S. A., & Izard, V. (2010). Beyond Core Knowledge: Natural Geometry. *Cognitive Science, 34*(5), 863–884. https://www.ncbi.nlm.nih.gov/pmc/articles/PMC2897178/.
Sterenburg, G., & McDonnell, T. (2010). *Learning Indigenous, Western, and Personal Mathematics from Place*. Canadian Council on Learning. https://www.researchgate.net/publication/265566546_Learning_Indigenous_Western_and_Personal_Mathematics_from_Place.

## Works Cited

Babcock, H. M. (2012–2013). "[This] I know from my Grandfather:" The Battle for Admissibility of Indigenous Oral History as Proof of Tribal Land Claims. *American Indian Law Review, 37*(1), 19–61.
Basso, K. (1996). *Wisdom Sits in Places: Landscape and Language Among the Western Apache*. Albuquerque: University of New Mexico Press.
Basso, K. H. (1990). *Western Apache Language and Culture: Essays in Linguistic Anthropology*. Tucson: The University of Arizona Press.
Beck, P. V., Walters, A. L., & Francisco, N. (1992). *The Sacred: Ways of Knowledge, Sources of Life* (Redesigned ed.). Tsaile: Navajo Community College Press.
Cajete, G. (2008). Seven Orientations for the Development of Indigenous Science Education. In N. K. Denzin, Y. S. Lincoln, & L. T. Smith (Eds.), *Handbook of Critical and Indigenous Methodologies* (pp. 487–489). Los Angeles: Sage.
Cajete, G. (2000). *Native Science: Natural Laws of Interdependence*. Santa Fe: Clear Light Publishers.
Chiswick, B. R., Patrinos, H. A., & Hurst, M. E. (2000). Indigenous Language Skills and the Labor Market in a Developing Economy: Bolivia. *Economic Development and Cultural Change, 48*(2), 349–367.

Cordova, V. (2004). Ethics: The We and the I. In A. Waters (Ed.), *American Indian Thought: Philosophical Essays* (pp. 173–181). Malden: Blackwell Publishing.

Cook, E.-D. (1989). Is Phonology Going Haywire in Dying Languages? Phonological Variations in Chipewyan and Sarcee. *Language in Society, 18*(2), 235–255.

Couture, J. (2008). Native Studies and the Academy. In G. J. Sefa Dei, B. L. Hall, & D. G. Rosenberg (Eds.), *Indigenous Knowledges in Global Contexts: Multiple Readings in Our World* (pp. 157–167). Toronto: Toronto University Press.

DiNova, J. R. (2005). *Spiraling Webs of Relation: Movements Toward and Indigenist Criticism*. London: Routledge.

Eglash, R. (2005). *African Fractals: Modern Computing and Indigenous Design*. New Brunswick: Rutgers University Press.

Errington, J. (2003). Getting Language Rights: The Rhetorics of Language Endangerment and Loss. *American Anthropologist, 105*(4), 723–732.

Harjo, J., & Bird, G. (Eds.). (1997). *Reinventing the Enemy's Language: Contemporary Native Women's Writings of North America*. New York: W. W. Norton.

Harrison, K. D. (2007a). *When Languages Die: The Extinction of the World's Languages and the Erosion of Human Knowledge*. New York: Oxford University Press.

Harrison, K. D. (2007b). *When Languages Die*. YouTube. Retrieved from https://www.youtube.com/watch?v=nmLYo8zQOVs.

Hester, T. L., Jr. (2004). Choctaw Conceptions of the Excellence of the Self, with Implications for Education. In A. Waters (Ed.), *American Indian Thought: Philosophical Essays* (pp. 182–187). Malden: Blackwell Publishing.

Hill, J. H. (1983). Language Death in Uto-Aztechan. *International Journal of American Linguistics, 49*(3), 258–276.

Holmes, L. (2008). Heart Knowledge, Blood Memory, and the Voice of the Land: Implication of Research Among Hawai'ian Elders. In G. J. Sefa Dei, B. L. Hall, & D. G. Rosenberg (Eds.), *Indigenous Knowledge in Global Context: Multiple Readings of Our World* (pp. 37–53). Toronto: Toronto University Press.

International Year of Indigenous Languages. (2019). https://en.iyil2019.org/.

Josephs, C. (2008). Silence as a Way of Knowing in Yolngu Indigenous Australian Storytelling. In E. B. Coleman & M. S. Fernandes (Eds.), *Negotiating the Sacred II: Blasphemy and Sacrilege in the Arts* (pp. 173–188). ANU Press.

Kovach, M. (2009). *Indigenous Methodologies: Characteristics, Conversations, and Contexts*. Toronto: Toronto University Press.

LaDuke, W. (2006). The People Belong to the Land. In J. Mander & V. Tauli-Corpuz (Eds.), *Paradigm Wars: Indigenous Peoples Resistance to Globalization* (pp. 23–25). San Fransico: Sierra Club Books.

Leitner, G., & Malcolm, I. G. (Eds.). (2010). *The Habitat of Australia's Aboriginal Languages: Past, Present and Future*. Berlin: Mouton de Gruyter.

Masolo, D. A. (2013). A Proverb Never Lies: On the Nature of Proverbs and How They Differ from Propositions. In C. Jeffers (Ed.), *Listening to Ourselves: A Multilingual Anthology of African Philosophy* (pp. 36–51). New York: SUNY.

Mbiti, J. S. (2006). *African Religions & Philosophy* (2nd enlarged ed.). Blantyre: Heinemann.

McIsaac, E. (2008). Oral Narratives as a Site of Resistance: Indigenous Knowledge, Colonization, and Western Discourse. In G. J. Sefa Dei, B. L. Hall, & D. G. Rosenberg (Eds.), *Indigenous Knowledges in Global Contexts: Multiple Readings of Our World* (pp. 89–101). Toronto: University of Toronto Press.

Mendoza-Mori, A. (2017). Quechua Language Programs in the United States: Cultural Hubs for Indigenous Cultures. *Chiricú Journal: Latina/o Literatures, Arts and Cultures*, 1(2), 43–55. Indiana University Press.

Meyer, M. A. (2008). Indigenous and Authentic: Hawaiian Epistemology and the Triangulation of Meaning. In N. K. Denzin, Y. S. Lincoln, & L. T. Smith (Eds.), *Handbook of Critical and Indigenous Methodologies* (pp. 217–232). Los Angeles: Sage.

Miller, B. G. (2011). *Oral History on Trial: Recognizing Aboriginal Narratives in the Courts*. Vancouver: UBC Press.

Mufwene, S. S. (2004). Language Birth and Death. *Annual Review of Anthropology, 33*, 201–222.

Oduyoye, M. A. (1995). *Daughters of Anowa: African Women and Patriarchy*. Maryknoll: Orbis Books.

Orbell, M. (1998). *A Concise Encyclopedia of Maori Myth and Legend*. Christchurch: Canterbury University Press.

Rolstad, K. (2001–2002). Language Death in Central Mexico: The Decline of Nahuatl and the New Bilingual Maintenance Programs. *Bilingual Review / La Revista Bilingüe, 26*(1), 3–18.

Romero-Little, M. (2006). Honoring Our Own: Rethinking Indigenous Languages and Literacy. *Anthropology & Education Quarterly, 37*(4), 399–402.

Silko, L. M. (1997). *Yellow Woman and a Beauty of the Spirit: Essays on Native American Life Today*. New York: Simon & Schuster.

Tryon, D. (2009). Linguistic Encounter and Responses in the South Pacific. In M. Jolly, S. Tchérkezoff, & D. Tryon (Eds.), *Oceanic Encounters: Exchange, Desire, Violence* (pp. 37–55). Canberra: ANU Press.

United Nations. (n.d.). *Together We Achieve*. The United Nations Permanent forum on Indigenous Issues. New York: United Nations. Retrieved from https://www.un.org/development/desa/indigenouspeoples/wp-content/uploads/sites/19/2018/04/Indigenous-Languages.pdf.

Urton, G. (1997). *The Social Life of Numbers: A Quechua Ontology of Numbers and Philosophy of Arithmetic*. Austin: University of Texas Press.

Viatori, M., & Ushigua, G. (2007). Speaking Sovereignty: Indigenous Languages and Self-Determination. *Wicazo Sa Review, 22*(2), 7–21.

White Hat, A. Sr. (1999). *Reading and Writing the Lakota Language* (J. Kampfe, Ed.). Salt Lake City: The University of Utah Press.

# 6

# Education

## Civiliza"tion"

*American Indians or Native Americans are broad terms for a collection of diverse people. The term European can no more define a Frenchman from a Swiss than the term American Indian can define a Seminole from a Navajo. No sane person would even try to lump all Europeans into one category, yet American Indians are lumped together, and no one seems to know the difference. No one but the Indians. And we know.*

*Go to Europe and ask, "Do you speak European?" and you would be laughed at. But American Indians are often asked, "Do you speak Indian?". Just as there is no "European language" to speak, there is no "Indian language" to speak, just a lot of different languages from all the different tribes.*

*As Native people, we really can't fault non-Indians for not knowing about our languages, cultures, or lifestyles, because we really haven't been that free with information. There's been too much borrowing from us already (borrowing is a friendlier word than stealing). Unless we tell them, how are they going to know? For that matter, how are the Indians who were unfortunate and lost their culture going to know? There needs to be a lot of educating done about us, and we need to be the ones doing it.*

*I used to teach something I called Indian 101 - a beginning course in college, like English 101 or Math 101. That's where you started in your coursework, with 101 courses. And many people needed Indian 101, not all of them white-skinned, either.*

*In fact, some of the things I taught were new to some Indians who had lost their ways through events such as boarding school; simple little facts about themselves that they had forgotten, but when reminded said they had already known. We had a good time about it, learning about ourselves and our tribal brothers and sisters. But it was serious business, too, because it made everyone aware of who and what an American Indian is.*

*Some students were quite interested to know how I knew some of those things I talked about. I laughed and said, after hanging around Mother Earth for nearly half a century I felt like I learned a few things just from being alive (it has been some 83 years now and it still makes me smile to think I know so little. Yet, I am willing to share what I have learned). But, some of these students wanted proof, Western style proof. Proof like research data. That meant we had to come up with it. And we did.*

*Another thing we need to understand is about the use of terms in this writing. We did a study in 1990 at Pow-wows, asking people which they wanted to be called, American Indian or Native American. This has changed over the years and from place to place. Some did not like American Indian because of the Columbus attachment and the atrocities of that era. But Native American is a contrived U.S. Government term invented because it would include Alaskans and Hawaiians, neither of which technically fit into the category of Native American. Most preferred to use traditional and tribal names, but these are not known outside of Indigenous populations and so make communications with non-Indigenous people continue to be difficult.*

*That study at Pow-wows taught us something else, too, that age made a difference. The majority of people who favored American Indian were older people (35 and up). The twenty-ish individuals favored Native American a lot more frequently than the older group.*

*Another word that we don't normally use often but will be brought up is "generalizations". I've made a lot of them. Sometimes you have to when you are writing about nearly two million people from over 500 cultures who speak more than 300 different languages or dialects. The word "we" is a generalization when I say "we had a good time". I try to use generalizations only when it can be said truthfully, like "we all have belly buttons". No one can argue with that generalization, but someone will surely argue with other statements I make. That doesn't upset me because I know where they are coming from, which is the do-you-speak-Indian frustration that lumps us all together. One of the first things I try to teach other cultures is that we are of different nations and tribes.*

*"We" also may refer to the interrelated and reciprocal ties of community. So, much must be done to understand the context. In this usage, "we" is not a generalization but a way of informing relational properties.—Carol Locust*

# Indian 101

*Often non-Indians know more about us as a collective group of people than we know about ourselves. For example, do you know how many tribal groups there are still in existence in the United States? At last count (February 1996) there were 536, with more groups doing their paperwork for recognition. Although each group has its own language, some of them can be called related or are in the same "language family" because they are similar. There are twenty-one language families, which indicates that at one time these "cousins" lived near each other, but over time some have drifted apart. For example, there is a language family called Dene; in it are Navajo and Apache (southwest), Haida (west coast), Athabaskan (northern Canada and Alaska). The languages of these tribes have similar structures, sounds, and some meanings of words are the same. But a Navajo cannot understand an Apache speaking his own language, nor can an Athapaskan from Alaska understand the Haida language.*

*People from one race often have trouble telling individuals from another race apart; they all seem to look alike. Actually, you can't say that about American Indians because there's a lot of variation in our physical appearances. At least to us, anyway; perhaps someone from Europe may not be able to tell a Sioux from a Hopi, but I bet most of us could. Some tribes have taller people, some shorter; there are round-heads and long-heads; some are darker skinned than others; some have low foreheads, others have high foreheads. These are but a few of the differences in our physical make-up that make us distinctly what we are.*

*Another way we are different is how we live, which is a product of where we live. Teepees are great for the plains but not for the everglades. Longhouses are great if you have big trees to make them from, but trees are rare on the southwest desert. The Tohono O'odham adobe houses would melt in the Seattle rains. And where we lived made a difference in our diet and our clothing, whether we had deer, buffalo, fish, or whale. Or squash and beans and cottontails. Our cultures developed in a relationship with Mother Earth and the creatures at the place of our being, which meant that our ceremonies and sacred rituals developed that way also. That is why some tribes avoid something that is sacred to another tribe. Or a tribe might have a special ceremony for an animal, and another will not have a ceremony for that animal, but for a different animal.*

*When a group of tribal people gets together for an intertribal pow-wow, the drums are different, and the drum rhythms are different. I was told that the reason was because the drum was the heartbeat of Mother Earth, and that the rhythm of the heartbeat was different in each part of Mother Earth. Some northern drums tend to be faster than some southern drums. Some drums are large and resonate deeply into Mother Earth. Other drums are small, if drums are used at all, as other instruments were also used to keep time to the Earth's heartbeat.*

*As a modern human, I've found another analogy to the heartbeat of Mother Earth, or more precisely, being out of step with it. We call it jet lag. Time zones may make a difference, but when you have to fly from place to place you suddenly arrive on Mother Earth at a spot where the Earth rhythm is different from where you just were. Of course, your body reacts to this difference. The best cure seems to be that once the plane lands and you've gotten where you need to be, is to find a place where you can walk on Mother Earth. Take time to attune yourself to the rhythms of that area, and you won't suffer those vague feelings of uneasiness and restlessness that often occur when you are away from home.*

*Now let's talk about how we are alike. These can be used as Western proof if one needs it and this is often used by Western anthropologists. First, many American Indians have something in common that most of us don't even know about: the shape of our front teeth. The two top front teeth tend to be wide and the back of the teeth is likely to be curved. Also, on the next tooth over (on the outsides of the two front teeth) there might be an extra bit of enamel, like a hard splint behind the tooth at the gum line.*

*Why are our front teeth like that? Physical anthropologists call it "shovel-shaped teeth" and identify that with American Indians. Why? I don't think anyone knows, except the teeth probably developed that way because of the diet. The fact is, many still have that characteristic today. The reason it is important is because if you have that particular physical characteristic, you are likely to have another.*

*The next thing one might have is important when you were little: short Eustachian tubes. The Eustachian are the tiny tubes that connect the ear with the throat, where excess fluid can drain away. When Native children are born those tubes are often horizontal instead of being slightly sloping like other babies. As Indian babies grow, the horizontal location does become more slanted, but even at adulthood the slope is often not as pronounced as those of non-Indians.*

*Also, the Eustachian tubes are often shorter among American Indians than in other populations. The combination of a more horizontal position and shorter tubes creates an environment that is ripe for middle ear infections, or otitis media. Indian Health pediatricians see more otitis media than any other condition among Indian children. Chronic otitis media can lead to hearing loss, which in turn affects language development, which then impacts learning.*

*If you have broad teeth and a history of otitis media, you might also have been born with a blue spot on your rear end. You will have to ask your family about that, because it tends to fade as you grow up. The technical name for it is the Mongolian Spot, and it occurs most often at the base of the spine, right where a baby's buttocks come together into the cute little v. Sometimes it is accompanied by dimples in that area, and sometimes the blue spots occur on other parts of the body, such as on the legs, arms, or parts of the back.*

*The reason it is important to be aware of this, and to teach non-Indians about it, is because many Indian parents have been accused of child abuse when physicians or nurses think the blue spots are bruises. If you are living off reservation and there's going to be an addition to the family, you might just happen to mention the blue spot to your doctor. Mention it to the attending pediatrician, too, because it is highly unlikely that an infant would be born with a bruise, yet the blue spot is there at birth.*

*Now we have three ways in which we are alike: our front teeth, our ears, and our rear-ends. If you have all three of these physical characteristics, chances are great that you have two others that are internal: problems with milk and sugar.*

*Milk, especially the powered kind that comes in commodity food boxes, has been called "white man's poison" because of the havoc it wreaks on Indian stomachs. We do not have an enzyme that helps us digest milk sugar called lactose. Therefore, few of us can drink milk without gastric upset, heartburn, gas, rumbling and the outhouse two-step. As a race of people, we never had cows like there were in European countries. The closest thing we had were the buffalo, and I, for one, would not want to try to milk a buffalo. If a culture doesn't have an element in the diet, bodies will not evolve to include that element, which is what we didn't do with milk. It is called milk intolerance, mostly intolerance to cow's milk. Mother's milk is all right, and I raised five children on goat milk.*

*The next internal problem is with sugar. Honey and sweet fruits were about the extent of native sugars. Our biological processes, including the pancreas, did not evolve to handle large amounts of sugar, and we develop diabetes (type II) in staggering numbers. Type II Diabetes is related to diet, which is different from type I, a heredity problem having to do with endocrine abnormalities. Type II is directly related to the changes in our diets since the coming of non-Indians to this land. We didn't have refined flour, sugar, and lard from cattle to fry foods in. One retired Indian Health physician said he could predict when a culture would develop diabetes among its population if he knew when the first non-Indians "discovered" that culture. That time from discovery to diabetes, as a rule, is about forty years. That is plenty of time to develop great problems from sugar, but not enough time for our bodies to adapt and evolve to include an efficient method of dealing with sugar.*

*It is strange that when we talk about teeth and ears and rear-ends, and then go on to milk and sugar, we get no arguments. But when we start talking about alcohol, tempers flare. Some people say, "you just gave them (tribal members) a reason to be a drunk", or "what you just said makes us different, and the next thing (white) people are going to say is that we are different/inferior as a race and just not as smart." And yet no one will argue with the milk and sugar problems, although the same type of information is available about alcohol that is available for them. The facts are simple: we can't handle milk, sugar, and alcohol. Our bodies were made differently, just like our teeth and ears and rear-ends. To stick our heads in the ground and deny that alcohol is a problem is to have a greater problem with it.*

*The problem, some physicians say, is not the alcohol but the addiction to it, which is shared by many persons in every culture. Others say that the depressive atmospheres on and around Indian reservations lead to despair and depression, which leads to alcoholism. And we would be fools not to recognize that these things are part of the problem. It is difficult to say which came first, social disorganization and then alcoholism, or if it was the other way around. It is also difficult to determine if the anger and rage from existing as conquered nations led to alcoholism, or if the true problems were grief and helplessness in the face of horrifying events and the conditions of war.*

*There are medical studies that indicate the livers of American Indians do not assimilate and detoxify alcohol in the same manner as non-Indian livers. But for every study of this nature, another one will determine the opposite. There are studies that indicate the problem is in the Indian diet, which is often marginal in terms of nutrition because of poverty. Certain nutritional deficiencies seem to trigger a need for alcohol, perhaps because it mimics serotonin in the brain which the body cannot manufacture if deficiencies exist. Instead, a type of depression occurs.*

*What we do know about alcohol is that it is a number one killer of our people, it maims and disables many of our children by FAS or FAE, it creates dysfunctional families and domestic violence, and has all but destroyed our Self- respect along with our cultures. So, whatever the underlying problem is, we do have a problem with alcohol. "We" being a generalized group of intelligent people who see the aftermath of alcohol consumption in our communities, and not necessarily "we" being the consumers of alcohol.*

*There is something else that we have in common, but this is not part of our physical make-up. It has to do with our histories and cultures, the stories that are passed down from grandparents to parents to children for generations. Each tribe, clan, and family has its own history, the telling and retelling of which can have a far greater influence on us than we ever thought possible. For example, as Cherokee people we were raised with stories of the removal; this historical experience is not limited to us but is common to many other tribes across the United States that suffered relocation. The horrors of relocation, starvation, disease, exposure to the elements, destruction of sacredness, and destitution of body, mind, and spirit are all part of our collective histories.*

*Unfortunately, we can't say that the suffering is limited to "history", because in many ways we live with it today. The boarding school experience, one that is shared by at least one or two members of almost every Indian family, created a destructive psychological pattern that far outweighs many of the positive educational features it presented. Then there were the social welfare programs that nearly destroyed Indian families, the work programs that created psychological issues in innocent Indian people, and this list could go on and on. This is the intergenerational trauma we face.*

*What we have done is to make a list of the "programs" that have dealt us the most misery in the past 500 plus years. I call them the "Tions" (shuns) of Indian Life - tion as in extermina"tion" ...*

- *Recognition*
- *Negotiation*
- *Extermination*
- *Infection*
- *Annihilation*
- *Civilization*
- *Christianization*
- *Relocation*
- *Reservation*
- *Education*
- *Assimilation*
- *Adoption*
- *Sterilization*
- *Termination*
- *Confrontation*
- *Domination*
- *Negation*
- *COLONIZATION*

–Carol Locust

## Educa"tion"

Historically, Indigenous education in colonized countries has had little to do with what one might now consider to be education. A majority of these programs functioned more as re-education facilities or internment camps used to change the hearts, minds, and souls of the children so that they could function in Western society. By defining Indigenous communities as "savage", "uncivilized", and "underdeveloped", Western communities justified in their own minds the removal, or stealing, of children, as early as age three,[1] and placing them in government-supported and Christian-run institutions for their own good and so they could "evolve" to the Western level of civilization. Ironically, the trauma inflicted on a large number of these children

---

[1] In Australia, some evidence notes the taking of children shortly after birth depending on skin color.

belies any concept of civilization as most of the facilities were run according to military standards and functioned more as workhouses than educational facilities.

The children were at times taught some reading and writing, but primarily so they could serve as proper domestic help, farm laborers, and factory workers. Meanwhile, the children spent months and sometimes years away from their families[2] and in some cases were never reunited with family, losing their culture, language, and the interrelationships needed for the understanding of reciprocity and spirit. These facilities, both the schools and the orphanages, were run by Western adults, but the children were primarily reared by older children.

The lack of community and kinship networks created generations of children detached from community and without Indigenous role models for raising their own children. Negative outcomes are not unexpected psychologically or sociologically when one studies the generations subjected to boarding school, orphanages, and workhouses. The intergenerational trauma is just as one would suppose. What is surprising is that, even in colonized countries such as Canada that have established reconciliation and admitted the violence and trauma inflicted on generations of children, the reality of the damage continues to be ignored and minimized. This chapter will briefly examine the history of boarding schools in North America and the stolen generations in Australia in order to understand the extent to which Western colonizing inflicted trauma on generations of Indigenous children in a way that supported the physical and cultural genocide of Indigenous cultures. The chapter will also examine issues of resistance and current attempts to decolonize and indigenize education in an attempt to heal intergenerational trauma resulting from these practices in an effort to advance Indigenous sovereignty and equity.

## A Brief History of Laws

According to President Jefferson, Indians had the capacity for civilization, but faced environmental deficits. Believing that the stages of social development moved from savagery through barbarism to civilization, he stated that it was the responsibility of White Americans to aid American Indians so that they could "advance" (Prucha 1984, pp. 136–138). According to Prucha, Jefferson saw "no contradiction or equivocation in working for the Indians'

---

[2]The stolen children of Australia commonly were never returned.

advancement and at the same time gradually reducing the land they held" (p. 139). Thomas L. McKenney, as superintendent of Indian trade and then head of the Office of Indian Affairs, whose influence on federal Indian affairs was unmatched between the War of 1812 and the removal of the Indians to west of the Mississippi after 1830" represented what Prucha called the "strong Christian influence" at that time (p. 141).

Indeed, attempts to Christianize Indigenous people were often the motivators of government policy. According to Prucha, McKenney focus on the Christianization of American Indians "sounded at times more like a missionary than a public official" (p. 148). The 1819 Civilization Fund Act established money to be used "at the president's discretion" to continue the civilization process (p. 151). While some in Congress disliked the fund and fought to eliminate it, McKenney continued his support and prevailed by reporting the success of the twenty-one existing schools that held some eight-hundred students. "In 1826 he recommended that the annual allotment be increased, so great were the benefits being derived from the schools. Annual reports showed a steady increase in the number of schools, the enrollment of Indian pupils, and the religious groups taking part" (p. 152).

According to Viola, McKenney used the existing missionary stations as evidence that "a plan commensurate to the object, would reform and save, and bless this long neglected, and downtrodden people" (1973, p. 35). Within the existing mission practices, the manner of conversion/education differed depending on which Christian group was involved.

According to Martin, the Quakers, Shakers, and Moravians "practiced a respectful style of proselytizing" (1991, p. 109). In the case of other Christian groups, the proselytizing was far less respectful and at times even violent as they forced children to convert. Using the Civilization Fund as leverage, McKenney fought for the inclusion of education in the treaties of this era arguing that the "creation of tribal school systems operated by white missionary teachers would culturally transform Native Americans in one generation" (Spring 1997, pp. 16–17). This intertwining of church and state established a pattern of American Indian education that continued into the twentieth century.

By the late 1820s, McKenney called for the removal of the Southeastern Nations, but he continued to advance the idea that "schools should be distributed over all their country. The children should be taken into these and instructed… [in] reading, writing and arithmetic, in mechanics and the arts, and the girls in all the business of the domestic duties" (Viola 1973, p. 335). Grande argues that these claims of assimilation through education were no more than a different face on the real objective of cultural or outright genocide (American 2004b).

According to Cotterill, the authorization of money to support civilization quickly followed by the Georgia Compact "foreshadow[ed] removal" (1954, p. 226). The removal period established multiple treaties that included promises of educational support, but these educational agreements rarely came to fruition, and, when they did, the education stressed American-European superiority as was expressed by Reverend James Ramsey.

> I showed them [on a map] that the people who speak the English language, and who occupied so small a part of the world, and possessed the greatest part of the wisdom and knowledge; that knowledge they could thus see for themselves was power; and that power was to be obtained by Christianity alone. (Coleman 1985, p. 42)

William P. Dole, commissioner of Indian affairs during the Civil War era, was primarily concerned with the consolidation of the reservations and the efficiency of government interaction. His vision was to segregate the American Indians away from the Whites to avoid conflicts and away from rival Indian communities to avoid interactions (Prucha 1994, pp. 463–464). According to Dole, "to civilize and reclaim" American Indians one had to "induce them to adopt the customs of civilization", which included "self-reliance". For this reason, he opposed indiscriminate allotment, but instead believed allotments should "be granted…only to an Indian who had demonstrated interest and ability". According to Prucha, Dole "acted out the role of Great Father, and part of that role was that of teacher", and as the Great Father, he promoted education in the form of "manual labor boarding schools" (p. 465). Enacting a paternalistic orientation toward American Indians, Dole believed firmly in the establishment and use of treaties to "make progress" in Indian territory.

When conflict continued between settlers and Native Americans, Pope supported the growing movement that charged the government to authorize a military solution. Pope favored military control especially in the southwest where treaties had not been put in place. His plan favored gathering American Indians and moving them "where the army would be left to deal with them without treaties" and without the interference of Indian agents (Prucha 1994, p. 273). Dole prevailed over Pope's military solution and the Treaty Era ended by 1871 leaving lands contested and communities in limbo. Prucha argues that "humanitarian attacks on the treaty system and the objections of the House of Representatives to the concentration of authority for dealing with

Indians in the hands of the Senate through its treaty-making power" brought the era to a close (1990, p. 136). Prucha's assessment provides some of the motivation for bringing the era to a close, but Takaki argues that the railroad lobby was a significant factor in ending treaty efforts as the reservations impeded railway progress.

With the military solution continuing to be a powerful voice in Washington, the focus on American Indian education was awarded to Richard Henry Pratt a former commander of black soldiers and an anti-segregationist. Pratt held that segregation was a "mistake" and that the only reason for education was to "complete assimilation" (Dippie 1982, p. 116). In 1822, the Secretary of War authorized the conversion of abandoned army facilities into "normal and industrial schools" for Native American children. According to Deloria and Lytle, the 1882 Act (22 Stat. 181) "can be said to demonstrate a major commitment by the United States to Indian education by taking established federal installations and converting them to schools" (1983, p. 11). During this same year, 1882, Hiram Price, Commissioner of Indian Affairs, stated that:

> Civilization is a plant of exceedingly slow growth, unless supplemented by Christian teaching and influences...In no other manner and by no other means, in my judgement, can our Indian population be so speedily and permanently reclaimed from the barbarism, idolatry, and savage life, as by the educational and missionary operations of the Christian people of our country...The Indian must be made to understand that if he expects to live and prosper in his country he must learn the English language, and learn to work. (Price 1882)

As documented by Prucha, there are two statements that can be understood to frame Indian education during this time in history. First, Commissioner Atkins' address reported in the House Executive Document for the 50th Congress, which stated:

> This language, which is good enough for a white man and a black man, ought to be good enough for the red man. It is also believed that teaching an Indian youth in his own barbarous dialect is a positive detriment to him. The first step to be taken toward civilization, toward teaching Indians the mischief and folly of continuing in their barbarous practices, is to teach them the English language. (1990, p. 176)

Following this statement, in 1889, Commissioner Morgan stated in the House Executive Document of the 51st Congress that:

> Especial attention should be directed toward giving them a ready command of the English language. To this end, only English should be allowed to be spoken, and only English-speaking teachers should be employed in schools supported wholly or in part by the Government…When we speak of the education of the Indians, we mean that comprehensive system of training and instruction which will convert them into American citizens. (1990, p. 179)

Prucha reports that, in his opening statements, Morgan argued that "the Indians must conform to 'the white man's ways,' peaceably if they will, forcibly if they must" (p. 179). In a later address at Lake Mohonk, Morgan stated that "[e]ducation should seek the disintegration of the tribes, and not their segregation" (p. 180). The implications of these statements can be observed in the boarding school requirements established to remove all traces of Indigenous cultures including cutting long hair, speaking only English, forced conversions to Christianity, and the isolation of the children from their families and communities. Morgan's views on Indian education can be encapsulated by his statement that the children "should carefully avoid any unnecessary reference to the fact that they are Indians" (p. 181). This statement resonated throughout what became the cultural and physical genocide perpetuated in the boarding school era.

By 1907, doubt began to arise as to the effectiveness of boarding schools, and Francis E. Leupp, Commissioner of Indian Affairs, favored on-reservation schools, reasoning that it was better to "take civilization to the Indian" with the hopes that it would influence the older generations to follow suit. Arguing that boarding schools bred further dependence, he stated that "was ever a worse wrong perpetuated upon a weaker by a stronger race?" (1990, p. 211). While the mid-1920s saw the closure of some boarding schools in favor of existing and new day schools on reservations, the 1928 Meriam Report became the catalyst for additional closings.

The Meriam Report chronicled the deplorable living conditions on the reservations along with the disturbingly inadequate care of American Indian children in boarding schools. The report documented a severe lack of hygiene, malnutrition, and untreated health epidemics. The graphic summaries of conditions and a general movement toward reform prompted the 1934-Wheeler-Howard Act (USL. 48.984), also known as the Indian Reorganization Act (IRA). The IRA was, in turn, followed by the Oklahoma Indian Welfare Act of 1936, which authorized the Wheeler-Howard Act in the previously exempted Oklahoma territory. Only the Osage Nation in Osage County remained exempt.

The termination period has been mentioned elsewhere in this text, but it is important to revisit it and understand its impact on education. During the termination period, the implementation of PL280 significantly changed the relationship between reservations and the American government, but the termination policies of the Eisenhower administration proved even more devastating. The appointment of Dillon S. Meyer, the former director of the Japanese-American internment camps, to Commissioner of Indian Affairs brought with it his idea to "free" the American Indians from dependence on the government and, in turn, free the government from the responsibility of its agreements to the Tribes and Nations.

"Congress was receptive to the Meyer's philosophy. Espousing a motive as laudable as it was illusive—to free the Indians from bureau paternalism and make them equal citizens of the United States—both Houses flirted with measures that would have repealed the Indian Reorganization Act outright before settling in 1953 on a remarkable concurrent resolution", House Concurrent Resolution No. 108 (Dippie 1982, p. 337).

> Congress proposed, 'as rapidly as possible,' to free 'from Federal supervision and control from all disabilities and limitations specially applicable to Indians' five tribes (the Flathead, Menominee, Klamath, Potawatomie, and Chippewa) as well as all the Indian bands located in California, Florida, New York and Texas, and to terminate the regional offices of the Bureau of Indian Affairs in these states. (pp. 337–338)

While cloaked in positive sentiment, termination policies of this era proved destructive to many Tribes and Nations and moved many communities from endangered to extinct, not because the populations ceased to exist, but rather because the government refused to recognize them as existing. For many Indigenous people, the termination era represented nothing more than veiled genocidal policy.

In 1973, the Menominee won a reversal involving elimination in USL 87:700 and soon after the Concurrent Resolution, Fred A. Seaton, Secretary of the Interior, spoke against the termination of a Nation or band unless that Nation or band agreed (Prucha 1990, p. 244). Three years later, a group of Native American leaders met at the University of Chicago and drafted a proposal calling for the official ending of termination and a focus on "economic development, health, welfare, housing, education, law, and other topics" to promote self-determination (p. 245).

In 1968, Johnson mandated a policy of self-determination, and in 1970, Nixon publicly renounced the policies of termination (p. 248). The 1969 subcommittee, headed by Robert Kennedy before his death and Edward Kennedy after, critiqued the state of American Indian education and proposed substantial policy changes "geared to making Indian education programs into models of excellence" (p. 255). This movement led to the Education Amendments Act of 1972 that "provided extensive support for the education of Indians and established new administrative structures in the Department of Health, Education, and Welfare to carry out the work" (p. 263).

While claiming advancements in Native American education, including the establishment of an advisory council made up of 15 Native Americans and Alaska Natives nominated by the Indigenous communities, Deloria and Lytle argue that the Act only formalized what was already in place and failed to address emergent problems, which increased bureaucracy and created additional issues (1983). The 1974 Student Rights and Due Process Procedure attempted to protect the rights of students in Bureau of Indian Affairs (BIA) schools followed by the 1975 Indian Self-Determination and Educational Assistance Act, which was intended to "provide maximum Indian participation in the Government and education of Indian people" (Prucha 1990, p. 274).

Further tribal control came with the 1972 Educational Amendments Act (PL 95-561) and the 1978 Tribally Controlled Community College Assistance Act (USL 92:1325). The former established standards for Indian schools regarding housing, construction, and basic education and the latter provided grants to establish community colleges. Self-determination was supported in full by the BIA in 1984 claiming that "the era of paternalism is dead" and the BIA would no longer "manage the affairs of the 488 federally-recognized tribes served by the organization" (1990, p. 309).

Currently, the policies of self-determination remain in place in the U.S., but the implementation of those policies has met with mixed results. There is criticism within Native American communities that these policies represent nothing more than hidden policies of termination as choosing to enact self-determination can mean the elimination of government treaty responsibilities particularly in terms of monetary support for institutions such as education.

Finally, it could be claimed that the U.S. has moved away from the sovereignty era into a new era involving the UN and international Indigenous movements. As the focus for evidence and argument expands to include international policies, American Indian strategy has become entwined with the global Indigenous rights movements as noted by Tsosie earlier in this book. However, such an era is relatively new limiting the analysis of an international policy impact on education. It is important to recognize, however, that while the American Indian communities are using international policies to support their claims and the U.S. government has officially supported international documents such as UNDRIP, there has been no effective implementation of these documents.

## Children, Boarding Schools, and Being Stolen

It is difficult to research, write, or read about the boarding school and the stolen children era without the faces and voices of those children haunting one's mind. Nonetheless, colonizing governments, history books, and dominant populations have too long ignored these policies and events and continue to ignore the resultant intergenerational trauma. It must be stated that experiences of the children removed or stolen varied with some claiming to have benefited by the experience. Others relate stories of mental, emotional, physical and sexual abuse, inedible and inadequate food, the lack of working toilets, dipping drinking water from the back of toilet tanks, and medical epidemics.

The differences in experiences represent, in part, the difference between the schools, but differing versions of the events may also reflect differing personalities, resiliency, and resistance among these children. Finally, the different experiences must be understood as reflecting age difference, the ability to interact with family, and the support of tribal communities before, during, and after "incarceration" as it has been called. One cannot solidify the boarding school and stolen generations' narratives into a single voice, as each voice deserves attention, and to claim a single voice as narrative would exacerbate the silencing of children who had already been silenced by the loss of their languages and cultures. With that in mind, this section will present only a few of the voices available in this broader collection of narratives and will focus not just on the American experience, but also on the Canadian and Australian boarding school and stolen children eras.

Understanding boarding school and the stolen children eras and policies can be done, as above, from the perspective of history, law, and pedagogy. In many ways, it is easier to look at the policies and the words of the colonizer. In doing so, one can distance oneself from the realities of these events. To venture into the experiences of the children requires one to imagine and empathize with children, often as young or younger than three, taken from their families and communities and placed in institutions run by people with different languages, ways of interacting, and beliefs.

These children were systematically groomed and redressed to destroy their original identity so that it could be replaced with a new identity and a new name. They were taught to speak a new language, worship a new god, and when they fell, were sad, or suffered from nightmares often had only other children to turn to for comfort.

Entering this area of study and listening to those, now grown, children describe their experience is often too difficult to fully imagine. This area of study embraces an existence where children suffered, became ill, and died surrounded and watched by other children without the comfort of family and community. The stories and pictures of these children question any Western claim to civilization. According to Adams, the American view was that education, either in the boarding schools or in the day schools, was to bring the children out of barbarism into civility. However, from the children's perspective, it was the removal from all that they knew and loved to a foreign and often unfeeling place filled with people they could not understand and rules that were wholly unfamiliar (1995, p. 97).

Children experienced a variety of ways in which they were removed and taken to the different institutions. Some volunteered while others claimed they were coerced, or tricked, and others experienced the "round-ups", which were marked by fear and force. To some extent, the differences in removal were a factor of time. By the 1920s, many Indigenous communities had experienced multiple generations of child removal creating a level of inevitability within the populations. The inevitability allowed parents to prepare children to the extent they could and allowed the children some comfort in knowing other children from the families and community had gone to these institutions and had returned.

There are cases of Indigenous individual and community resistance to child removal. These instances were met with varying levels of violence or imprisonment. In the case of the Hopi resistance, cavalry troops arrested nineteen "Hostiles" in 1894 and placed them in Alcatraz under hard labor until 1895 (Reyhner et al. 1989, p. 172). In 1892, the Navajo had a bit more success in protecting their children. When David L. Shipley, Navajo Indian Agent, came to fulfill his quota of thirty-four children, he was "dragged from a trading post….and beaten" (p. 175).

Reyhner and Eder recount various resistance tactics among the Navajo. They state that, while coercion was attempted with the promise of additional benefits, the tactics rarely worked. Research shows that families hid children in the mountains and when unable to protect all of their children from removal often were forced to choose one child for removal to save the others (pp. 175–176). The sacrifice of these children resulted in trauma for the children themselves as well as for the families and communities forced to make these decisions. Examples of the round-up trauma can be found in reports documenting police searches that moved from "hogan to hogan" and, when the children ran, police would fire a warning shot into the air to make them stop. The children were then "wrestled…to the ground, [the police] tied their legs and arms, and …put…[them] in the back part of the wagon, where they lay until Blair had gathered in the quota for the day" (p. 177). From the perspective of Indigenous populations, the removal and stealing of children represented an uncivilized violence against the children and against the community for the purpose of cultural and physical genocide. As reported by Reyhner and Eder, Indigenous communities such as the Navajo found Western-style schooling to be useless and so would often rotate the children who went in an attempt to keep their traditional ways of life intact (p. 177).

Canadian and Australian policies were similar to those of the U.S. in that officials "framed their efforts to remove indigenous children as benevolent acts of Christian charity" (Jacobs 2009, p. 41). However, Jacobs states that while U.S. policies claimed removal was for educational purposes, Australia made no such claims until confronted with criticism from some missionaries and reformers, who criticized the "government's failure to provide an adequate education for removed children" (p. 41). Australian rhetoric claimed that schools would provide "habits of industry" rather than the idleness exhibited in the camps where the children lived. Additionally, such rhetoric stated that children spent too much time in the camps listening to Aboriginal stories when they could be at school learning about the "good characters of history".

"In the camp, life is without meaning and labor without system: in the school, noble purposes were awakened, ambition aroused, and time and labor are systematized" (p. 43). In many cases, Australian child removal focused on "half-caste" children, children with White fathers and Aboriginal mothers. The removal of these children was understood to give them "a chance to lead a better life than their mothers" (p. 149). Jacobs argues that it was the removal of children "from their families and communities that made boarding schools in the United States and homes and missions for Aboriginal children in Australia instruments of violence, punishment, and control, and, in fact, often more effective…than military conquest alone" (p. 149).

According to Jacobs, official reports claim that Aboriginal women in many cases "dutifully, and gratefully, complied" with removal, but Aboriginal testimonials report a quite different scenario. She acknowledges that, as in the U.S. and Canada, there was no doubt some parents who did send their children thinking it the only possibility for survival or a better life and other parents who agreed because they were coerced. However, in many cases, children were simply rounded up by force or taken without parental knowledge.

Jacobs' research revealed that there is no way to know for certain how many parents "voluntarily gave up" their children or even how many children were stolen as "no statistics exist". Iris Burgoyne from South Australia reported witnessing "countless children stolen from mothers on the mission" (p. 171). According to Burgoyne, a nun would show up on a regular basis to take the "fair-skinned" children. She states that eventually the older children would flee into the bush with the younger children. Burgoyne reports that it was common to hear the mother "screaming" for her child's return and to witness the "struggl[e] with the policeman" only to be told something along the lines of "We will let you know where we put him. We will look after him better than you can" (p. 172). Jacobs chronicles stolen children narratives involving stories of tragic removal with the understanding that there was little hope of seeing their families again. Tragically, the initial separation from families was often followed by the separation of siblings according to skin color resulting in the isolation of these children from all family and community members.

Jacobs reports the dramatic means by which Indigenous parents attempted to hide their children in both the U.S. and in Australia. According to Jacobs, one mother attempted to hide her child from police by covering her in dirt except for her head and using blankets and dogs to conceal her (p. 174). Additionally, she states that while Indigenous parents in the U.S. had some recourse, at times, under informed consent laws, Aboriginal parents had no rights or avenues to fight State legislation regarding Aboriginal guardianship (p. 178).

Jacobs recounts one mother's attempt to reunite with her children. The response to the mother's letter was written on the back and stated, "I consider the girls are much better off where they are; No promise has been made to return them and it is better they should learn to earn their living outside". According to Jacobs, there are multiple archives with similar pleas for the return of children that went unanswered or received similar notations (pp. 179–180). Reports of parents and families attempting to find and reclaim their children by stealth exist, but also tended to result in failure. As a result, many parents moved to remain close by with the hope of maintaining some contact. Some missions did allow some parental contact but most others denied it (p. 181). While Jacobs does not deal with Canadian removal, policies were the same and the attempts to avoid removal and hide children were also the same with similar failed outcomes.

The U.S., Canada, and Australia also have reports of children agreeing to removal to save the family and community from reprisals, to follow siblings who were already removed, to find a way out of the poverty on reservations (reserves) and camps, and to find ways to support their families and communities left behind. These decisions tended to be made by older children rather than the younger ones. Adams reports the testimony of Ota Kte, Lakota, who was enticed into a shop with candy where Pratt was seeking volunteers. He said he was both "suspicious and intrigued". According to Ota Kte, he realized that he was reaching manhood and with no way of gaining traditional rites of manhood, such as war or hunting, this would be the way to show his bravery. He stated that he expected to die in the removal, and he wanted to prove he "could die bravely" (1995, pp. 97–98).

Once at the boarding schools and missions, the removed and stolen children were introduced to Western languages and ways of being. Aboriginal children were set to work in farming and industry settings, often with little or no effort in education. U.S. and Canadian boarding schools often used a work and education combination with children learning some reading, writing, and mathematics, but primarily only what was needed to obtain low-level service and farming work. The rest of the time the children spent in labor.

On arrival at the boarding schools, the students received haircuts supposedly to control lice, but Adams claims that "at the heart of the policy was the belief that the children's long hair was symbolic of savagism; removing it was central to the new identification with civilization" (p. 101). Given many Indigenous associations between hair and spirituality, the cutting of the children's hair was symbolic of subjugation and the stripping of kinship and reciprocal patterns of spirituality.

The children's clothing was taken and often burned or never returned along with any personal mementoes and spiritual items. They were given uniforms, many times sewn by other children at the institution, and in some cases issued a cross. While the timing and manner of renaming differed, the students were given new names, both proper and surnames. The loss of name for many was the most traumatic as it seemed an intimate both the erasure of identity and relations. The scholar Child argues that the name changes were "both practical and symbolic" in that Indigenous names were "unpronounceable, pagan, and sometimes even embarrassing. Symbolically, the casting off of the Indian name and the assumption of a 'Christian' name was the first sign that 'civility' had indeed touched the savage" (2000).

Staff and officials "taught students to be ashamed of their tribal names [and] their tribal languages" (pp. 28–29). Students were told never to speak their traditional languages, pray their traditional prayers, or find comfort in traditional mannerisms including sleeping in the same bed, which was a common practice for children in many Indigenous communities. Children found sleeping in the same bed in boarding schools were often accused of sexual impropriety and punished.

Illness and death were common occurrences among removed and stolen children. The number of deaths in the U.S. and Canada remains only partly documented as are the burial sites, but, in Australia, the lack of record keeping means that there is no way to estimate the number of children who fell ill or died while in custody. Child notes that the poor condition of most boarding schools along with overcrowding and poor sanitation led to issues such as tuberculosis, influenza, measles, and other communicable diseases that flourished and often went untreated.

In the case of tuberculosis, some children were sent to sanatoriums, often without parental consent or knowledge. Child reports that many times mail was screened especially in the case of an ill child so that the parents would not be informed (p. 39). Subterfuge came in several forms, but most often in the form of rhetoric. "In a year when the Haskell superintendent pronounced there were 'no serious outbreaks of disease at Haskell Institute,' he still cited numerous cases of measles and mumps, several cases of tuberculosis that required students to be sent away to sanatoriums, and two deaths due to meningitis" (p. 55). In 1935, Haskell alone "reported eighty-two students with measles, nine positive cases of tuberculosis, and several active cases of trachoma", but, again, no serious outbreaks were reported.

Child also reports that the Flandreau school superintendent, in one case, wrote a letter to the Commissioner of Indian Affairs stating, "that one of the teachers had 'a very pronounced case of small pox' and was 'broken out' while he met his classes". The letter stated that he hoped no "serious breakout" would occur. "Of the seventy-three Shoshone and Arapahoe students sent to the Carlisle, Genoa, or Santee boarding schools between the years 1881 to 1894, only twenty-six survived the experience", many died at school while others were sent home to die (p. 57).

In 1918, the influenza pandemic resulted in the deaths of numerous children but not a sufficient number to close the schools (p. 55). Regarding trachoma, estimates indicated that at times half of the boarding school populations were infected (pp. 57–58). It was often argued that it was better to leave the ill and exposed children at the schools so as not to infect Indigenous communities, but it is unclear that this was the actual reason. Reports indicate a lack of interest in child health at some schools and the unwillingness to spend money to send the children back home.

"Between 1885 and 1913, one hundred Indian students were buried in the Haskell cemetery alone…The youngest students interred at the cemetery were six and seven years of age". It should be noted that not all children who died at boarding schools were buried there, some bodies were returned to their families. Additionally, the records do not include those children who died after being sent to sanatoriums (pp. 66–67). In many cases, these dying children were attended and buried by other children, not their families and communities. The surviving children were left to grieve the loss without access to their spiritual understanding or rituals.

Haebich reports similar conditions in Aboriginal Orphan School (2000).[3] "By 1835 Robinson had gathered up the majority of Aboriginal children in Van Diemen's Land from their parents and masters and mistresses and from the streets...They were placed in the Orphan School in Hobart, the dormitories at Wybalenna and a few went to work... for prominent colonists" (p. 104). The institution was staffed by convicts, with reports of multiple scandals involving the misappropriation of the children's food and harsh punishments. The conditions were described as "brutal" and "Dickensian" (p. 106).

> In an era of general high child mortality, deaths exceeded those in the community outside. In 1835 five Aboriginal boys and three Aboriginal girls died. Epidemics swept through the crowded dormitories and, in 1843, fifty-six inmates died of scarlet fever. In the 1850s mortality rates were eight times higher than for other children in the colony. The children were also reportedly shorter and lighter than those on the 'outside'. In 1848 the superintendent noted that senior boys had many 'bodily and mental infirmities' and some were 'literally Dwarfs for their age." The quality of education and training for the children was also poor. Religious instruction formed an integral part of their learning, with church, daily prayers and religious instruction two afternoons a week. (p. 107)

Beyond the illness and deaths experienced by the removed and stolen children, there are countless reports of physical and sexual abuse associated with the schools and mission stations within the U.S., Canada, and Australia. The children had no protection from institutionally sanctioned or ignored violence and no legal recourse. With no means to understand that physical and sexual abuse was not part of the "civilizing process" along with the haircut and the new name, children suffered in silence. In many cases, it became the norm to experience physical and sexual abuse creating an intergenerational pattern of abuse. The haunting imagery described earlier by Deer is recalled as generations of boys and girls suffered repeated sexual assault. The

---

[3] While not discussed here, North American children could also be found in orphanages that were both mixed race and specifically Indigenous. The conditions were similar to those found in the boarding schools.

initial trauma, and resulting intergenerational trauma, suffered by many of the removed and stolen children by religious and political authorities in the name of "civilizing" them was, in no better word, savage.

When confronted with the evidence and testimonies from boarding schools and mission stations, several apologist responses are common including, "that was a long time ago" and "they didn't know any better back then, it was just the way things were done". Responses such as these fail logically as there were opponents of these policies, and similar practices of removal, stealing, and violence were not implemented universally among dominant educational practices. While such experiences occurred in wealthier White education, they were neither standard, nor systemic. Additionally, White children at least theoretically had legal recourse and family/community access that allowed physical and spiritual healing.

Whether in reference to the people of the past not knowing better or that people of the present do not know the history, Haebich views the "we just didn't know" claim to be disingenuous. Haebich states that she often gets these claims after presenting the information reported in *Bringing Them Home*, which chronicles the treatment of the stolen generations. Her reply chronicles the evidence of numerous newspapers that "uncovered hundreds of stories, letters and photographs" dealing with the stolen generations. She reports that "against a backdrop of apparent apathy or active and tacit approval, there is ample evidence in Australian newspapers of public opposition that was not only vocal but that also influenced governmental removal policies" (p. 564). The same is true in both America and Canada. Given the plethora of evidence, Haebich wants to know "How could you not know?" (p. 564).

## Resistance and Trauma

In understanding the resistance of the children removed or stolen, one must first remember that many of them were taken as young as three in the U.S. and as infants in Australia. Additionally, as Haebich reports in these institutions, "staff combined corrections, discipline, punishment, cruelty, and degradation in their efforts to control and mold the children, who were flogged with whips, canes, and even keys, and starved and shamed in front of their peers" (p. 108).

Intense indoctrination made it almost impossible for children to develop any advanced or well-organized strategies for dismantling these practices. Nonetheless, there are accounts of "absconding, by disobedience, insolence and theft, or by withdrawing into themselves" (p. 108). These acts of rebellion were often met with additional violence including practices such as forcing children to kneel in the snow and pray for hours, whippings, forcing the male students to dress in female clothing and encouraging taunts, or being struck on the head with a cross or a Bible. In many cases, disobedient youths were required to "pull down their pants" for whippings, a practice reportedly used on students well into their teens to ensure humiliation.

Running away from these institutions was a common form of resistance. Most of the children were caught and brought back by the institutional staff or by local settlers; other children died of hunger, exposure, and the occasional wild animal. A few found shelter with sympathetic communities, fewer still made it back to their families, but even these children were often found and returned to the institutions to receive punishment. The punishment was thought to deter further resistance from both the individual child and from the rest of the children.

On rare occasions, student resistance not only made headlines, but also worked to uncover the abuse and mistreatment of children at these institutions. One such case involved Zitkala-Ša (Enoch 2008). Called Gertrude Simmons while at boarding school and later as a teacher at Carlisle, Zitkala-Ša wrote three articles exposing the treatment and poor pedagogy being used within the system. When her articles came to light, Carlisle, and others, condemned her as a poor teacher implying that she was a former boarding school student with a grudge, regardless of the fact that these same people had praised her while she was in residence (pp. 91–95). Zitkala-Ša's publications in the *Atlantic Monthly* were primarily aimed at the "white financial supporters and Indian education sympathizers and asked them to observe a side of Carlisle's education that the *Indian Helper* would not publicize" (p. 95). Her claim was that the official reports coming out of Carlisle, and presumably other boarding schools, had been sanitized and propagandized to gain the support of White patrons.

Similarly, in her book *White Mother to a Dark Race*, Jacobs chronicles the work of women and women's organizations that supported the practice involving the removal and civilizing of Aboriginal children. She claims that these women and organizations often pursued removal for personal and political gain and to show their Christian charity. To this end, they would tout the few child "successes" and fail to mention any child resistance or failure. These women ignored the poor living conditions and health of the children while praising the silence and subdued nature of the former savages.

In some of the more insidious cases referring to what Jacobs calls the "Intimate Betrayals", White women and missionaries would befriend Aboriginal families in order to become "surrogate mothers to indigenous children" (p. 193). According to Jacobs, it was understood that "White women reformers themselves sought opportunities to carry out this maternal work, and government officials recognized that white women could be more effective than men as 'recruiters'" (p. 195). For Indigenous families and communities, the "association carried different meanings: they [surrogate mothers] signified bonds of reciprocity, trust, and responsibility... When white women failed to fulfill the motherly obligations and responsibilities...the families' trust often gave way to feelings of betrayal" (p. 194). This betrayal was felt not only by the parents who lost their children, but by the children who had trusted in the safety and protection of these White women. While the responses of children to these acts of betrayal differed, many claimed the impact of the event remained with them into adulthood.

Scott's research on resistance provides a window into some of the ways subjugated groups work to resist the oppressors (1990). Scott addresses the "public transcript", which is "the way of describing the open interaction between subordinates and those who dominate" (p. 2). According to Scott, there are three primary issues "in power relations":

> First, the public transcript is an indifferent guide to the opinion of subordinates...Second, to the degree that the dominant suspect that the public transcript may be 'only' a performance, they will discount its authenticity. It is a short step from such skepticism to the view, common among many dominant groups, that those beneath them are deceitful, shamming, and lying by nature. Finally, the questionable meaning of the public transcript suggests the key roles played by disguise and surveillance in power relations. Subordinates offer a performance of deference and consent while attempting to discern, to read, the real intentions and mood of the potentially threatening powerholder.

For Scott, both the subordinate and the dominant play a role that belies the "hidden transcript". In other words, the advantaged and disadvantaged may be observed as abiding by the proper "civilities". However, the hidden transcript for Scott is the "discourse that takes place 'offstage,' beyond direct observation by powerholders...it consists of those offstage speeches, gestures, and practices that confirm, contradict, or inflect what appears in the public transcript" (pp. 4–5; 284–303). Scott is quick to note that one should not "prejudge" such actions but understand that they are "produced for a different audience" (pp. 284–303).

The significance of these accounts is that the hidden transcript participates in resistance and defiance, in talk, in action, or both. Rather than participating in open defiance, the subordinates may choose small acts of defiance, which, depending on the dominate, or authoritative, power, may be tolerated as a strategy of control. Scott gives a detailed discussion of the psychological and social ramifications of these transcripts, but for this discussion it is sufficient to recognize that evidence of these types of public and hidden transcripts can be documented in the acts of removed and stolen children. As Scott notes, subjugated resistance ranges from small acts of "ignoring authority" to out-right revolt, and, while he primarily focuses on adult populations, it is interesting to observe similar behaviors in the subjugated communities of Indigenous children. While Apple also chronicles many acts of student resistance, he observes that many of these acts result in undesirable outcomes that serve to reinforce the dominant structure rather than dissolving it. When this occurs, the rebellious acts of these children may result in continued cultural and internal oppression (1995).

A great deal of scholarship has been devoted to the trauma in individuals, and in communities, related to the Jewish Holocaust. The impact on survivors and subsequent generations has been described in Jewish narratives and in trauma studies. Additionally, trauma scholars have equated the individual and social suffering stemming from these events as, at least as, equivalent to that observed from the dropping of the atomic bomb or from the 9/11 terrorist attack. While these studies are vital to the understanding of trauma on witnesses, survivors, and subsequent generations, Kleinman, Das, and Lock warn that:

> we must be cautious when trying to compare examples of individual or community suffering…universalizing instances of atrocity only diminishes their private impact. Understanding the differences is crucial… [they caution] us to view each atrocity within its own historical, geographical, cultural, and psychological context. (1997, p. 57)

Maria Yellow Horse Brave Heart is credited with the original scholarship involving colonization trauma in Indigenous cultures. Using trauma scholarship from studies involving the Jewish Holocaust and joining it with her recognition of intergenerational trauma including issues of addiction, violence, and high-risk behavior in Indigenous populations, she created a framework for understanding past and current phenomena in Indigenous populations. Her work recognized not only the trauma in individuals and families but recognized the subsequent trauma inflicted on the community as a whole.

As stated by Adelson, "social suffering, and responses to it, are social and political phenomenon" that remain relatively nationally and globally invisible (2001, pp. 76–77). As with Brave Heart's research, Adelson's research reports social trauma "manifest in excessively high rates of interpersonal violence, alcohol abuse, and related accidental deaths and suicides" in Canada's Aboriginal populations (p. 77).

Focusing on the James Bay Cree Nation, Adelson examines the social suffering, Aboriginal response, and issues of Indigenous renewal experienced in that community. According to this study, Cree communities are using traditional knowledge in the face of individual and collective trauma to create a path toward social healing. The path is not a return to the past that was stripped away, but an intertwining of the past and current social experiences. The articles in *PostColonial Disorders* further advance this discussion by examining the relationship between social and psychological expressions of trauma in colonized communities (Good et al. 2008). At the heart of the *Disorders* text "is the ongoing tension between modern, rational modes of subjectivity and selves and the 'traditional,' and the linking of this duality to colonial memories of power and humiliation" (p. 13).

## Decolonizing and Indigenizing Education

While the devastation of colonization involving removed and stolen children cannot be denied and should not be minimized, Indigenous communities and individuals are asserting their sovereign rights and attempting to regain balance by acknowledging themselves as Indigenous peoples as well as by critiquing colonizing institutions, histories, and politics. This section will examine ways in which Indigenous peoples are continuing to resist Western colonial patterns of education and community in order to assert their personal and communal ways of being by decolonizing and indigenizing of education.

The process of decolonization is debated by scholars along with its potential and actual success. According to some scholars, many Indigenous communities have lost all or most of their traditional ways making it impossible to regain the information. Other scholars note that generations of assimilation make decolonization unlikely because of an inability to "detangle" colonized and colonizer knowledge and ways of being. However, others claim that it is a necessary practice if communities are to heal and obtain recognition of Indigenous sovereignty, a practice that Indigenous peoples never ceded. For the work in this section, we will limit the understanding of decolonization to the practice of examining the assumptions, biases, and arguments embedded in dominant arguments and practices that lead to theories and practices involving Manifest Destiny, Social Darwinism, and claims involving hierarchical positions of superiority.

Decolonization is as much about deconstructing terms and theories involving dominant powers as it is advancing the knowledge claims and wisdom of colonized and subordinated populations. Decolonization scholarship, therefore, faces a great deal of resistance from political and economic institutions involved in preserving colonial dominance. Among these institutions are those associated with neoliberal political and economic thought which have long worked to unify knowledge in education and to eliminate what it claims to be fragmenting and victim-oriented educational practices.

In pedagogical terms, neoliberal education focuses on the need to create a nationalist identity that will advance an accepted way of being, primarily oriented to the understanding that economic progress represents a hierarchical positive. This model allows for diversity, but within a set of structured and acceptable guidelines. Under this model, educational disciplines such as African American Studies, Women and Gender Studies, and Indigenous Studies destabilize the unified national ways of being and promote individual identification with a victim mentality rather than embedding a proper individualistic and competitive mind-set. According to these ideals, intergenerational trauma is either not legitimate, or represents Indigenous desires to be "lazy" and to wait for "hand-outs" rather than pulling one's self up by her bootstraps and earning what she wants. Any trauma or unfortunate events are to be overcome with personal effort alone. Accordingly, colonization is a thing of the past and should be left as such so that assimilation can be completed (Lovern 2018).

In contrast, decolonization scholars tend to embrace theories such as critical pedagogy that advance diversity using difference as a valued and significant element in achieving social justice and Indigenous sovereignty rights. These scholars also tend to critique the assumed bias of Western claims of hierarchical superiority, which impairs the possibility of global equity. To understand the full extent to which colonization has infiltrated education, we begin with Willinsky's book *Learning to Divide the World*, which examines the way in which Western cultures divide phenomenal experience, things, and others.

In focusing on how "difference" as a concept is employed, Willinsky examines Western assumptions and constructions of superiority used to justify and continue acts of physical, political, and economic imperialism (1998). Willinsky argues that the manner in which difference is used to organize people, places, and things continues to be part of Western education so that each generation is taught to use this method of "differencing". This hidden curriculum reinforces categorical organization and hegemonic privilege through a process of educational indoctrination.

For example, why does the West differentiate people according to skin color? There are other human aspects such as the size of people's feet or the thickness of one's wrists that could equally difference people. The choice to focus on skin color is not argued, but rather assumed. Skin color eugenics is then similar to head shape and "bumpiness" eugenics, which have claimed that the size of one's head determines intelligence, and if one's head is "bumpy", she is likely to be criminally minded. The choices as to what bodily component is to be used to difference appear to be arbitrary and changeable over time. There is after all no evidence of early human differencing based on skin color or cranial bumps.

Until the eugenic agenda involving bodily differencing is dismantled, education will continue to support the indoctrination that certain colors of skin, eye color, hair, or cranial smoothness instantiate superiority and inferiority. According to Willinsky, the key to eliminating prejudicial differencing is in understanding the social constructions of difference in the past. "For a teacher to give an account of imperialism's educational legacy", one must examine "how the world was divided" by those in power and look at the continuing impact of those divisions (p. 251). Exposing the cultural construction of difference provides "the hope of dislodging what too often passes as the human nature of difference" (p. 253).

There is no evidence, for example, that human differencing involving skin color is a "natural" occurrence. One might claim that it is natural to notice skin color differences but interpreting that such observations justify hierarchal positioning regarding superiority has nothing to do with nature and everything to do with cultural and political construction and propaganda. Willinsky states that "asking the school to turn a self-critical eye toward its own practices and history, to how it has both participated in and managed to obscure the privileging of the West, is to ask the school for a level of educational courage" (p. 257).

While Western educational institutions continue to fight against the legitimacy and sophistication of Indigenous knowledge, Indigenous scholars have made some progress in the indigenizing of education. Indigenizing involves the building in of Indigenous knowledge and reclaiming the equity of Indigenous ontologies and epistemologies. According to Cajete:

> cultural mythos...forms the foundation for each culture's guiding vision, that is, the culture's story of itself and its perceived relationship with the world.

As its guiding vision, a culture isolates a set of ideals that guide and form the learning processes inherent in its educational system...these ideals reflect what that culture values as the most important qualities, behaviors, and value structures to instill in its members. Generally, this set of values is predicated on those things it considers central to survival. (1994, p. 25)

His book outlines an Indigenous educational structure using the science of interrelation, spiritual ecology, and place to form a sustainable structure for all beings in opposition to the existing Western educational system that emphasizes human-oriented science and technology in the advancement of material prosperity often at the cost of the environment.

Allen recommends a similar infusion of traditional knowledge involving Maori writings (2002). While primarily referencing literary and activist texts, Allen's use of Maori knowledge can easily be applied to knowledge transference in educational settings. According to Allen, "Carving releases ancestors from wood, from native trees grown in a soil imbued with the ancestors' bones...All representation must be conducted with the care of carving...its spiritually dangerous excess handled in accordance with Maori tradition" (p. 127). Applying these lessons to education, knowledge should be handled with care; it is neither trivial nor inanimate, and its misuse is dangerous.

Indigenizing both knowledge and education requires the understanding that the knowledge in the present involves the bodies of removed and stolen children in a way that changes how these events are handled when teaching history. Building our knowledge on the bodies and spirits of damaged and dead children creates a sacred trust that must be treated with respect and caution. This is a much different education than demonstrated in the first part of this chapter involving dates, places, and policies that led to and controlled boarding schools, workhouses, and missions. Even the terminology changes in the two paradigms. Allen explains that "contemporary Maori writers renew the indigenous past by refiguring it as a necessary part of the present", a way of bringing the past and present together (p. 158).

Referencing Grande, "red pedagogy is the manifestation of sovereignty" in which the "narratives assert the struggles of indigenous peoples and lived reality of colonization as a complexity that extends far beyond the parameters of economic capitalist oppression" (2004a, p. 175). She concludes that:

In the end a Red pedagogy embraces an educative process that works to reenchant the universe, to reconnect peoples to the land, and is as much about belief and acquiescence as it is about questioning and empowerment. In so doing, it defines a viable space for tradition, rather than working to 'rupture' our connections to it. (p. 176)

By engaging with Indigenous knowledge, education has the opportunity to indigenize and explore what Huston Smith refers to as the whole of human wisdom. This exploration of the totality of human understanding provides not only the ability to advance sustainability, but also to promote equity and justice on a global scale.

To this end, we see works such as *New World of Indigenous Resistance*, which is dedicated to the educational resistance of Indigenous communities and their work to incorporate Indigenous knowledge into the schools as an essential pedagogical reference (2010). The text suggests there is a possibility to unite Indigenous and Western education in a way that supports all children and communities. Additionally, works such as the *Indigenous Philosophies and Critical Education* continue to advance Indigenous issues of social justice in pedagogy (Sefa Dei 2011). Journals such as *the Australian Journal of Indigenous Education* have also taken up the fight for Indigenous sovereignty recognition and justice by addressing theoretical and practical impediments to Indigenous student success. According to all these works, the inclusion of Indigenous voice and knowledge is essential if governments are serious about reconciliation and Indigenous equity. One of the most significant advances in pedagogical work has involved the critique of scholarship and methodology in the study of Indigenous peoples and cultures. Books such as L. T. Smith's *Decolonizing Methodologies* are essential if Indigenous peoples and communities are going to be properly researched and represented in academia (2012).[4]

Using reciprocity ethics as a foundation, this chapter has focused on the divergent paradigms in Indigenous and Western models of education including the treatment of Indigenous removed and stolen children and their resistance efforts. The divergence in Indigenous and Western paradigms is marked not only by the way they "difference", but also by the understanding regarding the function and orientation of education. Western understanding of education, particularly the neoliberal models, focuses on individual completion and advancement using economic advancement to determine success. Indigenous education focuses on transferring ancestor and natural wisdom to subsequent generations so that they can experience interconnected lives of reciprocity and balance. Only the latter addresses the healing of intergenerational trauma.

---

[4]The lack of space required that we list some of the collections, books, and journal articles dedicated to Indigenous methodology in the additional readings at the end of this chapter.

## Additional Reading

Atkinson, J. (2002). *Trauma Trails Recreating Song Lines: The Transgenerational Effects of Trauma in Indigenous Australia.* Spinifex Pres Pty Ltd: North Melbourne.

Ball, J., & Janyst, P. (2008). Enacting Research Ethics in Partnerships with Indigenous Communities in Canada: 'Do It in a Good Way'. *Journal of Empirical Research on Human Research Ethics: An International Journal, 3*(2), 33–51. Sage.

Bensen, R. (Ed.). (2001). *Children of the Dragonfly: Native American Voices on Child Custody and Education.* Tucson: University of Arizona Press.

Brayboy, G. M. J., Faircloth, S. C., Lee, T. S., Maaka, M. J., & Rich, T. A. (2015). Sovereignty and Education: An Overview of the Unique Nature of Indigenous Education. *Journal of American Indian Education, 54*(1), 1–9.

Champagne, D., & Stauss, J. (Eds.). (2002). *Native American Studies in Higher Education: Models for Collaboration Between Universities and Indigenous Nations.* Altamira Press: Walnut Creek.

Chilisa, B. (2012). *Indigenous Research Methodologies.* Los Angeles: Sage.

Chun, N. M. (2006). *A'o: Educational Traditions.* Honolulu: University of Hawai'i.

Ezeanya-Esiobu, C. (2019). *Indigenous Knowledge and Education in Africa.* Springer.

Davoine, F., & Gaudillière. (2004). *History Beyond Trauma: Whereof One Cannot Speak, Therefore One Cannot Stay Silent* (S. Fairfield, Trans.). New York: Other Press.

Deloria, V., Jr. (1994). Second Printing. *Indian Education in America: 8 Essays by Vine Deloria, Jr.* Boulder: American Indian Science & Engineering Society.

Denzin, N. K., Lincoln, Y. S., & Smith, L. T. (Eds.). (2008). *Handbook of Critical and Indigenous Methodologies.* Los Angeles: Sage.

Fear-Segal, J., & Rose, S. D. (Ed.). (2018). *Carlisle Indian Industrial School: Indigenous Histories, Memories, and Reclamations.* University of Nebraska Press.

Flores, E., & Kihleng, E. (Ed.). (2019). *Indigenous Literatures from Micronesia.* University of Hawaii Press.

Fromm, M. G. (Ed.). (2012). *Lost in Transmission: Studies of Trauma Across Generations.* London: Karnac.

Goodyear-Ka'ōpua, N. (2013). *The Seeds We Planted: Portraits of a Native Hawaiian Charter School.* University of Minnesota Press.

Hansen, J. G. (Ed.). (2014). *Exploring Indigenous Social Justice.* Vernon: J Charlton Publishing Ltd.

HeavyRunner, I., & DeCelles, R. (2002). Family Education Model: Meeting the Student Retention Challenge. *Journal of American Indian Education, 41*(2), 29–37.

Hinton, D. E., & Hinton, A. L. (2015). *Genocide and Mass Violence: Memory, Symptom, and Recovery.* New York: Cambridge University Press.

Hirst, S. (2006). *I Am the Grand Canyon: The Story of the Havasupai People.* Grand Canyon: Grand Canyon Association.

Holt, M. I. (2001). *Indian Orphanages.* Lawrence: University Press of Kansas.

Kaya, H. O., & Seleti, Y. N. (2013). African Indigenous Knowledge Systems and Relevance of Higher Education in South Africa. *The International Education Journal: Comparative Perspectives, 12*(2), 30–44.

Kennedy, R. (2011). Australian Trails of Trauma: The Stolen Generations in Human Rights, Law, and Literature. *Comparative Literature Studies, 48*(3), 333–355. Special Issue Trials of Trauma.

Kievet, J. A. (2003). A Discussion of Scholarly Responsibilities to Indigenous Communities. *American Indian Quarterly, 27*(½), 3–45. Special Issue: Native Experiences in the Ivory Tower. University of Nebraska Press.

Klug, B. J., & Whitfield, P. T. (2003). *Widening the Circle: Culturally Relevant Pedagogy for American Indian Children.* New York: Routledge.

Knowles, F. E., Jr., & Lovern, L. (2015). *A Critical Pedagogy for Native American Education Policy: Habermas, Freire, and Emancipatory Education.* New York: Palgrave Macmillan.

Lomawaima, K. T. (2000). Tribal Sovereigns: Reframing Research in American Indian Education. *Harvard Educational Review, 70*(1), 1–21.

Lomawaima, K. T., & McCarty, T. L. (2006). *"To Remain an Indian": Lessons in Democracy from a Century of Native American Education.* Teachers College Press.

Philips, S. U. (1992). Colonial and Post-Colonial Circumstances in the Education of Pacific Peoples. *Anthropology and Educational Quarterly, 23*(1), 73–78.

Pio, E., Tipuna, K., Rasheed, A., & Parker, L. (2014). Te Wero-The Challenge: Reimagining Universities from an Indigenous World View. *Higher Education, 67*(5), 675–690.

Prakash, M. S., & Esteva, G. (1998). *Escaping Education: Living as Learning Within Grassroots Cultures.* New York: Peter Lang Publishing Inc.

Reed, J. L. (2010). Family and Nation: Cherokee Orphan Care 1835–1903. *The American Indian Quarterly* (A. J. Cobb-Greetham, Ed., Vol. 34. No. 3, pp. 312–343). University of Nebraska Press.

Reyhner, J., & Eder, J. (1989). *A history of Indian Education.* Billings: Montana State University-Billings and Council for Indian Education.

Sabzalian, L. (2019). *Indigenous Children's Survivance in Public Schools.* Routledge.

Schmidt, J. J., & Akande, Y. (2011). Faculty Perceptions of the First-Generation Student Experience and Programs at Tribal Colleges. *New Directions for Teaching and Learning* (127), 41–54.

Scott, J. C. (1985). *Weapons of the Weak: Everyday Forms of Peasant Resistance.* New Haven: Yale University Press.

Semali, L. M., & Kincheloe, J. L. (Eds.). (1999). *What Is Indigenous Knowledge? Voices from the Academy.* New York: Falmer Press.

Silltoe, P., Dixon, P., & Barr, J. (2005). *Indigenous Knowledge Inquiries: A Methodologies Manual for Development.* Warwickshire: Practical Action Publishing.

Smith, L. T., Tuck, E., & Yang, K. W. (2018). *Indigenous and Decolonizing Studies in Education.* Routledge.

Tobias, J. K., Richmond, C. A. M., & Luginaah, I. (2013). Community-Based Participatory Research (CBPR) with Indigenous Communities: Producing Respectful and Reciprocal Research.

Torrez, J. E. (2014). Edinizing, Naadizewin, Minomaadiziwin, Miinawaa Kendaasewin: Establishing an Urban Great Lakes Indigenous curriculum. *Journal of American Indian Education, 53*(2), 85–103.

Walter, M., & Anderson, C. (2013). *Indigenous Statistics: A Quantitative Research Methodology*. Walnut Creek: Left Coast Press Inc.

Warner, L. S. (2015). *Education in the Comanche Nation: Relationships, Responsibility, Redistribution and Reciprocity*. London: Routledge.

Woolford, A. (2018). *This Benevolent Experiment: Indigenous Boarding Schools, Genocide, and Redress in Canada and the United States*. University of Nebraska Press.

## Works Cited

Adams, D. W. (1995). *Education for Extinction: American Indians and the Boarding School Experience, 1875–1928*. Lawrence: University of Kansas Press.

Adelson, N. (2001). Reimagining Aboriginality: An Indigenous People's Response to Social Suffering. In V. Das, A. Keinman, M. Lock, M. Rampehle, & P. Reynolds (Eds.), *Remaking a World: Violence, Social Suffering, and Recovery* (pp. 76–101). Berkeley: University of California Press.

Allen, C. (2002). *Blood Narrative: Indigenous Identity in American Indian and Maori Literary and Activist Texts*. Durham: Duke University Press.

Apple, M. W. (1995). *Education and Power* (2nd ed.). New York: Routledge.

Australian Journal of Indigenous Education. (2020). https://www.cambridge.org/core/journals/australian-journal-of-indigenous-education.

Brave Heart, M. Y. H. (2000). Wakiksuyapi: Carrying the Historical Trauma of the Lakota. *Tulane University of Social Work*, 245–266. Retrieved from http://discoveringourstory.wisdomoftheelders.org/ht_and_grief/Wakiksuyapi-HT.pdf.

Brave Heart, M. Y. H. (2003). The Historical Trauma Response Among Natives and Its Relationship with Substance Abuse: A Lakota Illustration. *Journal of Psychoactive Drugs, 35*(1), 7–13.

Brave Heart, M. Y. H., Chase, J., Eikins, J., & Altschul, D. B. (2011). Historical Trauma Among Indigenous Peoples of the Americas: Concepts, Research, and Clinical Considerations. *Journal of Psychoactive Drugs, 43*(4), 282–290.

Cajete, G. (1994). *Look to the Mountain: An Ecology of Indigenous Education*. Skyland: Kivaki Press.

Child, B. J. (2000). *Boarding School Season: American Indian Families 1900–1940*. Lincoln: University of Nebraska Press.

Chomsky, N. (2010). *New World of Indigenous Resistance*. City Lights Publishers.

Coleman, M. C. (1985). *Presbyterian Attitudes Toward American Indians 1837–1893*. Jackson: University of Mississippi Press.

Cotterill, R. (1954). *The Southern Indians: The Story of the Civilized Tribes Before Removal*. Norman: University of Oklahoma Press.

Deer, S. (2015). *The Beginning and End of Rape: Confronting Sexual Violence in Native America* (3rd ed.). Minneapolis: University of Minnesota.

Deloria, V., Jr., & Lytle, C. M. (1983). *American Indians, American Justice*. Austin: University of Texas Press.

Dippie, B. W. (1982). *The Vanishing American*. Lawrence: University of Kansas Press.

Enoch, J. (2008). *Refiguring Rhetorical Education: Women Teaching African American, Native American, and Chicano/a Students 1865–1911*. Carbondale: Southern Illinois University Press.

Good, M. D., Hyde, S. T., Pinto, S., & Good, B. J. (Eds.). (2008). *Postcolonial Disorders*. Berkeley: University of California Press.

Grande, S. (2004a). *Red Pedagogy: Native American Social and Political Thought*. Lanham: Rowman & Littlefield Publishers Inc.

Grande, S. (2004b). American Geographies of Identity and Power: At the Crossroads of Indigena and Mestizaje. *Harvard Educational Review, 70*(4), 467–498.

Haebich, A. (2000). *Broken Circles: Fragmenting Indigenous Families 1800–2000*. Fremantle: Fremantle Arts Centre Press.

Jacobs, M. D. (2009). *White Mother to a Dark Race: Settler Colonialism, Maternalism, and The removal of Indigenous Children in the American West and Australia, 1880–1940*. Lincoln: University of Nebraska Press.

Kleinman, A., Das, V., & Lock, M. (Eds.). (1997). *Social Suffering*. Berkeley: University of California Press.

Lovern, L. L. (2018). *Fostering a Climate of Inclusion in the College Classroom: The Missing Voice of the Humanities*. Gewerbestrasse: Palgrave Macmillan.

Martin, J. W. (1991). *Sacred Revolt: The Muskogees' Struggle for a New World*. Boston: Beacon Press.

Meriam Report. (1928). *National Indian Law Library*. https://narf.org/nill/resources/meriam.html.

Price, H. (1882). *House Executive Document no. 1*. 47th Congress, 2nd session.

Prucha, F. P. (1984). *The Great Father: The United States Government and the American Indians* (unabridged ed., Vol. I and II). Lincoln: University of Nebraska Press.

Prucha, F. P. (Ed.). (1990). *Documents of United States Indian Policy* (2nd ed.). Lincoln: University of Nebraska Press.

Prucha, F. P. (1994). *American Indian Treaties: The History of a Poltical Anomaly*. University of California Press: Berkeley.

Reyhner, J., & Eder, J. (2006). *American Indian Education: A History*. Norman: University of Oklahoma Press.

Sefa Dei, G. J. (Ed.). (2011). *Indigenous Philosophies and Critical Education: A Reader*. New York: Peter Lang.

Scott, J. C. (1990). *Domination and the Arts of Resistance: Hidden Transcripts*. New Haven: Yale University Press.

Smith, L. T. (2012). *Decolonizing Methodologies: Research and Indigenous Peoples* (2nd ed.). London: Zed Books.

Spring, J. (1997). *Deculturalization and the Struggle for Equity* (2nd ed.). New York: McGraw-Hill Publishing.

Tsosie, R. (2013). Climate Change and Indigenous Peoples; Comparative Models of Sovereignty. *Tulane Environmental Law Journal., 26,* 239–257.

Viola, H. J. (1973). *Thomas L. McKenny: Memoirs, Official and Personal.* Lincoln: University of Nebraska Press.

Willinsky, J. (1998). *Learning to Divide the World: Education at Empire's End*. Minneapolis: University of Minnesota Press.

# 7

# Economics

## Aprons and Cradleboards

*The aprons project began with a gift of sharing and from that first moment it began to live its own life. Years ago, Carol and I began to look at projects for my daughters so that they could experience generations past. Without knowing what we had begun, we started collecting aprons for patterns. My daughters had learned to sew, with one having an interest in the older practices of embroidery. In the process of telling them about my grandmother, it occurred to me that stories of her tended to bring images of her aprons. She had one for hanging out clothes with pockets for the clothes pins. It tied around the waist and when we were old enough to hang the clothes ourselves, we would tie it on and set out to the back yard. Grandma had another apron, a full apron that covered her when she baked. This apron was my favorite as it meant sugar cookies or homemade chicken and noodles. The idea of recreating old apron patterns with my children seemed a wonderful way for them to create and give gifts for special occasions and to remember people and traditions.*

*Carol and I talked about this project and about aprons for hours. She remembered the aprons of her mother's and grandmother's generations, but she spent much of her time with her father and talked about his "aprons". These were then called toolbelts or when they were aprons they were often associated with leather meant to protect someone when working with metal or shoeing horses. Carol and I have spent countless hours talking about the different and practical ways such covers have been used to protect or to carry needed items.*

*The discussion seemed to take on its own life as we talked with others about aprons and pockets. It ranged, not only from descriptions but also included purposes.*

*Soon people were sending us aprons and patterns for collection and discussions involving old items made from animal skins. They described their purposes and their memories associated with such things.*

*Longer discussions of cradle boards and the need to keep infants close and warm were undertaken along with the "pockets" created to carry arrows and spearheads. The practicality of these items was always mixed with the traditions and the people to whom they were associated. An older Indigenous woman talked of the flour sacks they used to use for clothing and for aprons. She remembered the fun she and her sisters had in choosing the one they wanted as they often had different patterns or colors. An older Indigenous man talked of his apron that had come from his father to be used in the garden. It held all the tools for planting and tending and harvesting smaller vegetables. The people talked of the times spent in making and using these practical items and the community and traditions involved.*

*Carol took these discussions into the hospital where she worked with Indigenous people from various communities and she spoke of how the older people would light up as they talked of the memories and remembered the past and the comfort of being folded into an apron when injured or being pulled to the apron when the cloth came out for nose-wiping. Moments of love and humor and feelings of being enveloped once again in those times. Carol talked of a healing that seemed to take place with the re-visiting of these moments.*

*What always seemed to come through in these stories was the strength and resiliency of the people. Their ability to work with what they had to create what was needed. The ordinary and the extraordinary in the daily lives as far back as these story-tellers could remember. These were stories of all genders of people who watched over the families and communities. These were the people who always seemed to create a feast from empty pantries and seemed able to heal the wounds both physical and emotional. These women and men weren't saints necessarily, but certainly they could be said to create miracles at times.*

*When we meet with people or groups, we often open by asking about aprons and cradleboards. The reaction is almost always a smile and a softness of remembering on the faces and soon the stories emerge. The stories are different and the same. The telling and listening creates a new community and with luck carries the stories to the next generations.*

*We used this story to open this chapter because the stories with which we have been gifted revolve around industry and invention, resourcefulness and economy all of which are tied to the secular and the sacred, all of which are involved in the cosmologies, teaching, and environmental practices of the people. In this chapter we embrace the aprons.*

—Carol Locust, Lavonna Lovern

## Indigenous Economics

It is always interesting to talk with students and find out what they have been told about Indigenous cultures or what they have learned from the media. The stereotypes are not unexpected, but they are always a bit startling as one would think that by 2020 cultural competency would be more developed in the industrialized world. Nevertheless, student perceptions of Indigenous communities are often one of stagnation with little or no emphasis on innovation and productivity. Such stereotyping comes largely from Western linguistic associations with terms such as "developed/developing" and "industrialized/unindustrialized". This text has noted the binary hierarchy underlying Western verbiage and here we add two more binaries to the mix: industrialized and un-industrialized.

To begin, words such as industrial carry a positive Western connotation and tend to be associated with positive "work ethics" and "innovation". When used, the term "industrial" brings up mental images of creative, busy, and hard-working people, which also tend to be associated with upper and middle-class workers. In industrialized nations, then, the idea is that these working people will be rewarded with a comfortable lifestyle of their own choosing. However, terms such as "unindustrialized" or "non-industrial" tend to be paired with words such as lazy or simple-minded and associated with images of poverty, lower-class, and uninventive. As with terms such as "developed" and "developing", definition is everything when contributing to stereotypes, biases, and discrimination.

References in the media and in textbooks to the "industrialized world" in opposition to the "unindustrialized world", even though the latter is often implied and not explicitly stated, have imposed a set of stereotypes on generations of the world's children. When these children enter adulthood, they continue to difference individuals according to such indoctrination without realizing that such differences are neither objective nor accurate. There seems to be no evidence scientifically, sociologically, or anthropologically that any culture ever existed that had no industry or lacked inventive abilities. There also appears to be no evidence that any specific type of industry or inventive abilities are indicators of cultural superiority. Interestingly, even animals are part of industry and participate as inventive ability users. So, what exactly is being claimed in the terms "industrialized" and "unindustrialized"?

The designation difference in the West appears to be similar to the one discussed earlier between history and pre-history based entirely on written verses oral tradition. In this case, the terms appear to embody the concept, which defies actual evidence, that before Western contact Indigenous cultures had no industry or innovation. Perhaps it is not that none existed, but that it was the wrong type of industry or innovation. Either way, the assumed bias in the argument becomes obvious. How should "industrial" and "innovative" be defined?

There has been some separation between hunter/gatherers and agriculturalists that equates agriculturalists with a preferred level of hierarchical positioning. However, such judgments seem somewhat arbitrary as the needed industry and innovation for each is substantially different and both present sustainable possibilities for living. In fact, the hunter/gatherers are more environmentally sustainable according to Indigenous epistemologies. Falling back on theories such as Social Darwinism, there is an idea involving the evolution of cultures that tends to move from a "state of nature" to a "state of civilization" passing through different stages of development such as the agricultural stage.

However, these theories represent a cultural bias rather than a universal necessity as there is no evidence of any "naturally required" evolution of societies. The preference appears to be arbitrarily assigned based on "who is in power". Similar ranking models were used during the Cold War era, which assigned first, second, and third world nomenclatures based primarily on a culture's military ability to decimate the planet. Post-Cold War, the media and scholars have begun to talk of fourth-world cultures. The term is vague and often shifting, but largely used to reference Indigenous populations or to designate States within the borders of other States.

It is important to note that these hierarchical designations appear to be primarily political rather than scientific, and therefore largely dependent on the user of the word rather than on evidence and argumentation.[1] Hidden in these arguments is the requirement that one accept certain assumptions as to the type of culture, lifestyle, military prowess, or technological advancements that are superior and then use that bias to argue that such assumed superiority makes these superior. Should one assume the opposite, that these are inferior ways to exist on the planet, the argument could easily be run the other way and Western material lifestyles, military prowess, and advanced technology would be hierarchically inferior and environmental sustainability involving reciprocity and low carbon footprints would be in the superior position. Either version of the argument hides a logical fallacy and so should not be accepted as legitimate.

As referenced by Pascoe, these Western descriptors have become part of the educational erasure of Indigenous ingenuity and innovation (2015). Pascoe

---

[1] Interestingly, attempting to justify which type of industry and innovations are superior to others tends to involve fallacies and weak induction.

reports the absence of Aboriginal agricultural achievements within educational resources. He gives the example of the Brewarrina fish traps, which cannot be explained or duplicated by modern methods. Not only does this "engineering wizardry" continue to baffle scientists, but the length of time with which these traps have existed, and remain functional, stumps archaeologists and anthropologists. "The scientists who have examined the structure are still not sure how the locking principles work. How come the stones don't wash away in a flood? They know it has something to do with the node on the keystones but are not sure on which element of physics it relies" (p. 168).

According to Pascoe, many of these structures stood until colonization, which moved them aside for their own industry and, within a single season, two of the fish species in the area became extinct. While the Ngemba understanding of sustainability was predicated on reciprocity and ensured the survival of the different species, Western industry held no such sustainability requirement (p. 168). Boissoneault reports a similar linguistic feature in Arctic languages. She notes that Arctic languages are linked to the biodiversity of the region and to the peoples' knowledge of environment (2016). Accordingly, she acknowledges that one "Saami dialect" has 318 words for snow. The number of words references different relations between the people and the environment, which included reindeer herding and engineering innovations used for industry and the survival in the Arctic. With the advancement of Western industry and the ensuing global warming, many of these words are no longer in use as they no longer reflect the existing snow conditions, the terms and the snow types have become extinct.

Beyond these two examples, we have already noted the use of natural geometry and fractals in the construction of textiles, personal adornments, and city construction. Additionally, mathematical and geometrical knowledge have been noted in the advanced astrological engineering of the Chaco Canyon sites, the pyramids, global geoglyphs, and structures throughout the world that remain unexplainable according to Western science and innovation. Stonehenge and Manchu Pichu are two examples of ancient Indigenous engineering marvels that continue to confound modern Western science and technology. Other examples include China's hanging coffins, the hydroponic and tiered agricultural structures of the Andeans, and Indigenous trade routes, both on land and on sea that continue to defy modern explanation. Pascoe claims that, if these aspects of Indigenous cultures were taught regularly, colonizing cultures would not reference or define these cultures as "primitive", "uncivilized", "unindustrial", or "undeveloped". One need only look at the Nasca lines and geoglyphs in Peru to marvel at the industry, engineering, and innovation of these ancient Indigenous societies.[2]

Like claims of the industrial age's superiority, current Western claims of technological superiority are equally political. The ability to have computers, phones, and advanced weapons systems, like all technology, comes with a cost. These costs are environmental, communal, and can even be related to issues of personal identity. We are not claiming that technology is in itself bad, or that phones and computers have destroyed society, only that they have changed society and that not all of these changes appear to be positive or are advancing conditions to some type of evolutionary higher position or "utopia".

There are certainly advantages that have come from technological advancements in medicine and communication, but these advances are not without their downsides. What many Indigenous communities argue is that they do not want many Western technologies at the expense of sustainability or environmental balance. It is often difficult for Westerners to understand Indigenous preferences, but there are Indigenous communities that prefer to forgo Western innovation and technological advancement for their traditional ways of being. Other Indigenous communities may accept some aspects of Western technology but deny others. One Indigenous Elder stated that "technology and innovation needs to have a reason. It shouldn't be just for its own sake. If the community needs a new means of fishing or a new way to rotate crops, it is good to find that. But changing just because we can betrays our relationship with nature and other beings."

Western colonization brought with it the emphasis on scientific and technological advances. Along with the Western emphasis on progress, came the judgment that cultures not oriented in this manner are to be considered "backward" or "lazy" further justifying the need to educate and civilize them. This influence has led to the compromise, and in some cases the demise, of Indigenous communities and knowledge. Beyond the difficulties discussed elsewhere in this text, colonization has brought family and community divisions in the form of migrant workers. As the wealthier Western nations find themselves in need of farm and domestic workers, they are increasingly turning to poor and Indigenous communities to supply those needs.

An example of these economic drivers can be seen in the Philippines where approximately two-thirds of the migrant workers are women, most of whom

---

[2]Some may argue that not all these societies qualify as Indigenous, and that can be debated in another book, but what is clear is that Western structuring of these cultures, which are largely identified with Indigenous ancestral communities, have been incorrectly categorized and stereotyped as unindustrialized.

find jobs as Western domestic help (Parreñas 2003). In leaving their own families to care for wealthier Western families, these women have found a means of economic support. The cost for economic stability, according to Parreñas, is the significant changes to family and community involving a crisis in parent-child bonds. She reports that children are often caught between resentment for the mother's absence and sorrow for their mothers' "martyrdom". The loss of family solidarity and the difficulties faced by the children left behind is compounded by the fear of what the mothers face abroad. Parreñas argues that, because many of the host countries fail to recognize these migrant women and their contributions, they have little recourse legally or politically in cases of violence, sexual assault, and wage fraud. These women face additional human rights violations regarding employment status and low wages with little hope for advancement in pay or position (p. 54).

Migration patterns involving labor have prompted research into what has been designated the North and South economic divide. While we are placing this discussion in the economic section of this book, the divide applies to other areas such as education, healthcare, and community. A good deal of discussion has taken place as to why there appears to be "more advanced" economic growth in the Northern hemisphere. No definitive answer has been given, and, likely, there is no single answer to this question. However, many scholars attribute the divide largely to the Western colonial patterns that coveted and pursued the resources in the south.[3]

As with other difference designators, this divide is linguistically and factually controversial as it is largely predicated on how to assign North and South destinations. If the line is drawn at the equator, as some students suggest, there is far less land mass below the equator. Others refer, not to the actual hemisphere divide, but more to the economic division splitting below North America and Europe. This economic divide would more accurately match the discussions that places Mexico, South America, most of Africa, India, and part of Asia in the Southern region.

Students using the literal hemisphere division are often confused by the fact that such a split would potentially put Florida and part of Texas in that same grouping. Interestingly, this divide places Northern Africa in the North, which does support imagery found in Western education that recognizes this region, along with places such as the Egyptian pyramids, as more "Middle Eastern and less African". Students often forget or fail to realize that these

---

[3] A complete discussion of this phenomenon will be left for other works. It is placed here to recognize current economic issues between wealthier Northern nations and resource heavy Southern nations.

northern African countries are, in fact, African.[4] Eckl and Weber caution scholars regarding the use of the North/South designation as it may actually exacerbate negative perceptions of southern countries linguistically and culturally (2007).

In fact, the North/South designation is not so much geographical as it is economic. Toohey argues that globalization continues the "exploitation of impoverished countries resources", but, instead of creating a "balance of power", creates "asymmetric relationships" (2012, p. 74). Working specifically with Brazil's Indigenous and environmental issues, Toohey notes that Indigenous defenders of the environment face opposition from the Brazilian government, but also from "international financial organizations such as the International Monetary Fund (IMF) and the World Bank who represent a second wave of economic colonization of the Amazon and are not accountable to the Brazilian government" (pp. 74–75). Toohey argues that the foundation of these struggles can be found in the rise of neoliberal political and economic constructs.

Reuveny and Thompson support the North/South divide as being primarily economic claiming that it carries with it the old Cold War history that divided the world into first, second, and third world (2007). While they note that first and second world was primarily a West/East divide, they note that the designations have shifted since the end of the Cold War. After the Cold War, the second world designation was vacated leaving first and third world.[5] The new designations tend to be more North/South with the understanding that such countries are determined by their economic status and not their geographical location. As an example, they note that Russia, now designated as North, spent time under the third world designation. Additionally, Australia and New Zealand, both designated as first world, are located in the southern hemisphere. Reuveny and Thompson argue that in the twenty-first century the North/South divide will become a primary focus involving "morality and Justice" (p. 557). Their argument hinges on several

---

[4]The concern here is that students have been educated to think of African communities as primitive, giving them the impression that structures such as the pyramids were not created by Africans. In an attempt to counter these educational deficits, the four-part film *Lost Kingdoms of Africa*, and similar works, explore the histories and advances in African civilizations. This series documents Africa's technological, engineering, and archaeological advances in Great Zimbabwe, West Africa, Nubia, and Ethiopia.

[5]References to fourth world are a late designation referencing much of the Indigenous populations of the world. Often these are labeled as fourth world because they have a poverty level below what is commonly designated as third world or exist as a lower socio-economic class within other first or third world states.

factors including North nuclear power advantages as well as issues of migration, population growth, environment, and devastations involving infectious diseases.

One of the main problems with North/South designations is that they are determined by first world States and follow the developed/developing or civilized/uncivilized dichotomy. Given that first world States continue to make these designations and tend to use neoliberal models that emphasize economic and technological advancement rather than environmental sustainability, there is little opportunity for Indigenous populations to work their way out of third or fourth world status. According to Arrighi, the movement from international to transnational actions has created a Marxist style bourgeoisie and proletariat global divide (2001/2002, p. 469). Arrighi argues that North States claim that the divide will be lessened or negated. However, the statistics indicate rather than a convergence, there is greater divergence when considering many South states. Le Veness and Fleckenstien agree with the divergence and argue that the "obstacles" and "barriers" to South advancement are a result of North practices. They argue that any convergence will need to be precipitated by a "significant sacrifice by the North…[not] merely in terms of monetary contributions, but also in terms of limitations of consumption of the world's natural resources" (2003, p. 365). Their research highlights the need for an ethical implementation in the North that values both the people and the resources in the South as more than commodities (p. 367).

It is interesting that the North/South divide is often discussed and recognized more in South states, whereas North states tend to use developed/undeveloped designations. Regardless of the wording, there is ample evidence to support the claim that North states continue to view both people and resources in South states as commodities to be used to enhance the living standards of the North. Furthermore, as the first world/North/developed states have claimed the right to determine which States occupy a given designation, these determinations remain flawed. Among the logical fallacies involved in many of the first world/North/developed arguments is the idea that there is a necessary or natural definition of these terms that is universally accepted. Such assumptions fail to recognize that alternative definitions not only exist, but are equally viable, making determinations cultural and not universal.

Even after emancipation, many colonized regions remain economically tied to former colonial powers. In other cases, the colonial powers remain and continue to view former colonial possessions as resources for their use. In 1997, the controversial book *Open Veins of Latin America* was reprinted as a twenty-fifth anniversary edition (Galeano 1997). This text critiques both the Western practices of resource use in Latin America and the Latin American elite for pandering to Western economic consumption. Galeano argues that the Latin American bourgeois has catered to the Northern/Western capitalist demands for resources in a way that has kept Latin America indebted and impoverished. From discussions regarding the mining of led, silver, and zinc to the drilling of petroleum, Galeano condemns the resource drain for the benefit of the economically wealthy at the expense of the economically impoverished.

As noted, Galeno's book is a controversial work and considered somewhat dated, but it is one that continues to spark controversy involving international corporations in Latin America. These debates have been exacerbated under NAFTA, which many viewed as a way to gain cheap labor and to avoid governmental regulations in wealthier Northern nations. The issues are also a part of the current border crisis in the U.S. as people attempt to migrate north in pursuit of better living conditions or fleeing persecution. American attempts to stop the migration and to eject individuals working illegally within existing borders has become debated. As children are being separated, both at the border and within the U.S., from their parents and in many cases are being kept in detention camps, or what some have referred to as animal-type cages, human rights issues involving sleeping arrangements and hygiene are being legally debated.

Many Indigenous are evidencing continued colonial practices seen in early boarding school and stolen children policies. Scholars have pointed out that the current crisis is, in part, a result of U.S. political and economic interference in the region that was designed to benefit North America while destabilizing Central and South American societies. Counter arguments have claimed that these regions are unindustrialized and underdeveloped and, as such, contain inherently more violent populations. Ironically, the political ramifications of this debate are being played out in multiple areas one of which is the building of a border wall. Interestingly, the Indigenous communities fighting the border wall claim the U.S. has no right to build on their land. They are asserting their Indigenous sovereignty. These voices are being joined by non-Indigenous people fighting government intrusion and the taking of privately-owned property, specifically in Texas.

Supporting Galeano's argument and the North/South economic dynamic, the use of migrant workers and the implementation of NAFTA to supply affordable products to the U.S. and Canada evidence the impact of Western colonization in Central and South American regions. This may not be the only reason for regional issues, but the denial that there is some involvement is inaccurate and disingenuous. Brandt provides an account of these concerns by tracing the production of tomatoes from their origins in Mexico to their consumption in Canada (2008). Her work begins with the picking, crating, and scanning process largely done by women, many of whom are Indigenous. She then traces the economic and cultural impacts of tomato consumption.

Not surprisingly, the bulk of the economic gain is not seen by the women picking and processing the tomatoes but rather by the corporations and the retailers at the other end of production. Barndt argues that as the tomato has become a staple throughout Canada and America and can be grown, at least seasonally, throughout these regions, the marginalization of the female producers is not accidental nor is it because of any natural scarcity of resource. These patterns are also not a part of a natural evolution of cultures. In tracing the political impact of tomato routes, Barndt critiques the consequences of globalization and the continued economic patterns involved in using impoverished people to support the food consumption of wealthier nations.

The chocolate trade evidences similar patterns of colonization as well as a unique place in the history of food consumption in the North/West. Like tomatoes, early colonizers were skeptical about consuming cacao. In fact, some mistook the reddish liquid for blood, which created educational misrepresentations regarding widespread practices of human sacrifice and bloodletting in sacred ceremonies. This is not to claim that no humans were killed by Indigenous communities in the Americas or that forms of bloodletting for sacred events and healing did not occur, only to note that it was arguably far less than what is claimed in traditional Western scholarship and media propaganda. In fact, Western practices of human sacrifice exhibited in the Inquisition and Witch trials arguably represented a higher body count and what could be classified, using Western definitions of industry of innovation, and technology, more advanced torture procedures preceding these deaths.

Additionally, bloodletting and flagellation were also common practices in Western healing and religious practices. McNeil's edited volume exposes many of these misinterpretations involving cacao and its use in healing and sacred practices in Mesoamerica (2006). Some of the articles in McNeil's text also chronicle settler history involving cacao and the eventual commodification of the region. The work carries this history into the twenty-first century with a discussion of the political and economic impact of the cacao trade on modern Mayan communities. In the final chapter, McAnany and Murata examine the issue of *Fair Trade* production of *Maya Gold* (2006).[6] In general, the free trade movement has attempted to provide support to the growers, pickers, and initial handlers of the products to reverse the current models of economic profit that privilege the Northern countries. These fair-trade efforts have been met with mixed results. While some people within the wealthier States are committed to buying free trade products, others find the products too expensive and revert to the cheaper corporate versions.

Beyond the use of resources and the development of products, many impoverished and Indigenous areas have become tourist destinations, particularly among the Island nations. Visiting exotic places and viewing the Indigenous flora and fauna has always been a part of colonization, and it continues to be a part of the economic colonization by wealthier communities. The complexity of the economic situations has made the denial, or elimination of, tourist incursion difficult for many Indigenous and impoverished cultures as they are reliant on the money for survival. These populations often find themselves dependent economically on an influx of tourists. However, the price paid is often the need to demonstrate or display Indigenous or Aboriginal ways of being. Historically, this has often meant embracing the expected Western stereotypes when working with or selling to tourists.

In some cases, cultures have found economic relief by selling items, healings, and ceremonies to tourists. The Caribbean region is made up of people descended from African slaves, Indigenous islanders, and European colonizers making the cultures and spiritual beliefs of these populations a creolization of differing traditions. When tourists come to the islands, they want the "Native Experience", including, for example, the Vodou experience often without realizing or acknowledging the Christian elements in these belief systems. They wish to participate in or observe ceremonies and buy herbs, potions, and "voodoo dolls" along with T-shirts and trinkets embossed with sacred imagery to keep and take back as gifts. Some Indigenous people have described such practices as a kind of zoo mentality.

Regardless, the people have had to make decisions involving levels of participation in the selling of the sacred for community survival. Anderson talks of just such a practice in Haiti, which is regarded as the poorest nation in the hemisphere (1982). Anderson chronicles the differences between the ceremonies designed and scheduled for the tourists and the private ceremonies in local homes or in rural settings. The study notes that the tourist events are

---

[6]Cacao is grown, and chocolate produced, outside of Mesoamerica. The production and economic concerns are similar. For example, the harvesting in Western Africa has resulted in clear-cutting of forests and use of child labor to keep production costs low.

not inauthentic, as they do contain ceremonial activity, but they are not the ceremonies experienced by believers when they are beyond tourist eyes.

While this is an older article, its message is a long-standing one. Indigenous people have often been forced to sell their traditions for survival. In the U.S., there is a history of getting one's picture taken with "a real Indian" or buying what the public believes to be "authentic" ceremonial and sacred objects. Indigenous people, however, have shown their innovation in their creation of objects that resemble, but are not specifically related to, the sacred or specific ceremonial practices. As all things contain both the sacred and the secular, the selling of these is not misrepresentation, nor does it violate the tenant in many Indigenous moral codes that one does not sell medicine or sacred objects and that certain practices are not meant for public consumption. So, in many cases, what tourists buy is an artistic rendering of objects used in ceremony. For many Indigenous people, this compromise provides financial sustainability by meeting tourist expectations, while preserving the integrity of their traditions.

A Comanche Elder explained that tradition disallows the selling of ceremony or healing products, but that settlers, and later historians and anthropologists, wanted both. He stated that quite often only partial information was given for three reasons. First, many Indigenous people thought it funny to give misinformation and have the Western settler or academics who would attempt to perform the, non-existing, "dance" or herbal remedy made of ordinary corn, beans, and dung. He also noted that many Indigenous people delighted in having such things recorded by the academics who came to "study" them and subsequently passed on the information in academic narratives.

Second, he explained that those caught selling ceremonies or medicine would face punishment within the communities. Finally, he stated that sometimes partial, non-specifically sacred, medicines or ceremonies were given in return for money or goods needed to survive. Interestingly, he reported that many times people might want to preserve the information and so would pass it on. However, specific elements or ingredients would be withheld. The missing ingredients or elements would be easily recognized by other Indigenous people but would remain unnoticed by Westerners.

Choices involving survival and the sacred continue to plague Indigenous communities. The circumstances and the choices that were made vary, but the continuity of these situations remains the norm. Young reports the case of Rapa Nui, also known to the West as Easter Island. Young first notes that many people would most likely be surprised to know that Indigenous Rapa Nui still exist (2012). The Chilean colonization of Rapa Nui forced the people in 1889 from their traditional homes into Hanga Roa. One of the most offensive parts of this removal involved the forced labor of the Rapa Nui to build the wall that was to enclose them. The Rapa Nui were confined to this place, suffering poverty and health issues, until the 1960s (pp. 10–17). According to Young, this imprisonment, as the Rapa Nui called it, separated them from their named places.

> The entire island countryside is circumscribed by ancestral temples (ahu) punctuated by the iconic moai sculptures. Each Rapa Nui extended family (hua'ai) traces descent to a particular temple area—areas their families used to call home before Merlet imprisoned the people to make room for sheep. (p. 11)

Young provides an illustrative discussion regarding the different discourses used to describe the island of Rapa Nui. The first is the archaeological discourse which frames all discussions in terms of statues and dig sites. "Archaeology is principally a foreigner's discourse coded in foreign language" and is "managed by an international scientific academy in institutions outside of Rapa Nui" (p. 4). In this discourse, the Rapa Nui people are "informants", but not experts, meaning much of their knowledge is dismissed. The second discourse is that of tourists, who largely refer to the island as Easter Island, thus celebrating colonization. Young notes that for these people the island is about taking pictures by statures and learning information, including the Easter Island name that "reproduces" the understanding of the island as a place to be consumed. These vacationers fail to understand that "the [significance of the] island for the Rapa Nui was that it was the home of their grandchildren and future grandchildren, and where their remains would be buried among their ancestors" (p. 7).

The third discourse is that of Chile which sees the island as either a property or an Indigenous territory depending on the law referred to, but primarily it is considered a military asset. The final discourse is that of the Rapa Nui themselves, who talk of the sacred places, the statues, and the traditional ways of being before incarceration. Their discourse also encompasses the issues of language, illness, poverty, and an inability to continue traditional ways of being in the face of continued colonization.

The Rapa Nui describe the Pure Nahe community that confined those who suffered from Hansen's disease, and those that were exposed to it when they were imprisoned in the city. Young reports discussions of the place which were described as Hellish and containing The Chair, which can still be viewed. Individuals would be strapped into The Chair while limbs and teeth were removed without anesthetic. The general method described was "pulled from the body". "The cultural memory of Pure Nahe that he [an informant] related to me that day was in a sense one loud silent scream: a Munchian scream that continues to haunt me long after my departure from the island" (p. 14).

This scream remains a part of their intergenerational trauma. Young comments that "while [the] article has, on the surface, initially followed the precepts of cosmopolitan ethnography…it is not clear that 'entextualizing' Rapa Nui within this discourse genre is the most ethnographically, morally, and politically responsible way to place Rapa Nui" (p. 19). His recognition of his place in yet another layer of Rapa Nui discourse exposes the problematic role of academic work in Indigenous cultures. Young concludes his discussion by noting that the Chilean government has yet to return the island to the Rapa Nui as promised in the 1990s, "but has simply redistributed a few additional parcels of land within the modified 'Titulo Domino' land tenure system" (p. 20).

According to Western mythology, the ancient inhabitants of "Easter Island" were destructive and were forced to abandon the island after destroying all its resources. Current scholarship has set aside this myth and stated that the inhabitants were "sophisticated and peaceful" (Owoseje 2018). Another article written by Simpson, Tilburg, and Dussubieux's in *The Journal of Archaeology*, offers an updated narrative of the ancient people of the island, supporting the dismissal of earlier destruction narratives (2018). Regardless of this re-visioning of the archaeological and anthropological narratives, what is missing is the Indigenous voice.

Even when involved in scholastic projects, Indigenous voices are often given little deference. There are two films, which are widely shown in classes that illustrate this point. The first involves Chaco Canyon (Temple 2003). The film uses academic voices and Indigenous voices to explain the existence of the sites. What students often miss is that the Indigenous are giving a history and explaining the sites in both what is said and what is not said. The film however focuses on what is said by the academics, who claim that, even with scientific observation, they are unable to unlock the mysteries of the sites.

In a separate film, several scholars are brought to Manchu Pichu to explain how the great stones were taken up the mountain and placed in the highly engineered structures. All their scientific attempts fail. Ironically, no attempt was made to ask the descendants of the builders how it was accomplished. What is interesting about this film is watching the people in the background. These are largely Indigenous people, some of whom offer to help with the experiments. However, it is quite clear from the interaction and discussions of these people that they find these experiments amusing in their simplicity and inaccuracy. Several Indigenous students have commented on how much they enjoy the humor of the Indigenous people in the film and the shared jokes. One student stated that it appeared that the people shared the knowledge and the secret, but the attitude seemed to be "why tell them, they wouldn't believe us anyway". Ironically, the film goes on to show the ingenuity of the people as they create a bridge of rope made from grass intended to cross a deep mountain valley. The disbelief of the scholars as they watch the bridge take shape exemplifies Western narrative failures regarding Indigenous industry and invention.

## Economic Conflict and Sacred Sites

While admittedly brief, this section will highlight several global examples involving Indigenous sovereignty and sacred sites that are in conflict with different State economic claims. As mentioned before regarding definitions and recognitions of different forms of evidence, these conflicts showcase continued colonization patterns that pit diverse values, innovations, and industry against each other. Beginning with the Lepchas in Sikkim India, conflict has arisen concerning certain forest groves that are considered sacred and are to be left unharmed. The government, however, defines these areas as State commodities for conservation, meaning they are subject to governmental resource allocation. Between the Lepchas villages and Tholung, for example, there is a sacred forest that illustrates the larger regional conflict.

According to Arora, the forest protects Tholung, keeping evil away and thwarts attempts to steal sacred items (2006). The grove is said to cause death or insanity to anyone coming with evil intentions (2006). Even those on sacred pilgrimage are instructed to take nothing, not a twig or stone, from the area as the act would bring illness. More recently, these instructions have been ignored and Tholung faces the threat of modern looters and tourists (pp. 65–69). Similarly, when a hydroelectric project threatened both forest and biodiversity in West Sikkim, the Lepcha activists argued for the sacred forest. According to Arora, the Indigenous people understand that "the forest of symbols embodied in the idea of sacred landscape [as that which] legitimizes Sikkim's polity" (p. 71).

In this case, the government relented, citing religious sentiments as well as frequent landslides and escalating construction costs (pp. 73–74). It is unclear whether the project would have been dismissed purely on the basis of the sacred argument as the deciding factor seemed to hinge more on the landslides and construction costs. Even with this governmental reprieve, however, the sacred forests remain threatened by the state's desire for resources and by tourists' desires to witness unique communities.

In a similar issue, the government of Nepal instituted national parks to conserve areas within the Himalayan Mountains. While claiming to protect the region, "[t]he National Parks and Wildlife Conservation Act provides no recognition of indigenous peoples' right to consultation or to access their traditional lands and resources, while giving quasi-judicial powers to the park chief wardens" (Stevens 2013, p. 32). According to Stevens, this region is home to 37 of the 59 Indigenous communities in the country and, while the communities in the high regions were not relocated, their land was put under the control of the national park service. The Indigenous people retained their homes and fields but lost "governance and management authority" over communal lands causing them to become "economically, culturally, socially, and politically dispossessed and disadvantaged" (pp 33–34). While Steven chronicles Indigenous attempts to retain control over their land, sacred sites, and economic resources, he notes that many believe this to be a lost cause.

There are also many examples within North America that illustrate the conflict between Western concepts of progress and economic advancement and Indigenous sacred sites. When faced with progress and economic advancement, the American Indian Religious Freedom Act offers minimal protection. The two cases to be discussed involve Mauna Kea and Dzil Nchaa Si An. Both sites involve the building of telescopes.[7] In the case of Mauna Kea, Hawaiian Indigenous opponents claim the construction would desecrate sacred land, while the advocates claim construction would bring educational and economic advancement (Kelleher 2017).

Construction of telescopes on Mauna Kea began in the 1960s, but the recognition of Hawaiian opposition came largely in the 1990s when additional telescopes called the "Outriggers" were proposed (Swanner 2015, p. 153).[8] "According to the Native Hawaiian creation chant known as the *Kumulipo*, Mauna Kea itself is the place where all life originated" (p. 153). Hawaiian oral literature provided an abundance of evidence for the sacredness of the site. In this case, the oral evidence was accepted, but Western use of Mauna Kea continues. The Imiloa Astronomy Center has attempted to "integrate" both Western and Hawaiian narratives regarding Mauna Kea and the shared history of "discovery" and "exploration" (pp. 154–155). However,

---

[7] The Tohono O'odham site Kitt Peak could also be added. However, space limitation made it necessary to focus on only two sites. It should also be noted that environmentalists also fought against the use of these site, these claims also failed.

[8] According to Swanner, the use of the term "Outriggers" was part of the insult involved in the additional telescopes as it referenced part of the Polynesian canoes used in the area (p. 153).

many Hawaiians remain concerned about the Western connotations involved in the discussions of discovery and exploration.[9]

Construction of a new telescope on Mauna Kea was scheduled to begin in July 2019. According to scholars and the current Governor, David Ige, litigation over the site ended in the granting of a construction permit in 2018. Hawaiian protests, supported by global Indigenous groups, have resulted in Ige's declaration of a state of emergency, which is under suit, and the use of National Guard units. The protests have, so far, resulted in the arrest of a reported 33 Elders. There is a possibility of relocating the telescope to La Palma but it is a lower elevation which increases atmospheric turbulence. Still, many scientists have been persuaded by Hawaiian arguments that the benefits of the Mauna Kea location do not outweigh the cost. Growing accomplice support in academia may yet save this sacred site from further telescopic invasion.

In 1873, Dzil Nchaa Si An, also known as Mt. Graham, was declared public domain. What is unique about the Mt. Graham conflict is that it not only represents a conflict between Western science and Indigenous spirituality, but it also, and more fundamentally, represents conflict between two belief systems regarding the sacred, specifically Indigenous spirituality and the Vatican. As with Mauna Kea, the desire for scientific and educational advancements was the justification for the placement of telescopes on the site. The site was supported by the University of Arizona, but it also gained endorsement from the Vatican, which brought a form of supersessionism to Dzil Nchaa Si An.[10]

Father Coyne, the Jesuit emissary from the Vatican, was brought to the site to investigate Indigenous claims that the site was sacred and so should be left pristine. Father Coyne investigated the site and stated that he found no physical evidence to support Apache claims of sacredness. The absence of Western-style shrines and the lack of written documentation worked against Indigenous claims. According to Father Coyne, "[I]t is precisely the failure to make the distinctions I mention above [nature, earth, cultures, human beings] that has created a kind of environmentalism and a religiosity to which I cannot subscribe and which must be suppressed with all the force that we can muster" (Brandt 1995). Father Coyne's claim implied that, for a religion to be acknowledged, it must have the same structure as Christianity, specifically the Catholic faith. The lack of buildings, or religious

---

[9] Mauna Kea also represents a special case in regard to AIRFA as Native Hawaiians are not Native Americans and it has been argued the AIRFA does not apply to them.

[10] As explained in an earlier chapter, supersessionism, while officially focused on the Jewish religion, was used by Christianity to claim that non-Christian religions were "fulfilled", by Christianity.

structures recognizable to these Christian outsiders, damned the Indigenous and provided justification for the placement of telescopes.

For the Apache, to openly reveal the sacredness of the site was problematic, but it was the only hope to preserve it and their ancient traditions. However, these Apache efforts were dismissed by both the Vatican and the courts. The decision to place telescopes on "Mt. Graham", delegitimized Apache knowledge and spirituality. This discrimination was compounded by the additional insult of naming one of the telescopes for Columbus and the condescending statement by Father Coyne stating "We invite our Apache brothers and sisters to join in finding the Spirit of the Mountains reflected in the brilliance of the night skies" (Swanner 2015, p. 157).

While not all the projected telescopes have been built on the site, construction continues. In 2004, the University of Notre Dame dedicated its "Large Binocular Telescope" claiming it to be "the most technologically advanced ground-based telescope in the world" (Gilroy 2004). This act solidified the Vatican dominance over Indigenous spirituality and freedom of religion and denied the legitimacy of AIRFA. Brandt states that "ironically" the Dzil Nchaa Si An is subject to "cloud cover, monsoon storms, lighting strikes and turbulent wind, which create poor visibility and make astronomy difficult" (1995). Additionally, the site is subject to frequent wildfires that threaten the telescopes. Because of the politics and finances involving these telescopes, they continue to receive firefighting attention not received by Indigenous communities in the area. Additionally, the threat of fires and concerns for equipment have been used as justification for the denial of Apache access to ceremonial sites.

## Economic Sovereignty and Data Control

Continued Western control over "acceptable" evidence and "strong" arguments is exacerbated by the limited amount and type of data that exists regarding Indigenous populations. The inaccuracies involved in data collection and reporting have been used to limit or deny Indigenous claims including those to sacred land. One such argument continues to involve the misreporting of population numbers based on Western racial and ethnic identifiers. If a population is deemed too small, the needs and desires of the larger non-Indigenous population often sway the results of the conflict.

In many cases, who counts as Indigenous becomes a vital issue, and the use of Western definitions functions to bias the results. Both academic and governmental data collection continues to be primarily done by and in the service of non-Indigenous populations. Moreover, much of the data collection on Indigenous peoples is done without the consent of or collaboration with these communities. There have been recent movements to include Indigenous populations in the collection, interpretation, and dissemination of material, but much of what is gained is forced into Western frameworks to gain legitimacy. This section will examine some scholarly attempts to bring Indigeneity into academic and governmental systems of data collection, interpretation, and dissemination as a means of advancing Indigenous economic sovereignty. These attempts to reverse acts of colonial erasure are an essential part of healing collective trauma.

In a unique text, Kukutai and Taylor have brought together a collection of articles titled *Indigenous Data Sovereignty* (2016). This text acknowledges the global "data revolution" and uses UNDRIP, and supporting documents, to assess and develop strategies regarding

> Legal and ethical dimensions around data storage, ownership, access and consent, to intellectual property rights and practical considerations about how data are used in the context of research, policy and practice...and includes data generated or held by indigenous communities and organizations, governments, the public sector, international governmental organizations (IGOs), NGOs, research institutions and commercial entities. (p. 2)

By outlining the relation of UNDRIP to data sovereignty and the UN Forum on Indigenous Issues (UNPFII) regarding data collection and disaggregation, Kukutai and Taylor bring together information that both critiques existing governmental practices and provides strategies for decolonizing and indigenizing these practices.

They acknowledge that countries such as Canada, Aotearoa/New Zealand, and, to a lesser extent, the U.S. have made some attempts to become more inclusive and collaborative in Indigenous data collection, but they also argue that advanced and meaningful collection will "require a decolonization of existing nation-state statistical systems" and that "more thought and political work needs to go into identifying and validating appropriate loci of indigenous data sovereignty" (p. 15). Kukutai and Taylor recognize the advances made by the Canadian FNIGC, the U.S. Indigenous Data Sovereignty Network, as well as the Maori Data Sovereignty network, and call for expanded efforts. Kukutai and Taylor conclude their opening chapter by referring to the Maori Te Mana Raraunga charter as "the most complete expression to date of the basis for indigenous data collection" as "it recognizes that data form a living *taonga* or treasure" (p. 15).

Davis addresses the issue of Indigenous invisibility, especially in areas of Africa and Asia where they often have no "formal identification and recognition" (2016, p. 25). In addition to issues of invisibility, Davis reports that the membership of the UNPFII is comprised of,

> 16 members who are independent experts and serve for a term of three years. Eight members are appointed by the president of ECOSOC and represent the seven indigenous regions of the world: Africa; Asia; Central and South America and Caribbean; the Arctic; Central and Eastern Europe, the Russian Federation, Central Asia and Transcaucasia; North America; and the Pacific. The state members are elected by ECOSOC on the basis of the five UN regional groups: Africa, Asia, Eastern Europe, Latin America and the Caribbean, and Western Europe and other states. (p. 26)

Davis acknowledges that, even as the UNPFII and UNDRIP are seen as forward progression in the rights of Indigenous people, there are critiques from Indigenous populations that the "UNPFII domesticates indigenous issues within Western political structures and rigid working procedures and agendas to control the dissemination of information about human rights violations...and to avoid consideration of...self-determination" (p. 27).

Davis also recognizes that issues of Indigenous identity continue to be a problem in many Nation-States making representation of these people difficult, if not impossible.[11] According to Davis, there is some advancement with the development of the "Indigenous Navigator" project, which is "being developed by a collection of UN organons and NGOs" to allow for Indigenous perspectives on data sovereignty (p. 36). Section three of Davis' collection is devoted to the idea of "Data Sovereignty in Practice", which focuses on Indigenous oriented data collection, interpretation, and dissemination. The idea is to create, collect, analyze, and disseminate data based on the needs and wants of Indigenous populations and with their full consent, which forces the recognition that not all knowledge is to be known by all people. As mentioned before, many Indigenous populations recognize that individuals hold different information and that not all information is meant for all people.

To this end, Drahos and Frankel collected scholarship focused on Indigenous intellectual property rights (2012). Historically, Indigenous innovation

---

[11] An additional concern, not brought up by Davis, has been the make-up of the UNPFII and the situation of "appointment" and "voting" in terms of membership. While Indigenous concerns on these issues do not fall within the parameters of Davis' article, it is important to note that many Indigenous people have concerns as to the representation of global Indigenous concerns by the UNPFII. Some go so far as to claim the UNPFII is a further attempt to colonize or Westernize Indigenous concerns.

and intellectual property have been ignored or denied by colonizing groups that claim the right of discovery, not just over land, but over ideas, inventions, medicines, and crafts. It has also been a standard Western concept that there is a right to all or any knowledge one wishes to investigate. Drahos and Frankel state that the recognition of Indigenous property rights is relatively new politically and legally and that problems arise because a good deal of Indigenous innovations are "place-based innovation that is cosmologically linked to land and indigenous group's relationship with that place, rather than to laboratories" (p. 2). According to Drahos and Frankel, these Indigenous connections fail to be recognized in both Western academics and law making them easily dismissed along with oral testimony and other forms of traditional Indigenous knowledge.

Governmental and scholastic decolonization and indigenizing of data and the recognition of Indigenous sovereignty rights will, no doubt, require a change in the way information is gained, interpreted, and stored by colonizing States. Changing academic methodology to include Indigenous methodology as standard and creating Indigenous inclusion in State data systems will require a dedication to equity along with the reconciliation between colonizer and colonized. It will also require Western scholars and government officials to respect Indigenous traditions of consent and the right to deny access to information according to Indigenous standards. As Indigenous peoples believe that there is no inherent right to possess all knowledge, both scholars and governments will be required to accept what is offered and, even more, respect what is kept private.

According to Aikau and Spencer the Kanaka Maoli (Native Hawaiians) have had some success in limiting outside incursion and continue to control both economics and data on Moloka'i (2007). They argue that the "rational development theory" pursued by the State says that economic development will bring jobs to an impoverished area. For the Kanaka Maoli, economic development would threaten "the distinct society that grew out of the relationship between the land, sea, and people" (p. 2). The article states that declaring indigeneity can be an effective way to move a community toward "self-determination that can include control over governance, economic policies, land use, and natural resources" (p. 4). Data collection, interpretation, and dissemination along with intellectual property rights must be understood in terms of reciprocity ethics based in spirit and as foundational to sovereignty and self-determination.

To this end, the book *Research is Ceremony* offers a useful discussion for Westerners as they attempt data decolonization (Wilson 2008). If research becomes a relationship with the people involved and requires the ritual of ceremony in order to be done correctly, it becomes as much about the journey, or how the research is done, as it does about the conclusion. Tradition, cosmology, and paradigm narrative then become important elements in all research. After all, scholarly works and governmental collections of data are just smaller narratives embedded in the larger Western narratives. Following this model, research, at all levels, involves the reciprocity responsibilities of speaker and listener.

Finally, all research becomes relational, which means one must understand that it not only describes reality but creates it by participating in the sacred. Decolonizing and "Indigenizing the Academy" would, therefore, promote justice issues and allow equity values to become part of the education of all students (Mihesuah and Wilson 2004). Such practices may also allow for a revision and revitalization of the historic, and often stagnant, relationships between faculty and students, faculty and administration, and town and gown. Indigenous scholars often fantasize about an academy based in Indigenous structures of equity and complementarity that is devoid of hierarchical binaries which foster competition and territorialism. Such an academy would certainly broaden the possibilities of scholarship if it were open to what Huston Smith referred to as the totality of human wisdom.

Finally, decolonization and the indigenizing of data will require Western scholars and government officials to recognize Indigenous forms of complementarity and abandon systems of subordinate complementarity evidenced in Western hierarchical dualisms. If we are asking "what can Western communities learn from Indigenous communities" one answer would be that all people participate in economics, innovation, and data systems. Failing to recognize all of these contributions does not eliminate them, it simply inhibits them. For example, Támez describes the work of the Lipan Apache women as they work to maintain traditions and resist incursion (2010). These women are fighting to preserve the law of women within a culture that includes kinship orientations. They are fighting against the continued assault of colonization and the threat of replacement by Western law.

According to this article, TáNdeez notes that such endeavors are not feminist as there is no such word in their language. Instead, it is the traditional understanding of relatedness found in family, community, and economics. "Feminism-both the concept and the stereotypes of it- wedges uncomfortably" (p. 561). These women argue that their epistemic system is holistic based on their understanding of community.

> Where corporations, governments, state institutions, and their functionaries threaten our very existence as people—culturally, economically, socially, and politically—we must receive free and prior informed consent (FPIC) to

determine for ourselves the direction we will take in the stewardship of our cultural, social, economic, and political resources…The restoration of autonomy, respect, dignity, empowerment, and the sacredness of *Ńdeisdzáné* promotes the restoration of indigenous women's tribal law systems, where property and resources can be governed and protected. (pp. 566–567)

A similar regaining of identity and economic tradition can be observed in the Ainu women's reclaiming and advancement of traditional textiles (Lewallen 2016). Their use of the traditional patterns and ways of production not only honors and transmits tradition, but it has also established them as a modern economic force in Japan.

Data collection, innovation, and economic advancement remain communally bound. The recognition of these reciprocal ways of being must be at the forefront of governmental and scholarly work in Indigenous territories. Without this recognition, attempts to advance Indigenous rights and heal colonial intergenerational trauma will fail and, instead, will work to secure the status quo and reinforce trauma patterns.

## Additional Readings

Aikau, H. K., & Spencer, J. H. (2007). Introduction: Local Reaction to Global Integration—The Political Economy of Development in Indigenous Communities. *Alternatives, 32,* 1–7.

Alderete, W., Pacaldo, G., Huerta, X., & Whitesell, L. (1992). *Daughters of Abya Yala: Native Women Regaining Control*. Summertown: Book Publishing Company.

Anderson, T. L. (Ed.). (1992). *Property Rights and Indian Economies*. Lanham: Rowman & Littlefield Publishers, Inc.

Ball, J., & Janyst, P. (2008). Enacting Research Ethics in Partnerships with Indigenous Communities in Canada: "Do It in a Good Way". *Journal of Empirical Research on Human Research Ethics: An International Journal, 3*(2), 33–51.

Beckett, G., & MacPherson, S. (2005). Researching the Impact of English on Minority and Indigenous Languages in Non-Western Contexts. *TESOL Quarterly, 39*(2), 299–307.

Belton, K. A. (2010). From Cyberspace to Offline Communities: Indigenous Peoples and Global Connectivity. *Alternatives: Global, Local, Political, 35*(3), 193–215.

Brown, K. G., Doucette, M. B., & Tulk, J. E. (2016). *Indigenous Business in Canada: Principles and Practices*. Halifax: Nimbus Publishing.

Condevaux, A. (2011). Contextualization of Dances in Tourism: A Tongan Case Study. *The Journal of the Polynesian Society, 120*(3), 269–291.

Edmonds, E. V., & Schady, N. (2012). Poverty Alleviation and Child Labor. *American Economic Journal: Economic Policy, 4*(4), 100–124.

Forsyth, M. (2013). How Can Traditional Knowledge Best Be Regulated? Comparing a Proprietary Rights Approach with a Regulatory Toolbox Approach. *The Contemporary Pacific, 25*(1), 1–33.

Goodale, M., & Postero, N. (Eds.). (2013). *Neoliberalism, Interrupted: Social Change and Contested Governance in Contemporary Latin America*. Stanford: Stanford University Press.

Klemm, A., Henry, E., & Peredo, A. M. (Eds.). (2017). *Indigenous Aspirations and Rights: The Case for Responsible Business and Management*. London: Routledge.

Kristy, L. (2013). Invisible West Africa: The Politics of Single Origin Chocolate. *Gastronomica, 13*(3), 22–31.

Macpherson, C., & Macpherson, L. (2011). Churches and Economy of Sāmoa. *The Contemporary Pacific, 23*(2), 304–337.

Moretti, D. (2012). Gold, Tadpoles and Jesus in the Manger: Mythopoeia, Colonialism and Redress in the Morobe Goldfields in Papua New Guinea. *The Journal of the Polynesian Society, 121*(2), 151–179.

Pinel, S. L. (2007). Culture and Cash: How Two New Mexico Pueblos Combined Culture and Development. *Alternatives, 32*, 9–39.

Poblete, J. (2020). *Balancing the Tides: Marine Practices in America Sāmoa*. Honolulu: University of Hawaii Press.

Postero, N. G., & Zamosc, L. (Eds.). (2006). *The Struggle for Indigenous Rights in Latin America*. Brighton: Sussex Academic Press.

Radcliffe, S. A., Laurie, N., & Andolina, R. (2004). The Transnationalization of Gender and Reimagining Andean Indigenous Development. *Signs, 29*(2), 387–416.

Reilly, B. (2013). *Strategic Insights: Australia as a Southern Hemisphere Power* (pp. 1–15). Australian Strategic Policy Institute. Freedom House. https://www.files.ethz.ch/isn/167446/SI61Sthn_hemisphere_power.pdf.

Sturgeon, J. C. (2007). Pathways of 'Indigenous Knowledge' in Yunnan, China. *Alternatives, 32*, 129–153.

Valdivia, G. (2007). The 'Amazonian Trial of the Century': Indigenous Identities, Transnational Networks, and Petroleum in Ecuador. *Alternatives, 32*, 41–72.

Walter, M., Kukutai, T., Carroll, S. R., & Rodriguez-Lonebear, D. (2020). *Indigenous Data Sovereignty and Policy*. London: Routledge.

Webbink, E., Smits, J., & de Jong, E. (2013). Household and Context Determinants of Child Labor in 221 Districts of 18 Developing Countries. *Social Indicators Research, 110*, 819–836.

## Works Cited

Aikau, H. K., & Spencer, J. H. (2007, January–March). Local Reaction to Global Integration: The Political Economy of Development in Indigenous Communities. *Alternatives: Global, Local, Political, 32*(1), 1–8.

Anderson, M. (1982). Authentic Voodoo Is Synthetic. *The Drama Review: TDR*, 89–110.

Arora, V. (2006, January–March). The Forest of Symbols Embodied in the Tholung Sacred Landscape of North Sikkim, India. *Conservation and Society, 4*(1), 55–83.

Arrighi, G. (2001/2002). Global Capitalism and the Persistence of the North–South Divide. *Science & Society, 65*(4), 469–476; ProQuest.

Boissoneault, L. (2016, May 25). 318 Words for Snow: How to Preserve the Indigenous Languages of the Arctic. *Education and Society*. Retrieved from https://DAILY.JSTOR.ORG/INDIGENOUS-ARCTIC-LANGUAGES/.

Brandt, E. (1995). The Fight for Dzil Nchaa Si An, Mt. Graham: Apaches and Astrophysical Development in Arizona. *Cultural Survival Quarterly Magazine*. Retrieved from https://www.culturalsurvival.org/publications/cultural-survival-quarterly/fight-dzil-nchaa-si-mt-graham-apaches-and-astrophysical.

Barndt, D. (2008). *Tangled Routes: Women, Work, and Globalization on the Tomato Trail* (2nd ed.). Lanham: Rowman & Littlefield Publishers Inc.

Davis, M. (2016). Data and the United Nations Declaration on the Rights of Indigenous People. In T. Kukutai & J. Taylor (Eds.), *Indigenous Data Sovereignty: Toward an Agenda* (pp. 25–38). Acton, ACT: ANU Press.

Drahos, P., & Frankel, S. (Eds.). (2012). *Indigenous Peoples' Innovation: Intellectual Property Pathways to Development*. Canberra, ACT: Australian National University Press.

Eckl, J., & Weber, R. (2007). North-South?: Pitfalls of Dividing the World by Words. *Third World Quarterly, 28*(1), 3–23.

Galeano, E. (1997). *Open Veins of Latin America: Five Centuries of the Pillage of a Continent*. 25th Anniversary Edition, (C. Belfrage, Trans.). New York: Monthly Review Press.

Gilroy, W. G. (2004, November 8). *Astrophysicists Participate in Arizona Telescope Dedication*. Retrieved from Notre Dame News: https://news.nd.edu/news/astrophysicists-participate-in-arizona-telescope-dedication/.

Kelleher, J. S. (2017, September 28). *Telescope on Land Sacred to Native Hawaiians Moves Forward*. Retrieved from US News and World Report: www.usnews.com/news/news/articles/2017-09-28/hawaii-land-board-grants-permit-to-build-divisive-telescope.

Kukutai, T., & Taylor, J. (Eds.). (2016). *Indigenous Data Sovereignty: Toward and Agenda*. Acton, ACT: ANU Press.

Le Veness, F. P., & Fleckenstein, M. (2003). Globalization and the Nations of the South: Plan for Development or Path to Marginalization? *Journal of Business Ethics, 47,* 365–380.

Lewallen, A.-E. (2016). *The Fabric of Indigeneity: Ainu Identity, Gender, and Settler Colonialism in Japan*. Albuquerque: University of New Mexico Press.

McAnany, P. A., & Murata, S. (2006). *From Chocolate Pots to Maya Gold: Belizean Cacao Farmers Through the Ages*. Gainesville: University Press of Florida.

McNeil, C. L. (Ed.). (2006). *Chocolate in Mesoamerica: A Cultural History of Cacao*. Gainesille: University Press of Florida.

Mihesuah, D. A., & Wilson, A. C. (2004). *Indigenizing the Academy*. Lincol: Bison Books.

Owoseje, T. (2018, August 3). Easter Island Natives Were Sophisticated and Peaceful, New Study Reveals. *Independent*. Retrieved from https://www.independent.co.uk/news/science/easter-island-society-collapse-natives-revealed-study-rapa-nui-a8489476.html.

Reuveny, R. X., & Thompson, W. (2007). The North–South Divide and International Studies: A Symposium. *International Studies Review, 9*(4), 556–564.

Simpson, D. F., Jr., Van Tilburg, J. A., & Dussubieux, L. (2018). Geochemical and Radiometric Analyses of Archaeological Remains from Easter Island's Moai (Statue) Quarry Reveal Prehistoric Timing, Provenance, and Use of Fine–Grain Basaltic Resources. *Journal of Pacific Archaeology, 9*(2), 12–34.

Stevens, S. (2013). National Parks and ICCAs in the High Himalayan Region of Nepal Challenges and Opportunities. *Conservation and Society, 11*(1), 29–45.

Swanner, L. (2015). Contested Spiritual Landscapes in Modern American Astronomy. *Journal of Religion and Society*. In R. A. Simkins & T. M. Kelly (Eds.), Supplement 11, 149–162.

Támez, M. (2010). Restoring Lipan Apache Women's Laws, Lands, and Strength in El Calaboz Rancheria at the Texas-Mexican Border. *Signs, 35*(3), 558–569.

Temple, E. (Director). (2003). *The Mystery of Chao Canyon* [Motion Picture].

Toohey, D. E. (2012). Indigenous Peoples, Environmental Groups, Networks and the Political Economy of Rainforest Destruction in Brazil. *International Journal of Peace Studies, 17*(1), 73–97.

Parreñas, R. S. (2003). The Care Crisis in the Philippines: Children and Transnational Families in the New Global Economy. In B. Ehrenreich & A. R. Hochschild (Eds.), *Global Woman: Nannies, Maids and Sex Workers in the New Economy* (pp. 39–54). London: Granta Books.

Pascoe, B. (2015). Panara: The Grain Growers of Australia. In A. McGrath & M. A. Jebb (Eds.), *Long History, Deep Time: Depening Histories of Place* (pp. 163–170). Acton, ACT: ANU Press.

UNDRIP. (2008). *United Nations Declaration on the Rights of Indigenous Peoples*. New York: United Nations Publisher. Retrieved from http://www.un.org/esa/socdev/unpfii/documents/DRIPS_en.pdf.

United Nations Forum on Indigenous Issues. (n.d.). *Who Are Indigenous People? Fact Sheet*. New York: United Nations. Retrieved from https://www.un.org/esa/socdev/unpfii/documents/5session_factsheet1.pdf.

Wilson, S. (2008). *Reserach Is Ceremony: Indigenous Research Methods*. Halifax: Fernwood Publishing.
Young, F. W. (2012). 'I He Koe? Placing Rapa Nui. *The Contemporary Pacific, 24*(1), 1–30.

# 8

# Health

## Five Hundred Years and Three Seconds[1]

*We live with five hundred years of history laughing at us every day. I guess we all go through the three second thing at some time in our lives. Right now, it's my turn. Three seconds. Hell, after five hundred years you would think we'd be used to it, be stronger, be able to handle it. And yet there just doesn't seem to be any end to the shit we have to live with.*

*Oh, I know, tell me about how my ancestors were tough and rugged and how they fought to survive. Tell me that and I'll tell you how they suffered, how their hearts cried, how they wept from agony and loss. Tell me how they refused to give up or give in, and I'll tell you how many people they buried in shallow graves. Tell me about how they educated themselves and their children to the White man's world, and I'll tell you about the hell of living in a boarding school. Tell me about the 1996 New World Order called Welfare Reform and how it promotes equality, justice, and job opportunity for people of all colors in this country—tell me so I can laugh.*

*Don't be stupid, friend, you can see if you take off those rose-colored glasses and really look at what is happening around you. Welfare Reform and Managed Care. New terms for prejudicial systems that squeeze poor and minority people until their bones scrape against each other. Squeeze the life out of families, children, and the*

---

[1] For those unfamiliar with the three seconds Carol is referencing, she is speaking of the three seconds before taking one's own life. In those three seconds, one decides to stay here or to leave. For many Indigenous people, Intergenerational Trauma has made these three seconds a common occurrence as can be evidenced by the suicide rates, both attempted and completed, in Indigenous communities.

old. Squeeze us back to times recounted to us by our ancestors —times of hunger, cold, and constant struggle for survival. And three seconds. Too damned many three second ambushes staring you in the face.

What I feel now is anger; anger that a bigoted White man had the balls to call me racist, so he could have a reason to fire me from my job. Fire me because I told him what I thought about assholes who misuse money meant for Indian programs to benefit Red people, and that he was one of them. So, he used racism as a means to get rid of me. You know what I really did? I spoke the truth, and he didn't like it. Didn't like me not being a good Indian and saying yes sir all the time.

Remember what we were always taught when we were young? Don't rock the boat. Don't speak out. Don't make him (or her) angry because you or someone you love will suffer. I should have listened, should have kept my mouth shut, and I'd have a job. They hold the power, not us. They pull strings and we jump and dance. And they have the New World's Order of silent annihilation of "undesirable people" by way of Welfare Reform—and we have three goddammed seconds.

Damned three seconds! They ambush me, jump out and scream at me at any time, no matter what I'm doing or where I am. And I'm scared. Scared shitless. Yeah, I'm angry, too, but more scared. Scared because I can't control the seconds, can't make them go away. So far, I've been able to grab them fast enough to hold on, to shove them back into the dark shadows of my brain where they live. But I know they are there in my head waiting for some thought or action to trip the latch and let them out to ambush me again. Only I don't know what the thoughts are, or the actions that trip the latch. And I'm scared.

Is it just about my job? No, I don't think so. This one guy? No, he's a two faced, small minded piece of crap with the ego of a TV wrestler, but he has no real power. Privileged power perhaps. No, he can't create three seconds by his puny, arrogant self. But he is one of many others, over five hundred years, and still we Indians sit back and take their shit day after day, year after year, from situations at home on the rez to mealy mouthed bureaucrats in D.C. And I'm one of them. So, I decided to say something, and another Indian bites the dust in the working world. Creator help me!

I say I get ambushed by three seconds, but that's not really true. Three seconds are only the result of something else, of a totally unexpected, overpowering impulse to not be here. Not be anywhere. Oblivion forever.

The need to die. Creator...

Right out of nowhere, ambushed. God! A sniper hidden in the tree top, a forgotten land mine, a dark thought leaping out from inside my own head – ambushed! No time for defense, for rational thought. Can't mediate this, no deciding or choosing. There isn't time. Experience taught me that I had about three seconds to grab the impulse and crush it, otherwise I'm history. Oh God, I'm so scared...

Don't remember when I first got ambushed, just knew it scared the hell out of me. Must have been at least a year ago. Didn't start with my job, but the lay–off triggered lots more three–second episodes than I ever had before. Funny, too, that

*I don't feel depressed, never have, like you hear in the mental health commercials. In fact, most of the time I'm happy, laugh and joke a lot. So, what gives? I don't know. You tell me. I just hope I can keep catching the three seconds before they get away one day and I do something stupid… Creator! Help me…* —Carol Locust

## Post-colonization Stress Disorder

*If you look at mortality and morbidity rates among North American Indian people, you will find this prediction: without change, by the year 2100 the only place you will find many North American Indian tribes will be in a showcase in the Smithsonian Museum. Our people will continue to be decimated by accidents, alcoholism, diabetes, birth defects, and suicides. The 1990 census showed we have increased in numbers; what the census doesn't show is that we are dying young and that upwards of 1/3 of us are disabled. If we cannot stop the diseases and destruction of our people, many will vanish. And if I write these statistics for American Indigenous people, I know the same statistics occur among other Indigenous populations in the world.*

*What has caused the terrible statistics and the ominous prediction of 2100? We believe that the greatest contributor to our annihilation is Post-Colonization Stress. We also know that, without change, we face a continued downward spiral. Change must come. Indigenous people know this. Traditional medicine people have long predicted it. But, how does change come when colonization has taken the Old Ones and the Old Ways? When colonization continues to disallow land rights and religious freedom? When discrimination and bigotry make our young ones afraid or ashamed to admit who we are? The very structure of our communities has been altered by colonization. Old Way methods of appointing tribal leaders is no longer allowed by the colonizers. Choosing leaders now has to be done their way, by votes in elections. But, this is not the Old Way and those voted into leadership positions are not necessarily the tribal leaders. Despite what kind of self-governing system we are ordered to follow; each tribe of Indigenous people knows who its leaders are. Leadership is often a family lineage. Moreover, true leaders are men and women in the small villages who personally keep their communities together, who strive for peace and beauty, the ones to whom others go for advice and help. This traditional kind of leadership has not been destroyed! However, to exercise such leadership publicly will often call forth the wrath of the colonizers. Therefore, the real leaders are underground leaders, staying out of the public eye, not speaking up in meetings, sitting quietly until they can return to their community and function as leaders in the Old Way.*

*Having to elect Indigenous leaders "to satisfy the dominant race authorities" is not effective in the communities and often splits the communities it was intended to govern. The imposed government structures are not conducive to traditional*

*community leadership because it removes from traditional leaders their internal methods of support. Most of the rural/reservation/reserve communities function separately, still as clan or band groups, as autonomous units of the tribe as a whole. The leadership within these smaller groups is still strong, and this is where we can begin to bring change. Those in the cities and towns often continue to struggle to find identity and community. They search for what is lost and suffer physical and mental harm because of the loss. Because of the poverty, poor education, and lack of access to good healthcare, both reservation and non-reservation American Indians continue to suffer intergenerational trauma.*

*This trauma is lived and evidenced in the mental and physical health statistics that show the impact of what has been done to Indigenous people over the generations. Colonizers ignore the consequences of their actions saying, "it occurred a long time ago" and "we are no longer in the colonization era". But, the impact remains, and the Post-Colonization era continues the patterns of Indigenous destruction through assimilation, prejudice, and chosen ignorance. They simply choose not to see the consequences of past choices and actions.*

*Aside from statistics, the difference in the long run will be that the destructive pattern of PCSD will be changed, not by the colonizer, but by the colonized. Backs may still be against the wall, but the power to see a way out will be brought into the light. Indigenous peoples may be oppressed, but they will learn to look up and look to the Old Ways for healing. They will throw off colonial thinking and will begin to awaken traditional ways of knowing, making their choices, using their methods. Indigenous peoples will regain their pride and power. This kind of thinking will be there in the long run because once you unveil the mind, you free the Spirit. That is what we have to remind our young people, who they are and the beauty of the interrelation of self, land, and traditional knowledge.*—Carol Locust

## Healthcare

According to the 2016 *Lancet* mortality information,

> if [you are from an]... Indigenous tribe in Cameroon, you can expect to live until you are aged about 35 years, which is about 12 years less than for the non-Indigenous people there. In Greenland you would be better off, at 73 years, but nonetheless this figure is 9 years less than that for the Danish population...it makes no difference where you live if you are Indigenous-you will be worse off health-wise, regardless of the economic status of that country. (Indigenous Health, p. 104)

This chapter is divided into several sections dealing with Indigenous healthcare. It will begin with an examination of Indigenous health statistics that supports the UN claim that Indigenous populations are at risk because of colonial imposed poverty and the lack of access to healthcare standards enjoyed by dominant populations in the same regions. Indigenous populations not only suffer ill effects of "treatable" physical conditions such as colonization induced type II diabetes, but they also continue to suffer from the psychological effects of trauma.

The claim is not that such issues do not exist in dominant demographics, only that the rate and intensity of these situations are exhibited disproportionately in Indigenous populations. This chapter will partially examine the impact of colonization on mental and physical health but will also address genocidal issues associated with Western eugenic practices and forced sterilization in Indigenous populations. The chapter will conclude with an overview of Indigenous concepts of wellness and unwellness as an alternative perspective to Western constructions of health and illness. This final section will also address how these different paradigms define and react to body and mind differences.

## Indigenous Health Data

According to the notes prepared for the 2014 World Conference on Indigenous Peoples, "Indigenous peoples' health is an issue of concern in all countries, independently of their income" (p. 3). The report states that inadequate data collection and regional population differences including rural versus urban data create barriers to proper understanding, diagnosis, and treatment of Indigenous populations. Nonetheless, the existing data indicates wide-spread negative health issues and inadequate access to healthcare. This section will examine some of the existing data, including that published by the UN, to allow for a better understanding of Indigenous population health situations.

According to the World Conference documents,

> There are gaps in equity in comparison with non-indigenous peoples in terms of access to family planning services, delivery care for pregnant indigenous women as well as immunization coverage and the prevalence of illnesses associated with higher mortality rates for their children… Despite the significant decline in infant mortality rates in many regions, studies show systematic heightened mortality for indigenous children in comparison to the rest of the population. For example, in Latin America, infant mortality among indigenous children is 60 percent greater than for non-indigenous children… In many countries in the world, indigenous youth and adolescents have poorer mental health outcomes, and higher rates of disability due to injuries and accidents

than their non-indigenous counterparts… data that is available in the region of the Americas shows that the prevalence of depression is higher amongst indigenous communities than nonindigenous communities. (pp. 3–5)

The report also expresses concern regarding, what it deems, the insufficient collection of data on communicable diseases, nutrition, and disasters. According to the World Conference document, existing indicators of health differences are the direct result of colonization-imposed poverty and discrimination. This information is echoed in the 2013 UN *Indigenous Access to Health Services* report which states

> Indigenous peoples' health status is severely affected by their living conditions, income levels, employment rates, access to safe water, sanitation, health services and food availability. Indigenous peoples are facing destruction to their lands, territories and resources, which are essential to their very survival. Other threats include climate change and environmental contamination (heavy metals, industrial gases and effluent wastes). Indigenous peoples also experience major structural barriers in accessing health care. These include geographical isolation and poverty which results in not having the means to pay the high cost for transport or treatment. This is further compounded by discrimination, racism and a lack of cultural understanding and sensitivity. Many health systems do not reflect the social and cultural practices and beliefs of indigenous peoples. (SOWIP: Health 2009, pp. 182–155)

This document studied the UNPFII mandate involving access to healthcare in the regions of Africa, Asia, Arctic, Central/South America/Caribbean, North America, Pacific, and the Russian Federation. This research documents the economic, legal, environmental, and cultural issues that inhibit Indigenous access to health services that are available to their non-Indigenous counterparts in the same regions.

According to UN reports on morbidity and mortality in Indigenous populations,

> Indigenous peoples suffer from poorer health, are more likely to experience disability and reduced quality of life and ultimately die younger than their non-indigenous counterparts. The gap in life expectancy between indigenous and non-indigenous people in years is: Guatemala 13; Panama 10; Mexico 6; Nepal 20; Australia 20; Canada 17; New Zealand 11. (United Nations)

In attempting to establish "benchmarks" regarding Indigenous Healthcare, Anderson et al. noted two primary obstacles, limited data for Indigenous populations and a lack of "uniformity" in Indigenous populations (2016).

For example, relative to their respective benchmark populations, life expectancy at birth was 5 or more years lower for Indigenous populations in Australia, Cameroon, Canada (First Nations and Inuit), Greenland, Kenya, New Zealand, and Panama; infant mortality rates were at least twice as high in Brazil, Colombia, Greenland, Peru, Russia, and Venezuela; and high proportions of child malnutrition, child obesity, and adult obesity were documented in at least half of the populations for which we have data. By contrast, relative to benchmark populations, the Mon of Myanmar fared better in educational attainment and economic status and low birthweight data were significantly better among the Indigenous populations of Colombia and the USA. (p. 151)

The report notes that the "the inclusion of data from Scheduled Tribes in India for the first time is an important development in view of the population size", but that there remain significant "geographical gaps …particularly in China, Africa and Latin America" (p. 151). The report also cautions the use of data collections such as proxy measures based on language and geography. For example, the study specifically questions the proxy approach used in

Sweden where the geographical proxies are Sami Administrative Areas, with the Sami population 18 years and older of 9-13% of the total population. At this population density, we have concerns about the accuracy of this picture of Sami health status, in view of reports of increased rates of morbidity and mortality due to suicide, accident, and injury. Sweden's inability to disaggregate data by ethnicity means that it is unable to monitor the health status of its Indigenous population and respond accordingly through policy and service delivery. (p. 152)

In its conclusion, the report calls for better data collection using "close collaboration with Indigenous peoples" to gain a more detailed understanding of global Indigenous health situations. It also calls for documentation on all populations claiming Indigenous status regardless of their recognition by the colonizing States in which they are located. These recommendations would allow for data collection in groups such as the African San people who are "recognized by global bodies as Indigenous, but not by their governments" (p. 154). It would also allow for collection in areas such as China that asserted in the 1990s that they did not have Indigenous people, only minority groups (Hathaway 2016).

Anderson et al. attempted a comprehensive overview of Indigenous and tribal health in 2016. While the scope of this project is impressive, the authors recognize "gaps in geographical coverage…in Africa, Asia, and Latin America" and note that "contributors from occupied Palestine territory and Georgia withdrew" (p. 133). This report attempted to tackle a question asked in an earlier *The Lancet* article regarding "Indigenous peoples health—why are they behind everyone, everywhere?" The report concluded that because there is a lack of uniformity in global Indigenous populations, while their life expectancies, malnutrition, obesity rates and rates of disease were primarily more negative than their non-Indigenous counterparts, the rate with which they differed varied (p. 151).

The authors also recommended "that the development of Indigenous data systems be done in close collaboration with Indigenous peoples, so as to ensure that Indigenous values, health concepts, and priorities are reflected in them" (p. 154). Kirmayer and Bass, recognized the contributions of the Anderson et al. work, but note that it fails to account for "mental health, burden of chronic disease, or disability" and claim that "regional studies of Indigenous populations" also indicate "major disparities" within given geographical areas (2016, p. 105). Additionally, they argue that the Anderson et al's work failed to "account for complex migratory patterns and demographic shifts of Indigenous populations, including those associated with urbanization", meaning that it must be acknowledged that "Indigenous identity is a social and cultural construct that changes over time" rather than viewing Indigenous populations as "static" (p. 105).

According to Kirmayer and Bass

> The loss of control over one's own life as an individual, in communities, and whole populations, might be an especially toxic social process. Understanding the dynamics of disempowerment or loss of control over individual and collective destinies is important for identification of strategies for health promotion and recovery. (p. 106)

Kirmayer and Bass caution that the collection and discrimination of data is political and should be evaluated regarding the "recognition of specific local, social, cultural, and historical contexts" as these are essential components to understanding health care in Indigenous populations (2016, p. 106). Subsequent correspondence involving the Anderson article agrees that specific population data should be collected referencing the need, for example, to distinguish between India's 705 Scheduled Indigenous Tribes as the failure to collect data on each specific population inhibits health service by treating them as a single population (Saha et al. 2016, p. 2867). Subsequent reports, however, appear to support the Anderson et al. article's recommendation that "governments develop national policies with sustainable health targets focused on health service delivery, access, and Indigenous data systems". Discussions also agree that dominant governments fail to address the fact that the descriptive data, and attending reports, rarely result in "corresponding improvements in their [Indigenous population] health" (McCalman et al. 2016, pp. 2867–2868). In a final critique, Anderson et al. argues that collection of data continues to be done within Western paradigms and rarely results in any benefit to Indigenous populations (2016, p. 2868).

Indigenous/non-Indigenous health disparity was echoed in the World Health Organization's (WHO) symposium on social determinants and Indigenous health conducted in Adelaide (2007). The information reported at the symposium, again, decried the lack of sufficient data and the need to focus on Indigenous diversity involving location, State affiliation, and economic positioning. Overall, the symposium confirmed the Anderson et al. findings claiming that healthcare disparities among Indigenous populations, although remaining behind their non-Indigenous counterparts did vary within given regions. The symposium emphasized the impact of colonization, historically and currently, especially in connection with the loss of land stating that these were significant components involving the level of healthcare differences. Finally, the symposium reported that Western bias in the understanding of what is considered "health" exacerbated stereotyping, discrimination, and practices of blaming Indigenous populations for their negative health situations. They called for a global response to the health crisis in Indigenous populations beginning with an understanding of Indigenous paradigms and the need to address issues of human rights and of self-determination.

## Specific Statistics

Mortality and morbidity rates indicate significant disparities between Indigenous and non-Indigenous populations even when one recognizes the limited data and Western collection bias. By examining some of these disparities, one gains a picture of how different colonizers and colonized lives are. The statistics in this section, because of space and time, represent a rather randomized and limited example of the situations found in Indigenous communities. The specific issues covered also give credence to the above-mentioned diversity involving global Indigenous populations and the caution to not universalize situations and needs. What the examples do have in common is the connection between colonization practices such as land loss, cultural interference, and the loss of sovereignty recognition. These health issues then participate in what has been titled post-colonization stress disorders and impact both individuals and communities.

To begin, the impact of colonization stress is apparent when examining Indigenous suicide rates. While we are not claiming that suicide was non-existent in Indigenous populations before colonization or that all Indigenous suicides are the result of colonization stress, there is ample evidence that directly connects intergenerational trauma stemming from colonization to high rates of suicide in Indigenous communities.

According to Aho and Liu, "around the world, suicide rates for first nations (indigenous/aboriginal) peoples that have been colonized and positioned as a minority in their homeland are more than double that of other groups in the same country" (2010, p. 125). Acknowledging that the rates are under-reported, the available data indicates that

> suicide completion rates for indigenous populations are 1.5 to 4 times higher than those of other ethnic groups in the United States, Canada, Australia, and New Zealand…suicide rates among first nations compared to other ethnic groups in the same country; 1.7 times higher for American Indians and Native Alaskans, triple for Canadian Inuit and Metis in age-specific comparisons and double in gender-specific comparisons, three to four times higher for Australian Aborigines, and 1.5 times higher for New Zealand Maori. (p. 125)

Canadian Health reports support these inequities.

> In areas where there are many people who identify as Inuit, First Nations, and Métis, the suicide rates are, respectively, 6.5, 3.7, and 2.7 times higher than areas with a low concentration of people who identify as Indigenous. This means there are, respectively, 61.0, 29.2, and 18.6 more deaths by suicide per 100 000 people. Suicide rates are particularly high among males who live in areas where many people identify as Inuit (118.2 per 100 000). This represents 100.9 more deaths by suicide per 100 000 people. (2018, p. 11)

Echoing the above, the Australian health department claims that data in some Aboriginal populations is difficult to track because of the size and remote geographical areas (2013). However, the suicide rates among Aboriginal and Torres Strait populations have been "accelerating after the 1980s". According to the report, Aboriginals and Torres Strait suicides are twice that of the rest of the population and occur at younger ages. Additionally, the report states that the rate of intentional harm, non-completed suicide, is "many times higher" in Indigenous populations at a rate of 3.5 per 1000 for Indigenous populations as opposed to the 1.4 non-Indigenous rate (p. 10). According to the American Center for Disease Control (CDC), "the suicide rate among AI/AN [America Indians and Alaska Native populations] has been increasing since 2003, and in 2015 suicide rates in AI/AN [were] more than

3.5 times higher than those among racial/ethnic groups with the lowest rates" with a third of these deaths being between ages 10–24 (2018). Several of the reports also recognized the link between friend and family suicides as contributing factors to, what has been termed, clustered suicide events.

Discussions involving the increased rates of suicide, attempts, and completions, can be attributed to colonization impacts including loss of identity, land, tradition, and community. The destruction of culture and community appears to be increasing especially among younger demographics. Discussions among Indigenous scholars and medical personnel note increased suicide ideations, attempts, and completions in individuals reporting initial removal, such as boarding school and stolen status experiences, as well as those experiencing intergenerational trauma related to those events. What remains far less studied but indicated by these statistics is the rate of suffering and mental illness experienced by Indigenous populations that does not involve the attempt or completion of suicide.

While the above indicates the mental and emotional elements of post-colonization stress, the physical indicators are equally concerning. In 2009, Turnidge's research indicated a "high rate of *staphylococcus aureus* infection…in particular, a high rate of infection caused by methicillin-resistant strains of *S. aureus* (MRSA)". Turnidge references the Tong et al. article that indicates *S. aureus* is "6 times higher than that among the non-Aboriginal population" (p. 1416). Turnidge states that the increase may be because of rural geographic orientation along with "crowding and unreliable or deficient water supplies". Turnidge argues that prevention can be a simple matter of providing "access to clean water for bathing and showering" or installing and maintaining public pools to inhibit contraction and spread of the disease (p. 1417). While not wanting to over-simplify this health issue, the report does indicate that some treatments for communicable disease are within the controllable range for governments wanting to make a difference in Indigenous death rates.

A more prevalent and global epidemic in Indigenous populations that is directly attributable to colonization involves Type II diabetes. The Canadian health differential report claims that diabetes rates, I and II, on reserves and in Northern climates is 19% as opposed to the 6.8% in non-Indigenous populations. For Indigenous populations living off the reserve, the rate is 12.7%, Metis populations exhibit a rate of 9.9%, and Inuit populations report a rate of 4.7%. The Inuit rate which was not significantly different from the non-Indigenous rate (Pan-Canadian Health p. 195). However, there remains a concern regarding the Inuit data because of the population size and geographical region.

Aboriginal and Torres Strait statistics vary from 4% to 33% but these populations are listed as being three times more likely to suffer from diabetes I and II than their non-Indigenous counterparts. "In 2013, diabetes (excluding GDM) was the second leading underlying cause of death among Aboriginal and Torres Strait Islander people, with an age adjusted death rate six times higher than that for non-Indigenous people" (Australian Indigenous HealthReviews 2016, p. 3). According to *The Lancet*, the death rate from diabetes-related issues among Aboriginal and Torres Strait Islanders is "13 times greater" than in non-Indigenous populations (Clark 2011, p. 2066).

Colonization factors leading to the increase in Type II diabetes are largely attributed to the loss of land and traditional foods. Introduction of fatty foods, high levels of carbohydrates, and an emphasis on meat consumption on reserves, reservations, and in camps along with the later introduction of commodity boxes changed eating patterns. For example, while the Indigenous of the American Southwest ate a variety of beans before contact, post-contact rations and government organized crops focused on the use of pinto beans which are higher in carbohydrates than the more traditional tepary beans, which also contain higher protein concentrations (Nabhan et al. 1985). Some recent research has also indicated a potential connection between persistent organic pollutants (POPs) and the onset of Type II diabetes in Indigenous populations (Lovern et al. 2013). While POPs may not be the direct cause of Type II diabetes, they appear to be a potential trigger for the onset. Populations exposed to these environmental pollutants also exhibit higher levels of other issues such as cancers, birth defects, and loss of pregnancies.

While facing higher risks of specific illnesses, such as diabetes, stemming from the loss of traditional foods, individual Indigenous communities face unique health issues that must be addressed. For example, the Negev Bedouin Arabs in South Israel face the loss of seminomadic traditions which have been replaced by "government-directed urbanization". This community has "a median age of 15.9 years" and a birth rate of 5.45 compared with the general Arab population representing 22.2 years of age and a birth rate of 3.17 and Jewish populations that have an age of 31.8 years and a birth rate of 3.07. Additionally, "Infant mortality rates are 11.0 per 1000 births compared with 6.3 for all Arabic people and 2.4 for Jewish people" (Abu-Saad 2016, p. 1983).

Like other seminomadic and nomadic people, the Negev Bedouin populations continue to face problems of inclusion physically and the accuracy in data collection. In the case of the Negev Bedouins, this has also "excluded them from most of the national population, health, and welfare statistics" and "since 2012, the entire Negev Bedouin population, both in government-planned and unrecognized localities, has been excluded from national food security surveys" along with "labour force and poverty statistics" (p. 1983).

This statistical invisibility exacerbates the health disparity as well as the post-colonization trauma experienced within the Negev Bedouins. When States deny or ignore Indigenous populations, identity and land trauma become exacerbated and threaten communities with extinction.

Similar invisibility issues exist in African Indigenous populations. The African Commission on Human and Peoples' Rights (ACHPR) has worked to identify and promote the rights of these populations, but communities such as the Pygmies and the San continue to go unrecognized (Ohenjo et al. 2006, pp. 1037–1938). Unrecognized identity means unrecognized land rights, human rights, and loss of data inclusion. For the Pygmies of Central Africa, the destruction of forests has entailed the destruction of traditional ways of being. Additionally, "decades of violent conflict …subjected them to murder, rape, torture" (p. 1939). The loss of forests means the loss of traditional foods, medicines, and ceremonies used to reduce illness and discord. Without these traditional methods of healing, colonial diseases such as alcoholism and domestic violence have crept into communities (p. 1940).

For the San people of Botswana, similar issues involving the loss of land and traditional ways of being have resulted in physical and psychological trauma that remains largely unaddressed. The "controversial process of removing and resettling San from their lands in the Central Kalahari Game Reserve and dissolving their hunting and gathering rights" threatens their identity, health, and sovereignty rights (p. 1942). For the Namibian San, colonization "'meant incorporation as a landless underclass of farm labourers, domestic servants and squatters'". While a few individuals have been able to take control of small portions of land in the post-independent era, their way of life remains significantly altered (p. 1942). Research indicates that "health services [for both San and Pygmy populations] are at best inadequate for most and entirely absent for many" (p. 1943).

Colonization impacts have also been tracked within Latin America and the Caribbean beginning with population loss.

> The estimated total Indigenous populations dropped from up to 150 million (before European invasion in 1492) to 11 million…in many regions, particularly the tropical lowlands, populations fell by 90% or more in the first century after contact…the Caribbean…mortality rates in the Indigenous communities were as high as 900 per 1000 people. In tropical lowlands, Indigenous populations fell by more than 99%, in Peru from 9 million in 1520 to 670,000 (92%) in 1620, and in the Basin of Mexico from 1.6 million in 1519 to 180,000 (89%) in 1607. At the time of the Spanish invasion of Nicaragua in the 1520 s, there were 600,000 Indigenous people—in 1550 there were

only 45,000. At the end of the 16th century, Brazil had 1000 different Indigenous groups with 2-4 million people. Four centuries later the total Indigenous population had diminished to 220,000 individuals (Montenegro et al. 2006, p. 1861).

The destruction of populations had many components, but a large part of the population collapses have been attributed to the introduction of diseases including "smallpox and measles…influenza, yellow fever, and typhus".

Indigenous populations had no traditional medicines for these new diseases, and, before the needed medicines could be created, they were either dead or removed from lands that had the potential for traditional remedies. While the article notes some population recovery, it also notes the continued health disparity in the regions. The research indicates an increased standard of living when populations self-isolate and remain distanced from Western ways of life. For these populations, the struggle is to be allowed to maintain their land and access to resources against State and outside incursion (p. 1864). For populations that cannot self-isolate, the challenge is, as with all such Indigenous populations, to integrate traditional and colonial healthcare practices.

As research indicates, physical and mental health issues within Indigenous populations are at critical levels. Continuing sovereignty violations along with insufficient data collection, analysis, and dissemination exacerbate this crisis.

## Eugenics

One of the reasons that advancements in Indigenous global empowerment remain stymied is the failure of colonial States to recognize their responsibility in the creation of these situations. Canada, Australia, and a few other States have created reconciliation strategies and have admitted to past practices involving the destruction of Indigenous populations. However, equality efforts continue to be financially unsupported and, at times, are no more than political rhetoric. Neoliberal attacks on Indigenous land and resource rights continue to block Indigenous sovereignty assertions even as governments claim to support UNDRIP, the ILO, and related organizations focused on Indigenous rights. Additionally, limited scholarship and poor data collection erase or make invisible post-colonization trauma issues. In order to highlight colonial eugenics practices, this section will focus specially on how colonial eugenics strategies have violated Indigenous women's rights and functioned to eliminate Indigenous populations.

Beyond the diminishment of women's positions in traditional societies, colonizing powers must recognize their role and the continued consequences that have resulted from eugenics practices. It is not enough to say that events happened in the past and cannot be changed, as such claims dismiss the continuing impact of these historical events. As reported by Torpy, Galton's adoption of the term eugenics in 1883, along with claims of "improving the human race" established the foundation for later eugenics policies supporting forced sterilization (2000).

When connected with Mendel's theories of trait transmission, eugenics gave rise to theories that claimed, "individual maladies" and "social ills" could be transferred genetically. In 1927, these beliefs led to the upholding of *Buck v. Bell* creating an era of governmentally sanctioned involuntary sterilization (pp. 2–3). In addition to the physical sterilization practices imposed on "unfit" Indigenous individuals, policy eugenics strategies were also established as a means of "erasing" entire Native American communities deemed "not Indian enough" (Gonzales 2007, p. 54). We will first examine these policy eugenics before moving to the discussion of forced sterilization.

Walter Plecker is credited with spearheading policy eugenics and erasure techniques using the Racial Integrity Act of 1924. His justification stemmed from a belief that American Indian blood was "tainted" because of its prior mixture with "black blood". This identification of blood "color" caused him to fear the intermingling of American Indian blood with that of White blood. Using the practice of hypodescent, Plecker justified the documentary elimination of entire tribes by labeling them as "colored" (pp. 54–56).[2]

This reclassification eliminated American Indian identity at the time and continues to impact federal recognition for both individuals and tribes in Virginia. "Blood Quantum" along with physical features such as "skin color, facial features, hair texture, and body odor" became identifiers for "Indian" or "tribal" designation during the Indian Reorganization era. The Federal Acknowledgement Project in 1978 "provided both an administrative review process and mandatory criteria for any group seeking acknowledgement as a 'tribe' by the federal government" (p. 61).

In what may be some of the most unscientific measures imaginable for determining blood quantum, the science of eugenics turned to anthropometrics to identify "Indian" identity. Among these non-blood-related tests for determining blood-quantum was the "pencil test". According to this test, if a

---

[2] It is interesting to note that the term "colored" continues to be primarily associated with Black and African American communities. However, historically, this term referenced all non-Whites. So, when one references "colored" regiments, these regiments included demographics other than Black and African Americans. The failure to recognize the Indigenous involvement in such groups continues Indigenous invisibility and erasure.

pencil was placed in the person's hair and remained after "vigorous shaking" the person was not Indian. If the pencil fell, "it had fallen out of real Indian hair". Anthropometrics also included "size, shape, and width of the heads, teeth, skin, nose, [and] lips" as identifying Indian markers (p. 62).

While many of these anthropometric measures have fallen out of favor as identifiers of American Indians genetics, some "identifiers" continue to be used to justify migration theories such as the Bering Strait and other colonizing histories.[3]

> From 1924 until 1946, and relying on Virginia's Racial Integrity Act, Walter Plecker uniformly defined as 'negro' all Virginia Indian families who had been racialized in the ninetieth century as 'free people of color.' It was Plecker's opinion that no Virginia Indians were free of African ancestry; their Indianness therefore was considered null and void. Plecker then vigorously worked to further detribalize Virginia's Native peoples, including all divisions of the Monacan, Chickahominy, Rappahannock, Mattaponi, Nansemond, and Pamunkey by reclassifying them as 'Negro'. Plecker's methods were simple, direct, and effective. (p. 63)

Plecker worked to finalize Indigenous genocide by altering birth certificates issued before 1924 and by declaring that those who insisted on identifying as American Indian were "perpetuating racial fraud" for which they would face "felony charges" including a year in prison (p. 64). The continued adherence to the standards set in this era for "Indian" identification perpetuate stereotypes and ensure that individual and tribal recognition would remain "all but impossible" thus completing the "paper genocide" (p. 66). Paper genocide continues to be a problem for Indigenous identity especially in States that relied on eugenic markers. Australian Indigenous continue to face similar issues if they are lighter skinned. Claims of heritage are still often denied based purely on skin color.

As mentioned by Locust, there are some physical traits that can be observed in Indigenous populations, but they are not universal and they are not arbitrary factors such as hair type, skin color, or head size. The characteristics often used in these early genetic practices were both arbitrary and based on stereotyping of different Indigenous communities and individuals.

---

[3]An example of a modern anthropometric strategy has been used regarding a genetic marker that exists throughout many North American Indigenous and also in an isolated community in Asia. The interpretation of one team was that this "proved" Asian migration over the Bering Strait land bridge. As pointed out earlier in this text, such a conclusion runs afoul of Western logic that would indicate an equally logical conclusion would be that some American Indigenous migrated to Asia. Nonetheless, the use of this physical marker, along with skeletal markers, continue to be used as identifiers of American Indian identity.

According to Lawrence, eugenics guidelines and practices, such as those above, evolved into outright practices of involuntary sterilization in the U.S. which can be documented well into the 1960s and 1970s (2000). Lawrence examined Indian Health Services (IHS) policies and case law used to support enforced sterilization of "unfit" women including American Indian and women on welfare or in poverty. In 1976, the Government Accounting Office (GAO) recognized situations involving lacking or incorrect practices of informed consent regarding sterilization, but it failed to label these practices as coercive.

Instead, the report largely excused the practices as mistakes or because of the lack of knowledge of or a lack of uniformity of practices involving informed consent. In actuality, many of the practices involved active agency on the part of the medical staff as practices often included hysterectomies preformed while removing tonsils. In some cases, medical personnel claimed that sterilization procedures were reversible so that the women could choose to have children in the future.

In addition, language barriers, issues of literacy, and the lack of translators denied women adequate information necessary to give informed consent. One American Indian woman said she was handed a form after her baby was born and told it would help her get extra diapers and food. She later found out, when she could not get pregnant again, that they had sterilized her during what she thought was a routine post-pregnancy exam. When she denied knowledge, they produced the signed form.

Many of the forms used for consent gave no indication of what information had been conveyed to the patient allowing for a great deal of manipulation. When patients questioned the practices, examination boards were shown signed forms and could not scrutinize what patients were told as the information was unavailable (p. 407). In these cases, deference was given to the medical personnel rather than Indigenous patients. The assumption being that patients could not be reliable witnesses.

According to Lawrence, the GAO stated that the "forms did not adhere to the standards set by HEW" (2000, p. 406).

> The GAO investigators examined IHS records and found that the IHS performed 3,406 sterilizations during the fiscal years of 1973 through 1976. These numbers did not include those conducted in the Albuquerque area because contract physicians performed all sterilizations in that IHS region. GAO personnel did not interview any Native American women who had been sterilized during this period because they said they "believe [d] that such an effort would not have been productive." (p. 407)

Finally, the GAO report indicated that while some physicians failed to understand HEW guidelines for consent, others were independent practitioners and not subject to HEW regulations (p. 407).

Lawrence argued that Johnson's War on Poverty targeted Indigenous, African American, and Hispanic women for involuntary sterilization.

> ...studies revealed that the Indian Health Service sterilized between 25 and 50 percent of Native American women between 1970 and 1976. Dr. Connie Pinkerton-Uri conducted a study that revealed that IHS physicians sterilized at least 25 percent of American Indian women between the ages of fifteen and forty-four. Cheyenne tribal judge Marie Sanchez questioned fifty Cheyenne women and discovered that IHS doctors had sterilized twenty-six of them. She announced her belief that the number of women the GAO reported sterilized was too low and that the percentage was much higher than 25 percent. Mary Ann Bear Comes Out, a member of the Northern Cheyenne tribe, conducted a survey on the Northern Cheyenne Reservation and Labre Mission grounds. She found that in a three-year period, the IHS sterilized fifty-six out of 165 women between the ages of thirty and forty-four in the survey area. (p. 410)

Pinkerton-Uri's research further indicates that the Indian Health Service (IHS) "singled out full-blooded women for sterilization" and that "women generally agreed to sterilization when they were threatened with the loss of their children and/or their welfare benefits. Moreover, Pinkerton-Uri claims that many of these women gave consent when they were heavily sedated during a Cesarean section or when they were in a great deal of pain during labor. Finally, Pinkerton-Uri noted that the women often could not understand the consent forms as they were written in English at the twelfth-grade level" (pp. 411–412).

Lawrence explains that the loss of reproductive ability impacts both the identity and well-being of the individual and the community. She notes that as communities are unable to reproduce, they lose representation and economic sustainability making them easier targets for paper erasure.[4] While GAO statistics claim that 3,406 Indigenous women were sterilized between

---

[4] While relating this information to one of her classes, Lovern recalls a student becoming rather perplexed. When asked what she was thinking the student responded that she had been doing the math. Beginning with the 3,406 Indigenous women sterilized between 1973 and 1976 she extrapolated the potential loss of children given birth rates at the time between 2 and 4. Additionally, the 3,406 number was limited by the GAO because it chose only a few IHS centers for study. The subsequent studies that list between 25 and 50% in some areas represents an even greater loss of generations. The student agreed that some of these procedures may have been therapeutic and others a matter of consensual choice. Nonetheless, the student noted that the numbers are staggering.

1973 and 1976, additional scholarship argues that the GAO limited its investigation to only a few IHS centers. Subsequent studies indicate that between 25 and 50% of Indigenous women were involuntarily sterilized within certain populations effectively eliminating generations of Indigenous children.

In A. Smith's research on American Indian women's reproductive issues, she quotes Hernandez-Avila and Stannard, who claim that the targeting of American Indian women was a systematic attempt to continue colonization practices following Chivington's statement to "kill and scalp all little and big" as "nits make lice" (2005, pp. 79–80). A. Smith acknowledges the research estimating 25–50% sterilization rates in areas might appear unbelievable but points out that many women were sterilized after having two or more children.

A. Smith chronicles the experiences of these women including one, who was told that her headaches would be cured with sterilization, only to find out after sterilization that she, in fact, had a brain tumor (p. 83). A. Smith also notes that sterilization strategies were not limited to the U.S. but existed in other colonized areas. "In Peru, the Health Ministry recently issued a public apology for sterilizing 200,000 indigenous people (primarily Quechua and Aymara) without consent during the presidency of Alberto Fujimori…The majority of operations were undertaken without anesthesia and without aftercare" (p. 85). According to A. Smith estimates are that only 10% of the sterilizations in Peru between 1996 and 2000 were voluntary (pp. 85–86).

Stote reports that Canada employed "coercive sterilization …in several provinces but only two, Alberta and British Columbia, enacted formal legislation" (p. 5). Stote chronicles the eugenics arguments in Canada including its use as treatment for mental illness and as a way to control high rates of infant mortality in poor populations (pp. 15–16). According to Stote, Alberta established a Sterilization Act and installed a Eugenics Board to oversee the sterilization of Aboriginal patients. She reports that "the proportion of Aboriginal peoples sterilized by the Act rose steadily from 1939 onward, tripling from 1949 to 1959…despite the stipulation that consent be obtained, it was only sought in 17 percent of Aboriginal cases" (p. 49).

Stote also reports that in 1973 the Canadian Broadcasting Corporation produced the show *Weekend* that charged the Canadian system with attempting to undermine Inuit birth rates by coercing sterilization (2015). The program also claimed that the government supported such practices "for their own good" and the known language barriers represented a governmentally sanctioned undermining of the population. These charges were denied by the Minister of National Health and Welfare, but allegations continued (pp. 71–75). Stote acknowledges that the government may not have actively sanctioned the "systematic sterilization of Aboriginal people", but she argues that it was complicit based on the "policies and legislation affecting other aspects of Aboriginal life… making sterilization more likely… through its financial support of provinces" (p. 92).

A. Smith claims that modern U.S. strategy has turned from surgical sterilization to sterilization by hormonal contraceptives such as Norplant and Depo-Provera, which largely target poor women and women of-color regardless of the often-extreme side-effects (pp. 88–96). It should be noted that Norplant was eliminated from use in the U.S. around 2002 after sizable lawsuits but was continued in use overseas in many "developing" countries. Even as the drug continues to be controversial, there are discussions of reintroducing it, or similar products, with slight changes and under a different name. Depo-Provera has faced its own controversy including a marketing strategy claimed to target women of-color in the U.S. and areas such as sub-Saharan Africa. Beyond issues of markets and side-effects, part of this controversy revolves around some studies that indicate the drug might increase the likelihood of contracting HIV. While the debate over the use of drugs such as these has yet to be "scientifically" concluded, the potential impact on colonized women and communities remains concerning.

Stote's concluding chapter on the UN definition of genocide explains how States, especially those admitting their acts under reconciliation agreements, will never be held accountable for these policies and practices (2015). According to Stote, States escape being charged with genocide by employing careful wording and ambiguous definitions in documents such as the UN document on genocide. Given that the alleged perpetrators of these practices were responsible for crafting the UN documents, and other legislation involving genocide, it is not surprising that they built in a loophole. Stote explains that Canada, for example,

> will not likely be subject to the scrutiny of the international community within a criminal court, nor will they be weighted according to the internationally accepted definition of genocide. The role Canada has played in shaping current understandings of genocide has limited the avenues for justice available to Indigenous people within national borders and abroad…Canada played a role in rendering the Genocide Convention ineffective through its involvement in its formation at the United Nations and on the national level by enacting domestic legislation that has attempted to confine genocide solely to instances of physical destruction. (p. 152)

The issue here seems to be one of spirit verses letter of the law. While colonizing countries such as Canada and the United States supported eugenics legislation, current definitional standards, set largely by these colonizing countries, deny the use of the term "genocide". However, it is difficult not to equate the systemic eugenics practices involving "paper erasure" and sterilization along with boarding schools, military removals from land, and massacres perpetuated because of religious difference as anything other than genocide. Given that these were planned, organized, and carried out against Indigenous populations, such practices clearly fit within the spirit of the UN definition of genocide, if not the letter. Western study of genocidal practices such as those listed directly above tends to be compartmentalized so that boarding schools are not studied in conjunction with sterilization or land loss. The compartmentalization of these topics ensures topic isolation and avoids any recognition of the cumulative pattern. Moreover, when the patterns can be clearly observed in multiple Western colonized countries, it is difficult to deny that these patterns involve a strategy of the genocide of global Indigenous populations.

"American Indians face emotional challenges such as depression, substance abuse, collective trauma exposure, interpersonal loss and unresolved grief, and related problems within the lifespan and across generations" (Brave Heart et al. 2011, p. 282). In looking at the history of colonization ranging from boarding schools to involuntary sterilization, the patterns of intergenerational trauma and distrust become clear. Additionally,

> …traditional American Indian/Alaska Native mourning practices and cultural protective factors were impaired due to the federal prohibition around 1883 against the practice of traditional ceremonies, which lasted until the 1978 American Indian Religious Freedom Act. However, parts of Indigenous practices related to traditional burials are still not permitted. (p. 284)

Faced with the plethora of historical and current policies designed to actively or complicity limit Indigenous sovereignty, it is no wonder that there exists a vast distrust by Indigenous populations regarding both governments and governmental sponsored or supported healthcare (Lovern, 2011). Indigenous populations are aware of past and current governmental and medical practices. They recognize the impact of eugenics and legal legislation to limit their sovereignty assertions to land, religious freedom, and to children, both born and unborn. What continues to be frustrating is the fact that colonizing States choose to remain unaware and apathetic when faced with the results of their own systemic practices that they would classify in other states as patterns of genocide.

## Indigenous Peoples on Wellness

In many ways, the entirety of this book has been leading to this chapter recognizing the impact of colonization on Indigenous individuals and communities both physically and mentally. This section recognizes these impacts but will focus primarily on traditional Indigenous concepts of wellness and the attempts by many communities to continue or re-orient in order to rebalance both individual and community.

Before focusing on Indigenous knowledges involving wellness, two concepts need to be clarified. First, what constitutes wellness is culturally dependent. As with most Indigenous ideologies, there are different standards and ideas on how to "define" a "well" person. There remains, however, a significant difference between Indigenous concepts of wellness and Western concepts of health.[5] Similarly, there are distinct differences between unwellness and illness. Some of these differences will be discussed in this section, but what is important to note here is that these terms, and the conditions to which they are assigned, are culturally dependent.

Recalling Western binary constructs, health is constructed as being in opposition to illness with health being the preferred, or "normal", position and illness being the negative, or "abnormal", position. Additionally, Western medicine has primarily taken a reductive approach in dealing with illness and the abnormal. This approach isolates what is abnormal with the intention of eliminating it or "fixing" it. While holistic approaches to the human and to illness do exist in Western medicine, these perspectives have yet to become the norm. Treatment of illness is then targeted against what is considered abnormal, or "ill", with less focus on the entirety of the individual in relation to the abnormal virus, disease, infection, or anomaly. Even less emphasis is placed on the relationship between the individual and the community and how this illness or disease impacts that relationship.

Using Indigenous approaches to wellness, it becomes clear that culture must be considered in defining health and diagnosing and treating individual and communal physical and mental well-being. Second, the impact of colonization has significantly altered traditional Indigenous definitions, diagnoses, and the treatment of unwellness. Removal from and destruction of land has impacted Indigenous peoples' abilities to relate to, care for, and be in balance with environmental elements necessary for the promotion of wellness and the treatment of unwellness.

---

[5] We will use the concept of wellness to refer to Indigenous constructs and health to refer to Western constructs. The term "health" could be employed for both, but we wish to avoid confusion as to the definition of "health".

Loss of religious freedom has also inhibited traditional ceremonies and rituals necessary to maintain balance and wellness and to avoid both individual and communal unwellness. Fragmented social structures and the loss of community have damaged and eliminated Indigenous traditional interaction creating rifts and undermining family and social structures needed to perform the required ceremonies and to maintain traditional knowledge. The loss of language means that prayers, chants, sings, and sacred utterances to promote wellness are not available, and the assimilation into Western knowledge and education has significantly inhibited or destroyed thousands of years of healing knowledge. Finally, the loss of traditional economies and trade has meant that what was once available to assist traditional healers is now controlled by Western laws or often no longer in existence because of environmental destruction.

Post-colonization stress can be observed in the bodies and minds of Indigenous people globally. As stated by Milburn, "as populations adopt Western diet and lifestyle patterns, [a] distinct pattern of diseases began to emerge" (2004, p. 413). Milburn identifies some of these diseases as "obesity, Type II diabetes, hypertension, coronary heart disease, peripheral vascular disease, varicose veins, diverticulosis, appendicitis, kidney stones, and some forms of cancer" (p. 413). He notes that these are largely related to the introduction of the Western diet, and he claims that obesity, following from this diet, is what often leads to a myriad of health problems.

Milburn also notes that "Indigenous populations are often disproportionately affected by changing diet and lifestyle patterns" but also argues "that major lifestyle change can not only prevent but even begin to reverse Western diseases over a matter of weeks" (pp. 414–416). According to Milburn, adoption of Indigenous diets requires cultural and bioregional sciences focused on a "wholistic worldview". "Traditional food ways are based on an intimate and spiritual connection to the land and entail a reciprocal relationship that must be actively maintained" (p. 421). He points out that this integrated Indigenous science allowed the Inuit to understand and treat scurvy, which, in turn, allowed them to treat Jacques Cartier's crew in 1535 (p. 422).[6] Living sustainably is a foundational component of Indigenous ways of being, making reciprocal aspects of sustainability a large part of Indigenous wellness.

Cajete lists several foods and medicines introduced by Native American communities to Western communities including, but not limited to, corn, cotton, rubber, pumpkins, peanuts, strawberries, and avocados (2000, pp. 133–140). As mentioned in a previous chapter both tomatoes and cacao,

---

[6] Jacques Cartier and his crew were colonizers and were among the many groups of colonizers who suffered from and had no knowledge of how to treat diseases such as scurvy.

originating in Indigenous communities, have become Western staples, but in addition medicines such as tobacco, quinine, and pain relievers were also Indigenous discoveries later usurped by colonizing forces (pp. 133–140). Voeks reports that

> The roots of *Cephaelis ipecacuanha*, known in colonial times by the Tupi name *ipecacuanha*, was employed medicinally for its antihemorrhage properties. It later became the source of pharmaceutical *ipecac*. Pilocarpine, the major treatment for glaucoma, was derived from the local medicinal shrub *jaborandi* (*Pilocarpus jaborandi*). The enzyme papain was extracted from papaya and used as a digestive aid as well as a meat tenderizer...A few, however have retained their original names and continue to be employed for their perceived medicinal properties. These include *capeba* (*Pothomorphe umbellata*, fedegoso (*Senna occidentalis*), *embauba* (*Cecropia pachystachya*), alfavaquinhade-cobra (*Peperomia pellucida*) and jurubeba (*Solanum sp.*). (Voeks p. 39)

Additional collections of Indigenous pharmaceuticals can be found in works such as Lewis and Jordan's *Creek Indian Medicine Ways* and Moerman's *Native American Ethnobotany* (2002; 1998). Beyond these collections are traditional Asian understandings of food as medicine, acupuncture, yoga, and energy practices. While Western cultures have bastardized many of these practices, making them into martial arts competitions or exercise classes, their roots originate in spiritual practices of wellness.

Milburn concludes by noting that Indigenous science and medicine can work to advance not only Indigenous wellness, but also non-Indigenous concepts of health (2004). For example, the use of the "three sisters" (beans, corn, squash), not only creates an environmental wellness by balancing the soil and discouraging infestations, but also works to promote individual wellness by balancing nutrition and avoiding pesticides. Use of the three sisters can also assist in community economic balance by producing healthier crops without depleting the soil (p. 423). Finally, the growth of beans and corns combine to create a protein that takes far less acreage for larger output than animal-based protein such as beef or chicken, that is if the animals are allowed to roam.

Talamantez explains that for Indigenous people "to be moved away from her place means to be living an unhealthy life, out of balance and harmony" (2006). While Talamantez is speaking specifically of the Apache concepts of healing, the sentiments are replicated throughout Indigenous research.

> Acknowledging the interconnectedness of all living entities is central to what it means to be indigenous to a place and to be of good health... An Apache

knows, when she is ill, that it is because she is out of harmony with the universe. She knows that if a ceremony has effected a cure for someone else, it can also cure her. The performance reassures her that something can be done to reestablish a proper balance between her and the spiritual and physical environment. She is instructed as well as informed by the medicine man or medicine woman, that the cure will be achieved if the 'patient' will behave in the prescribed way—the way the supernaturals behaved in the beginning of time. (p. 119)

To understand what Talamantez is saying, it is important to return to the understanding of spirit in Indigenous epistemology. As always, this is a generalization used to aid in understanding and not a universal or essentialist claim as each Indigenous community will have a unique understanding of spirit, reciprocity, and wellness. However, the generalization will serve to highlight the difference between Indigenous and Western constructs. Focusing on the concept of reciprocity and the ethics involving connectivity, one can begin to understand the complexity of Indigenous concepts of wellness. Beginning with the understanding that all things participate in spirit and are therefore connected one to the other, the wellness of the individual is tied to all one's relations including community, environment, and spiritual realms.

The idea of wellness is then to be in balance, or harmony, with all those to which the individual is related. Unwellness is, in turn, being out of balance, or harmony, with one's self or one's relations. Ceremonies, rituals, prayers, and medicines work together to maintain wellness and to avoid or treat unwellness. "Ritual is for the purpose of restoring balance, the essence of health, to individual and community" (Somé 1998, p. 183). Within this system, individuals are careful in word, thought, and action as these create reality and impact the wellness of their relations. Such an ethic is complex in that one must consider the position of all others before choosing and, in choosing, one must accept the consequences of that choice.

While some communities discuss the abilities of a medicine person to "draw out" that which is causing the unwellness, many Indigenous communities refer to the medicine person as the "helper". In other words, the individual is responsible for her own wellness, or balance but may need the assistance of the medicine person and, in turn, need the assistance of the community. According to Somé's article, African rituals and healing commonly emphasize the importance of community (pp. 86–100). Ceremonies and rituals may also include relations from the plant, animal, spiritual, and human realms working together to assist in a person's return to balance. It is however important to remember that balance is not a state of being so much as a process that changes from moment to moment requiring constant adjustments.

Within many Indigenous communities, often only specific individuals are charged with the knowledge of medicine, ritual, or ceremony because with this knowledge comes the knowledge to harm. The information may be passed in families, from a teacher to initiate, or be appointed by community at birth. Nonetheless, often, knowledge is held within specific members of the community. Additionally, there may be multiple medicine people within a community, each with a specialty or simply with different "clients". In the case of the Sami, secrecy was held regarding the most sacred healing knowledge and was not to be shared or "withdrawn". The practices were considered powerful enough to cause harm to anyone attempting to appropriate the knowledge. The *noaidi* traditionally practiced these secret healing events. However, colonization and the death penalty for "Sami Sorcery" changed the practice as well as the transmission of the traditional healing knowledge (Miller 2015).

Similar problems have occurred in other Indigenous communities as colonizing forces have intentionally and unintentionally misinterpreted traditional knowledge and medicine. For example, Western colonizing interpretations and translational limitations continue to frame traditional medicine as "magic" or "sorcery", which equates it with "evil" in Western dichotomous religious beliefs. According to one Creek medicine woman, "most of the knowledge is common sense if one pays attention to the land, the plants, and the animals. They will tell you what heals and what harms. Watching and listening closely is a large part of the medicine, the rest is taught from one healer to another or from Spirit, but it is a life-long quest as things change."

A Cherokee medicine woman reported that there are

> …three main causes of unwellness. First, one fails to be careful and follow the right path or do things in a good way. There are consequences to this as mentioned in the stories. Second, there is unintentional harm. Unintentional harm occurs when one says something without thinking or does not realize the harm an action could do to another. Even being too happy can cause harm to one whose energy is in the wrong place. Finally, there is intentional harm. This occurs when one intends to inflict damage physically, emotionally, or mentally. (Lovern et al. 2013, pp. 41–54)

Intentional harm has often been associated with the English term "witching", which is partly a matter of Western religious bias and partly because of translational insufficiencies in the English language. When understood from an Indigenous perspective, both intentional and unintentional harm can "witch" a person as these can both inflict harm on another. Understanding how this works goes back to the understanding of Spirit as the primary way in which beings interact. If Spirit connects all things, it impacts all things.

Using the knowledge of Spirit in either its spiritual or physical manifestation to harm another is found in many Indigenous understandings and is associated with negative practices and the violations of reciprocity ethics. Within the differing languages, however, the terms referring to such practices are more complicated than Western depictions of "witches". Unintentional harm also comes with consequences but is often viewed less negatively depending on the situation and individual, particularly if the individual is a child. Nonetheless, children are taught early to be careful with words, actions, and thoughts as they can cause harm.

Part of being brought up Indigenous is to learn to avoid unintentional harm. It is also often understood that any type of conflict will cause imbalance and a lack of harmony, which allows unwellness to occur (Lovern et al. 2013, pp. 41–48). So, conflict is avoided. While controversy may be discussed and is understood as part of life, conflict is considered childish and one is responsible for growing in wisdom and learning to compromise or avoid conflict. This is a wisdom sought and worked toward as one ages.

## Body and Mind Differences

Returning to the understanding that wellness is culturally constructed, it is important to place this in the context of mind and body differences. In Western construction, difference imposes the dichotomy of abled/disabled with abled being in the preferential position. This ableist construction further idealizes the abled position by imagining some body orientation involving "perfect" or "absolute" health. The idea is to be free of any disease, disability, or disfigurement. While such a Platonic form might be imaginable, it is not clear that such a form exists. Rather, what appears to exist is a collection of humans each falling below the "perfection" standard be it from near-sightedness, diabetes, missing limbs, or mental illness.

Clare argues that Western understandings of difference frame the issue according to "who's healthy and who's not" and attempts to "clarify the relationship between health and disability" (2017, p. 14). Clare also argues against the medicalization of disability and its subsequent emphasis on "cure", as this construction of being invokes images of lesser beings and emphasizes the "need to fix" what is "wrong". Clare states that "for some of us, even if we accept disability as damage to individual body-minds, these tenants quickly become tangled, because an original nondisabled state of being doesn't exist...Rather it arises from an imagination of what I would be like, from some definition of *normal* and *natural*" (p. 15). Clare's book challenges the concept of cure and explores the imagery assigned to body-mind differences in Western constructions of wholeness and health.

What Clare's discussions bring to light is the need for alternative ways to envision mind-body differences. Indigenous understandings offer just that, an interpretation of body differences in a way that neither judges a difference as "abnormal", nor requires a "cure". It is interesting to note that many Indigenous languages have no words for disability, crippled, or similar Western terms. There are no constructions of abled/disabled or idealized understandings of what a human should be. Instead, it is understood that differences are a part of human reality, with no two humans being exactly alike. Describing humans is then like the 300 words used by the Sami to describe snow, each is accurate and unique. One way to think about differences involves the idea of talents. Somé have a talent for singing or for walking, while others may have a talent for painting or for hearing. Not being able to see, hear, or think quickly is no more than a difference in talents. According to Locust, many Indigenous people believe that "everyone is made exactly as the Creator intended. To want to be different or to fret over a perceived lack is to question the Creator's wisdom. Others believe that each of us knew the form we would take before birth. We had a choice and chose this life for the lessons that could be learned or that which could be taught, but it was a choice."

Another description of difference is that, while bodies may be unique, one must remember that the spirit is whole. So, someone with a difference in mental ability, an issue with anxiety, or who is unable to communicate verbally with others still participates in a wholeness of spirit. It is possible to have a spiritual unwellness or damage to one's spirit as evidenced by colonization trauma and intergenerational trauma, but these are a unique type of spiritual damage. Cases of physical or mental differences do not necessitate or indicate a spiritual difference or damage.[7]

While some traditions claim that body and mind differences allow special qualities to be recognized, others understand that such people have lessons to learn or to teach. Still others claim that a strong spirit is needed to inhabit a severely different body. Regardless, body differences neither define the individual, nor do they necessarily impact the spirit. Additionally, differences do not necessitate a cure. While cures are often both possible and welcome,

---

[7]It is important to remember here that Indigenous ontologies often use concepts of mind, body, and spirit or mind, body, spirit, and emotion. Unwellnesses are thus manifested differently and can involve or impact the spirit in different ways but may also be entirely distanced from the spirit.

some cases are chronic or can be repeated. These differences are then part of the balancing process. They are just part of the person's lived experience. As some differences require continued adaptation, balance will shift with the changes. Indeed, even individuals with only minor or non-permanent differences such as colds or the flu find that, if they live long enough, they will suffer additional differences as they age (Wendell 2008, p. 828).

Body differences are a part of interdependence and reciprocity ethics. The talents of all members are part of the whole of society. As one Elder stated, when the child, or any person, with differences needs something, the entire community is there to help. The family need not ask; it is just a part of being a community (Patterson 1997). The community will also need to balance with the needs involving the differences in people. While disability is framed in the West as an individual situation needing to be dealt with and "overcome" by the one disabled, Indigenous communities understand difference as a way of life and so part of reciprocity ethics involving community responsibilities. It is also important to note that differences do not define an individual within a community, it is simply a part of the individual and both the individual and the community need to come to balance with the difference, thus the understanding of lessons and teachings. Locust talks of a Piki bread maker who, despite having hip dysplasia and severe back trauma, was known for her expertise in making Piki bread. At times she needed assistance to attend the baking, but her talent was revered in the community (Lovern et al. 2013, pp. 95–96).

In cases of mental differences, Somé explains that in Africa

> There is a similar respect for the person who is experiencing a psychological crisis. This crisis is seen as the result of an intense interaction with the other world, making the person think and act crazily. Resolving the crisis, in an indigenous community, results in releasing that person's gift to the community—the very gifts won through the person's intense dealings with Spirit…The difference is that in the modern world, errant behavior in a person is regarded as a personal problem, concerning only that individual. The possibility that there is a larger meaning to be found in the person's experiences, which might translate into something meaningful for that person's community, is rarely considered. (p. 97)

According to Somé, "the community supports the person through ritual" (1998, p. 99). In talking about Indigenous ways of wellness, the authors of this book have had many Westerners respond to these descriptions with shock and with incorrect interpretations such as "crazy people are allowed to run around and do what they pleased and harm themselves or others". Such statements are not only patently false, but simpleminded. When communities come together to support a person in crisis, Indigenous practices involve love, respect, and assistance. It is true that they do not regularly lock away the person in crisis or remove them from the community. Instead, the individual often becomes well-attended in a way that instills dignity and community embeddedness and eliminates, as much as one can, any possible harm to self or others. It must be noted that neither in Indigenous nor in Western systems can harm to self and others be completely eradicated.

Waugh, Szafran, and Triscott, in addressing cultural competency issues in Western medicine, refer to the fact that "the majority of diagnostic tests are based on cognitive assessments not validated within various cultural contexts" (2011, p. 19). For example, they explain that "not all cultures accepted the medical concept of dementia. The Bigstone Cree did not recognize dementia as an illness" (p. 31). According to this research,

> there is no direct Cree word to designate the illness we identify as dementia, the closest being *wongigiskit,* meaning forgetfulness…forgetfulness and memory loss were related to a stage in life, rather than to a disease. The community suggested that to treat such a person as being 'ill' was a degradation of their personal worth in their community and removed them from tasks that they could and should be doing…Absent-mindedness at a certain level was regarded as 'normal' for those dealing with issues 'from the other side'. (Triscott 2011, p. 180)

This is a system of balance and reciprocity. As changes occur with age, accident, or exist from birth, balance will need to be sought by the individual, family, and community. The balance is integrated and will require continual healing practices including ritual and ceremony.

B. H. Miller advocates for the "relatively new field of transcultural psychiatry" that denies the modern "one-size-fits-all…diagnostic system for mental disorder" noting that "transcultural psychiatry shows that mental disorder may manifest differently in different parts of the world" (2015, p. 100). The creation of fields such as transcultural psychiatry represents a move forward in Western colonization as these cultures begin to explore inclusive models even as they fall short of fully recognizing the reciprocity ethic represented in Indigenous concepts of balance and wellness.

This chapter has focused on health issues in Indigenous cultures stemming from historical and current practices of colonization including governmentally sanctioned eugenics and involuntary sterilization. We have also examined the issues involving the failure to properly collect, interpret, and disseminate Indigenous data. A common theme in all these practices has been the lack of adequate consent by Indigenous individuals and communities. The final sections of this chapter explored a bit of what wellness means in Indigenous populations and its relation to reciprocity and balance.

This chapter, and indeed the wholeness of this book, has been leading to the discussion of wellness and balance in Indigenous cultures. While understanding the historical and current trauma within Indigenous communities and suffered by Indigenous individuals, it is important to recognize that traditional ways of being continue to exist as both individuals and communities are working to heal. In the face of intergenerational trauma and the continuation of sovereignty denial, many Indigenous communities and individuals have advanced wellness traditions as they attempt to balance with intergenerational colonization trauma in a way that creates both individual and community wellness.

## Additional Readings

(2010). *Addressing the Housing Needs of Native American Veterans with Disabilities: Field Hearing before the Subcommittee on Housing and Community Opportunity of the Committee on Financial Services U.S. House of Representatives.* One Hundred Eleventh Congress, Second Session. Serial No 111-119. Washington: U.S. Government Printing Office.

(2006). "African Commission on Human and Peoples' Rights (ACHPR)". *Indigenous Peoples in Africa: The Forgotten Peoples?* (pp. 1–29) Copenhagen: International Work Group for Indigenous Affairs.

Anderson, W. (2008). Indigenous Health in a Global Frame: From Community Development to Human Rights. *Health and History, 10*(2). The physician as Historian. Australian and New Zealand Society of the History of Medicine, Inc. 94–108.

Barnsley, I. (2006). The Right to Health of Indigenous Peoples in the Industrialized World: A Research Agenda. *Health and Human Rights.* The President and Fellows of Harvard College on behalf of Harvard School of Public Health/Francois-Xavier Bagnoud Center for Health and Human Rights, pp. 43–54.

Bennett, B., & Green, S. (Ed.). (2019). *Our Voices: Aboriginal Social Work* (2nd ed.). Red Globe Press.

Biddle, N., Al-Yaman, F., Gourley, M., Gray, M., Bray, J. R., Brady, B., Pham, L. A., Williams, E., & Montaigne, M. (2014). Indigenous Australians and the National Disability Insurance Scheme. *Key Issues for Disability Service Delivery Models for Remote Indigenous Communities.* ANU Press.

Brown, E., Godden, C., & Sopheak, N. (2006). Uniting Indigenous Communities in Cambodia to Claim the Right to Maternal Healthcare. *Gender and Development, 14*(2), 211–222.

Bruchhausen, W. (2017). The Human Right to Health and Primary Health Care (PHC) Policies. In S. Klotz, H. Bielefeldt, M. Schmidhuber, A. Frewer (Eds.), *Healthcare as a Human Rights Issue: Normative Profile, Conflicts and Implementation* (pp. 145–166). Transcript Verlag.

Chenhall, R., & Senior, K. (2009). 'Those Young People all Crankybella': Indigenous Youth Mental Health and Globalization. *International Journal of Mental Health, 38*(3). Globalization and Mental Distress (pp. 28–43). Taylor & Francis, Ltd.

Danieli, Y. (1998). *International Handbook of Multigenerational Legacies of Trauma.* Plenum Press.

Dodsworth, S. (2011). The Challenge of Respecting Indigenous Peoples' Rights: Comparing Experiences from Africa, Latin America and North America. In *International Conference, McGill University, Montreal* (pp. 2–16). Institute for the Study of International Development.

Freemantle, J., et al. (2015). Indigenous Mortality (Revealed): The Invisibility Illuminated. *American Journal of Public Health, 105*(4), 644–652.

Goodkind, J. R., et al. (2012). 'We're Still in a Struggle': Dine Resistance, Survival, Historical Trauma, and Healing. *Qualitative Health Research, 22*(8), 1019–1036.

Haskins, J. S., & Stifle, J. M. (1980). *…He Will Lift Up His Head: A Report to the Developmental Disabilities Office on the Situation of Handicapped Navajos and the Implications Thereof for All Native Americans.* Department of Health, Education, and Welfare.

Jolivette, A. J. (2016). *Indian Blood: HIV and Colonial Trauma in San Francisco's Two-Spirit Community.* University of Washington Press.

Jolles, C. Z., with Oozeva, E. M. (2002). *Faith, Food, and Family in a Yupik Whaling Community.* Seattle: University of Washington Press.

Keenan, T. (2009). Colonization and the Indigenous People of Australia, Aotearoa, and Rapa Nui. *Rapa Nui Journal, 23*(1), 18–25.

Lechner, A., Cavanaugh, M., & Blyler, C. (2016). *Addressing Trauma in American Indian and Alaska Native Youth* (Mathematica Policy Research Report).

Lewis, D., Jr., & Jordan, A. T. (2002). *Creek Indian Medicine Ways: The Enduring Power of Mvskoke Religion.* Albuquerque: University of New Mexico Press.

Mihesuah, D. A., & Hoover, E. (2019). *Indigenous Food Sovereignty in the United States: Restoring Cultural Knowledge, Protecting Environments, and Regaining Health* (Vol. 18). University of Oklahoma Press.

Moerman, D. E. (1998a). *Native American Ethnobotany.* Portland: Timber Press.

Priest, N., Paradies, Y., Stevens, M., & Bailie, R. (2012). Exploring Relationships Between Racism, Housing and Child Illness in Remote Indigenous Communities. *Journal of Epidemiology and Community Health (1979-), 66*(5), 440–447.

Ranzijn, R., McConnochie, K., & Noland, W. (Ed.). (2008). *Psychology and Indigenous Australians: Effective Teaching and Practice.* Cambridge Scholars Publishing.

Rees, S., Tsey, K., Every, A., Williams, E., Cadet-James, Y., & Whiteside, M. (2004). Empowerment and Human Rights in Addressing Violence and Improving Health in Australian Indigenous Communities. *Health and Human Rights,*

8(1). The President and Fellows of Harvard College on behalf of Harvard School of Public Health/Francois-Xavier Bagnoud Center for Health and Human Rights(pp. 94–113).
Sarche, M., & Spicer, P. (2008). Poverty and Health Disparities for American Indian and Alaska Native Children: Current Knowledge and Future Prospects. *NIH Public Access. Annals of the New York Academy of Sciences*, 126–136. https://doi.org/10.1196/annals.1425.017.
Smith-Morris, C. (2006). *Diabetes Among the Pima: Stories of Survival*. Tucson: The University of Arizona Press.
Thatcher, R. W., & Knowles, F. E., Jr. (2014). *The Circle Fellowship: A Members Guide to Organizing and Participating in a Sobriety Support Group in Native American, First Nations, Inuit and Metis Communities*. Vernon: JCharlton Publishing Ltd.
Valery, P. C., Coory, M., Stirling, J., & Green, A. C. (2006). Cancer Diagnosis, Treatment, and Survival in Indigenous and Non-Indigenous Australians: A Matched Cohort Study. *The Lancet*, 1842–1848.
Velarde, M. C. R. (2017). Addressing Double Layers of Discrimination as Barriers to Health Care: Indigenous Peoples with Disabilities. *Ab-Original, 1*(2), 269–278.
Walker, J. L. R., Kukutai, T., Jones, C., & Henry, D. (2017). Indigenous Health Data and the Path to Healing. *The Lancet, 390*, 2022–2023.
Walder, R. J., & LaDue, R. (1986). An Integrative Approach to American Indian Mental Health. In *Ethnic Psychiatry* (pp. 143–194). Plenum Medical Book Company.

## Works Cited

Abu-Saad, K. (2016, October 22). Indigenous Data Matter: Spotlight on Negev Bedouin Arabs. *The Lancet, 388*, 1983–1984.
Aho, K. L.-T., & Liu, J. H. (2010). Indigenous Suicide and Colonization: The Legacy of Violence and the Necessity of Self-determination. *International Journal of Conflict and Viloence, 4*(1), 125–132.
Anderson, I. et al. (2016, July 9). Indigenous and Tribal Peoples' Health (The Lancet-Lowitja Institute Global Collection); A Population Study. *The Lancet*, 131–157.
Anderson et al. (2016, Dec 10). Authors' Reply. *The Lancet, 322*, p. 2868.
Australian Indigenous HealthReviews. (2016). *Review of Diabetes Among Aboriginal*. Australian Indigenous HealthInfoNet. no. 17. Retrieved from https://healthinfonet.ecu.edu.au/healthinfonet/getContent.php?linkid=590810&title=Review+of+diabetes+among+Aboriginal+and+Torres+Strait+Islander+people.
Brave Heart, M. Y. H., Chase, J., Eikins, J., & Altschul, D. B. (2011). Historical Trauma Among Indigenous Peoples of the Americas: Concepts, Research, and Clinical Considerations. *Journal of Psychoactive Drugs, 43*(4), 282–290.

*Buck v. Bell.* https://www.lexisnexis.com/community/casebrief/p/casebrief-buck-v-bell.

Butler, M., & Snowden, W. (2013). *National Aboriginal and Torres Strait Islander Suicide Prevention Strategy.* Australian Government: Department of Health and Aging. https://www1.health.gov.au/internet/main/publishing.nsf/content/1CE7187EC4965005CA25802800127B49/$File/Indigenous%20Strategy.pdf.

Cajete, G. (2000). *Native Science: Natural Laws of Interdependence.* Santa Fe: Clear Light Publishers.

Clare, E. (2017). *Brilliant Imperfection: Grappling with Cure.* Durham: Duke University Press.

Clark, S. (2011, June 18). Health Initiatives by Indigenous People in Australia. *The Lancet, 377,* 2066–2067.

Gonzales, A., Kertësz, J., & Tayac, G. (2007). Eugenics as Indian Removal: Sociohistorical Processes and the De(con)struction of American Indians in the Southeast. *The Public Histrian, 29*(3), 53–67.

Hathaway, M. J. (2016). China's Indigenous Peoples? How Global Environmentalism Unintentionally Smuggled the Notion of Indigeneity into China. *Humanities, 5*(54), 1–17.

Indigenous Health: A Worldwide Focus. (2016, July 9). *The Lancet,* 388(10040). Retrieved from www.thelancet.com.

International Labor Organization. (n.d.). *Who Are the Indigenous and Tribal People?* Retrieved from http://www.ilo.org/global/topics/indigenous-tribal/WCMS_503321/lang–en/index.htm.

International Work Group for Indigenous Affairs. (2006). *Indigenous Peoples in Africa: The Forgotten People?* The African Commissions Work on Indigenous People in Africa. New Jersey: Transaction Publishers. Retrieved from www.iwgia.org.

Kirmayer, L. J., & Bass, G. (2016, July 9). Addressing Global Health Disparities Among Indigenous Peoples. *The Lancet,* 105–106.

Lawrence, J. (2000). The Indian Health Service and the Sterilization of Native American Women. *American Indian Quarterly, 24*(3), 400–419.

Lewis, D., Jr., & Jordan, A. T. (2008). *Creek Indian Medicine Ways.* New Mexico: University of New Mexico Press.

Lovern, L., & Locust, C. (2013). *Native American Communities on Health and Disability: Boarderland Dialogues.* Palgrave Macmillian.

McCalman, J., Bainbridge, R., Tsey, I. K. K., Lawson, K., Lui, F. W., & Cadet-James, Y. (2016, December 10). Indigenous Tribal Peoples' Health. *The Lancet, 388,* 2867–2870.

Milburn, M. P. (2004). Indigenous Nutrition: Using Traditional Food Knowledge to Solve Contemporary Health Problems. *American Indian Quarterly, 28*(3–4 Special Issue: The Recovery of Indigenous Knowledge), 411–434.

Miller, B. H. (Ed.). (2015). *Idioms of Sami Health and Healing.* Edmonton: The University of Alberta Press.

Moerman, D. E. (1998). *Native American Ethnobotony.* Limited edition. Timber Press Incorporated.

Montenegro, R. A., & Stephens, C. (2006). Indigenous Health 2: Indigenous Health in Latin America and the Caribbean. *The Lancet, 367,* 9525. ProQuest. 1859–1869.

Morbidity and Mortality Weekly Report. (2018). *Suicides Among American Indian/Alaska Natives—National Violent Death Reporting System, 18 States, 2003–2014.* Center for Disease Control and Prevention. Retrieved from https://www.cdc.gov/mmwr/volumes/67/wr/mm6708a1.htm.

Nabhan, G. P., Weber, C. W., & Berry, J. W. (1985). Variation in Composition of Hopi Indian Beans. *Ecology of Food and Nutrition, 16,* 135–152.

Ohenjo, N., Willis, R., Jackson, D., Nettleton, C., Good, K., & Mugarura, B. (2006). Indigenous Health 3: Health of Indigenous People in Africa. *The Lancet, 367,* 1937–1946.

Pan-Canadian Health Inequalities Reporting Initiative. (2018). *Key Health Inequalities in Canada: A National Portrait.* Public Health Agency of Canada. Retrieved from https://www.canada.ca/content/dam/phac-aspc/documents/services/publications/science-research/key-health-inequalities-canada-national-portrait-executive-summary/hir-full-report-eng.pdf.

Patterson, J. M. (1997). Meeting the Needs of Native American Families and Their Children with Chronic Health Conditions. In S. H. McDaniel & T. L. Campbell (Eds.), *Families, Systems & Health: The Journal of Collaborative Family Healthcare* (pp. 237–241).

Permanent Forum on Indigenous People. (2009). *State of the World's Indigenous People.* Department of Economics and Social Affairs; Division for Social Policy and Development. New York: United Nations. Retrieved from http://www.un.org/esa/socdev/unpfii/documents/SOWIP/en/SOWIP_web.pdf.

Saha, K. B., Saha, U. C., Sharma, R. K, Singh, N. (2016). Indigenous and Tribal Peoples' Health. *The Lancet, 388.*

Smith, A. (2005). *Conquest: Sexual Violence and American Indian Genocide.* Cambridge: South End Press.

Somé, M. P. (1998). *The Healing Wisdom of Africa: Finding Life Purpose Through Nature, Ritual, and Community.* New York: Penguin Putnam Inc.

Stote, K. (2015). *An Act of Genocide: Colonialism and the Sterilization of Aboriginal Women.* Halifax: Fernwood Publishing.

Talamantez, I. M. (2006). Teaching Native American Religious Traditions and Healing. In L. L. Barnes & I. Talamantez (Eds.), *Teaching Religion and Healing* (pp. 114–126). New York: Oxford University Press.

The Commission on the Social Detriments of Health. (2007). *Social Determinents and Indigenous Health: the international experience and its policy implications.* Report on the specially prepared documents, presentations and discussions at the International Symposium on the Social Detriments of Indigenous health. Retrieved from http://www.who.int/social_determinants/resources/indigenous_health_adelaide_report_07.pdf.

Torpy, S. J. (2000). Native American Women and Coerced Sterilization: On the Trail of Tears in the 1970s. *American Indian Culture and Research Journal, 24*(2), 1–22.

Triscott, J. A. C. (2011). Reflections on Langauge in the Management of Dementia. In E. H. Waugh, O. Szafran, & R. A. Crutcher (Eds.), *At the Interface of Culture and Medicine* (pp. 173–188). Edmonton: The University of Alberta Press.

Turnidge, J. D. (2009, May 15). High Burden of Staphylococcal Disease in Indigenous Communities. *Journal of Infectious Diseases, 199*, 1416–1418.

United Nations. (n.d.). *Together We Achieve.* The United Nations Permanent forum on Indigenous Issues. New York: United Nations. Retrieved from https://www.un.org/development/desa/indigenouspeoples/wp-content/uploads/sites/19/2018/04/Indigenous-Languages.pdf.

United Nations. (2008). *United Nations Declaration on the Rights of Indigenous Peoples.* New York: United Nations Publisher. Retrieved from http://www.un.org/esa/socdev/unpfii/documents/DRIPS_en.pdf.

United Nations. (2013). *State of the World's Indigenous Peoples: Indigenous Peoples' Access to Health Services.* New York: United Nations. Retrieved from https://www.un.org/development/desa/indigenouspeoples/wp-content/uploads/sites/19/2018/03/The-State-of-The-Worlds-Indigenous-Peoples-WEB.pdf.

United Nations. (2018). *UNDESA Division for Inclusive Social Development Indigenous People.* Retrieved from https://www.un.org/development/desa/indigenouspeoples/.

United Nations Forum on Indigenous Issues. (n.d.). *Who Are Indigenous People? Fact Sheet.* New York: United Nations. Retrieved from http://www.un.org/esa/socdev/unpfii/documents/5session_factsheet1.pdf.

Voeks, R. (1997). *Sacred Leaves of Candomblé: African Magic, Medicine, and Religions of Brazil.* Austin: University of Texas Press.

Waugh, E. H., Szafran, O., & Triscott, J. A. (2011). Impact of Cultural/Ethnic Perspectives on Dementia and End-of-Life Care in Five Communities in Northern Alberta. In E. H. Waugh, O. Szafran, & R. A. Crutcher (Eds.), *At the Interface of Culture and Medicine* (pp. 19–33). Edmonton: The University of Alberta Press.

Wendell, S. (2008). Toward a Feminist Theory of Disability. In A. Bailey & C. Cuomo (Eds.), *The Feminist Philosophy Reader.* Boston: McGraw Hill.

World Health Conference: Inter-Agency Support Group on Indigenous peoples' Issues. (2014). *The Health of Indigenous People.* New York: United Nations. Retrieved from http://www.un.org/en/ga/president/68/pdf/wcip/IASG%20Thematic%20Paper%20-%20Health%20-%20rev1.pdf.

# 9

# We Are More Than Our Trauma

## Time and Healing

*The heart of this book and the commitment to bringing it about comes directly from Carol or more specifically from her son Kee. In the introduction, there was mention of a family trauma that changed things in Carol's life. Carol had always been dedicated to Indian education and healing Indian trauma, but it was Kee's journey that focused her more specifically on wellness and medicine. Back in the day, the American government placed poison outside of the reservations, often inside smaller animals, so that the larger animals not wanted in the area would eat it and die. Kee's dog found this poison and came home with it on his fur. As Kee petted his dog and played with him, the poison was absorbed into the little boy's body. The resulting seizures and body trauma caused severe mental differences that lasted the rest of Kee's time here before he moved on.*

*During his time, he continued to experience seizures and spent a great deal of time working to balance with his situation. While not able to walk or move on his own and being limited in his communication, he taught strength and happiness and joy. His body was forever changed but his spirit was whole and strong. Carol struggled to balance with the pain her son experienced and the challenges he faced simply getting the support he needed, like a wheel chair that would fit his body. The family and the community also worked to support the gaining of balance. Part of her balancing with the situation was done by immersing herself in the medical world and studying brain functioning and knowledge of brain differences. She began to work with people with differences and to help them, their families, and their communities find the resources that would help with balance. She brought joy in the traditional ways. Along the way she found what another of her sons called the Hope Warriors. It is to these Hope Warriors, past, present, and future, that we dedicate this work, as well as to Kee, who, for the short time he was here, gave so much and brought such joy, light, and teaching to the world. His Spirit continues to guide our work and inspire our lives.—Lavonna Lovern*

## Healing

*Healing means remembering, speaking the past into the present and learning from the ancestors and from the spirit of those around us. It is knowing the past and respecting the present and hoping for the future. Remembering these connections and the reciprocity owed to all beings is the way to heal the trauma from the past that continues in the present and threatens the future. Above all, it means changing the patterns. Changing the patterns means to stop doing what was done before. We are repeating old patterns that will cause the same trauma for generations.*

*During the work on this book, the Trump administration announced that it would re-authorize the use of "cyanide bombs" to kill coyotes and dogs that were unwanted. It is said that this move will protect livestock herds. The use of these places children like Kee in jeopardy as the cyanide can't be contained or limited to just "unwanted animals". More children, more families, and more communities will face the impact and will experience the trauma of a beautiful child struggling in his own body because of the choices of others. The environment will suffer trauma and the Spirit will have to work harder to heal the larger community. We have not learned the lessons of the past.*

*We are taking children from their parents, young children—babies, at the border. We are separating them from the love and support they have come to depend on. Their suffering cries out to the children of the past taken for boarding schools and stolen for workhouses. They are experiencing an unimaginable trauma surrounded by only other children to console them. And as some die in captivity, children mourn children, again. We have created the pattern for intergenerational trauma again as these memories will not be forgotten by these children. As we remove parents from children and deport them while the children are in school leaving children alone and afraid, we are creating trauma that will survive into the future. The fear and trauma felt by these children is now a part of them and will be passed to the next generation as fear of government separation remains a part of our governmental policies. We have not learned the lessons of the past.*

*We are facing global warming and still we are stopping regulations to protect Mother Earth and all our relations. We have created dead portions of the ocean and dumped garbage until our relations in the sea are threatened. Our relations on land and in the sky are threatened by pollution and our human relations suffer from the damage we have caused to our relations that have supported us from the beginning of time. We have not taken care of our relations, and we continue on the path without thought as though such things do not matter and there are no consequences to our actions. We have forgotten the lessons of reciprocity ethics. We have not learned the lessons of the past.*

*And now we face the 2020 pandemic and there is a clear divide between those that focus on personal liberty and those that focus on community wellness. The struggle in this pandemic is substantial and the price in relations is devastating to families and communities. The loss of Elders and the loss of their knowledge is devastating. The loss of young people damages the future of our communities. People are focusing more on their rights, rather than their responsibilities. Reciprocity ethics do not rule the day, but we do see some signs of it breaking through. Yet, we struggle. There is fear as we go back to work and to classes. What will be the cost? Who will pay the price? Who will survive? We have not learned the lessons of the past.*

*In the U.S. we are seeing racial divides and protesting reminiscent of the Civil Rights era. People are tired of division and racism. People crave equality and fairness, human dignity, and self-determination. People crave understanding and recognition of the harms of the past and how these created intergenerational trauma. They are crying out for healing and asking for justice. We hear the chants of hatred and love fighting for the soul of the country. Anger and upset continue to twist the minds of many and they act in ways that harm individuals and communities creating more trauma. We have not learned the lessons of the past.*

*Yet, as we struggle with the darkness there is kindness. There are people helping and working for others. Small kindnesses are turning into larger movements as people come together in community. We can see the lessons of the past and we see many trying to learn and to change so as to change the future. Many see light in the midst of the darkness and a true change that can bring about social justice and equity and wellness for all. Many are learning the lessons of the past.*

*We must build the Hope Warriors and continue to work for our relations and for the survival of the future. We must balance with the impact that we have created and build a future that supports life rather than diminishes it. Coming to balance is a constant struggle and requires constant adjustments, but we have the knowledge of the Old Ones. We have the traditional ways that have laid a road and have given us a map. We are not without guidance from them and from Spirit. We are not alone in what we need to do. There has always been a line of Hope Warriors, and that line will continue into the future. We can bring the past into the present to create a balanced future for all our relations. We must honor the ways of all the people and cultures of this world to heal and to create a global wellness. Indigenous people are vital to the survival of all, their ways and their knowledges are essential. We must come together to balance the world in community. We must remember that we are the ancestors of our descendants. What knowledge and tradition are we going to pass on to them? We must learn the lessons of the past.—recent spirit conversations with Carol Locust*

## 2020 Pandemic

> *Working on this book during the pandemic and wanting to make sure it reflects the wisdom of Carol and global Indigenous people around the world has given me great pause. As I look at the suffering of all the people but also hear of the devastation to Indigenous populations, I am deeply saddened and troubled for the future. And while Carol at 83 has suffered from health issues, she continues to bring light, hope, and inspiration to this work. Her energy and wisdom are essential for the completion of this work and for the community of Hope Warriors. It is my profound hope that this final chapter does justice to the knowledge and wisdom of Indigenous communities around the world in difficult times. It is an attempt to bring the past into the present, to give courage and comfort to make the proper choices for the future. It is an attempt to bring together all our relations and join in a wholeness of community and balance that promotes harmony and wellness. This is Carol's vision and my task. Together we offer this final chapter as a gift from Spirit that unites all relations in all directions.—Lavonna L. Lovern*

## Beyond Trauma

Given the discussions of the differing paradigms as well as the understanding and use of different evidence to build ontological and epistemic narratives regarding reality, one may be left with some confusion as to what is to count as "history" and how global communities should orient themselves now and in the future. This text does not intend to answer any of these questions, nor does it intend for the reader to come to a set or given conclusion as the authors do not believe that a single answer or position is possible. The diversity of paradigms and the uniqueness of the cultures involved in these paradigms precludes any claim to "a single truth or a final claimant to the throne". Instead, there appear to be multiple and equal claims when considering truth and reality. The question, for us, is not which one should be chosen, as we continue to see the violence and discrimination associated with such hierarchically minded power grabs. The question is how the multiplicity can engage in equitable dialogues to promote social justice.

Can Indigenous diversity and inclusion provide a global political and cultural alternative to the Western hierarchical binary? The neoliberal assumption continues to be that diversity and multiculturalism cannot produce equity but instead produces chaos and anarchy by teaching division and victimization. Alternatively, Western critical theorists and Indigenous scholars claim that radical inclusion and multiculturalism is the only path to global equity. According to neoliberals, no such state has existed in recorded history, at least not in a developed or civilized culture. At this point, Indigenous cultures and scholars beg to differ, and it is here that this chapter will diverge from Western narrative tradition, while attempting to also bring it along in a style that does not deny Western reality but positions it alongside other relations' realities.

To assist with developing an inclusive dialogue, this chapter will focus on the concepts of Long History and Deep Time.[1] Specifically, the chapter will focus on Smail's question regarding how one is to reconcile Western claims that Aboriginals migrated to Australia 50,000 years ago and Aboriginal claims that they have always been there (Smail 2015, pp. xi–xv)[2]. Inspired by the 2013 *Deepening Histories of Place Symposium,* Smail opens the book edited by McGrath and Jebb with this question. The edited work brings together Indigenous and Western paradigms and scholarship to discuss the concepts of history and temporality in a way that allows for the possibility of creating and maintaining an inclusive and equitable dialogue.[3]

We have chosen this work as the foundation for this concluding chapter, not because the text "solves the problem", but because it begins a dialogue, one which is bound to surprise many Western governments and scholars. The book questions Western constructs and expands the possibilities involving history, reality, and truth. The text also functions to uncover many of the Western assumptions and scientific biases hidden and considered sacrosanct in academia. These assumptions continue to be taught to children as "proven, facts, or certainties". The politics of such sacrosanct curriculum is that it serves to maintain Western claims to hierarchical positioning and intellectual and cultural dominance.

Discussions involving constructs such as long history call into question the preferential positioning of any single culture as long history places humans not in the primary position of history but as a small part in a much longer history. This in turn minimizes any culture's claim to dominance as any single culture represents only a very minor position in the long history of the Earth. By placing the significance of history within Western written human history, Western cultures elevate their historical positioning. However, when one views human history or any given culture within the long history of

---

[1] Long History has been used to refer to the time before Western claims of written history. The idea embraces the understanding that history existed from the beginning of the planet and only a small part of it relates to humans and an even smaller part to Western recorded human history.
[2] In Western thinking, these different narratives are in conflict and one must win in the quest for priority positioning.
[3] By not participating in a hierarchical binary, Indigenous epistemology encourages non-duality thinking in a way that offers alternatives to conflict and win/lose strategies in the face of controversy.

the Earth itself, events and cultures become nothing more than minor Earth events.

Indigenous cultures tend to mark history beginning with creation of the Earth itself. Origin narratives begin with creation and move to the present and include the future of beings on and around the Earth. The principle organizer of long history is then Spirit rather than Western calendar or yearly organizations. Spirit is not held to linear temporal constructions. Humans exist within this long history but exist only as part of the history alongside all other beings, which represents a significant difference between Indigenous and Western historical accounts. While Western origin narratives also begin with the creation of the Earth, they focus religiously and scientifically on the dominance of humans and their place in history as though the Earth was created primarily for humans. Indigenous narratives do not give humans primacy but rather place humans within history as a part of the long line of beings that have been and will be housed in or on the Earth.

Histories of plants, animals, and other beings have equal importance and are often considered more important in that these educate humans on how to sustainably exist on this planet. Indigenous long history, therefore, looks beyond human existence to events that have or will occur with equal considerations of significance. Such an understanding often places humans as not only relatively new to history, but also as the younger, and less wise, sibling among Earth's vast relations.

The difference between Western and Indigenous views regarding history appears to be a matter of perspective. One views one's place in history differently when understood in long time and as part of the larger community of relations. Humans in general hold only a small place in that history. Indeed, any single culture or empire holds an even smaller and any individual exists for only an instant. While Western readers may find this upsetting or even depressing, Indigenous people tend to celebrate this understanding as an important part of the spiritual becoming that is the process of life itself. This is not to say that Indigenous people do not value human existence, cultures, or individuals. It is to say that they do not over value them. All that has come before and all that will come after holds value in the same proportion. No being or set of beings holds a privileged place in long history or with the Creator.

## Academic Transparency

There is a need for academic honesty and transparency that, while known within scholarly realms, is often not communicated in neoliberal-controlled education. As mentioned earlier in this text, Western knowledge is taught with an air of "certainty, proof, and absolute". What Western scholars often fail to acknowledge is that these terms have been loosely used and often completely misconstrued for political reasons. Western knowledge, like that in other cultures, is a series of continually debated theories. One need only go to a regional, national, or international conference to encounter these debates. These debates exist in journals, disciplines, and academic departments. In fact, these debates are necessary for the continuation of processes such as tenure and promotion. Publishing is paramount, which means one must find something entirely new or a new way of perceiving something old in order to get paid.

There is little, if any, information within a given discipline that is agreed to by all scholars in the field. Nonetheless, college students continue to experience surprise on entering university classrooms and finding out that "facts" are contingent and "proven", when applied to empirical data, is at best highly probable but never certain. The reasons for this disconnect between scholars and students are a discussion for another text, but the phenomena involving student disillusionment continues. Discovering that Columbus is not revered by all, that Western colonizers enacted genocide, or that Indigenous cultures continue to exist and have possessed advanced languages, mathematics, and sciences for thousands of years often makes students question the legitimacy of their prior education.

The transparency and academic honesty, that may aid in avoiding this disillusionment, could also allow for a more rigorous treatment of terminology and logic in earlier education. Understanding that, logically, "facts" are contingent and do not represent anything that is either "certain or absolute" may assist students. Additionally, teaching that theories are inductive arguments, meaning that the conclusion follows from the premises as a matter of probability, not necessity, would also assist students in more fully understanding advanced scholarship. Knowing the reality of Western logic allows for diversity and inclusion by noting that knowledge, for the most part, is no more than a matter of strong probability. This means that multiple knowledge paradigms could, without logical issue, have the same or similar levels of probability. With this understanding hierarchical positioning becomes both impossible to determine and unnecessary.

Students' surprise in understanding that Western logic itself precludes "absolute or proven" facts continues to undermine confidence in advanced scholarly endeavors. As students are informed that "beloved ideas and facts" are contingent or simply matters of probability, the concern for intellectual anarchy in the form of relativism often undermines the legitimacy of academic scholarship. Students often come to the conclusion that if there is no absolute or certainty of information, then no knowledge can possibly exist. Again, this is a rather simplistic view that has been critiqued in Western post-modern philosophies. Saying we lack absolute empirical truth does not deny that highly probable arguments and theories do exist. Within a given cultural paradigm, the highly probable may stand in the position of truth, but "truth" in this sense does not entail "absolute" or "certain". The words are not synonymous. The realization that empirical data being "proven" only means it has been replicated or that it holds a position of high probability continues to backfire in higher education as well as in Western political agendas.

Ironically, these reactions tend to stem from the foundational assumption that existence is and should be understood to fall on a hierarchical binary. In other words, there has to be a knowledge winner and a knowledge loser, there can be only one truth and all else is false, and one culture must dominate at the top of the pyramid with the others being subservient. The binary pattern itself, however, creates a fallacy of false dichotomy, or bifurcation. This fallacy occurs when two positions are given as mutually exclusive. One of the positions is argued against, so it must be the case that the other is correct. However, if there is even a single alternative to the dichotomous exclusive, the argument fails. In this case, Indigenous knowledge offers at least one other possibility, a paradigm that allows for the diversity and inclusion of multiple paradigms and multiple knowledge systems in a natural democracy.

Fear of multiple and equitable paradigms and knowledge systems has long inspired Western political and academic claims involving cultural destabilization stemming from relativism. Indeed, neoliberal claims have often decried allowing equity of paradigms and knowledge as creating a slippery slope into anarchy, arguments riddled with false cause fallacies. Politicians and social groups have continued to support these fallacies in order to promote the idea that a single truth or theory must be chosen or established to keep order and peace. Within many neoliberal theories, social and political stability are predicated on the understanding that there must be core knowledge or ideals. Not surprisingly, this core tends to be Western. However, no conclusive inductive argument is given for claiming that the Western knowledge set or paradigm construction is the "correct" system, or should be the heir apparent. Rather the assertion of Western dominance tends to be an assumption made based largely on power from colonization.

Western foundational beliefs are primarily asserted as truth and knowledge without justification or proper logical argumentation. One could say that this is the case for all cultures and paradigms and likely this is true within given paradigms or sub-paradigms. However, at issue here is the forcible imposition of Western paradigm beliefs on paradigms with differing knowledge systems. Colonization is the process of erasing one culture's truths and inserting another culture's truths, which leads to questions of social justice and the possibility of eliminating stereotypes and discrimination.

Colonization justifies itself using primarily poor logic and weak inductive arguments that defy the very standards of Western logic that claim to make the West superior to other "less logical" or "savage" cultures. What Indigenous scholars continue to point out is that different logical standards are applied to Indigenous, and non-Western, cultures than are applied to Western cultures. These scholars, then, call for an equity of logical application and standards as promoted in many post-modern theories. As Indigenous scholars argue, doing so will open academic scholarship to global knowledge opportunities and promote inclusion and diversity in all social institutions including academic and political.

Academic transparency would require that education at all levels accurately portray Western scholarship and theories for what these are, inductive arguments involving contingent facts based on paradigm assumptions, politics, and ontologies brought together to form a largely coherent epistemology. In other words, Western knowledge informs Western narratives of reality. Within its own system, the narrative is largely coherent while still debated. However, the Western paradigm is a single system in a long and diverse set of human paradigms, each of which is largely coherent within itself, none of which have the ability to claim superior positioning outside of its own coherent paradigm. What this means is that any hierarchical position works only within a given narrative that accepts hierarchical positioning as an ontological/epistemological foundational component. Beyond that narrative, such constructs are meaningless. Any assumption of narrative dominance is culturally bound and should not be extended to other narratives or cultures. Dominance is then neither "absolute", "proven", nor "necessary" even according to Western logic. In the end, Western logic itself states that "different from" fails to imply "better than" or "worse than". "Different from" only implies "different from". Normative claims of "better" or "worse" come from subjective determinations within a given paradigm.

## Equity and Inclusion

This section focuses on the need to eliminate Western narrative's hierarchical positioning and colonization arrogance as a way to promote inclusion and to promote Indigenous sovereignty as well as to heal the intergenerational trauma of colonization. Bringing all cultural narratives into dialogue requires the creation of trust and a respect for difference. Such dialogues also require the understanding that all members are equal and that the positions of those in the conversation represent legitimate truths.[4] Humility is required for this endeavor to work as discussion members must agree that other paradigms are equal to or potentially superior to their paradigm in some ways. The idea being that there is knowledge to be learned from all paradigms and that knowledge could possibly advance other paradigms in some way. Certainly, some knowledge will be rejected by different dialogue members. However, controversy does not logically entail conflict, so agreeing to disagree is an option. Additionally, this method does not have as its goal a creation of a single, combined, or hierarchically superior paradigm, which eliminates the need for necessary conflict.

Given this dialogue structure, students inevitably ask "what if a situation arises where two dialogue members are at complete odds", what would be the course of action? This is indeed a dilemma and the dialogue participants may need to address such situations and how they are to be resolved before the dialogue begins. For the Western participants, there are a number of ethical theories that may assist in solving such dilemmas. Western existentialism may serve, for example, when conflict arises between dialogue partners as it does not claim the existence of an absolute truth or solution, only that each dialogue member take responsibility for his or her choices. Complete freedom of action comes with complete responsibility for the consequences of that action. According to Habermas, the solution to disputes would have to be negotiated as a part of communicative action. Indeed, this type of negotiation is not unprecedented in Western solutions to dilemmas.

---

[4]It is logically possible that an agreement could be made between a set of dialogue members that a specific narrative or paradigm is not legitimate. However, such a designation would require, under this model, that there be sufficient evidence, logic, and justification for a paradigm to be labeled as inferior or illegitimate. Additionally, under the standards for such inclusive dialogues, any position designated as inferior or illegitimate would not be included in the inclusive dialogue as only equal members may participate. It is difficult to say what would occur to create a situation where several dialogue partners determined that another potential partner was inferior or illegitimate. However, as we have established that there exist no absolutes in empirical theories, such a scenario could occur. Within reciprocity ethics, exclusion of a paradigm from the dialogue would be highly unlikely but is logically possible.

Indigenous responses to such a dilemma would differ according to community but would involve reciprocity and considerations of the interrelatedness of all things. The dialogue community as well as any impacted community would need to be considered and discussed before a solution could be determined. Indigenous paradigms tend to strive for compromise through negotiation as controversy does not entail conflict. Nonetheless, the predilection for avoiding conflict, which is seen as damaging to the spirit of all involved, may be the result. For most Indigenous communities, a conclusion involving conflict is not only the last resort but is entered into with great sorrow. A distinction is often made in that harm, violence, or killing is never to be honored. While the reasons, such as protection of one's people, may be honored, the use of violence costs the perpetrator part of her spirit and invokes more trauma on all the relations impacted by the violence. Balance will be difficult to reestablish in the aftermath, and both individual and community spirit, on all sides, will require healing.[5] Healing is then not complete in any specific community until all related to the conflict, including non-humans, are healed. Healing requires that individuals and communities take responsibility for the harm inflicted on the Other and work to heal that harm. The difficulty involved in such a process and the primacy of Spirit helps to explain Indigenous resolve to avoid conflict, as it comes with great responsibility.

For many of our Western students, this is a difficult position to understand. Many want to know why American Indians did not destroy the European invaders or the early settlers. The understanding of reciprocity ethics, interrelatedness, and Spirit work to answer this question. First, when one meets another, she is meeting Spirit and owes respect and hospitality to that spirit. Second, assuming the worst of someone, hating a person, or doing someone harm damages one's own spirit. This damage is difficult to heal and often creates serious negative physical and mental consequences for the individual acting negatively. Third, when another causes harm, one is required to allow her to attempt the healing of her spirit by helping to heal the harm caused. Finally, reciprocity ethics require that one view all beings as relations, even if not close relations, that come from Spirit. So, reciprocity ethics require that to the best of one's ability one must harm none and to the best of one's ability one has to help all one's relations.

Again, turning to Western logic, "different from" does not entail "better than" or "worse than", only different from. Bringing all narratives into a

---

[5]Again, we are not claiming that similar sentiments do not exist in Western paradigms. However, given the independent aspects of Western cultures that support competition, often using conflict as a motivator, the paradigms experience a significant difference.

dialogic circle will require that narrative equity be recognized and respected. As represented throughout this text and in the plethora of scholarship beyond this text, Indigenous narratives contain both complex and advanced knowledge systems. Examples of such knowledge include aspects of natural geometry, Chaco Canyon, Machu Picchu, and the Nazca Lines, which still baffle Western knowledge.

Employing dialogic models of communication, advances inclusion and respects diversity in a way that can benefit all humans. This benefit may even work to extend human existence in the long history of the Earth. The authors do not expect a utopia, only, to borrow Western narrative terms, an "evolution" beyond the barbarism currently being experienced by many humans and their relations culturally and environmentally.

## Decolonizing

The purpose of this section is not to overwhelm the reader with historical theory, but to give an example of how the Western academic narrative continues to participate in colonization. The use of the Western paradigm and subsequent definitions, many discussed earlier in this book, continue to frame the history of humanity on Earth. If the study of history is bound by Western constructs, then any claim that falls outside those constructs is considered irrelevant or insignificant. Indigenous constructs, however, examine the long history involving becoming and existence of all relations to the Earth. This section is then an example of the possible decolonization and indigenizing of the academy that promotes diversity and offers a more inclusive understanding of existence on this planet.

Returning to *Long History, Deep Time* as the guiding element of this chapter, it seems important to do more than simply mention Western knowledge debates to assist in the promotion of narrative understanding and academic inclusion. The use of *Long History* is then a case study in dialogic scholarly inclusion. The book begins by giving an example of the decolonization of knowledge, but, more importantly, it gives an example of how to indigenize scholarly discussions. According to Porr, current Western models of human existence claim that "modern humans" began in Africa "around 150,000 and 200,000 years ago and subsequently migrated" throughout the world making it to, for example, "Australia by about 50,000 years ago" (2015, p. 203).

Porr notes that Western theories involved two models of migration "'Out-of-Africa I' (connected to *Homo ergaster/erectus* around two million years ago) and 'Out-of-Africa II' (connected to *Homo sapiens sapiens* about 100,000 years ago)". These models are supported by DNA analysis that was established in the 1980s called the "mitochondrial 'Eve' hypothesis" (p. 203). However, Porr notes that "revised genetic evidence for inter-breeding within Africa of supposedly archaic and modern humans, as well as the persistence of archaic populations" have "complicated" these narratives.

Porr claims that the "evidence from molecular genetics is mainly regarded as having influenced the debate between Multiregional and Out of Africa views of recent human evolution in favor of the former" (p. 204). So, advanced genetic testing now favors a multiregional science of human origin. It is less important to this discussion that the reader understand all of the specifics of these Western debates than that the reader recognizes that the debates exist. Did all human life begin in Africa and migrate out or did human life begin in different regions and eventually intermingle? There continues to be debate as to where life began as well as the patterns of reproduction, which Porr refers to as involving the issue of an "essentialist" narrative. Claiming a specific point of origin and migratory route tends to reveal a great deal about the people who make these claims. Each claim then includes the idea that individual scientists may favor one version over another for non-scientific reasons such as loyalty or indoctrination.

When discussing the theories involving Western concepts of "modern man", Porr states that "there is actually no morphological definition of our own species that allows us to clearly identify what an anatomically modern human is in biological taxonomic terms", which leads to claims that the distinction of "modern man" is not a matter of "physical appearance or morphology" (p. 207). Given the difficulty in finding a definitive physical trait for determining who is "modern man", Porr argues that scientists have turned to behavior for answers.

Porr argues that the use of behavioral traits or capacities to identify "modern man" exhibits two primary problems. First, behaviors and intellectual capacities can neither be "observed…in fossil human remains nor in archaeological artifacts". Second, any attempt to use behaviors and capacities becomes tainted by current authors' projecting "modern abilities" and paradigms into the past, thus tainting the evidence and "creating a narrative that sees humanity as a slow unfolding of an essential human capacity" (p. 208). In other words, the use of behaviors and capacities to mark "modern man" is potentially no more than cherry-picking and the biased collection, interpretation, and dissemination of data.

Evolutionary moves from "savage to civilized" or from "hunter/gathering cultures to technologically advanced cultures" therefore become suspect. The inductive probability of the conclusion becomes threatened by fallacies such as begging the question, false cause, strawman, and missing the point. Interestingly, Waters notes the same fallacies in her discussion of the Bering Strait narrative (2004).[6] What becomes clear from Porr's discussion is that the theories involving the origin of "modern man" and subsequent migration narratives are debated inductive arguments and should not to be taken as deductive[7] or necessarily the case. While general agreements may be found, such as an underlying commitment to evolution narratives, the details continue to be debated lessening the inductive probability involving any specific variation of the general narrative. Thus, various contender theories provide "reasonable doubt" regarding the evidence and construction of each competing theory.

H. Allen corroborates the difficulties in Western theories of cultural development beginning with a chronicling of Aquinas' use of Aristotle's teleology. Allen notes that Aquinas used teleological ideals to justify "that non-Greek peoples were 'natural slaves' on the grounds that, while they had the capacity to think rationally, they chose not to" (Allen 2015, p. 171). Allen argues that "[i]n later historical works, the secular goal of continuous human progress replaced spiritual improvement, transforming Aristotle's psychological/developmental theory into a historical one" (p. 172).

The convergence of teleological theory and theories of evolution has created a Western narrative that interprets history and all within it as "moving forward" or as "improving" in a way that promotes the idea that humankind, cultures, and even political and economic institutions are advancing over time to some "perfection", "end", or "telos". "However, in incorporating growth from simple beginnings to a more complex maturity with time broken up into Ages, they [Western scholars] form a template for the historicist theories which follow" (p. 172). Allen critiques the use of "stages" in anthropological theories by noting the difficulty in defining such stages. Additionally, he examines problems in identifying stage teleological/evolutionary "development", and the difficulty in aligning such stages in one part of the globe with those in another part.

---

[6] As of the writing of this book, new archeological evidence has come out of Cooper's Ferry that dispels the Bering Strait narrative noting human activity before the "official" migration date and that migration may have taken place by water and not by land. Such evidence is added to other, often ignored, evidence that the Bering Strait myth should be rethought as it is a myth long denied by Indigenous knowledge and evidence.

[7] A deductive argument has a set of premises that necessarily lead to the conclusion. When dealing with matters involving the world, or the empirical, deductive arguments may be part of larger arguments, but inductive arguments are the primary source of information as arguments about the empirical world contain assumptions and empirical facts which are contingent.

Beginning with the identification of stages, Allen argues that "the process of change [is] under-theorized", noting that identification of the "moment" of shift from one stage to the next is largely non-identifiable although it is continually accepted as a reality. Allen further argues that "[a] survey of anthropological and archaeological books published during the twentieth century reveals that the term 'Stone Age' was commonly used to describe contemporary Australians" while a debate continued as to the classification of early Australian Aborigines. The debate centered on whether the Aborigines were at the "Middle or Upper Paleolithic technological stage, that is whether they should be considered archaic Mousterians or [whether they were] members of modern *Homo sapiens*?" (p. 181).

Allen later explains that in identifying early Aboriginal cultures there are

> two dimensions to the 'Neolithic Problem' ...The first involves attempting to explain why Australian Aborigines had not...'achieved' agriculture. The second attempts to account for the presence of polished stone axes in Australia. Polished stone was the defining artefact of 'Neolithic' gardeners, yet the Australians were clearly hunters and gatherers. The latter problem, however, only emerges when archaeologists approach stone artefacts from an essentialist point of view, as the defining criteria of a stage of human development. (p. 184)
>
> Similar problems involved explanations for the presence of small stone spear points and microliths in Australia. For example, small, leaf-shaped stone points are a hallmark of the Upper Paleolithic Solutrean culture in Europe, while microliths and various other backed implements first appear in Europe during the European Mesolithic and are definitional for that period. Because of their status as markers of progress in the European sequence, their presence in Australia has been taken to indicate Aboriginal advancement to a higher level of technical production and social organization. (p. 185)

Allen's description of the empirical evidence and of the alignment of stages represents the continued debate regarding how advanced Australia's Aboriginals were when "discovered" and why their cultural "advancements" failed to track European development stages. There are, of course, a plethora of theories to explain these anomalies, but, as with the above, the purpose of this section is not to determine the "right" answer but to bring to light some of the inductive arguments in Western anthropological narratives that continue to be debated and how such debates require that such theories be understood as inductive arguments of probability rather than deductive arguments of certainty. According to Allen, "[e]scaping the ideological baggage of our colonial past represents a daunting task". He references Shryock and Smail's claim that "to comprehend the immensity of human time and its dynamic of change, we need new frameworks based on kinshipping, webs, trees, fractals, spirals, extensions and scalar integration" (p. 191).

The purpose of relating these Western debates involving anthropology and archaeology is neither to discount them as disciplines nor to claim that Western narratives are wrong but rather to begin the task of decolonizing and indigenizing academic scholarship to make it both transparent and inclusive. Western tradition contains a group of theories discussing the origin of humans and their migration throughout the world. However, these theories have yet to establish "The Final Theory" even within the Western paradigm, let alone within the plethora of paradigms of other cultures. Western colonization has been supported by the arrogance attached to its claims of intellectual, evolutionary, and narrative dominance. However, such claims are indicative of a "rigged" game.

Western control of definitions, stages, models of development, and evidentiary standards, has created a game that denies other paradigms, sciences, evidence, and knowledge. The denial is not based on objective or logical standards, but, instead, it embraces subjective phenomenal experience along with biased assumptions that deny the possibility that non-Western knowledge has legitimacy. Understanding Western narratives as fallible and incomplete, undermines the hierarchical positioning advanced in colonization, which continues to be sacrosanct in modern Western education and politics.

Placing Western narratives alongside, rather than above, other cultural narratives not only reaffirm Western standards of logical argumentation, but also recognizes the potential value of Indigenous cultures whose narratives, many of which date back at least 50,000 years and according to Indigenous knowledge even farther. With the completion of the examination involving the decolonization of *Long History*, we move into an example of indigenizing scholarship by examining *Deep Time*.

## Indigenizing

Recognizing the limitations of Western knowledge does not entail that Indigenous knowledge should take a preferential position hierarchically. Each paradigm may be understood to contain wisdom and truth within its own boundaries but must also be recognized as limited by its own assumptions.[8]

---

[8]Logically, if one considers the foundation of each argument to be a set of assumptions, which by their nature are assumed and not argued, then the subsequent inductive argument, even when properly argued, is shaped by these base assumptions. Change the foundational assumptions, and the argument itself is changed.

However, if we take seriously Huston Smith's understanding regarding the totality of human wisdom, then it is the collection of the differing paradigms that represents a greater knowledge. The difficulty is creating a dialogic method that respects the various paradigms, even when disagreeing.[9] Such a dialogic method requires not only a humility to admit what is not known, but an openness to consider diverse perspectives. In this way, we introduce the indigenizing of Earth's deep time.

This section will consider various narratives involving the topics of time, place, and spirit as a way to illustrate how indigenizing scholarship and the academy can advance knowledge and establish inclusion equity. The emphasis will be on ways in which different narratives and theories can stand together without conflict even when controversy exists.

First, when constructing a narrative of temporality, language is essential. Western constructs of quantum mechanics have expanded interpretations of time; however, the standard remains a version of the linear construction involving past, present, and future.[10] In this way, Western constructions of time tend to reference a set of discrete "connected" units in a continuous linear sequence. Understanding that much of the world thinks about and references temporality differently is important as these differences change how individuals and communities interact with the world and each other.

Linguistic usage of temporal designators creates an opening in this discussion as there is a uniqueness involving time that both describes and influences cultural institutions and interactions. To this end, Moore references Armas' discussion of cultural descriptions of time.

> Depending on one's culture, one interacts with time in a very distinct fashion. One example which gives some cross-cultural insights into the concept of time is language. In Spanish, a watch is said to 'walk.' In English, the watch 'runs.' In German, the watch 'functions.' And in French, the watch 'marches.' In the Indian culture of the Southwest, people do not refer to time in this way. The value of the watch is displaced with the value of 'what time it's getting to be.' Viewing these five cultural perspectives of time, one can see some definite emphasis and values that each culture places on time. (2006, p. 473)

---

[9] There will be those that assert the "problem of relativism" in that we can come up with paradigms that are horrific or call for such destruction of relations or groups that many would not want to give them a seat at the table or to be approached with respect. These are significant topics for concern. We recognize the need for these discussions but reserve them for other books and refer back to earlier discussions of conflict resolution.

[10] The generalization of quantum theories is done to advance the conversation, not to claim there is a single or essentialist notion of quantum time.

These descriptors are significant as they explain how people experience and organize time. In this way, cultural experiences referencing "running time" and those referencing "what time it is getting to be" evidence vastly different ways of being in the world. To further this point, Mbiti describes the difference between Western and many East African concepts of time.[11] He states that Western communities view the concepts of "time as a commodity which must be utilized, sold and bought; but in many traditional African life, time has to be created or produced. Man is not a slave of time; instead, he 'makes' as much time as he wants" (1999, p. 19).

Mbiti further distinguishes African conceptions of time as containing "Notime", that which "has not taken place or what has no likelihood of an immediate occurrence" and "potential time", that which "is certain to occur, or what falls within the rhythm of natural phenomena" (p. 16).[12] He argues that these conceptions of time orient around the past and present. The future is "practically foreign" as time is marked by events that have existed or are existing and nothing exists in the future. He states that "[i]n the east African languages …there are no concrete words or expressions to convey the idea of a distant future" (p. 17). This is not to say that these cultures have no conception of the future, only that they do not orient to the future as it holds no events and thus no reality. Nothing has occurred in the future and so orientation is toward that which has or is occurring. Contrast that with the West which primarily orients towards the future and one acquires a better understanding of the difficulties in communication and of the negative impact of colonization on African communities.

In yet a different understanding of time, James describes the Aboriginal conception of *Tjukurpa* which "is not relegated to a past 'Dreamtime', but rather is an active continuous time" (James 2015, p. 33). James describes "history as written in the land" (p. 33).[13] "The land itself is imbued with religious significance. The interconnectivity of humans and the sentient land is celebrated in song, story and dance" (p. 34). James describes an annual returning to the "country of my spirit" in which there is a

---

[11] Mbiti is clear that he is not equating his discussion of time with all African interpretations. He is referencing specific tribal understandings of time in order to explain African/Western differences in ontology and epistemology.

[12] Mbiti states his work is primarily done within Eastern African languages.

[13] Dreamtime references the Australian Aboriginal origin narratives. These narratives exhibit a significantly different orientation of time and spirit involvement regarding creation. The time differences reported here are complex and deserve further explanation. However, the difference in temporal construction is used to explore non-Western paradigms regarding time and existence.

renewal of relationship with *Tjukurpa* ancestors and the spirits of forebears who have passed into the rocks and trees of their home-country…[it] is like walking into the land as a multi-dimensional text…the imprint of a body on the ground where a person slept holds both the physical and spiritual memory of that person. The desert winds, rain and harsh sun may erase physical traces of humans in this landscape over time, but the spiritual imprint of their soul is absorbed into the land, and remains there…it is not the built environment that marks and holds people's history; rather it is the land itself that holds the history of creation and the people who have walked upon it". (pp. 34–35)

James challenges people oriented to Western and the written word to "lift their eyes from the page and attune their aural senses to other ways of knowing history" (p. 35). According to James' description, *Tjukurpa* encompasses all things "being, knowing, substance, essence, cause, identity, time and space" and is understood as "an unfolding mystery". Additionally, the understanding is "acquired throughout one's lifetime, where individuals earn the right to progress through stages of initiation into ever more complex layers of cultural knowledge. Outsiders looking into this metaphysics of being can only partially understand its complexity" (p. 35).

James addresses the concerns with terms such as "Dreamtime" and "Dreaming" noting that such concerns tend to be "limited" and are often associated with "unreality". However, she argues that her purpose in this discussion is not to critique the terms, but to "expand the understanding of *Tjukurpa*…the 'eternal dreamtime' [which] is not an endless succession of time-periods rather… [it is] an ever-present spiritual reality" (p. 36). According to James, "the physical, spiritual and moral worlds are all shaped by the *Tjukurpa*. Sacred time exists concurrently with secular time" (p. 43). Time is then "multi-dimensional", to use a Western phrase, in a way that understands creation as both having occurred and as constant and continuing.

For many Indigenous peoples, the complexity of time is compounded by the relationship to place.[14] As indicated by James, one must learn to "read history in the land".

Nganyinytja tells us the *Tjukurpa* was laid down all over Australia *iriti*, long time ago, and it was put there by *nganana*, we the first peoples of Australia. Angu *Tjukurpa* does not refer to a beginning time before sentient life on earth, rather it tells us of the time when totemic beings walked the earth. The *Tjukurpa* in inhabited by the first creative beings that were both animal

---

[14]This is not to claim that Western constructions of space-time are not complex.

and human, and who purposefully created landforms, trees, food plants, water sources and fire. These beings were *tjukuritja*, of the *Tjukurpa*, and are the direct ancestors of Anangu living today. The creative ancestors were beings with extraordinary powers that were able to shift their shapes between animal, plant, rock, tree and human form, thus establishing the Anangu Law of continuous connectivity between humans and the natural environment. Anangu living on their lands today sing and dance the song sagas of the *Tjukurpa* to keep their country, the plants, animals and human beings alive. (p. 39)

This connectivity establishes a continuous reciprocity. The multi-dimensionality of time connected to the physical place, which often embodies a reality unfamiliar to Western cultures. Where Western cultures may talk of rocks "being 'like' people or representing them; the Aboriginal knowledge states that they 'are' the person" (p. 41).

Porr describes the relationship between Aboriginal concepts of time and place as a "timelessness of identity and an ongoing presence of a mythological past" (p. 205).[15] In this way, Porr explains "that people are so intimately connected to Country that they are one and the same, and thus neither 'arrived' nor came from somewhere else. The stories that bind people and Country together are timeless and always present, and the people who know the stories have always been in the Country" (p. 205). Similar descriptions to those of James and Porr can be found throughout Indigenous ontologies. These experiences of time and place create a reality where multiple-dimensions and continuous creation are connected to an understanding of the relatedness to all things allowing for the possibility of real and intimate knowledge of both long history and deep time.

For many Indigenous people, they understand that their people have always inhabited their Country. They offer ample evidence that they are part of the continuing creation of the place and are directly related to the historical and current beings of that land. There is no limiting to the construct of "modern man" or *Homo sapiens sapiens*. Some may translate this into Western constructs of cells and evolution from earlier species to a later species created from the land, animals, and water that formed the individual pre-birth and continue to create each cell post-birth. Many Indigenous peoples have no problem with such a narrative as prior beings are our ancestors; we come from them and will go back to them.

The land, animals, and water were also created from prior generations, and, as each generation dies, it becomes the Earth which is ingested to create

---

[15]The use of the term "mythological" does not refer to "unreal". It refers to an earlier, but continuing, creative time. It is understood to be spiritually and physically real phenomena.

the next generation of relations. Additionally, many Indigenous cultures are not tied to the superiority of the human form, so do not find the idea of having been created from, or shifting from, non-human beings to "modern" human beings to be problematic. Indeed, many Indigenous cultures continue to recognize shape shifters as part of reality. Being created from prior beings into current beings is both natural and respected. In this way, one comes to understand the deeper time of the planet as part of a continuing and ever-present reality. The self is then a compilation of all that came before, part of what is now, and part of what will come after. Reciprocity ethics can then be tied to a longer history and a deeper time creating a multi-layered reality in which past, present, and future reside simultaneously in a given place with beings having access to one, a few, or all levels.[16] One may imagine a web of relations that centers itself in a time and place and radiates outward while at the same time folds each strand back into that single, yet continuing, creative moment of reality.

In many ways, it is the third component discussed in this section, Spirit that holds this web together and makes possible the phenomenal experience of the continuing creative moment and the ability to be both self and other, or human and nature, in the same place. An Indic leader once attempted to describe the indescribable in a symposium of Indigenous and Western scholars and activists. She stated that one must begin to understand that there is no real individuation between beings. All beings are the same being with the experience of individuality, or individuation, no more than an illusion. She explained her statement noting its comprehension difficulty. Her explanation of this narrative was that reality requires that one embrace the self as not simply an individual, but also as the multitude of beings, the totality of all that is, and the singular unity of the ultimate.

One may ask the significance of discussing long histories and deep times. For Indigenous people, the reasons are obvious and significant as they are part of the continuous becoming of individuals, communities, and the Earth. Rifkin references a reason that may be easier for some to grasp in that Indigenous peoples should be allowed temporal sovereignty. Temporal sovereignty is an often-overlooked aspect of sovereignty discussions but may be of primary importance. In his book *Beyond Settler Time,* Rifkin argues that defining all of history according to Western standards is prejudicial and inaccurate (2017). Rifkin states that "the insistence that Native people be recognized

---

[16] To be clear, the use of the term "levels" does not imply any hierarchical designation. It is simply used to provide a limited illustration of that which, in many Indigenous narratives, can neither be accurately imagined, nor accurately discussed. It is, therefore, a metaphor or an illustration to help the reader envision the narrative.

as contemporary or modern…and the refusal to pursue non-native recognition on the basis that it is part of the colonizing interpellation of Indigenous peoples into settler social forms and dynamics" denies temporal sovereignty and perpetuates unjustified discrimination against Indigenous peoples (179). Forcing Native people into settler time forces history, government, and social orientations into "non-native interests and trajectories" (182). Rifkin argues that until Indigenous peoples are allowed to represent themselves in their own temporality with an understanding of their own interests and trajectories, there is no chance of social or legal justice. The denial of temporal sovereignty denies the legitimacy of Indigenous knowledge and continues to deny Indigenous peoples' equality as modern humans.

Indigenous people often find themselves forced into settler time because of colonization and so forced to live by standards, politics, laws, and technology that Western paradigms claim define "modern humans". However, these same Indigenous peoples often fully embrace non-settler temporalities, meaning that time and history are not bound by human or colonial standards. Long history goes beyond colonial contact and embraces multiple layers of time that often enfold phenomena in a way that allows experience to inhabit multiple temporalities.

It may be Indigenous constructs of deep time that are the most difficult for Westerners in that these experiences and events exist beyond settler understandings of linear time. Deep time allows for knowledge involving and from various and multiple temporal realities and connects these realities to place. Although Indigenous constructs of temporality can encompass linear constructions of past, present, and future, it also allows for additional temporal realities that allow for a combination of the three or the experience of multiple times at once. The difficulty in describing Indigenous phenomenological experiences of the temporal is that the concepts often do not translate into other paradigms or languages. Deep time is not something observed, but experienced and as mentioned above can be phenomenologically individual, communal or both.

In taking Spirit seriously and placing it as a/the primary organizer, Indigenous peoples are the past, present, and future of the land, or the land made manifest. They belong to the land; the land does not belong to them. Furthermore, since the land is animate as it contains spirit, the experience, knowledge, and creation of all that is does not follow Western defined trajectories. Deep time is not so clearly defined but tends to involve the acceptance of multiple realities experienced separately or together. Furthermore, as all things are primarily connected by Spirit, no knowledge becomes extinct even if it lays dormmate for centuries. For many Indigenous peoples, this is the time designated for a remembering of the long histories and reconnecting with the understanding of the deep times as they embrace a becoming beyond settler time and settler being.

The discussion of various understandings of time, place, and spirit exhibited here represent only a small section of a larger conversation, but it is enough to recognize that the variations in constructs and evidence provide significantly different experiences of reality and ways of being in the world. It is not difficult to understand how the various existences and realities could, and do, create controversies between the peoples and communities around the world. The question is whether these controversies must, of necessity, result in conflict or whether those who hold these differing positions can stand together in an understanding of equality and social justice.

## Concluding Thoughts

Part of exploring Indigenous concepts of place, time, and Spirit is to reassert what has been dismissed, threatened, or destroyed because of colonization and the subsequent discrimination and genocide of Indigenous people around the world. Recognizing what has disappeared, even if this disappearance is temporary, and what remains is significant not only to Indigenous peoples, but also to the totality of human knowledge. Predictions have existed in many Indigenous communities long before colonization that, following the siege and destruction, Indigenous knowledge and ways of being would resurface, reunite, and heal.

In an era faced with climate change, ocean death, the destruction of our relations, and now a pandemic, Indigenous knowledge of environment and medicine can help find solutions. Some Indigenous predictions claim that the world will face a level of environmental collapse, which is human caused. These will be the consequences of our choices. Ignoring balance and reciprocity ethics has consequences. Recognizing the value of Indigenous knowledge and its healing capacity may not eliminate issues such as climate change, as many say it is too late to stop the process, but it may assist in bringing to balance what is already occurring.

As with other chronic illnesses, environmental chronic illness can be balanced, according to many Indigenous narratives. To begin the balancing, however, humans must authentically admit their breaking of reciprocity ethics and actively work to reestablish balance by admitting responsibility for the consequences of their individual and collective actions and by working to heal the wrong done. Humans will have to, as Locust explained, come to the fire with the right heart.

Part of the global healing will also require the healing of colonization wounds. It is not possible to "undo" what has been done, but authentic steps need to be taken to regain balance. While actions such as UNDRIP and Reconciliation agreements represent a beginning, they remain unactualized. In many cases, the words are not good as they are not followed with policy change. In other cases, these words have been used to support colonization while claiming to be "Indigenous friendly". For example, one young Indigenous scholar recently attended a conference which featured two panels on Indigenous issues. Two issues of import were revealed in the panel discussions.

The first issue involved the non-Indigenous scholars' identification as settlers. This Indigenous scholar reported an interesting pride represented by one of the panelists when he claimed settler descent identity and indicated that he was now working on Indigenous issues. The Indigenous scholar noted that the individual may indeed have good intention but failed to see the irony in his statement. While these scholars discussed their research, there was a detachment that often comes with Western academics. The scholars were working on projects that would help them in careers, giving little discussion of what the Indigenous communities being studied wanted, approved, or would gain from the scholarship. What struck this Indigenous scholar was the continued colonial undertones. It is not that non-Indigenous scholars cannot or should not participate in Indigenous scholarship, they can be, in fact, important accomplices. What struck this young scholar was the way in which scholarship was being approached and the Western manner in which Indigenous issues were being oriented and examined. It was all couched in settler time.

Again, this young scholar noted a concerning trend in a panel where each panelist began their remarks by thanking the people and spirits of the land on which the conference took place. In some panelists, this scholar noted a type of rote recitation, rather than genuine addresses. She admitted it might be because of nerves but was concerned that such practices have now become expected or "trendy" at conferences. While the practice of thanking the people and the Spirits of the ancestors is a common and important aspect of Indigenous introductions, there is concern that such sacred practices might be becoming colonialized versions of "proving one's authenticity", forgetting that how something is done is as important as the doing. For many Indigenous people, the issue of authenticity continues to be of great importance. Questions such as for whom this work is being done, why is it being done, and is the work being done in a correct manner are important to Indigenous people.

There is a significant difference in Indigenous communities between work done for self and that done for the people. Similarly, thanking the people, ancestors, and relations of the area is meaningful only if done for the right reason and in the right way.

For settler decedents (if this is how they wish to be identified) and States, the question is one of authenticity. For whom is the work being done and how is it being done? Have reconciliation agreements simply opened new avenues for academic advancement and a means of winning elections, or will the agreements result in policy changes and the recognition of Indigenous sovereignty and self-determination? Good words require more than well-crafted verbiage. It is what happens in the silences that reveal the spirit of the words.

According to Indigenous ideals, it is understood that both the colonizer and the colonized require healing as they are becoming and that authentic admission and the acceptance of responsibility must occur in a manner that is located within Indigenous ways of being. Attempting to "make amends" within colonizer ways of being fails on the grounds of both authenticity and reciprocity. Meeting Indigenous peoples in a place of equity and dialogue requires the complete recognition of past, present, and future involving Indigenous knowledge and sovereignty. It involves the recognition, if not the understanding, of constructs such as long histories and deep times. The realization must be that Indigenous communities have continued and maintained traditional ways for thousands of years and have access to multi-dimensional, multi-level knowledge, allowing them access to non-settler places, temporalities, and knowledge.

Additionally, having been subjected to acts of cultural and physical genocide and intergenerational trauma, Indigenous peoples have knowledge of an ability to access and implement healing from various relations and from Spirit. For these reasons, it should not be seen as a threat to Western knowledge or communities to say that Indigenous peoples have knowledge that is different from theirs. Indeed, different Indigenous peoples have different knowledges from each other. There need be no threat in such claims and, indeed, such claims may promote a larger healing. As indicated by Deer, Indigenous peoples are more than colonization trauma. Indigenous peoples are that which existed from the beginning of time and place, in conjunction with long history, and that which continues to become, according to deep time.

## Works Cited

Allen, H. (2015). The Past in the Present? Archaeological Narratives and Aboriginal History. In A. McGrath & M. A Jebb (Eds.), *Long History, Deep Time: Deepening Histories of Place* (pp. 171–202). Acton Act: Australian National University Press.

Deer, S. (2015). *The Beginning and End of Rape: Confronting Sexual Violence in Native America* (3rd ed.). Minneapolis: University of Minnesota.

Habermas, J. (1985). *The Theory of Communicative Action* (Vol. I & II, T. McCarthy, Trans.) (Reprint ed.). Boston: Beacon Press.

James, D. (2015). *Tjukurpa* Time. *Long History, Deep Time: Deepening Histories of Place* (pp. 33–45). Acton Act: Australian National University.

Mbiti, J. S. (1999). *African Religions & Philosophy. Second revised and* (2nd rev. and enlarged ed.). Blantyre: Heinemann.

Moore, R. B. (2006). Racism and the English Language. In T. E. Ore (Ed.), *The Social Construction of Difference and Inequality: Race, Class, Gender, and Sexuality* (3rd ed.). Boston: McGraw Hill.

Porr, M. (2015). Lives and Lines. In A. McGrath & M. A. Jebb (Eds.), *Long History, Deep Time: Deepening Histories of Place* (pp. 203–219). Acton Act: Australian national University.

Rifkin, M. (2017). *Beyond Settler Time: Temporal Sovereignty and Indigenous Self-Determination.* Durham: Duke University Press.

Smail, D. L. (2015). Preface: 'The Gift of History'. In A. McGrath & M. A. Jebb (Eds.), *Long History, Deep Time: Deepening Histories of Place* (pp. xi–xv). Acton Act: Australian National University Press.

UNDRIP. (2007). *United Nations Declaration on the Rights of Indigenous Peoples.* New York: United Nations Publisher. Retrieved from http://www.un.org/esa/soc dev/unpfii/documents/DRIPS_en.pdf.

Waters, A. (2004). *That Alchemical Bering Strait Theory; America's Indigenous Nations and Informal Logic Courses* (A. Waters, Ed.). Malden: Blackwell Publishing.

# Index

**A**
Abidogun, J. 106, 107
Aboriginal
    Aboriginal Orphan School 173
    Aborigine 226, 267
Abu-Saad, K. 228
Academia 3, 16, 17, 59, 132, 182, 206, 257. *See also* Education
Adams, D.W. 168, 171
Adelaide 225
Adelson, N 178
Africa 13, 70, 80, 103, 106, 135, 141, 195, 196, 200, 209, 222, 223, 229, 236, 245, 264, 265
African Commission on Human and Peoples' Rights (ACHPR) 103, 229
African Court on Human and Peoples Rights (AfCHPR) 67
Agtuca, J. 102
Aho, K.L-T. 226
Aikau, H.K. 210
Ainu 212
Allen, C. 181
Allen, H. 266, 267

Amazon 39, 75, 196
America
    Central 62
    North 32, 160, 195, 198, 205, 209, 222
    South 33, 34, 195, 209, 222
American 1882 Act (22 Stat. 181) 163
American Convention on Human Rights (ACHR) 68
American Indian 1, 11, 14, 33, 59–62, 72, 101, 102, 105, 108, 124, 125, 135, 147, 153–156, 158, 160–166, 219, 220, 226, 231–235, 237, 263
American Indian Church 62. *See also* Native American, Church
American Indian Movement (AIM) 61
American Indian Religious Freedom Act (AIRFA) 62, 63, 205–207, 237
Ancestors 22, 44, 59, 61, 69, 71, 74, 76, 80, 90, 138, 143, 144,

147, 181, 182, 202, 217, 218, 254, 255, 271, 272, 276, 277
Ancient One 74, 75
Andean 106, 193
Anderson, T.L. 200, 202
Anthropometrics 231, 232
Aotearoa 133, 208. *See also* New Zealand
Apache 99, 125, 144, 147, 148, 155, 206, 207, 240
Apple, M.W. 177
Appropriation 65. *See also* Misappropriation
Arapahoe 172
Arawak 69
Arctic 39, 41, 193, 209, 222
Armas' 269
Arora, V. 204
Arrighi, G. 197
Ashanti 80
Aspin, C. 106
Assimilation 1–3, 5, 10, 14–16, 27, 34, 37, 61, 65, 86, 90–92, 94, 99, 105, 112, 125, 127, 130, 131, 161, 178, 179, 220, 239
assimilationist 8, 55
Atkins 163
Australia 7, 37, 75, 87, 92, 100, 110, 133, 147, 159, 160, 169, 170, 172–174, 196, 222, 223, 226, 230, 257, 264, 267, 271
Australian Indigenous HealthReviews 228
Austronesian 129
Awas Tingni 68
Aymara 235

B

Babcock, H. 92
Babcock, H.M. 139
Balance 21–23, 42, 43, 62, 78, 95, 105, 115, 134, 178, 182, 194, 238–241, 245–247, 253, 255, 256, 263, 275, 276
Balawag, G. 10
Ballantyne, T. 66
Bass, G. 224
Basso, K.H. 138, 144, 147, 148
Battiste 133
Beck, P.V. 77, 136
Bendremer, J.C. 71
Benin 69
Bennett, N. 113
Bering Strait 30–34, 74, 232, 266
Bikini 40
Binary 94, 97, 104–107, 191, 238, 260
Biolsi, T. 77
Bird, G. 149
Blood memory 10, 145
Blood quantum 90, 101, 231
Boissoneault, L. 193
Bolivia 113
Borrero, R. 10
Botswana 229
Brandt, E. 206
Brave Heart, M.Y.H. 11, 177, 178, 237
Brewarrina 193
Brysk, A. 113
*Buck v. Bell* 231
Buffalo Soldiers 99
Bureau of Indian Affairs (BIA) 165, 166
Bureau of Justice 109

C

Cajete, G. 42–44, 56, 57, 77–79, 94, 137, 143, 144, 180, 239
Cameroon 220, 223
Canada 7, 38, 39, 68, 87, 100, 110, 111, 139, 142, 155, 160, 169, 170, 172–174, 178, 198, 199, 208, 222, 223, 226, 230, 235, 236

Candomblé 69
Canons of Construction 102
Caribbean 15, 32, 61, 69, 70, 200, 209, 222, 229
Carlisle 172, 175
Center for Disease Control (CDC) 226
Chaco Canyon 136, 141, 193, 203, 264
Cherokee 1, 59, 60, 100, 146, 242
Cheyenne 234
Chickamauga 61
Child, B.J. 171, 172
Chilisa, B. 17
Chiswick, B.R. 131
Ciboney 69
Ciudad Juarez 110
Civilization Fund Act 161
Clare, E. 243, 244
Clark, S. 228
Coleman, M.C. 162
Collins, M.B. 31, 33
Colonization 1–3, 5, 9–16, 23, 25, 27, 33, 34, 37, 54, 55, 58, 61, 65, 66, 69, 70, 75, 90–94, 99, 103–106, 110, 111, 113–115, 127–131, 136, 139, 177–179, 181, 193, 194, 196, 198–202, 204, 211, 220–222, 225–229, 235, 237, 238, 242, 244, 246, 247, 261, 262, 264, 268, 270, 274–277
Colville Reservation 74
Comanche 201
Complementarity 104, 106, 114, 115, 141, 211
Concurrent resolution 165
Cook. E-D. 130
Cordova, V. 145
Cotterill, R. 162
Couture, J. 137
Coyne, Fr. 206, 207
Cree 178, 246
Creek 242

Cremo, M.A. 31
Creole/creolization 69, 70, 115, 129, 130, 200

D

Das, V. 177
Davis, M. 209
Dawes Act 60, 101
Dean, A. 110, 111
Decolonization 3, 4, 17, 29, 76, 90, 92, 113, 115, 116, 178, 179, 208, 210, 211, 264, 268
Deep Time 257, 269, 272–275, 277
Deer, S. 91, 92, 104, 108, 109, 112, 114, 115, 173, 277
de Las Casas, B. 5, 27
Delaware 60
Deloria, V. Jr. 32, 33, 35, 76, 77, 79, 92, 94, 95, 101, 163, 166
DeMallie 35
Denzin, N.K. 17
The Department of Health 166
Diabetes 38, 157, 219, 221, 227, 228, 243
Dialogue 2, 5, 12, 17, 18, 38, 54, 56, 76, 133, 141, 256, 257, 262, 263, 277
DiNova, J.R. 144, 145
Dippie, B.W. 163, 165
Disappeared Women 110
Dispossession 25–27, 58, 59, 91
Diversity 2, 24, 106, 114, 116, 131, 133, 145, 179, 225, 256, 259–261, 264
Doctrine of Discovery 6, 25, 26, 35, 100
Dole, W.P. 162
Dominant 3, 7, 13, 17, 54, 69, 91–93, 103, 131–134, 167, 174, 176, 177, 179, 221, 224
Dragging Canoe 61
Drahos, P. 209, 210
Dreamtime 270, 271

Dualism 116, 211
Dunbar-Ortiz, R. 99–101
Dussubieux, L. 203
Dzil Nchaa Si An 205, 206, 207. See also Mount Graham

E

Echo-Hawk, W.R. 35, 62, 63, 74, 102
Eckl, J. 196
*Economic Opportunity Act* 102
Ecuador 39, 113, 134
Eder, J. 168, 169
Education 1, 4, 16, 18, 44, 56, 58–61, 91–93, 99, 107, 111, 112, 127, 132, 134, 146, 147, 159–166, 168, 169, 171, 173–175, 178–182, 195, 211, 220, 239, 253, 259–261, 268. See also Academia
Educational Amendments Act (PL 95-561) 1972 166
Eglash, R. 140, 141
Eisenhower 165
*Employment Division v. Smith* 64
Energy 24, 42, 43, 79, 123–125, 143, 240, 242, 256. See also Spirit
Enewetak 40
Enoch, J. 175
Environment/environmental 13, 18, 23–25, 28, 30, 33–42, 51, 95, 156, 160, 181, 192–194, 196, 197, 222, 228, 238–241, 254, 271, 272, 275
Equal
 equality 22, 69, 92, 99, 115, 217, 230, 255
 equity 12, 17, 30, 42, 94, 105, 114, 132, 134, 160, 179, 180, 182, 210, 211, 221, 255, 256, 260–262, 264, 269, 274, 275, 277

Errington, J. 127–129
Essential/essentialism/essentialist 3, 5, 6, 15, 18, 22, 29, 34, 38, 43, 60, 63, 80, 96, 112, 113, 116, 134, 144–146, 182, 208, 222, 224, 241, 255, 256, 265, 267, 269
Ethiopia 70, 196
Eugenics 109, 180, 221, 230–233, 235–237, 246
European Convention on Human Rights (ECHR) 68
Excellence 146, 147, 166

F

Federal Acknowledgement Project in 1978 231
Fernández, S. 113
Fienup-Riordan, A. 79
First Amendment Free Exercise Clause 36
First Nations 12, 38, 110, 223, 226
Fishman 132
Food and Drug Administration (FDA) 63
Foster, L. 63
France 40
 French 54, 69, 269
Francisco, N. 77
Frankel, S. 209, 210
Free Exercise Clause 62–64

G

Ga 80
Galeano, E. 198
Galton 231
Genoa 172
Genocide 4, 26, 27, 55, 87, 94, 104, 107, 109, 110, 160, 162, 164, 169, 232, 236, 237, 259, 275, 277
 paper genocide 232

Geoglyphs 136, 193, 194
Ghana 69
Ghost Dance 61, 62, 101
Gilley, B.J. 105
Gilroy, W.G. 207
Gonzales, A. 231
Gonzales, T.A. 44
Good, B.J. 11, 178
Good, M.D. 11, 178
Government Accounting Office (GAO) 233–235
Grande, S. 161, 181
Great Zimbabwe 196
Grim, J.A. 44
Guatemala 222
Guinea 69

H

Haebich, A. 173, 174
Haida 141, 155
Hale 133
Hansen, J.G. 202
Harden, M.J. 43
Harjo, J. 145, 149
Harmony 16, 18, 21, 22, 34, 42, 43, 58, 80, 95, 240, 241, 243
Harrison, K.D. 133
Haskell 172
Hathaway, M.J. 223
Havasupai 43, 149
Hawaii
 Hawaiian 154, 205, 206
 Native Hawaiian 35, 205, 206, 210
Heal/healing 2, 11, 12, 19, 22, 54, 63, 64, 71, 80, 93, 106, 107, 112, 115, 116, 127, 143, 147, 160, 174, 178, 182, 190, 199, 201, 208, 229, 239–242, 246, 247, 253–255, 262, 263, 275–277
Henare, M. 44
Hernandez-Avila, I. 235

Hester, T.L. Jr. 146, 147
Hierarchy/hierarchical 6, 30, 94, 107, 108, 115, 116, 130, 135, 179, 192, 211, 257, 259, 261, 262, 268, 273
 hierarchical binary 105, 211, 256, 257, 260
Hill, J.H. 128
Hinton, A.L. 11
Hinton, D.E. 11
Hirst, S. 43
Holmes, L. 137, 138
Holocaust 11, 27, 177
*Holy Piby* 70
*Homo sapiens* 265, 267, 272
Hopkins, D.M. 31
House Concurrent Resolution No. 108 165
House Executive Document for the 50th Congress 163
House Executive Document of the 51st Congress 163
Howell, T.L. 105
Human rights 4–6, 9, 15, 25, 36–38, 62, 63, 68, 103, 111, 112, 127, 128, 195, 198, 209, 225, 229
Hurst, M.E. 131

I

Igbo 106, 107
Ige, D. 206
Imiloa Astronomy Center 205
Inca 32, 114, 135
Inclusive 66, 208, 246, 257, 262, 264, 268
India 195, 204, 223, 224
Indian Appropriations Act 60
Indian Civilization Fund 58
*Indian Civil Rights Act* 102
Indian Claims Commission 74
Indian Health Service (IHS) 233–235

Indian Religious Crimes Code 60
Indian Removal Act 59, 100
Indian Reorganization Act (IRA) 101, 164, 165
Indian Self-Determination and Educational Assistance Act 1975 166
Indianz 100
Indic 135, 273
Indigeneity 2, 3, 13, 14, 91, 208, 210
  indigenize 17, 160, 182, 264
Indigenous Data Sovereignty Network 208
Indigenous Environmental Network (IEN) 24
Indigenous health 220, 223, 225
Inter-American Court of Human Rights (IACtHR) 68, 113
Intergenerational trauma 1, 3, 10, 11, 14, 34, 37, 54, 55, 58, 61, 71, 80, 90, 91, 93, 100, 108, 112, 127, 160, 167, 174, 177, 179, 182, 203, 212, 217, 220, 226, 227, 237, 244, 247, 254, 255, 262, 277. *See also* Trauma
*International Justice Research Center* 8
International Labor Organization (ILO) 6, 13, 103, 113, 230
  Convention 169 6, 13
International Work Group for Indigenous Affairs 103
Interrelation 28, 30, 43, 56, 91, 139, 142, 181
  interrelatedness 94, 142, 263
Inuit 39, 223, 226, 227, 235, 239
Irwin, L. 60, 61

J

Jacobs, M.D. 169, 170, 175, 176
Jamaica 70
James, D. 270–272
Jebb, M.A. 257

Jefferson, Thomas, Pres 72, 160
Joffe, P. 8
Johnson, Pres 165, 234
*Johnson v. McIntosh* 26
Jordan, A.T. 240
Josephs, C. 147
Joseph, S.J. 66

K

Kalahari Game Reserve 229
Kanaka Maoli 210
Kelleher, J.S. 205
Kennedy, E. 165
Kennedy, R. Pres 165
Kenya 66, 67, 223
King Phillip's War 58
Kinship 11, 12, 99, 160, 171, 211, 268
Kirchner, S. 68
Kirmayer, L.J. 224
Kitt Peak 205
Kleinman, A. 11, 177
Knowles, F.E. 103
Kongo 69
Kovach, M. 96, 137
Ktunaxa 68
  *Ktunaxa Nation v. British Columbia* 67
Kukutai, T. 208
*Kumulipo* 205
Kwakiutl 141

L

LaDuke, W. 24, 76, 137, 138
Lakota 66, 101, 149, 171
Lambert-Pennington, K. 75
*Lancet* 220, 224, 228
Langi 80
Language 3, 7, 8, 12, 13, 15–17, 41, 42, 53, 56–58, 77, 80, 87, 92, 94, 105, 107, 123–125, 127–140, 142–149, 155, 156,

160, 162–164, 167, 171, 193, 202, 211, 223, 233, 235, 239, 242–244, 259, 269, 270, 274
  linguistics 12, 29, 56, 127–133, 191, 193, 269
La Perouse 75
Latin America 113, 131, 198, 209, 221, 223, 229
Lawrence, J. 233, 234
Leitner, G. 133
Leon-Portilla, M. 57, 58
Lepchas 204
Leupp, F.E. 164
Le Veness, F.P. 197
Lewallen, A-E. 212
Lewis, D. 240
Linklater, R. 12, 115
Lipan Apache 211
Lock, M. 177
Locust, C. 1, 4, 14, 116, 139, 140, 145, 146, 276
Long History 257, 258, 264, 272, 274, 277
Lorde, A. 114
Lovern, L. 97, 110, 179, 228, 234, 237, 242, 243, 245
Lytle, C.M. 101, 163, 166

M

*Major Crimes Act* 101, 102
Malcolm, I.G. 133
Manchu Pichu 193, 203
Manifest Destiny 26, 34, 55, 94, 105, 179
Mankiller, W. 43
Mansee 60
Maori 66, 106, 133, 141, 143, 181, 226
  Maori Data Sovereignty 208
Marginalized 10, 65, 128
Marinucci, M. 17
Markus, H.R. 96
Marshall Islands 40

Marshall Trilogy 6, 26
Martin, J.W. 161
Marubbio, M.E. 107, 108
Masolo, D.A. 148
Mauna Kea 205, 206
*Mayagna (Sumo)Awas Tingni Community v. Nicaragua* 113
Mayan 110, 141, 199
Mbiti, J.S. 79, 80, 140, 270
McAnany, P.A. 199
McCalman, J. 225
McGrath, A. 257
McIsaac, E. 137
McKay, R. 110
McKenney, T.L. 161
McNeil, C.L. 199
Medicine 41, 44, 56, 58, 59, 63, 64, 69, 73, 78, 106, 116, 143, 194, 201, 210, 229, 230, 238–242, 246, 253, 275
  medicine people 4, 58, 60, 86, 116, 125, 242
Mendel 231
Mendoza-Mori, A. 132
Menominee 165
Meriam Report 60, 101, 164
Methodology 16, 17, 132, 182, 210
Metis 226, 227
Meyer, D.S. 165
Meyer, M.A. 79, 138
Micronesian 129
Migrate/migration 28, 30–34, 74, 103, 112, 130, 195, 197, 198, 232, 257, 264–266, 268
Mihesuah, D.A. 211
Milburn, M.P. 239, 240
Miller, B.G. 139
Miller, B.H. 242, 246
Misappropriation 14, 65, 75, 173. *See also* Appropriation
Mithun 133
*Modoc Indian Prisons* 100
Moerman, D.E. 240
Moiwana 68

Moloka'i 210
Montenegro, R.A. 230
Moore, R.B. 269
Moravians 161
Morbidity and mortality 222, 223
Morgan 60, 163, 164
Morgensen, S.L. 105, 106
Mount Graham 206, 207. *See also* Dzil Nchaa Si An
Mount Wheeler 104
Mufwene, S.S. 129, 131
Murata, S. 199
Murrell, N.S. 69

N

Nabhan, G.P. 228
Nagy, R. 110, 111
Nahe 202
Nahuatl 132
Namunu, S.B. 44
Nasca lines 194
National Sami Parliaments 68
Native American
    Church 62, 64
    Graves Protection and Repatriation Act (NAGPRA) 73. *See also* American Indian Church
Natural geometry 57, 127, 139–141, 193, 264
*Navajo* 153, 155, 168, 169
Negev Bedouin Arabs 228
Nelson, M.K. 44
Neoliberal 29, 112, 130, 179, 182, 230, 256, 259, 260
Neolin 61
Neolithic 267
Nepal 205, 222
Newman, D. 68
New Zealand 7, 133, 196, 208, 222, 223, 226. *See also* Aotearoa
Nez Perce 74
Nicaragua 68, 229
Nigeria 69, 106

Nixon, Pres. 165
Nkai 66, 67
Noaidi 242
Non-Governmental Organizations (NGOs) 208, 209
    Non-Governmental Organization Conference on Discrimination against Indigenous Populations in the Americas 6
Nubia 196

O

Obeah 70
Oceania 40
Oduyoye, M.A. 148
Ogiek 67
Ohenjo, N. 229
Oklahoma Indian Welfare Act of 1936 164
Old Settlers 59
*Oliphant v. Suquamish* 102
Olmos, M.F. 70
O'Neill, C.A. 42
Oppressed 3, 4, 115, 220
    oppressor 3, 115, 176
Orbell, M. 143
Ota Kte 171
Otavalo 113
Owoseje, T. 203

P

Pacific 130, 141, 209, 222
    Pacific Islands 32, 129
Panama 222, 223
Pan-Canadian Health 227
Pandemic 28, 110, 172, 255, 256, 275
Papal Bull 25
Papounhan 60
Papua New Guinea
    Papuan 129

Paradigms 12, 15–17, 23, 29, 30, 33, 37, 42, 44, 55, 56, 71, 75–77, 79, 93, 94, 96, 97, 104, 116, 127, 181, 182, 211, 221, 225, 256, 257, 259–265, 268–270, 274
Parreñas, R.S. 195
Pascoe, B. 192, 193
Patrinos, H.A. 131
Patterson, J.M. 245
Paulik, S. 64
Peace Policy 60
Pequot 58, 99
Permanent Forum on Indigenous Issues (PFII) 9
Persistent Organic Pollutants (POPs) 38, 228
Peru 39, 113, 194, 223, 229, 235
Petroglyphs 136
Peyote 62–64
*Peyote Way Church of God v. Thornburgh* 64
Philippines 194
Piki 245
Pinkerton-Uri, C. 234
PL 280 102
Platt, T. 72, 73
Plecker, W. 231, 232
Polynesian 129, 205
Pommersheim, F. 5–7
Pope 162
Pope Alexander VI 26
Porr, M. 264–266, 272
Post-colonization 9–11, 14, 90, 219, 220, 225, 227, 229, 230, 239
Powell, S. 72
Powers, K.V. 106
Pratt, R.H. 99, 163, 171
Preston, J. 8
Price, H. 163
Prucha, F.P. 160–166
Pueblo 77, 144
Pygmy 229
  Pygmies 229

Q
Quakers 161
Quechua 132, 142, 235
Queensland 103
Quetzalcoatl 56, 57
Quichua 113

R
Racial Integrity Act of 1924 231, 232
Racism 10, 11, 111, 218, 222, 255
Ramsey, J. Rev. 162
Rapa Nui 201–203
Rastafarianism 70
Raya, Mairin Iwanka 112
Reciprocity 22, 23, 28, 30, 34, 41, 44, 56, 80, 86, 91, 96, 114, 116, 138, 140, 145, 148, 160, 176, 182, 192, 193, 210, 211, 241, 243, 245–247, 254, 255, 262, 263, 272, 273, 275, 277
Rees, S. 11
Relation(s) 94, 95, 123, 131, 136, 137, 140, 148, 208, 238, 247
relational 11, 154, 211
Religious Freedom Restoration Act 36, 64
Removal 11, 25, 26, 34, 39, 40, 42, 55, 59–61, 67, 91, 92, 99, 100, 110, 113, 158, 159, 161, 162, 168–171, 174, 175, 202, 227, 237, 238
Repatriation 70, 71, 73–75
Reuveny, R.X. 196
Reyhner, J. 168, 169
Richman, K.A. 71
Riding In, J. 74
Rifkin, M. 273, 274
Roa, Hanga 202
Robinson 173
Rolstad, K. 132, 133
Romero-Little, M. 134
Rongelap 40

Ruozzi, E. 68

S

Sacred 32, 54, 55, 57, 60–65, 67, 68, 70, 76–78, 80, 85, 86, 97, 100, 123, 135, 138–140, 147, 155, 181, 190, 199–202, 204–207, 211, 239, 242, 271, 276
   sacred sites 36, 59, 62, 63, 65, 67–69, 97, 204, 205
Sahneyah, D. 102
Samburu 66, 67
Sami 41, 68, 223, 242, 244
San 223, 229
   Namibian San 229
Santee 172
Santeria 69
Scheduled Tribes 223
Scott, J.C. 176, 177
Seaton, F.A. 165
Selassie, Haile 70
Self-determination 4–6, 8, 13, 15, 23, 36–39, 68, 91, 98–103, 113, 127, 134, 165, 166, 209, 210, 225, 255, 277
Settler 35, 54, 57–60, 62, 90, 99, 162, 175, 199, 201, 263, 274–277
Seward, T. 113
Shakers 161
*Sherbert v. Verner* 64
Shilluk 80
Shipley, D.L. 168
Shrubsole, N. 67, 68
Sikkim 204
Silko, L.M. 143, 144
Sillitoe, P. 17
Simpson, D.F .Jr. 203
Smail, D.L. 257, 267
Small pox 28, 172
Smith, A. 109, 235, 236
Smith, H. 64, 182, 211, 269

Smith, L.T. 17, 182
Snake, R. 64
Social Darwinism 26, 34, 55, 72, 92, 94, 130, 179, 192
Somé, M.P. 241, 244, 245, 272
South Pacific 141
Sovereign 37, 98, 160, 178
   sovereignty 4, 5, 14, 15, 23, 34–42, 70, 71, 74, 91, 93, 97–103, 109, 112–114, 127, 134, 139, 149, 166, 178, 179, 181, 182, 198, 204, 208–210, 225, 229, 230, 237, 247, 262, 273, 274, 277
Space 2, 149, 181, 182, 205, 225, 271, 272
Spanish 27, 69, 106, 131, 229, 269
Special rights 63
Spencer, J.H. 26, 210
Spirit 8, 21, 22, 32, 42–44, 67, 69, 73, 76, 77, 79, 80, 86, 91, 94–97, 116, 123, 135, 137–140, 142, 143, 149, 160, 207, 210, 220, 237, 241–245, 253–256, 258, 263, 269, 270, 273–275, 277. *See also* Energy
Spring, J. 161
Standing Wolf 146
Stanford, D.J. 31
State of the World's Indigenous People (SOWIP) 9, 24, 25
Sterilize/sterilization 104, 112, 221, 231, 233–237, 246
Stevens, S. 205
Stonehenge 193
Stote, K. 235, 236
Straight, B. 66, 67
Student Rights and Due Process Procedure 1974 166
Sun Dance 61
Supersessionism 65, 66, 69, 206
Surinam 68
Swanner, L. 205, 207
Szafran, O. 246

## T

Taino 69
Takaki, R. 163
Takatapui 106
Talamantez, I.M. 240, 241
Talbot. S. 58
Támez, M. 211
Taylor, J. 208
Te Ao Hurihuri 66
Teller, H. 60
Te Mana Raraunga 208
Temple, E. 203
Termination 98, 101, 102, 164–166
The Truth and Reconciliation Commission of Canada 8
Tholung 204
Thompson, R. 31
Thompson, V.C. 95
Thompson, W.R. 196
Time 2, 4, 7, 14, 18, 21, 23, 24, 31, 37, 40, 54, 56, 58, 59, 61, 69, 72, 76, 80, 86, 88, 97, 101, 110, 111, 124, 125, 127–129, 133, 135, 137, 139, 142–144, 146, 148, 149, 154–157, 160, 161, 163, 168–173, 180, 189, 190, 193, 196, 201, 218, 220, 223–231, 234, 240, 241, 245, 253, 254, 256–258, 266, 267, 269–277
*Tjukurpa* 270–272
Tlingit 141
Tohono O'odham 125, 155, 205
Toohey, D.E. 196
Torres Strait 226, 228
Traditional Environmental Knowledge (TEK) 24, 25, 36, 41, 42
Trail of Tears 59, 60, 100
Trauma 10, 11, 18, 19, 24, 25, 75, 91, 93, 104, 107–109, 112, 115, 130, 159, 160, 168, 174, 177–179, 208, 212, 220, 221, 229, 230, 237, 244, 245, 247, 253–255, 263, 277. *See also* Intergenerational trauma
Treaty of Hopewell 59
*Tribal Law and Order Act* 102
Tribally Controlled Community College Assistance Act (USL 92:1325) 1978 166
Triscott, J.A. 246
Truth and Reconciliation Act 8
Truth Commission Digital Collection 8
Tryon, D. 129, 130
Tsosie, R. 35–37, 166
Turnidge, J.D. 227
Turtle Island 32–34, 54
Two-Spirit 105, 106

## U

Umitilla Nation 74
United Nations (UN)
  Declaration on the Right of Indigenous Peoples (UNDRIP) 2, 6–9, 25, 36, 37, 68, 98, 99, 103, 104, 167, 208, 209, 230, 276
  Forum on Indigenous Issues 12, 13, 103, 208
  General Assembly 7
  Human Rights Council 111
  Permanent Forum on Indigenous Issues 9, 103
  State of the World's Indigenous Peoples 9, 24
United States (US) 26
  House of Representatives 162
Universal
  universalist 3, 128
  universalization 3, 113
University of Arizona 1, 206
University of Notre Dame 207
Un-wellness 221, 238, 239, 241–244
Urton, G. 142
Ushigua, G. 134

USL 87:700 165

**V**

Vancouver 110
Van Diemen's Land 173
Van Tilburg, J.A. 203
Vatican 66, 100, 206, 207
Viatori, M. 134
Viola, H.J. 161
Violence Against Women Act (VAWA) 110
Vodou 69, 200
Voeks, R. 27, 240

**W**

Wanapum 74
Water rights 38
Waters, A. 32, 266
Waugh, E.H. 246
Weber, R. 196
Wellness 18, 115, 221, 238–241, 243, 245–247, 253, 255, 256
Wendell, S. 245
West Africa 196
Wheeler-Howard Act (USL. 48.984) 164
White Face, C. (Zumila Wobaga) 8

White Hat, A. Sr. 149
Willinsky, J. 179, 180
Willis, F.M. 113
Wilson, S. 210
Winthrop 58
*Worcester v. Georgia* 35
World Conference on Indigenous Peoples 221
World Health Organization (WHO) 225
Wounded Knee 61, 101

**Y**

Yakama Nation 74
*Yakye Axa indigenous community v. Paraguay* 113
Yellow Bird, M. 14
Yolngu 147
Yoo, J. 100
Yoruba 69
Young, F.W. 201–203
Yunupingu, M. 43

**Z**

Zápara 134
Zitkala-Ša 175
Zuni 105

The manufacturer's authorised representative in the EU is Springer Nature Customer Service Centre GmbH, Europaplatz 3, 69115 Heidelberg, Germany. If you have any concerns regarding our products, please contact ProductSafety@springernature.com

Printed and bound by CPI Group (UK) Ltd, Croydon, CR0 4YY

25/03/2026

02078197-0005